The Death of Jesus in Early Christianity

THE DEATH OF JESUS IN EARLY CHRISTIANITY

JOHN T. CARROLL AND JOEL B. GREEN

WITH
ROBERT E. VAN VOORST, JOEL MARCUS,
DONALD SENIOR, C.P.

HENDRICKSON PUBLISHERS

ISBN 1-56563-151-X

First Printing — October 1995

Library of Congress Cataloging-in-Publication

Carroll, John T., 1954–
    The death of Jesus in early Christianity / John T. Carroll and Joel B.
Green; with Joel Marcus, Donald Senior, and Robert E. Van Voorst.
    Includes bibliographical references and indexes.
    ISBN 1–56563–151–X
    1. Jesus Christ—Crucifixion—History of doctrines—Early church,
ca. 30–600.   2. Bible.   N.T. Gospels—Criticism, interpretation, etc.
3. Bible.   N.T.—Criticism, interpretation, etc.   4. Bible.   N.T.—Extracanonical parallels. I. Green, Joel B., 1956–.   II. Title.
BT450.C347 1995
232.96′3–dc20   95-4951
                                                                      CIP

    The authors acknowledge with thanks the permission of Westmin-
ster/John Knox Press to include in ch. 11 materials adapted and re-
printed from *The Way of the Lord: Christological Exegesis of the Old
Testament in the Gospel of Mark* by Joel Marcus © 1992. In ch. 8,
quotations from the *Ascents of James* are taken from Robert E. Van
Voorst, *The Ascents of James*, © 1989 by Scholars Press. Used by
permission.

CONTENTS

PREFACE

Few subjects have so captured the imagination of historians of early Christianity, so inspired art and liturgy through the centuries, or so stimulated theological reflection and Christian self-understanding as the crucifixion of Jesus. Recent scholarship has moved beyond a preoccupation with the task of tracing the historical traditions tapped by the Gospel writers to address the interpretation of Jesus' death within the Gospels as coherent narratives. Moreover, employing methods drawn from the social sciences and guided by greater sensitivity to the context of late Second Temple Judaism, scholars have cast new light on the profound struggle of the first generations of Christians to make sense of the scandal of the cross. And in the light of contemporary Jewish-Christian dialogue, historical and theological issues surrounding the death of Jesus—particularly the historical question of responsibility for that death—have assumed increasing importance.

In November 1988 the Passion Narrative and Tradition in Early Christianity Group, a research unit newly formed by the Society of Biblical Literature, convened for the first time, under the leadership of a steering committee composed of John Carroll, Marty Soards, and Joel Marcus. Over the next seven years, this group of scholars met each year to take stock of important research on the passion narratives and to chart new directions for study of the early Christian interpretation of Jesus' death. The work of this group prompted two of its members, John Carroll and Joel Green, to attempt to harvest for the benefit of both exegetical specialists and serious nonspecialist readers the fruits of recent study of the death of Jesus. Rather than present a loose collection of essays representing diverse points of view, we made it our aim to offer a cohesive statement developing a particular interpretive approach to the death of Jesus in early Christianity.

The authors wish to acknowledge with thanks the stimulus given their research by the work of other members of the Passion Narrative and Tradition in Early Christianity Group. In particular, we express our profound gratitude to three of these colleagues who agreed to write chapters for this volume: Robert Van Voorst (ch. 8), Joel Marcus (ch. 11), and Donald Senior (ch. 12). Their essays have immeasurably improved the book. The product of the collaboration of the coauthors and these three scholars is, we hope, a coherent contribution to the contemporary challenge of interpreting the death of Jesus.

The authors acknowledge with gratitude the courtesy extended by Passion Group colleague Raymond E. Brown, who made available in advance of publication the manuscript of his magnum opus *The Death of the Messiah*. We also thank Jeffrey S. Siker, who read a draft of ch. 10 and offered helpful critical comments. Above all, we thank Patrick H. Alexander of Hendrickson Publishers, who enthusiastically endorsed the proposal that led to this book, and carefully shepherded it to publication.

J. T. C. and J. B. G.
September 15, 1994

It has been a delight to collaborate with Joel Green in the research and writing of this book. The many discoveries of shared perspectives and convictions along the way afforded a satisfaction that more than compensated for those few areas of scholarly disagreement requiring some negotiation. I thank my coauthor for what he has taught me and for the friendship that has accompanied our work on this project. I am grateful, too, to colleagues at Louisiana State University and Union Theological Seminary in Virginia whose friendship and support of my work over the last decade have undergirded the writing of this book. It is a pleasure, as well, to acknowledge the stimulus given my own thinking by students at these two schools and by friends at University Presbyterian Church, Baton Rouge; First Presbyterian Church, Baton Rouge; and Ginter Park Presbyterian Church, Richmond. My parents, James R. and Mildred L. Carroll, have read with interest the drafts of several chapters and offered helpful suggestions; for their help and encouragement I am thankful. First and last, though, I express my profound appreciation to my wife, Cindy Walker, and to our children, Andrew and Anna. They have followed each step of the project with curiosity and patience, and their unfailing love and truthfulness keep calling me back to what really matters.

J. T. C.

Work on this project has been accompanied by numerous serendipities, two of which deserve special mention. The first is the joy of authorial koinonia—sometimes challenging, alway stimulating. It is a pleasure to record my gratitude to John Carroll for his friendship and collegiality. Second, as is often the case in these waning years of the twentieth century, changing paradigms have led to controversial and provocative perspectives on the significance—ancient and contemporary—of the cross of Christ. After devoting years of doctoral research to the narrative tradition of Jesus' passion, it has been delightful to revisit those narratives and other materials along different avenues. Work on this project has been formative for me not only for these reasons but also because of my interactions with my students at New College Berkeley, the American Baptist Seminary of the West, and the Graduate Theological Union and with other friends, especially at St. Luke's United Methodist Church, Richmond; Thousand Oaks Baptist Church, Berkeley; First Baptist Church, La Jolla; and Redwood Christian Park. My friends and colleagues Rev. Mike Walker and Dr. James Chuck read drafts of some of this material. I owe a great debt of gratitude to them as well as to my family, Pam, Aaron, and Allison.

J. B. G.

ABBREVIATIONS

I. GENERAL ABBREVIATIONS

alt.	alteration from the NRSV (used in ch. 11)
B.C.E.	Before the Common Era (B.C.)
ca.	circa
C.E.	Common Era (A.D.)
cf.	*confer*, compare
ch(s).	chapter(s)
ed(s).	edition; editor(s); edited by
e.g.	*exempli gratia*, for example
esp.	especially
ET	English Translation
et al.	*et alii (aliae)*, others
i.e.	*id est*, that is
n(n).	note(s)
no.	number
n.s.	new series
LXX	Septuagint
MT	Masoretic Text (of the OT)
NT	New Testament
orig.	original
OT	Old Testament
par.	parallel
rev.	revised (by)
trans.	translated by
vol(s).	volume(s)
v(v).	verse(s)
§(§)	section or paragraph number(s)

II. ANCIENT LITERATURE

A. Biblical Books with the Apocrypha

Old Testament

Gen	Genesis
Exod	Exodus
Lev	Leviticus
Num	Numbers
Deut	Deuteronomy
Josh	Joshua
Judg	Judges
Ruth	Ruth
1-2 Sam	1-2 Samuel
1-2 Kgs	1-2 Kings
1-2 Chr	1-2 Chronicles
Ezra	Ezra
Neh	Nehemiah
Esth	Esther
Job	Job
Ps(s)	Psalm(s)
Prov	Proverbs
Eccl	Ecclesiastes
Cant	Song of Solomon
Isa	Isaiah
Jer	Jeremiah
Lam	Lamentations
Ezek	Ezekiel
Dan	Daniel
Hos	Hosea
Joel	Joel
Amos	Amos
Obad	Obadiah
Jonah	Jonah
Mic	Micah
Nah	Nahum
Hab	Habakkuk
Zeph	Zephaniah
Hag	Haggai
Zech	Zechariah
Mal	Malachi

Apocrypha

1-2 Esdr	1-2 Esdras
Tob	Tobit
Jdt	Judith
Add Esth	Additions to Esther
Wis	Wisdom of Solomon
Sir	Sirach (Ecclesiasticus)
Bar	Baruch
Ep Jer	Epistle of Jeremiah
Pr Azar	Prayer of Azariah
Sus	Susannah
Bel	Bel and the Dragon
Pr Man	Prayer of Manasseh
1-4 Macc	1-4 Maccabees

New Testament

Matt	Matthew
Mark	Mark
Luke	Luke
John	John
Acts	Acts
Rom	Romans
1-2 Cor	1-2 Corinthians
Gal	Galatians
Eph	Ephesians
Phil	Philippians
Col	Colossians
1-2 Thess	1-2 Thessalonians
1-2 Tim	1-2 Timothy
Tit	Titus
Phlm	Philemon
Heb	Hebrews
Jas	James
1-2 Pet	1-2 Peter
1-3 John	1-3 John
Jude	Jude
Rev	Revelation

B. Pseudepigrapha and Early Christian Writings

Eusebius

Hist. Eccl.	*Historia Ecclesiastica*

Irenaeus

Haer.	*Adversus haereses*

Justin Martyr

Dial.	*Dialogus cum Tryphone Judaeo*

Origen

Comm. John	*Commentary on John*
Comm. Matt.	*Commentary on Matthew*
Hom. Jer.	*Homily on Jeremiah*

Other Writings

A.J.	*Ascents of James*
Gos. Pet.	*Gospel of Peter*
Gos. Thom.	*Gospel of Thomas*
Rec.	*Pseudo-Clementine Recognitions*
T. Judah	*Testament of Judah*

C. Dead Sea Scrolls and Related Texts

1QH	*Hôdāyôt,* or Thanksgiving Hymns, from Qumran Cave 1
1QS	*Serek hayyaḥad,* or *Rule of the Community,* or *Manual of Discipline,* from Qumran Cave 1
1QSa	Appendix A, *Messianic Rule,* to 1QS
4QFlor	*Florilegium,* or *Eschatological Midrashim,* from Qumran Cave 4
4QpNah	*Pesher on Nahum* from Qumran Cave 4
4QPs^f	Fragment of the Psalter from Qumran Cave 4 (also 4Q88)
4Q285	*Serek ha-milhamah,* or Pierced Messiah, or Messianic Leader, from Qumran Cave 4
11QTemple	*Temple Scroll* from Qumran Cave 11

D. Targumim

Tg. Neb.	Targum of the Prophets

E. Rabbinic Literature and Tractates

b.	Babylonian Talmud
Ḥul.	*Ḥullin*

Pesaḥ.	*Pesaḥim*
Sanh.	*Sanhedrin*
Sukk.	*Sukka*
t.	Tosepta

F. Other Ancient Authors and Writings

Josephus

Ag. Ap.	*Against Apion*
Ant.	*Antiquities of the Jews*
J.W.	*Jewish War*

Philo

Flacc.	*In Flaccum*
Post. C.	*De Posteritate Caini*
Somn.	*De Somnis*
Spec. Leg.	*De Specialibus Legibus*

Tacitus

Ann.	*The Annals*

III. MODERN LITERATURE

AB	Anchor Bible
ABD	*The Anchor Bible Dictionary.* 6 vols. Ed. David Noel Freedman
ABRL	The Anchor Bible Reference Library
AMT: BBB	Athenäums Monografien: Theologie; Bonner biblische Beiträge
AnBib	Analecta biblica
AS	Advances in Semiotics
ATANT	Abhandlungen zur Theologie des Alten und Neuen Testaments
BA	*Biblical Archaeologist*
BAR	*Biblical Archaeology Review*
BETL	Bibliotheca ephemeridum theologicarum lovaniensium
BibLeb	*Bibel und Leben*
BibRes	*Biblical Research*
BibRev	*Bible Review*

BJRL	*Bulletin of the John Rylands University Library of Manchester*
BJS	Brown Judaic Studies
BNTC	Black's New Testament Commentaries
BTB	*Biblical Theology Bulletin*
BTS	Biblische theologische Studien
BWANT	Beiträge zur Wissenschaft vom Alten und Neuen Testament
BZ	*Biblische Zeitschrift*
BZNW	Beihefte zur *ZNW*
CBQ	*Catholic Biblical Quarterly*
CEP	Contemporary Evangelical Perspectives
CI	*Critical Inquiry*
ConBNT	Coniectanea biblica, New Testament
CRINT	Compendia rerum iudaicarum ad novum testamentum
CurTM	*Currents in Theology and Mission*
DJG	*Dictionary of Jesus and the Gospels*, ed. Joel B. Green and Scott McKnight
DPL	*Dictionary of Paul and His Letters*, ed. Gerald F. Hawthorne, Ralph P. Martin, and Daniel G. Reid
EDNT	*Exegetical Dictionary of the New Testament*. 3 vols. Ed. Horst Balz and Gerhard Schneider
ETL	*Ephemerides theologicae lovanienses*
FB	Forschung zur Bibel
FF	Foundations and Facets
FRLANT	Forschungen zur Religion und Literatur des Alten und Neuen Testaments
FTS	Frankfurter theologische Studien
GBS	Guides to Biblical Scholarship
GNS	Good News Studies
GP	Gospel Perspectives
HDR	Harvard Dissertations in Religion
HT	*History and Theory*
HTR	*Harvard Theological Review*
IBC	Interpretation: A Bible Commentary for Teaching and Preaching
IEJ	*Israel Exploration Journal*
Int	*Interpretation*
IRT	Issues in Religion and Theology
JAAR	*Journal of the American Academy of Religion*
JBL	*Journal of Biblical Literature*
JSHRZ	Jüdische Schriften aus hellenistisch-römischer Zeit
JSNT	*Journal for the Study of the New Testament*

JSNTSup	Journal for the Study of the New Testament Supplement Series
JTS	*Journal of Theological Studies*
LCBI	Literary Currents in Biblical Interpretation
LCL	Loeb Classical Library
LTPM	Louvain Theological and Pastoral Monographs
NABPRBS	National Association of Baptist Professors of Religion Bibliographic Series
NAS	New American Standard Version
NCV	New Century Version
NIGTC	New International Greek Testament Commentary
NIV	New International Version
NovT	*Novum Testamentum*
NovTSup	Novum Testamentum, Supplements
NRSV	New Revised Standard Version
NTAbh	Neutestamentliche Abhandlungen
NTS	*New Testament Studies*
NTT	New Testament Theology
OBT	Overtures to Biblical Theology
PS	The Passion Series
QD	Quaestiones disputatae
RB	*Revue biblique*
RSV	Revised Standard Version
SANT	Studien zum Alten und Neuen Testament
SB	Sources bibliques
SBEC	Studies in the Bible and Early Christianity
SBLA	Society of Biblical Literature Abstracts
SBLDS	Society of Biblical Literature Dissertation Series
SBLMS	Society of Biblical Literature Monograph Series
SBLSBS	Society of Biblical Literature Sources for Biblical Study
SBLSP	Society of Biblical Literature Seminar Papers
SBLSS	Society of Biblical Literature Semeia Series
SBS	Stuttgarter Bibelstudien
SecCent	*Second Century*
SJ	Studia judaica
SNTSMS	Society of New Testament Studies Monograph Series
SNTU	Studien zum Neuen Testament und seiner Umwelt
SNTW	Studies of the New Testament and Its World
SP	Sacra pagina
SPB	Studia postbiblica
SSG	Studies in the Synoptic Gospels

SSS   Special Studies Series
Str-B   H. Strack and P. Billerbeck, *Kommentar zum Neuen Testament*
TDNT   *Theological Dictionary of the New Testament.* Ed. Gerhard Kittel and Gerhard Friedrich
TI   Theological Inquiries
TPINTC   Trinity Press International New Testament Commentary
TS   *Theological Studies*
WBC   Word Biblical Commentary
WUNT   Wissenschaftliche Untersuchungen zum Neuen Testament
WW   *Word and World*
ZNW   *Zeitschrift für die neutestamentliche Wissenschaft*
ZSNT   Zacchaeus Studies: New Testament

Part One

*The Death of Jesus
and the Gospels*

⊕ ONE

THE GOSPELS AND THE DEATH
OF JESUS IN RECENT STUDY

CHANGING PARADIGMS

As with Gospels study more generally, so with inquiry into the death of Jesus in the Gospels, the hegemony of strictly historical methods has waned in recent decades, allowing for a wider range of questions to be addressed.[1] Perhaps most importantly, the loss of a narrow focus on tradition- and historical-critical concerns has opened up fresh paths for exploring the significance of the crucifixion of Jesus as this event is related to the entirety of Jesus' life and mission.

In previous generations, the study of Jesus' passion drew upon a now predictable inventory of questions. What actually happened "on the night when Jesus was delivered up"? What was the role of the Jews in Jesus' trial? How did the passion tradition develop? What sources did the evangelists have as they wrote their own passion accounts? What was the nature of those sources—oral or written, reliable or capricious? And so on. Even if questions such as these continue to be debated, it is nevertheless true that reflection on the death of Jesus has taken a decisive turn in recent years. The passion narratives of the four Gospels are studied less as discrete units of tradition, more as accounts integrated into the narratives in which they participate. What is more, study of "the death of Jesus in Matthew" (for example) now takes with utmost seriousness not simply the account of Jesus' death in Matt 26–27 but the whole of Matthew's Gospel as it impinges on our understanding of the death of the Messiah.

---

[1]See Anthony C. Thiselton, "New Testament Interpretation in Historical Perspective," in *Hearing the New Testament: Strategies for Interpretation*, ed. Joel B. Green (Grand Rapids: Eerdmans, 1995).

This notable shift in the investigation of the Gospels as literary texts has been accompanied by a further innovation, the proportions of which are still being measured. This is the rediscovery of the Jewishness of Jesus.[2] It may seem odd to persons at the turn of the twenty-first century that Jesus' social, national, and religious identity as a Jew needed "rediscovering"; after all, this has been the subject of many recent studies in the wake of a new and more general appreciation of one's "context." But decades of questing after the historical Jesus prior to the 1980s had generated a kind of stand-alone Jesus, a universal figure outside history. Life-of-Jesus research had turned up a portrait of a person who had not felt the winds blowing off the Sea of Galilee or experienced, as a member of first-century Judaism, the winds of change arising from three centuries of cultural imperialism (Greek) and several decades of foreign rule (Roman). Chiding a major stream of New Testament study (and theological reflection based thereon) for its failure to let Jesus be a first-century Jew, David Batstone has recently urged that "the historical coordinates which frame Jesus' cause and led him to his death on a cross [must] serve as the criteria for determining the truthfulness of every Christology."[3]

Our purpose in this chapter is to locate contemporary readings of the death of Jesus in the Gospels on the horizon of recent research. By "recent" we refer above all to the final decades of the twentieth century. Some readers may find such an excursion of little value—an unnecessary rehearsal of bygone chapters of study. A report of this nature has significance in at least three ways, however. First, it will serve as a kind of introduction to the chapters that follow—indicating what issues have become prominent and how they have achieved notoriety. Second, it will suggest how newer readings of the passion of Jesus are indebted to older ones. The questions raised and assumptions made today build on, if sometimes by reacting against, earlier generations of attempts to make sense of the ignominy of the crucifixion of God's Messiah. Finally, for persons interested in pursuing questions of the sort raised in these chapters, this summary may serve as an entry point and bibliographic prologue to ongoing deliberation.

---

[2]This emphasis in contemporary study was heralded especially by Geza Vermes, *Jesus the Jew: A Historian's Reading of the Gospels* (Philadelphia: Fortress, 1973).

[3]David Batstone, *From Conquest to Struggle: Jesus of Nazareth in Latin America* (Albany: State University of New York, 1991) 147.

THE GOSPEL AND THE PASSION

From Martin Kähler to Frank Matera

"To state the matter somewhat provocatively, one could call the Gospels passion narratives with extended introductions."[4] Writing a century ago (1896), Martin Kähler perhaps quite unintentionally thus set the twentieth-century agenda for study of the accounts of Jesus' last days. With this assertion, Kähler hoped to draw attention away from the Gospels as biographies designed to show the development of Jesus' self-consciousness. This emphasis on Jesus' growth as a person, Kähler thought, is contrary to the concerns of those responsible for the completion of the Gospels; the ancient church highlighted not Jesus' person but his work. Hence, the Gospels devote substantial space to the passion account, and with the onset of the passion, the Gospel narratives become relatively more detailed.

In the twentieth century, Kähler's "provocative" comment was taken as axiomatic.[5] Whatever its original meaning, this statement was made to participate in a segregation of the accounts of the death of Jesus from those of his life—a segregation helped along by the efforts of form criticism through the 1960s. Dividing the Gospels into series of pericopes, each with its own tradition history, each serving its own particular purpose in the early church, form critics worked with such categories as "miracle story" and "pronouncement story," but they were generally unsuccessful at subjecting the passion narratives to similar analysis.[6] They tended to assume the very early provenance of a passion account, noting the narrative's self-sufficiency and internal coherence and its indications of time and topography.[7]

That is, the isolation of the accounts of Jesus' suffering and death from the study of the Gospels more generally grew out of concerns with tradition and history. The consequence has been the further separation of the passion accounts from the Gospels with respect to theological interests and theme. In fact, Etienne Trocmé went so far as to insist that

---

[4]Martin Kähler, *The So-Called Historical Jesus and the Historic Biblical Christ* (ET; Philadelphia: Fortress, 1964) 80 n. 11.

[5]This is especially true of study of the Second Gospel, with Kähler's statement often misquoted as referring only to the Gospel of Mark.

[6]Cf. esp. Martin Dibelius, *From Tradition to Gospel* (ET; Cambridge: James Clarke, [1933] 1971) 22–23, 178–80; Rudolf Bultmann, *The History of the Synoptic Tradition* (ET; 1963; reprint, Peabody, Mass.: Hendrickson, 1994) 275; Vincent Taylor, *The Formation of the Gospel Tradition* (London: Macmillan, 1949) 49–62.

[7]Cf., e.g., T. A. Burkill, *Mysterious Revelation: An Examination of the Philosophy of St. Mark's Gospel* (Ithaca, N.Y.: Cornell University, 1963) 219–20.

chs. 14–16 of the Gospel of Mark are unrelated theologically to Mark 1–13 and that the original edition of the Second Gospel ended with ch. 13.[8] Separate from other Gospel accounts in tradition history, the passion accounts, it was thought, need not cohere with their respective Gospel narratives in theology, character development, narrative strategy, geographical interest, or otherwise.

It may not be surprising, then, that some of the first chinks in the armor of the form-critical consensus on the ancient, autonomous existence of the passion narrative came from studies locating bridges—especially christological—from Mark 1–13 to Mark 14–16.[9] Flank attacks of this sort did not stop the advance of tradition-historical study, especially of the Markan passion account, however. The 1970s saw the publication of several fastidious and minutely detailed studies of Mark 14–15, dividing verses and half-verses among multiple layers of tradition and redaction.[10] Nevertheless, it was increasingly clear that the more Mark 14–16 looked *Markan*, the less easy or necessary it was to argue for a thoroughgoing, pre-Markan passion account.[11]

As has become increasingly obvious, the shape of this discussion on the origins of the passion narrative was itself problematic. The reason is that it tended to pit tradition and interpretation, history and theology against each other as though they were mutually exclusive categories.

---

[8]Etienne Trocmé, *The Formation of the Gospel according to Mark* (London: S.P.C.K., 1975) esp. 215–59; and idem, *The Passion as Liturgy: A Study in the Origin of the Passion Narratives in the Four Gospels* (London: SCM, 1983) 7–19.

[9]E.g., Johannes Schreiber, *Theologie des Vertrauens: Eine redaktionsgeschichtliche Untersuchung des Markusevangeliums* (Hamburg: Furche, 1967) 22–82; Eta Linnemann, *Studien zur Passionsgeschichte* (FRLANT 102; Göttingen: Vandenhoeck & Ruprecht, 1970).

[10]E.g., Ludger Schenke, *Studien zur Passionsgeschichte des Markus: Tradition und Redaktion in Markus 14,1–42* (FB 4; Würzburg: Echter, 1971); and idem, *Der gekreuzigte Christus: Versuch einer literarkritischen und traditionsgeschichtlichen Bestimmung der vormarkinischen Passionsgeschichte* (SBS 69; Stuttgart: Katholisches, 1974); Detlev Dormeyer, *Die Passion Jesu als Verhaltensmodell: Literarische und theologische Analyse der Traditions- und Redaktionsgeschichte der Markuspassion* (NTAbh n.s. 11; Münster: Aschendorff, 1974); and idem, *Der Sinn des Leidens Jesu: Historisch-kritische und textpragmatische Analysen zur Markuspassion* (SBS 96; Stuttgart: Katholisches, 1979). On this and related study, see the surveys in John R. Donahue, "From Passion Traditions to Passion Narrative," in *The Passion in Mark: Studies on Mark 14–16*, ed. Werner H. Kelber (Philadelphia: Fortress, 1976) 1–20; Joel B. Green, *The Death of Jesus: Tradition and Interpretation in the Passion Narrative* (WUNT 2:33; Tübingen: J. C. B. Mohr [Paul Siebeck], 1988) 9–14.

[11]See, e.g., Werner H. Kelber ("Conclusion: From Passion Narrative to Gospel," in *Passion in Mark*, 153–80 [157]): "*The understanding of Mk 14–16 as a theologically integrated part of the Mkan Gospel calls into question the classic form critical thesis concerning an independent and coherent Passion Narrative prior to Mk*" (italics original); Frank J. Matera, *The Kingship of Jesus: Composition and Theology in Mark 15* (SBLDS 66; Chico, Calif.: Scholars, 1982).

Of course, Willi Marxsen had noted, early on, the possibility that the Gospels were written *backwards*, so to speak: "Mark thus prefixes the passion story with the traditions of Jesus, and prefixes that tradition with the tradition about the Baptist."[12] Such a procedure could explain both the existence of a pre-Markan passion account and the existence of theological and narrative coherence between these two sections of Mark. But this does not address the more fundamental problem to which we have pointed. This is the reality that in the last decades of the twentieth century, the positivist segregation of "what actually happened" and "what was perceived to be meaningful" has become obscured. That is, significance is attributed to events even as decisions are made about *what* will be remembered and *how*, and this process of meaning making does not await the efforts of those, like Mark or Luke, who write it down.[13] To the degree that these efforts proceeded along a line of investigation hoping to find uninterpreted "events" under the rocks of theological interests, then, such efforts were flawed from the outset.

Urs Sommer's recent study, *Die Passionsgeschichte des Markusevangeliums*, underscores this transformation.[14] He notes that the characterization of the Gospels in general and the passion narratives in particular as faith documents is problematic precisely because it seems to pit "objective history" against "subjective faith." His historical and theological analysis of the Markan account of Jesus' suffering and death leads him to adopt the expression "testimony to faith" as a description of this narrative material, but only with qualifications. This is not testimony devoid of historical content, as though historical narrative necessarily lacks rhetorical aim. The passion narratives are theological discourse grounded in the narrative history of the passion of Jesus.

In recent years a number of other scholars have developed the significant literary and theological integration of Mark 14–15 with the rest of the Gospel while at the same time assuming that in narrating Jesus' passion, the second evangelist worked with a traditional account.[15]

A major shift in the study of the passion narratives was marked by the publication of *Passion Narratives and Gospel Theologies* by Frank J.

---

[12]Willi Marxsen, *Mark the Evangelist* (Nashville: Abingdon, 1969) 31.

[13]See, e.g., Hayden White, "The Value of Narrativity in the Representation of Reality," *CI* 7 (1980–81) 5–27; idem, "The Narratization of Real Events," *CI* 7 (1980–81) 793–98; idem, "The Question of Narrative in Contemporary Historical Theory," *HT* 23 (1984) 1–33; Mary Douglas, *How Institutions Think* (The Frank W. Abrams Lectures; Syracuse, N.Y.: Syracuse University, 1986).

[14]Urs Sommer, *Die Passionsgeschichte des Markusevangeliums: Überlegungen zur Bedeutung der Geschichte für den Glauben* (WUNT 2:58; Tübingen: J. C. B. Mohr [Paul Siebeck], 1993).

[15]E.g., Christopher Bryan, *A Preface to Mark: Notes on the Gospel in Its Literary and Cultural Settings* (New York/Oxford: Oxford University, 1993) 112–19.

Matera.[16] He does not eschew tradition-historical concerns but (1) provides an overview of each of the synoptic passion accounts, briefly addressing the question of sources; (2) provides a commentary on each synoptic passion account, attending especially to primary theological themes; then (3) traces the development of selected themes of each passion account through the Gospel narrative as a whole. The result is a deliberate move away from narrowly defined *historical* concerns toward the *theological* integration of each passion account within its respective Gospel.

The class of study represented by *Passion Narratives and Gospel Theologies* accents the role of the Gospels as whole narratives in the interpretation of Jesus' death. In his discussion of the theology of Jesus' death in the Gospel of Luke, for example, Matera underscores four motifs: "The Passion as the Destiny of Jesus," "The Passion as a Model of Discipleship," "The Passion as the Rejection of Jesus the Prophet," and "The Passion as the Death of God's Royal Son." This is not to say that contemporary Gospel study has fallen prey to what Kähler had opposed a century ago. Inquiry into the theologies of Jesus' death in the Gospels today is not especially motivated by an attempt to grapple with Jesus' development as a *person* or to discern the nature of his emerging *self-consciousness*—against which Kähler argued; rather, students of Jesus' passion now attempt to take with more seriousness the ways in which the evangelists characterize Jesus of Nazareth and demonstrate the relationship between his mission and his execution. This is the burden of Matera's monograph, but also of Donald Senior's "Passion Series" (see below) and the lengthy essay by Joel B. Green in *DJG*.[17]

Before surveying recent monographs treating the passion narratives of each Gospel, we draw attention to the encyclopedic treatment in *The Death of the Messiah* by Raymond E. Brown.[18] Altogether, Brown devotes some 1600 pages in two volumes "*to explain in detail what the evangelists intended and conveyed to their audiences by their narratives of the passion and death of Jesus.*"[19] Given this objective, Brown surprisingly

---

[16]Frank J. Matera, *Passion Narratives and Gospel Theologies: Interpreting the Synoptics through Their Passion Stories* (TI; New York/Mahwah, N.J.: Paulist, 1986).

[17]Donald Senior, *The Passion of Jesus in the Gospel of Matthew* (PS 1; Wilmington, Del.: Michael Glazier, 1985); idem, *The Passion of Jesus in the Gospel of Mark* (PS 2; Wilmington, Del.: Michael Glazier, 1984); idem, *The Passion of Jesus in the Gospel of Luke* (PS 3; Wilmington, Del.: Michael Glazier, 1989); and idem, *The Passion of Jesus in the Gospel of John* (PS 4; Collegeville, Minn.: Liturgical, 1991); Joel B. Green, "Death of Jesus," *DJG*, 146–63.

[18]Raymond E. Brown, *The Death of the Messiah—from Gethsemane to the Grave: A Commentary on the Passion Narratives* (2 vols.; ABRL; New York: Doubleday, 1994).

[19]Brown, *Death of the Messiah*, 1.4; italics original.

elects to read the passion narratives of the four Gospels "horizontally" rather than "vertically"—that is, he examines each episode of the passion in all four Gospels simultaneously rather than treating each passion narrative on its own merits. This does not mean Brown is uninterested in the passion theology of each evangelist. He provides general introductions to the perspective each Gospel writer gives to the death of Jesus, then weaves into his episodic structure an ongoing discussion of the outlook of each Gospel account. It does mean, however, that one is unable easily to follow the development of, say, John's passion theology from the beginning of his passion account to the end. Moreover, as the subtitle, "From Gethsemane to the Grave: A Commentary on the Passion Narratives," suggests, Brown devotes relatively little space in his book to the passion theology of the whole of each Gospel, including material on Jesus' suffering and death occurring proleptically, prior to the onset of the passion accounts. Finally, Brown is not concerned primarily with questions of a historical nature. He does not accord privilege to the question, What actually happened? Although he addresses questions of historicity (and also of composition), Brown's principal intent is to comment on the text and not on its prehistory. In some ways, then, *The Death of the Messiah* provides a bridge from tradition-critical inquiry into a more narrative-oriented study of the death of Jesus in the four Gospels.

The Gospel of Matthew

Perhaps because of its similarities to the Gospel of Mark—on which, most scholars believe, the first evangelist was dependent—Matthew's presentation of the death of Jesus has not received the attention given Mark's or Luke's. Two studies can be mentioned nevertheless.

First, Donald Senior has built on a previous study of the sources and redaction of the Matthean passion narrative with a second book exploring further the passion theology of Matthew.[20] The latter book, *The Passion of Jesus in the Gospel of Matthew*, is structured in three parts—(1) a survey of the first twenty-five chapters of the Gospel in order to show how the death of Jesus has been looming before the reader almost from the very beginning of Matthew's narrative of the good news; (2) a scene-by-scene exploration of the passion narrative of the Gospel; and (3) a relatively brief section constructing a synthesis of Matthew's passion theology.

---

[20]Donald Senior, *The Passion Narrative according to Matthew: A Redactional Study* (BETL 39; Louvain: Leuven University, 1975); and idem, *Passion of Jesus in Matthew*.

As helpful as it is in distilling contemporary Matthean scholarship into a highly informative and readable format, Senior's commentary on the passion narrative is not the chief contribution of his study. This lies elsewhere, especially in showing the degree to which the death of Jesus is integral to his identity and mission in the First Gospel ("the cross reveals the inner core of Jesus' commitment to give his life on behalf of the many")[21] and in outlining the shape of Matthew's message of Jesus' suffering. Thus, Senior demonstrates how Jesus' passion is related, e.g., to *Christology* (revealing Jesus as God's faithful Son whose suffering and death is both redemptive and exemplary); to *discipleship* (underscoring the role of the disciples as people of "little faith" in Matthean perspective and highlighting the admirable faith of such "little people" as Mary Magdalene, "the other" Mary, and Joseph of Arimathea); and to *the suffering of God's people.*

More recently, John Paul Heil has attempted "A Narrative-Critical Reading of Matt 26–28."[22] His point of departure is his understanding of the Gospels as "artistic, literary communications" designed to produce a "rhetorical effect" for their implied readers. Without employing the technical language of narrative criticism or rhetoric, Heil comments on the death and resurrection accounts of the Gospel of Matthew in order to explore how Matthew summons his audience to respond to the events unfolding before them. In fact, Heil participates more in a new-literary "close reading of the text" than in narratology, though he is able to suggest some illuminating relationships among the episodes in Matt 26–28. These narratives, he surmises, lead us into the story of the conflict of the human and divine and so better prepare us for a similar challenge in our own lives. Will we, like Jesus' enemies and friends, oppose or abandon God's plan in the midst of suffering? Will we, like Peter and Judas,[23] repent of our failings and follow the model of Jesus, who undergoes suffering without abandoning trust in God? Will we follow the line of faithful witnesses from the cross to the empty tomb and so be led into authentic faith in the crucified but risen Lord?

The Gospel of Mark

Senior's examination of the Markan passion account proceeds along a line similar to that already noted for Matthew—namely, a major section noting the ways Mark 1–13 prepares for the passion narrative, then a more detailed analysis of the Markan passion narrative itself, and

---

[21] Senior, *Passion of Jesus in Matthew*, 31.

[22] John Paul Heil, *The Death and Resurrection of Jesus: A Narrative-Critical Reading of Matthew 26–28* (Minneapolis: Fortress, 1991).

[23] Heil argues that Matthew presents Judas as repenting in the face of Jesus' innocence (*Death and Resurrection*, 67–69).

finally a thematic discussion of Mark's message of Jesus' suffering and death.[24] Senior is not concerned much with questions of sources or historicity but employs composition criticism to shed light on Mark's literary and theological achievement.

In order to clarify the profound degree to which Mark prepares for the passion account, Senior addresses four themes from Mark 1–13: the passion of John the Baptist, narrated in such a way as to anticipate Jesus' own trial and death; the plot against Jesus, which surfaces as early in the narrative as Mark 3:6; the journey of Jesus and the disciples in Mark 8–10, with its emphasis on Jesus' predictions of execution; and, very briefly, the warning of impending ordeal for the church. Here and in his appraisal of the Markan passion narrative itself, Senior underscores how Jesus cannot be understood or authentically confessed as Christ apart from his fundamental identity as the Crucified One.

Although he is fully aware of the importance of the cross for Mark's Christology, Senior's examination is also of interest for the way it draws out the implications of Jesus' suffering for those who wish to follow Jesus. This, too, is the concern of a recent book by Joel B. Green entitled *The Way of the Cross*, the approach of which is also literary-theological.[25] Green maintains throughout his exploration of Mark that the second evangelist's concern is pastoral; Mark encourages his readers to ground their understanding of discipleship in their understanding of Jesus, and he roots his portrait of Jesus as God's Son in his divine mandate: "He is God's Son, and this means above all being obedient to God in sacrificial service, even when the way of God leads to Golgotha."[26]

These two books, by Senior and Green, are written with the purpose of bringing the insights of biblical scholarship to a wider audience. A further monograph, by Joel Marcus, is itself an important contribution to Markan study and, in terms of our interest in the death of Jesus, is significant for its exploration of the use of the OT by the second evangelist.[27] Marcus devotes a complete chapter to OT citations and allusions in Mark 14–16, focusing on four bodies of OT literature: Zech 9–14, Dan 7, the Psalms of the Suffering Righteous, and the Isaianic Servant Songs. He turns a sensitive ear to the many echoes of these OT texts in the Markan passion account and is thus more open than some twentieth-century scholarship to the imaginative interplay of passion narrative and OT prefigurations. He is also able to show how the use of the OT in the Markan narrative—some uses of which he takes to be

---

[24] Senior, *Passion of Jesus in Mark.*

[25] Joel B. Green, *The Way of the Cross: Following Jesus in the Gospel of Mark* (Nashville: Discipleship Resources, 1991).

[26] Green, *Way of the Cross*, 43.

[27] Joel Marcus, *The Way of the Lord: Christological Exegesis of the Old Testament in the Gospel of Mark* (Louisville: Westminster/John Knox, 1992).

traditional, others he attributes to Markan innovation—portrays Jesus' suffering in an apocalyptic context that invites believers to see in their own suffering an invitation to cross bearing and an anticipation of divine vindication.

We have already had occasion briefly to mention a recently completed German dissertation by Urs Sommer on the passion narrative in the Gospel of Mark.[28] In some ways, Sommer's examination is reminiscent of earlier study concerned with historical questions and the contribution of Mark to the story of Jesus' execution. His analysis of Mark 14–16 is framed, however, by a quite distinct agenda, represented in the subtitle of his work: "Reflections on the Significance of Historical Narrative (*Geschichte*) for Faith." That is, Sommer wants to know how faith (and unbelief) might be related to the narrated history of the suffering of Jesus. In this way he navigates between simplistic categorizations of the Markan passion account as "fiction" or "fact" and queries how the reader might respond to this historical narrative.

The Gospel of Luke

The Third Gospel has attracted perhaps more than its share of attention among those interested in the death of Jesus. This is due to a number of factors—e.g., the enigma of Luke's presentation of Jesus' crucifixion, apparently devoid of soteriological meaning;[29] the concomitant view that Luke's Jesus dies the death of a martyr;[30] and the widespread but much-debated view that Luke 22–23 preserves an account of Jesus' passion that is not dependent on the Gospel of Mark.[31]

Taking as his point of departure an assumption of the unity of Luke and Acts and working within the rubrics of new literary criticism, Joseph Tyson has investigated how the third evangelist portrays the death of Jesus in Luke–Acts.[32] Interestingly, he does so not by focusing narrowly on the passion narrative of Luke but by tracing Luke's depiction of Jesus'

---

[28] Sommer, *Passionsgeschichte*.

[29] Cf., e.g., Hans Conzelmann, *The Theology of St. Luke* (ET; New York: Harper & Row; London: Faber & Faber, 1960; reprint, London: SCM, 1982) 201.

[30] See the discussion in Brian E. Beck, "'*Imitatio Christi*' and the Lucan Passion Narrative," in *Suffering and Martyrdom in the New Testament: Studies Presented to G. M. Styler by the Cambridge New Testament Seminar*, ed. William Horbury and Brian McNeil (Cambridge: Cambridge University, 1981) 28–47.

[31] This view is supported, e.g., by Vincent Taylor, *The Passion Narrative of St. Luke: A Critical and Historical Investigation*, ed. Owen E. Evans (SNTSMS 19; Cambridge: Cambridge University, 1972); Green, *Death of Jesus*, esp. 24–104.

[32] Joseph B. Tyson, *The Death of Jesus in Luke–Acts* (Columbia: University of South Carolina, 1986).

relations to others within the narrative—the Jewish public, the Jewish leaders, and Jerusalem and the temple—before examining in more detail the trial of Jesus. This allows him to bestow special significance to the motif of conflict in the Gospel[33]—conflict that adds to the dramatic interest in the narrative, accents Jesus' legal innocence over against the Jewish leadership, and creates an arena in which Luke can emphasize his conviction regarding the divine necessity of Jesus' death. All of this suggests for Tyson that Luke's passion theology is controlled by the identity of his own community, a Christian community that was anti-priestly and pro-Roman and, though perhaps regretting its segregation from Judaism, blamed this break on the Jews.

Robert Karris has also adopted a literary approach in his presentation of "Luke's Passion Account as Literature."[34] How does Jesus get to the cross, according to Luke? This is a central question for Karris, and his answer lays special stress on Jesus' eating habits—or, at least, on Jesus' commitment to justice and faithfulness as this is embodied in his table fellowship with outcasts.

As with his other contributions to the Passion Series, Senior's *Passion of Jesus in the Gospel of Luke* sets Luke's interpretation of the death of Jesus within the context of the larger Lukan narrative. Hence, he devotes the first major section of his book to Luke 1–21, exploring how Luke's narrative of the birth and ministry of Jesus prepares for and interprets the passion. Senior draws special attention to the challenge of justice, breaking the boundaries, Jesus as the rejected prophet-martyr, the test of evil, and the divine destiny of Christ. Study of these themes accentuates Senior's view that "death comes as no surprise to Jesus but as part of his God-given mission, a fearful yet inevitable climax to a prophetic destiny,"[35] and leads to an engaging, scene-by-scene commentary on Luke 22–23. How is Jesus' death related to Luke's overall portrayal of Jesus? Senior believes Luke does present Jesus' death as integral to his redemptive mission, and he draws particular attention to the fate of the repentant criminal on the cross (Luke 23:43).[36] He also develops Luke's concerns with Jesus' death as the obedient and trusting Son of God, with God's validation of Jesus' mission and message even in the jaws of death, and with the conquest of evil in Jesus' passion.

---

[33] See also Joseph B. Tyson, "Conflict as a Literary Theme in the Gospel of Luke," in *New Synoptic Studies: The Cambridge Gospel Conference and Beyond*, ed. William R. Farmer (Macon, Ga.: Mercer University, 1983) 303–27; cf. Jack Dean Kingsbury, *Conflict in Luke: Jesus, Authorities, Disciples* (Minneapolis: Fortress, 1991).

[34] Robert J. Karris, *Luke: Artist and Theologian. Luke's Passion Account as Literature* (TI; New York/Mahwah, N.J./Toronto: Paulist, 1985).

[35] Senior, *Passion of Jesus in Luke*, 17.

[36] Similarly, cf. Joseph A. Fitzmyer, *Luke the Theologian: Aspects of His Teaching* (New York/Mahwah, N.J.: Paulist, 1989) 203–33.

Shunning any narrow commitment to questions of historicity or Luke's sources, Jerome Neyrey bases his *Passion according to Luke* on his view of Luke as "a learned and creative author," "a master of literary styles."[37] Compared with the previously noted books, Neyrey's is significant for its greater attention to the relation of the passion narrative to parallels in the Acts of the Apostles; he finds in Luke's second volume, e.g., analogues for Jesus' farewell address and trial. Nevertheless, vis-à-vis the Third Gospel, his study is concerned more narrowly with Luke 22–23, and he provides a detailed redaction-critical analysis of these chapters. In spite of his characterization of the third evangelist as "learned and creative," Neyrey is unable to find any common interpretive threads by which to hold together Luke's presentation of Jesus' passion.

In 1990, Dennis Sylva edited a collection of essays entitled *Reimaging the Death of the Lukan Jesus*, a primary purpose of which was to call into question the often repeated notion that Luke presents Jesus' death as that of a martyr.[38] Although these essays follow no common method, they do surface other key questions in the contemporary study of Jesus' death in Luke—a theological rationale for the lack of atonement theology in Luke–Acts coupled with an unparalleled stress on the divine necessity of the Messiah's death; the attitude of Luke toward the Jewish people as this is worked out in Luke's narration of Jesus' rejection and execution; and the implications of Jesus' message (including his death) for the Roman Empire. These are not settled issues, however, and studies of Jesus' death in Luke–Acts must revisit them.

The Gospel of John

The passion account of the Fourth Gospel has always presented special problems, most related to the distinctive character of the Gospel of John vis-à-vis the Synoptics.[39] For example, although the first three Gospels locate material related to Jesus' suffering and death in a tightly woven narrative, John disperses some of this same material throughout his Gospel. The prayer in Gethsemane in Mark 14:32–42 has a parallel earlier in John's Gospel, in 12:27–30; the anointing of Jesus in Mark's account occurs two days before Passover (14:3–9), according to John six days before (12:1–8); and so on. Second, even though the passion narrative proper in John is often judged to commence with Jesus' trial in ch. 18, almost one-half of the Gospel is given over to Jesus' last week

---

[37] Jerome Neyrey, *The Passion according to Luke: A Redaction Study of Luke's Soteriology* (TI; New York/Mahwah, N.J.: Paulist, 1985) 1–2.

[38] Dennis D. Sylva, ed., *Reimaging the Death of the Lukan Jesus* (AMT:BBB 73; Frankfurt am Main: Anton Hain, 1990).

[39] Cf. Green, *Death of Jesus*, 105–34.

(John 12–21), with five chapters devoted to Jesus' final discourse (John 13–17). Third, it is in the passion material that John's Gospel is closest to the synoptic tradition, so this has been the focus of discussion on the possible literary relationship between the Synoptics and John.[40] Finally, within the passion narrative itself, John's portrayal of Jesus departs from that of the other canonical Gospels by its heightened emphasis on irony and Jesus' majesty.

These and other important motifs are developed helpfully in Donald Senior's final contribution to the Passion Series, *The Passion of Jesus in the Gospel of John.* The format of his study is now familiar: a general overview of the Gospel to show how John's narrative prepares for, and is integrated with, the passion of Jesus, followed by a more detailed analysis of the passion account itself, with a concluding section devoted to John's passion theology. The distinctive character of John's account allows Senior to focus on such themes as the role of the execution of Jesus in his journey as God's Son from incarnation to glorification; Jesus and his opponents; and the suffering of Jesus and discipleship.

The significant integration of Jesus' death into the overall Johannine story of Jesus has also been examined by Godfrey C. Nicholson.[41] Jesus has come from God, and in the passion narrative Jesus is shown to return to God; John's concern was to situate the death of Jesus within the context of the movement of the Son back to his Father. Hence, for John the death of Jesus was not an inexplicable calamity, but neither is John's presentation controlled by the categories of sacrifice and atonement (even if these are present—cf. John 1:29).

> Rather, the Johannine Passion Narrative is presented in terms of victory and glory: Jesus gives himself up to his arrestors, he becomes the judge, he is crowned as king and his cross becomes his throne. When he is ready to die (and not before), having put his own house in order, he lays down his life before anyone can take it from him (cf. 10:17f.).[42]

Carrying forward his ongoing study of the shape of Christian persuasion in the Roman world, Richard Cassidy's "new perspective" on John's Gospel includes an interesting study of the Johannine report of

---

[40]See D. Moody Smith, *John among the Gospels: The Relationship in Twentieth-Century Research* (Minneapolis: Fortress, 1992) 111–37; also Anton Dauer, *Die Passionsgeschichte im Johannesevangelium: Eine traditionsgeschichtliche und theologische Untersuchung zu John 18,1–19,30* (SANT 30; Munich: Kösel, 1972); Till Arend Mohr, *Markus- und Johannespassion: Redaktions- und traditionsgeschichtliche Untersuchungen der Markinischen und Johanneischen Passionstradition* (ATANT 70; Zurich: Theologischer, 1982).

[41]Godfrey C. Nicholson, *Death as Departure: The Johannine Descent-Ascent Schema* (SBLDS 63; Chico, Calif.: Scholars, 1983).

[42]Nicholson, *Death as Departure*, 3.

Jesus' Roman trial.[43] He regards this section of the Gospel as carefully plotted, dramatic in its presentation, as it shows how "Jesus comes to be tried before the Roman governor because he insists upon his own exalted identity and sharply attacks the Pharisees and the chief priests ('the Jews') for refusing to accept him."[44] On the one hand, Cassidy notes the evangelist's interest in the salvific consequences of Jesus' death, highlighted in an ironic way in the words of Caiaphas (John 11:47–53). On the other, through a series of six interchanges between Pilate and Jesus' adversaries—especially the Pharisees and chief priests—a more distinctively political element is brought into relief. Jesus is portrayed as sovereign in a way that supplants any possibility of support for the worship of the emperor, but also in a way that allows no room for violent resistance against Rome. Christians on trial *as* Christians are challenged to follow Jesus' example—calling into question the supremacy of Rome, bearing witness to the truth of the good news, inviting Rome and its representatives to faith.

In contrast to such readings of John's passion theology, J. Duncan M. Derrett argues that the fourth evangelist presents Jesus as a willing sacrificial victim.[45] Jesus is thus the victim in a double sense—the one executed at Israel's behest and the one whose sacrificial death was a vicarious atonement for the sins of the nation. As is typical of Derrett's other works, this one reexamines an important aspect of the Gospel from a vantage point very much outside the mainstream of Gospel study. In this case, the author is particularly influenced by his perception of sometimes quite evasive allusions to the OT, discerned between the lines of the Johannine narrative.

FAMILIAR QUESTIONS

If studies of the death of Jesus have focused more and more on the individual passion theologies of each evangelist and if a wide-angle lens has been used in such studies to situate the suffering and rejection of Jesus more fully in the narrative portrayal of his life in each Gospel, this does not mean that older and more familiar questions have been discarded completely. The question of the origin of the passion narrative

---

[43]Richard J. Cassidy, *John's Gospel in New Perspective: Christology and the Realities of Roman Power* (Maryknoll, N.Y.: Orbis, 1992) 40–53. Cf. his earlier *Jesus, Politics, and Society: A Study of Luke's Gospel* (Maryknoll, N.Y.: Orbis, 1978); and idem, *Society and Politics in the Acts of the Apostles* (Maryknoll, N.Y.: Orbis, 1987).

[44]Cassidy, *John's Gospel*, 41.

[45]J. Duncan M. Derrett, *The Victim: The Johannine Passion Narrative Reexamined* (Shipston-on-Stour, England: Drinkwater, 1993).

continues to be raised, in spite of premature conclusions in some, especially North American, circles that this had been resolved in favor of the hypothesis that the second evangelist was its architect. Moreover, the debate over the relation of the Scriptures of Israel to the passion accounts—creative or interpretive agent?—persists. Jesus studies, and especially the recovery of Jesus' social context in ancient Palestine, have brought into focus a third, now ongoing issue of a more narrowly historical sort. Why was Jesus executed? Pursued along *historical* lines, this issue nonetheless is implicated in profoundly significant *theological* concerns.

The Origin of the Passion Narrative

In the last decade or so, investigation of the origin of the passion narrative has been carried on less in order to isolate the possible sources of Mark 14–15;[46] instead, more attention has been paid to the possibility of non-Markan sources behind the Johannine and Lukan passion narratives. Till Arend Mohr, for example, argues that the Markan and Johannine passion accounts are independent of one another, with John's source actually the more primitive of the two.[47] Matti Myllykoski also focuses on the passion narratives of the second and fourth Gospels;[48] he assumes their independence and so, in his analysis of the Markan material, turns repeatedly to the Johannine for verification of his proposals about the traditional material employed by Mark. He believes that an old passion report began with the entry of Jesus and the Twelve into Jerusalem, followed by the scene of provocation at the temple, moving to the conspiracy scene of Mark 14:1–2, 10–11, then to the arrest scene and the examination of Jesus before the high priest. In vol. 2 of this study of "The Last Days of Jesus," he argues that this "old passion account" extended to include, in the briefest terms, a hearing before Pilate and a report of the crucifixion. This passion report accorded privilege to the question of Jesus' identity as "King of the Jews"—a focus consonant with its beginning in the early Christian mission, where the death of Jesus was characterized as the death of the Messiah. In his view,

---

[46] See, however, the recent conclusion in favor of a pre-Markan passion narrative in Adela Yarbro Collins, *The Beginning of the Gospel: Probings of Mark in Context* (Minneapolis: Fortress, 1992) ch. 4. C. Clifton Black (*The Disciples according to Mark: Markan Redaction in Current Debate* [JSNTSup 27; Sheffield: JSOT, 1989]) has shown how easily efforts at discerning redaction and tradition in Mark belie the preconceptions of those doing the discerning.

[47] Mohr, *Markus- und Johannespassion.*

[48] Matti Myllykoski, *Die letzen Tage Jesu: Markus und Johannes, ihre Traditionen und die historische Frage* (2 vols.; Suomalaisen Tiedeakatemian Toimituksia, Annales Academiae Scientiarum Fennicae B/256 and B/272; Helsinki: Suomalainen Tiedeakatemia, 1991–1994).

this account evolved into "an expanded passion narrative," which was then developed independently by Mark and John into their passion narratives.

The source-critical study of Marion Soards centers on the possibility that the third evangelist had access to a non-Markan passion source.[49] He concludes that Luke 22:1–71 represents Luke's redaction of the parallel material in Mark, together with "special Lukan material" (e.g., 22:3a, 15a–16c, and 19a–20c) derived either from Lukan composition or Luke's access to oral tradition. Etienne Trocmé, on the other hand, holds that Luke's narrative of Jesus' suffering and death is not at all based on the Gospel of Mark; in addition, he finds that the Fourth Gospel includes a passion account built along the same lines as, but not dependent on, the synoptic narratives.[50] Trocmé goes on to argue that an archetypal account of the passion, used independently by Mark, Luke, and John, dates back to the period before 40 C.E. and had its beginnings in the liturgical commemoration of Jesus' death by Christians during the Jewish celebration of Passover.

Three broadly conceived studies have been written by John Dominic Crossan, Joel B. Green, and Wolfgang Reinbold.[51] Of these, the most provocative is Crossan's. He argues that the earliest stratum of the apocryphal *Gospel of Peter* was a self-contained narrative of Jesus' passion and resurrection. This primitive account—the "Cross Gospel," according to Crossan—was composed of three narrative units: (1) crucifixion and deposition of Jesus, (2) tomb and guards, and (3) resurrection and confession. Mark's passion account has as its sole source this Cross Gospel; Matthew and Luke made use of both Mark's narrative and the Cross Gospel; John used all three synoptic accounts together with the Cross Gospel; and the *Gospel of Peter* was produced by the combination of the Cross Gospel with material from the four canonical Gospels. Crossan supports his theory in a detailed exegesis of each scene of the *Gospel of Peter*, drawing on a wide array of, especially, extracanonical Christian literature. For him, the dominant influence in the process of constructing the passion narratives was *passion prophecy*—i.e., the fabrication of passion events from OT texts.

By comparison, Green's work is more traditional. He regards the *Gospel of Peter* as secondary, dependent on the canonical Gospels.[52] He

---

[49] Marion L. Soards, *The Passion according to Luke: The Special Material of Luke 22* (JSNTSup 14; Sheffield: JSOT, 1987).

[50] Trocmé, *The Passion as Liturgy.*

[51] John Dominic Crossan, *The Cross That Spoke: The Origins of the Passion Narrative* (San Francisco: Harper & Row, 1988); Green, *Death of Jesus*; Wolfgang Reinbold, *Der älteste Bericht über den Tod Jesu: Literarische Analyse und historische Kritik der Passionsdarstellungen der Evangelien* (BZNW 69; Berlin/New York: Walter de Gruyter, 1994).

[52] Joel B. Green, "The *Gospel of Peter*: Source for a Pre-canonical Passion

thus builds his analysis of a precanonical passion narrative on the basis of (1) his arguments for Luke's use of a non-Markan passion account in addition to Mark and for the literary independence of Mark and John and (2) a detailed comparison of these three "sources" of the passion tradition. In his view, the early and ongoing practice of the Lord's Supper in the life of the church provided the setting for the development of the narrative tradition of Jesus' passion.

Like Green, Wolfgang Reinbold regards the *Gospel of Peter* as secondary and argues for the basic literary independence of John and the Synoptics.[53] Against Green, though, Reinbold regards the hypothesis of a special, Lukan passion source as unnecessary and so treats the Gospels of Mark and John as "primary tradition" for Jesus' passion. This analysis leads to the designation of "the earliest passion account" in nine scenes: resolution to have Jesus executed; entry into Jerusalem; last meal with the announcements of betrayal and denial; arrest; hearing before the high priest and denial of Peter; hearing before Pilate and the Barabbas episode; scourging and mockery; crucifixion and death; and burial. According to Reinbold, this account was available in written form as a report of historical narrative, a "narrative concerning the death of Jesus Christ" (διήγησις περὶ τοῦ θανάτου Ἰησοῦ Χριστοῦ, *diēgēsis peri tou thanatou Iēsou Christou*.)

Early on in his analysis, Reinbold insists that the issue of historical veracity must be kept separate from the literary identification of an early passion tradition. Not surprisingly, then, he devotes part 2 of his monograph to a more narrowly focused historical analysis—first of the various scenes of "the oldest passion account," then of various secondary elements in the wider passion tradition and relevant testimony about Jesus' death elsewhere in the NT and beyond. Interestingly, Reinbold finds that the theological concerns emphasized in the unhistorical material of "the earliest passion account" underscored Jesus' innocence according to the Roman perspective and the complicity of the Jews in the crucifixion of Jesus.

The Old Testament and the Gospel Passion Accounts

Early in the twentieth century, Martin Dibelius had postulated the formative role of the OT in the developing passion tradition. Some more recent critics have pushed Dibelius's hypothesis to the limit, arguing that the earliest passion accounts had little or no historical basis but are based entirely on contemplation of the OT. As we have noted, this is the view of Crossan, and on this point he is joined by others, including

---

Narrative?" *ZNW* 78 (1987) 293–301.
[53]Reinbold, *Der älteste Bericht über den Tod Jesu*.

Werner Kelber.[54] Whether the OT served above all as the basis for the creation of passion material in the absence of historical memory or was most prominent for its interpretive agency has thus become a topic of discussion, taken up at length by Douglas Moo.[55]

Moo locates his examination of the use of the OT in the Gospel passion accounts within a larger exploration of contemporary Jewish hermeneutics. Appealing to a range of biblical interpretations within the period of Second Temple Judaism, Moo argues against the assumption that biblical texts might exercise a creative influence at the point of application. Even though OT texts were often conscripted for the interpretive agenda of Jewish writers and communities, narrative does not appear to have been created on the basis of Scripture. Rather, Moo points out, more evidence exists for emendation of the scriptural text in order to make it fit more closely the shape of recent events.

One other point about recent study of the OT and the passion theology of the Gospels is worth mentioning. This is the growing recognition of the phenomenon of intertextuality in the NT materials as a whole and in the passion accounts in particular. Previous scholarship had insisted on plain, explicit evidence for the deliberate citation of OT materials and often treated the use of OT texts in an atomistic way. As illustrated, for example, by the study of Joel Marcus (noted above, and see ch. 11 below), students of the Gospel passion accounts are more and more ready to explore how these narratives are engaged in an interplay of other texts and so exist as nodes within a larger literary and interpretive scriptural network.

What Killed Jesus?

Until recently, the question, What killed Jesus? was especially related to Jesus' foreknowledge or intent: Did Jesus "intend" his death? Did he anticipate his death? Did he interpret his death?[56] Contemporary installments to the quest of the historical Jesus have given this matter a new twist, however. In fact, John Meier, whose recently published tome covers only matters preliminary to a discussion of the historical Jesus, goes so far as to list as a criterion for determining what

---

[54]Werner H. Kelber, *The Oral and the Written Gospel: The Hermeneutics of Speaking and Writing in the Synoptic Tradition, Mark, Paul, and Q* (Philadelphia: Fortress, 1983) 196–97.

[55]Douglas J. Moo, *The Old Testament in the Gospel Passion Narratives* (Sheffield: Almond, 1983); cf. R. T. France and David Wenham, eds., *Studies in Midrash and Historiography* (GP 3; Sheffield: JSOT, 1983).

[56]Cf., e.g., Joachim Gnilka, "Wie urteilte Jesus über seine Tod?" in *Der Tod Jesu: Deutungen im Neuen Testament*, ed. Karl Kertelge (QD 74; Freiburg/Basel/Vienna: Herder, 1976) 13–50; Rudolph Pesch, *Das Abendmahl und Jesu Todesverständnis* (QD 80; Freiburg/Basel/Vienna: Herder, 1978).

material actually comes from Jesus the "Criterion of Rejection and Execution": what historical words and deeds of Jesus can explain his trial and crucifixion as "King of the Jews"?[57]

Why did Jesus have to die? Several answers have been given. Jesus had to die as a religious deceiver and false prophet, according to Deut 13.[58] Jesus, in his saying about the Son of humanity (ὁ υἱὸς τοῦ ἀνθρώπου, *ho huios tou anthrōpou*) seated at the right hand of God, committed blasphemy, a capital violation.[59] Jesus' teachings threatened the sensitive coexistence of Jewish and Roman authority, and even Roman sovereignty itself[60]—though this is not necessarily to characterize Jesus as a "zealot."[61] And so on.

The magnitude of the question, What killed Jesus? for historical scholarship arises out of the virtual certainty of Jesus' execution by means of crucifixion—a form of capital punishment ordinarily reserved for Roman military and political punishment—by the Romans.[62] And it is against this question that contemporary attempts to present the historical Jesus will be measured.[63]

---

[57]John P. Meier, *A Marginal Jew: Rethinking the Historical Jesus*, vol. 1, *The Roots of the Problem and the Person* (ABRL; New York: Doubleday, 1991) 177. Cf. Ellis Rivkin, *What Crucified Jesus? The Political Execution of a Charismatic* (Nashville: Abingdon; London: SCM, 1984); Francis Watson, "Why Was Jesus Crucified?" *Theology* 88 (1985) 105–12.

[58]Cf. Graham N. Stanton, "Jesus of Nazareth: A Magician and False Prophet Who Deceived God's People?" in *Jesus of Nazareth: Lord and Christ. Essays on the Historical Jesus and New Testament Christology*, ed. Joel B. Green and Max Turner (Grand Rapids: Eerdmans; Carlisle: Paternoster, 1994) 164–80; Peter Stuhlmacher, *Jesus of Nazareth—Christ of Faith* (Peabody, Mass.: Hendrickson, 1993) 42–47.

[59]Darrell L. Bock, "The Son of Man Seated at God's Right Hand and the Debate over Jesus' 'Blasphemy,'" in Green and Turner, *Jesus of Nazareth*, 181–91.

[60]Nils A. Dahl, "Messianic Ideas and the Crucifixion of Jesus," rev. Donald H. Juel, in *The Messiah: Developments in Earliest Judaism and Christianity*, ed. James H. Charlesworth (Minneapolis: Fortress, 1992) 382–403. E. P. Sanders (*Jesus and Judaism* [London: SCM, 1985]) relates Jesus' political threat to his prophetic act against the Jerusalem temple.

[61]See the thoroughgoing denial of the characterization of Jesus as a revolutionary in Ernst Bammel and C. F. D. Moule, eds., *Jesus and the Politics of His Day* (Cambridge: Cambridge University, 1984).

[62]Cf. A. E. Harvey, *Jesus and the Constraints of History* (Philadelphia: Westminster, 1982) 11–12.

[63]Thus, e.g., Stephen Mitchell's "historical Jesus" fails to convince. In *The Gospel according to Jesus: A New Translation and Guide to His Essential Teachings for Believers and Unbelievers* (New York: HarperCollins, 1991) he allows no room for the historical Jesus to have provoked opposition sufficient to lead to his death by execution.

Conclusion

Clearly, this central ingredient of Christian faith, the death of Jesus, continues to excite the interest of students of the NT. For study of the enigma of his crucifixion, multiple methods are being engaged—literary and narratological, literary-theological, social-scientific, and more traditional, historical approaches. This is a consequence of the several levels of meaning contemporary study seeks to discern, for the focus today is both on why the historical Jesus was executed in so brutal and dishonorable a manner and on how those early Christians worked to make sense of his ignominious demise.

 **TWO**

THE DEATH OF JESUS IN THE GOSPEL ACCORDING TO MARK

INTRODUCTION

"The death of Jesus broods over the entire Gospel [of Mark]."[1] This observation is as true as it may be surprising, given the focus of Mark's early chapters on Jesus the wonder-worker and herald of God's kingdom. Jesus, after all, is the one over whom the crowds gush, "A new teaching—with authority!" (1:27) and, "We have never seen anything like this!" (2:12). "He has done everything well!" they cheer (7:37). This is the one whose fame spread throughout Galilee (1:28), so that he was unable even to enter a town openly (1:45). Nevertheless, it is true: already near the outset of Jesus' public ministry as Mark narrates it, the Pharisees turn against him and begin to conspire with the Herodians how to destroy him (3:6).

To a significant degree, how we understand the death of Jesus in Mark's Gospel depends on how we learn to correlate these two sides of Mark's portrait of Jesus. Although it is easy enough to divide the Gospel as a whole into two major thematic sections—the first highlighting Jesus the miracle worker and authoritative teacher, the second centering on Jesus who embraces his divinely appointed death on a Roman cross—in fact these two motifs are juxtaposed throughout the whole Gospel, from beginning to end. The miracle worker is the Suffering Servant. The herald of the advent of God's kingdom is the stone the builders rejected. The authoritative teacher is he who stands silent

---

[1] Ernest Best, *Mark: The Gospel as Story* (SNTW; Edinburgh: T. & T. Clark, 1983) 66.

before his accusers and the Roman governor. The one whom God declares to be "my son" is the one whose last declaration is, "My God, my God, why have you forsaken me?"

What purpose do these paradoxical images serve? What needs are served by the foregrounding of these apparent incongruities? What does Mark, the narrator of the Second Gospel,[2] hope to communicate in this way about Christology? discipleship? Such questions as these will occupy our attention in this chapter.

FOREBODINGS

With the introduction of new literary criticism to Gospel research, Norman Petersen pointed out the significant place of prediction and anticipatory allusion in the Second Gospel.[3] Narratives generally move forward as possibilities are introduced, whether to be frustrated, actualized, or left unfulfilled in the ensuing script. Jesus' passion, as an aspect of Mark's narrative strategy, is introduced as early as 2:18–20. Asked why he does not instruct his disciples to fast in a manner similar to the followers of either the Pharisees or the Baptist, Jesus replies that the presence of the bridegroom precludes fasting. "The days are coming," he continues, "when the bridegroom will be taken away from them, and then they will fast on that day." A similar turn of events is recounted in 2 Esdr 9:38–10:4: after God's provision of a long-awaited son, when he entered his wedding chamber on the day of the feast, he fell down and died, giving rise to mourning and fasting. Hence, although the verb Jesus uses (ἀπαίρω, apairō, "travel") connotes nothing particularly tragic, this thematic echo intimates his unexpected departure.

Jesus returns to the subject of his impending death, albeit in a veiled way, in 6:4, where he identifies himself as a prophet. That he does so in the context of his being rejected by his townspeople underscores his proleptic identification with the fate of all the prophets—rejection and death (e.g., Neh 9:26; Jer 2:30). What is more, this scene in Mark is followed immediately by the account of the beheading of John (6:14–29), himself a prophet.[4]

---

[2]As with the other canonical Gospels, the Gospel of Mark is anonymous, although early tradition attributed its writing to Mark, companion of Peter (Papias, cited in Eusebius *Hist. Eccl.* 3.39.15; cf. the anti-Marcionite prologues; Irenaeus *Haer.* 3.1.1). In this chapter, we employ the name "Mark" to refer to the narrator of the Second Gospel without bias as to the actual authorship of this document.

[3]Norman R. Petersen, *Literary Criticism for New Testament Critics* (GBS; Philadelphia: Fortress, 1978) 49–80.

[4]Note also the impressive parallels between John's passion and Jesus', as

These are relatively allusive anticipations of Jesus' death from early in the Second Gospel. Within their immediate cotexts,[5] however, their meaning and impact are more obvious. On the one hand, given the overwhelming success of Jesus' ministry, these more negative notes are heard more sharply. On the other, even in the early chapters of Mark, the response to Jesus is not homogeneous. In addition to his great following, he attracts adversaries. Mark thus introduces a theme of conflict that adds texture to Jesus' own hints of calamity and initiates an important element of dramatic tension to the narrative, driving the reader forward to discover how this conflict will be resolved.

As we will see later in this chapter, this theme of conflict serves another, perhaps even more significant role: it fosters for Mark's audience a point of decision. It becomes clear almost immediately that Jesus' ministry does not encourage fence sitting. Nevertheless, for readers of the Second Gospel, determining with whom to side concerning Jesus will not be easy because, as the narrative progresses, it becomes increasingly difficult to determine who really is for Jesus. Even his closest followers appear at times in the garb of opponents.

Conflict and Plots

The first hint of conflict raises its head in 1:14 with the mysterious, offhand report that John had been arrested. We are told neither by whom nor for what reason he was taken into custody, only that this took place prior to Jesus' public ministry in Galilee. The degree to which the work of John and Jesus have already been interrelated—in the Isaianic citation (1:2–3), in the characterization of John as forerunner and his prediction of a coming Powerful One (1:4–8), and in Jesus' baptism by John (1:9–11)—nurtures doubts about whether we are to understand the relation between John's arrest and the onset of Jesus' mission as merely temporal. If the one who prepares the way is imprisoned, what will happen to the one for whom the way had been prepared?

Any such suspicions are quickly suspended by the subsequent account of Jesus' ministry, for in his opening forays into Galilee he is enormously successful and esteemed. With the most unadorned invitation,

---

both are narrated by Mark: (1) the Roman authority is sympathetic toward his prisoner, whom he regards as innocent (6:20; 15:14); (2) he pronounces the death sentence only at the instigation of others (6:26; 15:15); and (3) the body of the executed is sought, taken, and laid in a tomb (6:29; 15:42–47). Cf. Senior, *Passion of Jesus in Mark*, 16–20. It is true that, on a first reading of Mark 6, one would not recognize in these parallels an anticipation of Jesus' passion; rereading, however, would make this evident.

[5]"Cotext" refers to the string of linguistic data within which a text is set, the relationship, say, of a sentence to a paragraph or of a pericope in Mark's Gospel to the larger Markan narrative.

fishermen are ready to set aside their lives to follow him (1:16–20). He teaches and heals, even manifesting power over the demonic and cleansing a leper (1:21–44). As a consequence, his reputation and area of influence proliferate (1:45).

It is only with Mark 2 that the renewed theme of antagonism begins to spill again into the open. Here there is a progression of hostility—from scribes "questioning in their hearts" (2:6–7), to open queries of the disciples about Jesus' behavior (2:16), to open confrontation with Jesus about his disciples' behavior (2:18, 24), and finally to a collective attempt by the Pharisees to catch Jesus in a religious infraction (3:2). This malevolence reaches its crescendo finally in 3:6: "Immediately the Pharisees went out and with the Herodians conspired against him, how they might destroy him."

Departing town, Jesus wins for himself a brief respite (3:7–19a), but controversy finds him again upon his return to Capernaum (3:19b–35). Even the momentary lull in the clash between Jesus and his detractors advances the theme of conflict for the reader, however, for among the apostles Jesus chooses is one about whom Mark gives warning ahead of time: "Judas Iscariot, who betrayed him" (3:19). We might think that around the protagonist would gather his allies, persons who would assist him in his mission from God; instead, even among his helpers one is cast in the role of opponent. Are the boundaries between helpers and adversaries so porous? Apparently so, since in the immediately adjacent scene even Jesus' family—his own mother, brothers, and sisters—come to restrain him, believing he is out of his mind. In this way they appear in league with the Jerusalem scribes, similarly blind to the activity of the Spirit manifest in Jesus. Unlike his family, who believe Jesus has lost his senses, the scribes attribute his behavior to satanic incursion. This leads to a fundamental redefinition of Jesus' family: his inner circle consists of "whoever does the will of God" (3:35).

Again by the sea, away from town, Jesus enjoys a respite from enemy challenge, teaching a large crowd together with his disciples (4:1–34). Even this proves to be a less safe place than anticipated, however, for we learn that in spite of privileged instruction (4:10–12, 33–34), his disciples respond to him in ignorance (4:35–41). Failing to recognize who their master is, they substitute fear for faith, proving how ill-suited they are to serve his mission.

As the story continues with Jesus farther away from the town of his detractors, he is again successful against diabolic forces, even gaining a herald of the good news in the area of the Decapolis (5:1–20). Demonstrating that a leading Jew might respond with open faith, Jairus seeks and receives help from Jesus, as does an unclean woman (5:21–43); having returned to the town of his upbringing, however, Jesus again encounters resistance, this time from his own neighbors and kin (6:1–6). Following this, he sends his disciples to engage in ministry, but not before preparing them for rejection, too (6:7–13; esp. v. 11). Might they not participate in the fate of John, who went before them (6:14–29)? Again, in spite of their positions of privilege around Jesus, the disciples prove themselves slow to learn, and they respond to him with misunderstanding and fear (6:37, 50).

The Pharisees and Jerusalem scribes locate Jesus anew as he travels among the villages and towns, and not surprisingly, given their past toxic relations, this leads immediately to confrontation. As in the past, so now the focus of controversy is the interpretation of God's commandments (7:1–23). Following an argument with the Pharisees, again intent on testing Jesus (8:11–13), Mark narrates a lengthy interlude where Jesus' interactions are more focused on his disciples (8:27–10:52, though cf. 8:31; 10:2, 33). This change of focus does not signal an end to the theme of conflict, however, for the disciples continue to demonstrate their lack of understanding, even lack of support, of Jesus' divine mission (8:32; 9:5–6, 18–19, 28–29, 32, 33–40; 10:13–14, 32, 35–45). In this way, they show themselves to be people of the same generation as the Pharisees (8:12; 9:19)—unbelieving, slow to discern and align themselves with God's purpose.

Upon Jesus' entry into Jerusalem, dramatic tension is further exacerbated. This is true, first, because Jesus has foretold his death in Jerusalem (10:33), but also because he has entered the territory of his chief opponents (recall that the scribes who had tested him in Galilee were themselves Jerusalemites). Thus, a series of Jewish groups question him during his ministry in the temple (11:27–12:34), and the active plotting against Jesus reappears in 11:18; 12:12. Standing in the way of attempts to do away with Jesus is his popular support (11:18; 12:12; 14:1)—an obstacle surmounted by the collusion of Judas, one of the Twelve (14:10–11—about which we have been forewarned). With this convergence of persons hostile to Jesus with a defecting member of his shaky inner circle, the passion begins. The progression of Jesus' public mission has been overtaken by forces working against it.

Predictions

In Mark's Gospel, Jesus is not oblivious to the hostile forces sweeping around him. On the contrary, he engages in open criticism of his opponents, predicts his own suffering and death, and, most important, interprets this fatal turn of events as integral to God's redemptive purpose.

In Mark's rendering, Jesus is the Spirit-directed herald of the good news who carries out his divine commission. This commission he receives at his baptism (1:9–11), then repeatedly clarifies in "wilderness experiences" and prayer (1:12–13, 35–39; 6:30–46; 14:32–42). Thus, there is a deliberateness about his journey to Jerusalem in the face of hostility, and he seems almost driven to this destination, where he will fulfill God's purpose.

This journey to Jerusalem and its meaning are the particular focus of the lengthy section extending from 8:27 to 10:52. Repeatedly we are informed that Jesus is travelling, on "the way" (8:27; 9:33, 34; 10:17, 32, 46, 52)—an echo of "the way of the Lord" proclaimed by the Isaianic herald whose appearance Mark promulgates (1:1–3). This way leads to Jerusalem, but more especially it leads to the fulfillment of the divine purpose. "The journey is the way of God. Being 'on the way' means more than moving through a physical landscape to Jerusalem; it also means that Jesus moves toward the goal God has set before him: death in the service of proclaiming God's rule."[6] Controlling this journey and inter- preting it is a series of predictions of Jesus' suffering, death, and resurrection (8:31; 9:31; 10:33–34; cf. 9:12). In each, Jesus outlines the coming events but also emphasizes their divine necessity: "the Son of humanity [ὁ υἱὸς τοῦ ἀνθρώπου, ho huios tou anthrōpou] must [δεῖ, dei] suffer many things." In one sense this situates Jesus' passion within the rubric of divine fiat: Jesus must suffer because God wills it. In another sense Mark situates this suffering in a particular context—at the hands of the Jewish leadership in "this adulterous and sinful generation" (8:38; cf. 8:12; 9:19). We might ask, What other fate might those who follow God receive? (See the story of the Baptist!) In yet a further sense, this suffering is necessary because it is critical to the drama by which God brings redemption. This sense arises from our recognition that within Judaism innocent suffering was not without meaning. It was regarded as *efficacious*.[7] What is more, Jesus' recognition of the centrality of the cross to God's plan and his obedience in embracing this plan situate the cross squarely at the heart of his own mission. It is against such a backdrop that Jesus interprets his suffering as the acme of his divine mission. His mission is this: to win salvation for others (10:45; 14:22–24). By refusing to save his own life, he saves others (15:31; cf. 8:35).

WHO DO PEOPLE SAY THAT I AM?

A Question of Identity—Perspectives

Alongside, often overlapping, the theme of conflict in Mark is a further emphasis—namely, the question of Jesus' identity. The ques-

---

[6]David Rhoads and Donald Michie, *Mark as Story: An Introduction to the Narrative of a Gospel* (Philadelphia: Fortress, 1982) 64.

[7]See, e.g., Isa 52:13–53:12; 1 Macc 2:27–38; 2 Macc 6:18–7:42; 4 Macc 6:28–29.

tion, Who is Jesus? breaks out into the open in 8:27, 29, where Jesus asks of his disciples, in turn, "Who do people say that I am?" and, "Who do you say that I am?" But this issue has been a pivotal one from ch. 1. The crowds ask of one another, "What is this? A new teaching—with authority!" (1:27). Demons do not ask, but they seem to perceive already who Jesus is—"I know who you are, the Holy One of God!" (1:24); "What have you to do with me, Jesus, Son of the Most High God?" (5:7; cf. 1:34). Yet Jesus silences these voices. Though diabolical spirits recognize him, their acclamations are empty: they serve another.

Jesus' adversaries, too, worry over his identity. In particular, they wonder by what authorization he says what he says and behaves as he does: "Where did this man get all this? What is this wisdom that has been given to him?" (6:2). "By what authority are you doing these things?" (11:28; cf. 2:7, 16, 24; 3:21–22; 6:14–16).

Most puzzling to the reader and frustrating to Jesus is the failure of Jesus' own disciples to grasp his identity. Even after receiving private instruction, they are stunned by his mastery of the storm and sea: "Who then is this, that even the wind and the sea obey him?" (4:41). When he comes to them walking on the sea, they take him for a ghost (6:49).

God, on the other hand, is clear about Jesus' identity. Twice God claims Jesus as "my son, the beloved" (1:11; 9:7), and Jesus affirms this relationship in his Gethsemane prayer: "Abba, Father" (14:36; cf. 13:32). This perspective is also shared by the narrator, Mark (1:1), so it is surely of consequence that it is shared by no other human being until the very end of the story. It is true that Peter acclaims Jesus as Messiah (8:29), but his understanding of this title is clearly deficient (8:27–33); in any case, "Messiah" is not a title Jesus ever uses as a self-description in Mark, and he allows it otherwise only when properly nuanced. No, it is only the centurion, and he only when facing the cross and observing the manner of Jesus' death, who recognizes Jesus as God's Son (15:39). This underscores unambiguously the necessary correlation between Jesus' identity and his crucifixion. Without the passion, Jesus cannot be understood.

Jesus, Wonder-Worker

This is not the whole story, however. In understanding Jesus in the Gospel of Mark, one must also account for the heightened interest in Jesus as authoritative teacher and popular miracle worker. Indeed, at times it appears that Mark is more interested in portraying Jesus in this way than in relating the content of that teaching or the details of those miracles. That is, Mark often resorts to *telling* rather than *showing*, taking advantage of the device of summary. Thus, e.g., in 1:32–34; 3:7–11; 6:53–56 the exact nature, the what and how, of his healing ministry is not delineated. Rather, the spotlight pinpoints that healing activity's magnitude, made glaringly obvious through such descriptive phrases as "the whole city gathered," "he cured many," "he cast out many demons," "all who had diseases pressed upon him," and "all . . . were healed."

Nevertheless, stories of Jesus' power abound. He manifests authority over cosmic forces (1:23–27; 4:35–41; 5:1–20; 6:47–52; 7:24–30; 9:14–30); after all, Jesus has plundered the house of the devil (3:27). He cures all manner of diseases—fever (1:29–31), leprosy (1:40–45), paralysis (2:1–12), a withered hand (3:1–5), hemorrhaging (5:25–34), deafness (7:31–35), and blindness (8:22–26; 10:46–52); he even restores a dead girl to life (5:35–43).

His miraculous power extends further, to include the feeding of thousands (6:33–44; 8:1–10), the cursing of the fig tree (11:12–27), and prescience (11:1–6; 14:12–16). Other miraculous activity accompanies his ministry—e.g., his transfiguration (9:2–8), the darkness and rending of the temple veil at his death (15:33, 38), and, of course, his resurrection (16:6).

What is particularly remarkable about this conglomeration of powerful manifestations is their fundamental characterization in Mark as expressions that Jesus teaches as one having authority. This is highlighted initially and decisively in his opening and prototypical appearance in the Capernaum synagogue (1:21–28). There the label "teaching" is used to describe both instruction (1:21–22) and exorcism (1:23–27).

What is the function of these miracle stories and miraculous ingredients worked into the larger narrative?[8] Most essentially, they function to portray Jesus as the powerful teacher who manifests the power of God, the herald of the kingdom in whose ministry God's own restorative power has come to open expression. Some miracle stories go on to demonstrate that the redeeming grace of God at work in Jesus' ministry is available to Gentiles as well as Jews, for Jesus performs in the region of the Gentiles the same kinds of miracles (exorcism and feeding miracles—5:1–20; 8:1–10) he performs among the Jewish people.

What is more, from Mark 2 onward it becomes clear that Jesus' activity as authoritative teacher and agent of miraculous power is the impetus for the negative attention he receives from his opponents. Though recognizing his power, some attribute it to the devil (3:22) while others test him, asking for a sign (8:11). As Edwin Broadhead claims, "The power of Jesus' words and deeds seals the death plot against him." Indeed, that both passion-oriented statements and evidences of miraculous power are interspersed throughout the Markan narrative, including

---

[8]See, most recently, Edwin K. Broadhead, *Teaching with Authority: Miracles and Christology in the Gospel of Mark* (JSNTSup 74; Sheffield: JSOT, 1992).

the passion narrative itself, is illustrative of the integration of these into one coherent portrait. They do not so much stand in tension as they merge together in order to signify the full nature of his mission. On the one hand, "Jesus is the powerful proclaimer whose wondrous teachings lead to his death."[9] On the other, in his words and deeds of power and in his suffering and death we see the expression of the one mission of God's Son, whose life is given for the redemption of others.

THE MOMENT OF REVELATION

According to Mark, in the midst of his journey to Jerusalem and in conversation with his disciples, Jesus interpreted his death as the zenith of his mission: "The Son of humanity came . . . to give his life a ransom for many" (10:45). In its immediate cotext (10:35–45), this assertion serves as the ultimate object lesson for the disciples who have been slow to learn Jesus' message about the sort of life that honors the way of the Lord—an other-centered life, especially oriented toward those of low status and in need (cf. 9:33–41; 10:13–16). As such, it also documents the centrality of the cross for Jesus' messianic message and so directs our attention to the Markan account of Jesus' passion and death.

In sharpest focus is the scene of Jesus' death, Mark 15:33–39, for it stitches into one fabric two narrative threads that reach back into the larger Gospel. The first we have already mentioned; this is the question and meaning of Jesus' identity as God's Son. The second is also of importance, however; this relates to the Jerusalem temple. In the Markan account of Jesus' last moments, these two issues are addressed as direct, parallel consequences of Jesus' death:

> (1) Then Jesus gave a loud cry and breathed his last, and the veil of the temple was torn in two, from top to bottom (15:38).

> (2) When the centurion who stood facing Jesus saw that in this way he breathed his last, he said, "Truly this man was God's Son!" (15:39).[10]

The death of Jesus, then, is a critical moment of revelation in the Second Gospel, for in his dying breath Jesus' kinship with God is manifest and he replaces the now defunct temple. "In Jesus' death on

---

[9]Broadhead, *Teaching with Authority*, 208, 213.

[10]Contra David Ulansey ("The Heavenly Veil Torn: Mark's Cosmic *Inclusio*," *JBL* 110 [1991] 123–25), Jesus' death does not lead to the torn veil, and the torn veil to the centurion's confession. Mark narrates the centurion's words as a response to "how Jesus thus died" (ὅτι οὕτως ἐξέπνευσεν, *hoti houtōs exepneusen*); cf. the repeated ἐξέπνευσεν (*exepneusen*, "expired," vv. 37, 39).

the cross, the regal presence of God is revealed."[11] How does the Markan narrative prepare for this climactic point?

Jesus and the Temple

The import of the temple to Mark's presentation of the crucifixion is confirmed by his multiple references to it in the passion account. In his Jewish trial scene, false witnesses are brought forward to certify, "We heard him say, 'I will destroy this temple made with hands, and in three days I will build another, not made with hands' " (14:58). At Jesus' crucifixion, passersby wag their heads at Jesus, saying, "Aha! You who would destroy the temple and build it in three days, save yourself, and come down from the cross!" (15:29–30). Third, as a consequence of Jesus' death, "the veil of the temple was torn in two, from top to bottom" (15:38).

At the same time, the temple material in the Markan passion account is not without precedent in the Second Gospel. By intercalating the story of the cursing of the fig tree within that of Jesus' obstruction of the normal activity of the temple (11:15–21), Mark interprets Jesus' action in the temple not merely as its cleansing but as its cursing. For him, the time of the temple is no more, for it has lost its fecundity. Indeed, read in its immediate cotext, Jesus' subsequent instruction to the disciples, "Truly I tell you, if you say to this mountain, 'Be taken up and thrown into the sea . . . ' " (11:23), can refer only to the mountain on which the temple was built!

What is Jesus' concern with the temple? Why does he regard it as extraneous to God's purpose? Hints may be found in the mixed citation of Mark 11:17, part of which derives from Isa 56:7, the other from Jer 11:7. Intended as a house of prayer for all the nations, the temple has been transformed by the Jewish leaders in Jerusalem into a den of brigands. That is, the temple has been perverted in favor of both socioreligious aims (the exclusion of Gentiles as potential recipients of divine reconciliation) and politico-economic purposes (legitimating and consolidating the power of the chief priests, whose teaching might be realized even in the plundering of a poor widow's livelihood—cf. 12:41–44).

The reference to Jer 11:7 is significant in a second way. Jeremiah had railed against those who, after committing atrocities, sought sanctuary in the temple; such behavior will lead to the destruction of the temple, he avowed. Jesus intimates this same fate for the Jerusalem

---

[11]Linnemann, *Passionsgeschichte,* 163; cf. Paul Christoph Böttger, *Der König der Juden—das Heil für die Völker: Die Geschichte Jesu Christi im Zeugnis des Markusevangeliums* (Neukirchen-Vluyn: Neukirchener, 1981) 90–91.

temple by his allusion to Jeremiah. The coming destruction of the temple is highlighted elsewhere—by Mark's placement of this saying in the midst of his account of Jesus' cursing of the fig tree (see above), by the direct prophecy of destruction in 13:1–2, and also by the temple charge that surfaces twice in the passion narrative (14:58; 15:29–30).

What is more, Jesus apparently expects the construction of a replacement for the temple, even if it is one not made with human hands. This is the force of 12:10–11: a stone rejected by the builders of the temple has been made its cornerstone. In this pericope, Jesus uses temple imagery from Ps 118 to refer to his own rejection and vindication and, in the process, documents his expectation of a new temple, inclusive of "others" (12:9; Gentiles?). This is the community of his disciples.[12] With this background it becomes clear that in the passion account Mark announces the replacement of the old temple in Jesus' death—ironically in the charges brought against Jesus at his trial and the words of mockery at his crucifixion, straightforwardly in his report of the rending of the temple veil.

Jesus, Son of Humanity, Son of God

If the death of Jesus is the climax of the passion account, the scene of Jesus' struggle in prayer (14:32–42) is clearly its turning point. Here Jesus discerns and submits to the will of God, conjoining Mark's emphases on Son of God and Son of humanity into one. By this emphasis on Son of humanity, we have in mind above all the dual stress on Jesus' authority, evident especially in controversy stories, and on Jesus' suffering and death, manifest in his passion predictions. Previously we have been told, "the Son of humanity *will be* delivered up"; in Gethsemane, "the Son of humanity *is* delivered up" (14:41). The identification of Jesus as God's Son was made initially by the evangelist in 1:1, then confirmed by God at Jesus' baptism and transfiguration (1:11; 9:7). Now, in addressing his prayer to "Abba, Father" (14:36), Jesus himself acknowledges this relationship. Undoubtedly, it is as Son of humanity that Jesus is Son of God, and vice versa. Suffering and death are not inconsistent with power and authority, or even incongruous with resurrection and return (8:31; 9:31; 10:34; 13:26), for all of these are only elements in the life of the one fully obedient to God's redemptive purpose, the Son of God.

We may also add that just as Gethsemane serves as the turning point in the passion narrative, it also functions as the crisis in the life

---

[12] See Marcus, *Way of the Lord*, 119–28; cf. Donald Juel, *Messiah and Temple: The Trial of Jesus in the Gospel of Mark* (SBLDS 31; Missoula, Mont.: Scholars, 1973) 159–68.

of the Son of God. As Feldmeier has seen, it is here, in prayer at Gethsemane, that Jesus first experiences the silence of God, a divine estrangement that comes to full expression on the cross, in Jesus' final words, "My God, my God, why have you forsaken me?" (15:34). In effect, these words are the completion of the prayer begun in Gethsemane, "not what I will, but what you will" (14:36), as the Son affirms his unwavering trust in his Father even while experiencing the horror of encroaching death.[13]

DISCIPLESHIP AND THE CROSS

It is perhaps shocking that the centurion, not one of Jesus' followers, identifies Jesus as God's Son. We have no history of him in the narrative. He is not one of the Twelve. He is given no name. He is a Gentile.

On the other hand, that a nameless Gentile receives this revelation is consonant with the shape of the Markan narrative as a whole. Repeatedly, people who appear at the periphery in Mark, "little people," have flashes of insight; they understand far more than perhaps they should, certainly far more than Jesus' chosen inner circle. A Gentile demoniac recognizes the hand of the Lord at work in Jesus' healing activity (5:19–20). An unclean, sick woman believes and receives healing (5:25–34). A synagogue ruler appears in Mark 5, too, at a point in the narrative where Mark's audience may have been tempted to give up on Jewish leaders as hopelessly taken up with their own agenda; yet Jairus, concerned for the health of his daughter, pleads with Jesus, and he restores her to life (5:21–24, 35–43). A nameless, Syrophoenician, Gentile woman bests Jesus in verbal exchange, resulting in the casting out of a demon from her daughter (7:24–30). A blind man, held back by the crowds, recognizes Jesus and, after being healed, follows him on "the way" (10:46–52). A woman proleptically anoints Jesus' body for burial, showing that she understands better than his disciples the nature of his mission (14:3–9). Simon of Cyrene, previously unknown to us, "takes up his cross" (15:21; cf. 8:34). Women are found at the cross after the disciples have all fled (15:40–41). To children belongs the kingdom (10:14).

Contrast these "success stories" with the characterization of the disciples in Mark! Though called and equipped to share in his mission, they are repeatedly found to be woefully inadequate in their under-

---

[13] See Reinhard Feldmeier, *Die Krisis des Gottessohnes: Die Gethsemaneerzählung als Schlüssel der Markuspassion* (WUNT 2:21; Tübingen: J. C. B. Mohr [Paul Siebeck], 1987); also Senior, *Passion of Jesus in Mark*, 123–24.

standing of Jesus. Thus, rather than gaining recognition for their solidarity with him and his divine mission, more often than not they appear to be working at cross-purposes (see above).

This routine of discipleship failure is continued in the passion account itself. Disciples scold the woman who anoints Jesus' body for burial and thus receive a reprimand from Jesus (14:5–9). True to Jesus' prophecies, one betrays him, one denies him, and all desert him (14:18, 27–31, 43, 50, 66–72). Their failure is highlighted further in comparison with the parallel account of John's passion. After his execution "his disciples . . . came and took his body, and laid it in a tomb" (6:29); after Jesus' execution his disciples are conspicuously absent, so that a Jewish leader serves this role.[14]

In the midst of a narrative of discipleship failure, which finds its acme in the passion account, the tableaus of faithfulness we have reviewed are all the more astonishing. What might this portend for Mark's understanding of the nexus between the cross of Christ and the community of his followers?

The Community of Mark

The Gospel of Mark has no "address," of course, nor does it divulge (in an explicit way, at least) its date of composition. Hence, it is not possible to pinpoint with precision the audience to whom this Gospel might have been addressed. For our purposes, however, a couple of inferences help us to detect the sort of audience implied by the narrative. First, this is an audience with some familiarity with, or expectation of, persecution.[15] Thus, e.g., the courtroom scene portrayed in 8:34–38 suggests situations where disciples might be called upon to disavow their relationship with Jesus, himself known for his execution as a political threat.[16] What is more, legal interrogations before Roman and Jewish authorities are the fate of Jesus' followers (13:9). We may refer, too, to the added reference to persecutions in the list of "gifts" received by those who give up everything to follow Jesus in 10:38–39, the warning about trouble and persecution in 4:17, and the menacing portent in 13:13: "You will be hated by all because of my name."

---

[14]Contrary to an often repeated view, Joseph of Arimathea is not portrayed by Mark as a disciple of Jesus. He is a pious Jew responding to the longstanding Jewish concern that no corpse be left unburied. That he is "awaiting the kingdom" does not identify him as a disciple—cf. the similar language in 12:34 and his role as a member of the body that demanded the death penalty in Jesus' case. See Joel B. Green, "Burial of Jesus," *DJG*, 88–92 (90–91).

[15]Cf. Martin Hengel, "The Gospel of Mark: Time of Origin and Situation," in *Studies in the Gospel of Mark* (London: SCM, 1985) 1–30.

[16]Cf. ch. 9 below.

Whether formal or informal, whether regional or local, affliction and unrest seem to be among the qualities characteristic of Mark's implied audience.

Second, one can at least raise the question whether Mark envisions a community among whom are those who, in the context of trials, have already (to use Mark's language) renounced Jesus rather than deny themselves. That is, it may be that Mark envisions a community struggling with concrete expressions of discipleship failure in their midst.[17] This would help to explain the emphasis he places on the failure of the members of Jesus' chosen inner circle.

Persons in such circumstances might hear Mark's message as transformative news. On the one hand, the failure of Jesus' own disciples, together with Jesus' prediction of their restoration in the community and ongoing mission (e.g., 14:27–28; 16:7), would have been good news indeed. On the other, Mark's Gospel would thus be seen to be situating the possibility of the suffering of believers in a larger interpretive context. Jesus, as a part of his divine mandate, journeys to Jerusalem in the foreknowledge that Jerusalem held for him only a heinous death. Mark's narrative does not in this way seek to glorify suffering, as though true discipleship could be realized only by replicating Golgotha. On the contrary, Jesus' family are those who do the will of God (3:35), and true discipleship is measured by faithfulness to the divine will. Jesus' own experience is that as he fulfills God's purpose, as he carries on his ministry of authoritative teaching, he attracts opposition. Jesus' aim is to serve God's redemptive will; in doing so he becomes the object of controversy. So, too, disciples are called upon by the second evangelist to reckon with the cost of living a life oriented toward God in the midst of a "sinful generation" (8:38). Obedience to God may lead to cross bearing—literally for some of Mark's readers, as they carry their own crossbeams, for the sake of the gospel (8:35), en route to the place of execution.

Messianic Woes, Messianic Suffering

The suffering of Jesus' followers is not without meaning according to Mark. Even it can be gathered up into the larger mission of the Messiah, for the second evangelist shows how these two, suffering and mission, are related. For him, the passion of the community of believers has already begun in the final suffering of Jesus. He demonstrates this by building a bridge of parallels between Mark 13 (with its predictions of coming crisis before the end) and Mark 14–15 (the beginning of that crisis):[18]

---

[17]Cf. Senior, *Passion of Jesus in Mark*, 152–53.

[18]Cf. Dale C. Allison, Jr., *The End of the Ages Has Come: An Early*

Mark 13	Mark 14–15
The destruction of the temple (v. 2).	The destruction of the temple (14:58; 15:29, 38).
Disciples to be delivered up to Jewish and Roman authorities (vv. 9–13).	Jesus is delivered up to Jewish and Roman authorities (14:10–11, 18, 21, 41–42; 15:1, 10, 15).
Disciples to be betrayed by kin (vv. 12–13).	Jesus is betrayed by a table intimate (14:10, 20, 43).
The sun to be darkened (v. 24).	Darkness covers the land (15:33).
The Son of humanity to be seen coming in clouds with great power (v. 26).	The Son of humanity to be seated at the right hand of the Power and to come with the clouds (14:62).
No one knows the hour (vv. 22, 33).	The hour has come (14:41).
Watch! (vv. 5, 9, 23, 33, 35, 37).	Watch! (and failure) (14:34, 37–38).
"Therefore, keep awake—for you do not know when the master of the house will come, in the evening, or at midnight, or at cockcrow, or at dawn" (v. 35).	Throughout 14:17–15:1, these time designations are used: evening, midnight, cockcrow, early morning.
Master comes and finds you sleeping (v. 36).	Jesus comes and finds disciples sleeping (14:37–38).

On the one hand, these parallels encourage an interpretation of Jesus' death as the inauguration of the long-awaited new epoch. On the other, and more to the point here, they locate the sufferings of persecuted believers within the framework of the messianic sufferings of Jesus—and, indeed, within the wider context of God's bringing redemption to the whole world.

Life on "the Way"

A further way in which Mark addresses the community of disciples is his reminder that the cross of Christ is, for the ongoing work of the church, a turning point. This is true in at least two senses. First, the journey may be continued with *fresh understanding*, for the redemptive mission of the Son of God takes on new meaning, deeper tones, in light

---

Interpretation of the Passion and Resurrection of Jesus (Philadelphia: Fortress, 1985) 36–38.

of his crucifixion. Second, the journey must be continued, for it does not culminate at Golgotha but persists beyond the cross. Thus Jesus instructs his disciples to return to Galilee, where they will be restored and where they will understand (14:28; cf. 16:7: "see").[19]

Of course, their new lives will be lives shaped by Jesus' teaching about, and death on, the cross. This message of the cross, as Mark presents it, stands radically opposed to the sort of status-seeking, power-wielding behavior characteristic of the disciples earlier in the Gospel. This is the behavior of Jesus' opponents and is unbecoming those who "deny themselves" and "welcome children." In addition, this new life will be one of openness to outsiders, remembering the many unknown, peripheral characters within the narrative who exemplify true insight and manifest authentic faith. Discipleship will entail continuing the mission of Jesus—for to this were the disciples first called and subsequently prepared (cf. 1:16–20; 3:13–15; 6:7–13); moreover, before the Parousia "the good news must first be proclaimed to all nations" (13:10). In all of this, Jesus will be with his disciples (14:28; 16:7), just as he called them, first and principally, to be with him (3:14).

---

[19]For "to see" as a metaphor for perceptive faith, see Paul-Gerd Müller, "Βλέπω," *EDNT*, 1.221–22.

 # THREE

"His blood on us and on our children":
THE DEATH OF JESUS IN THE
GOSPEL ACCORDING TO MATTHEW

Matthew's presentation of the death of Jesus might register with the hearer as "Variations on a Theme by Mark." Prominent structural and thematic patterns of the Markan narrative reappear in Matthew, yet not without important variations that transform the reader's experience of the passion. The motif of the blood of Jesus weaves its way as a bright red thread through the Matthean passion account, riveting readers' attention on the question of responsibility for the death of Jesus but at the same time enabling readers to probe the deeper layers of the event's meaning.

The characters in the drama—Jesus, Judas, Peter, Pilate and his wife, the priestly elite, Joseph of Arimathea—enact for the reader sharply divergent responses to issues of life and death that overtake them. In this parade of characters are glimpsed models of trust and fidelity, of loyalty and courage. Yet alongside them one cannot miss their sometimes horrible, sometimes tragic counterparts, paradigms of treachery and cowardice, of infidelity and coercive power. That is, Matthew confronts the reader with fundamental issues of human character and purpose when he brings the characters of his story face-to-face with the death of the Messiah.

Moreover, the author deftly ties together the opening and closing chapters of Jesus' life, with clear echoes of the infancy narrative guiding readers of the passion story to new appreciation of the significance of Jesus both for Israel and for the nations. And the culmination of Matthew's passion narrative clearly trumpets the epochal, indeed cosmic, significance of this royal Messiah's death. These are the dimensions of Matthew's account of the death of Jesus that we will explore in this chapter.

NARRATIVE PREPARATION FOR THE DEATH OF THE MESSIAH

Birth and Death: Narrative Correlations

The genealogy with which Matthew's Gospel opens (1:1–17) presents Jesus to the reader as the Messiah (Christ), in whom Israel's history, laden with both promise and failure, finally reaches its goal. Appropriately, then, the unusual circumstances surrounding Jesus' birth define that event as the fulfillment of a scriptural promise of divine presence with the people—"Emmanuel" (1:22–23). Of particular interest is the angel's disclosure to Joseph, through the medium of a dream,[1] that Mary's son will "save his people from their sins" (1:21) and should be named accordingly ("Jesus"). Jesus' public career and especially his death will confirm for Matthew's readers the truth of this message: through Jesus, God saves the people. Indeed, Jesus will interpret his approaching death as a covenant enactment that offers forgiveness of sins (26:28). Then, even as he dies on the cross, the religious leaders will mock him as one who "saved others" but "cannot save himself" (27:42).

Not until the episode of Herod and the magi (ch. 2), however, does the reader meet the first clear anticipations of the story's denouement. A chorus of voices, featuring magi from the East, Herod the Great, chief priests and scribes of the people, and the prophet (Micah), identifies Jesus as one born to be "King of the Jews," as Messiah and ruler of Israel. Only the (Gentile) magi, though, evidence any joy at the advent of this extraordinary child. In fact, "all Jerusalem" shares Herod's distress (2:3), and when the magi do not provide him with the information he needs to eliminate a potential rival to power, the violent force of his rage is not spent until he has murdered all the infant boys in the region of Bethlehem.[2]

Jerusalem—including the religious leaders and the whole people— already at the outset of the story is deeply etched in the reader's imagination as a menacing place where the divinely named ruler of the people receives none of the honor due him and where, in fact, his life is endangered. So when Jesus does return to Jerusalem at the end of the story, the reader has been well prepared for the outcome of that fateful encounter. Outsiders (the magi, Pilate, and his wife) may well discern and publicly acclaim the special status of the "King of the Jews," but the

---

[1] The Matthean narrative employs dreams as vehicles of divine disclosure and guidance (see 1:20; 2:19–20, 22; 27:19). This literary pattern itself echoes Scripture. See Robert Gnuse, "Dream Genre in the Matthean Infancy Narratives," *NovT* 32 (1990) 97–120.

[2] It is significant that the angel, in a later dream message to Joseph, speaks of the death of those who sought the child's life (2:20). The narrative does not suggest any dissent to Herod's denial of "one who would be king" on the part of Jerusalem's leadership or populace.

people of Jerusalem and their leaders will spurn him, seeking not to honor but to destroy him. And the king whom they will repudiate is none other than God's own Son, who as a child is summoned out of Egyptian exile (2:15) and who as an adult is condemned to die (26:63–66) and later ridiculed (27:40, 43) precisely as "Son of God."

Conflict Precipitated by Jesus' Public Ministry

The Matthean passion echoes patterns of the infancy narrative, but it also marks the culmination of Jesus' public ministry to "the lost sheep of the house of Israel" (15:24). The escalating conflict that greets Jesus' work of proclamation, teaching, and healing finally issues in his death.[3] Controversy erupts for the first time when Jesus, in "his own city," pronounces a paralyzed man's sins forgiven, prompting already the charge of blasphemy (9:1–8).[4] By the end of the chapter, Pharisees have joined the chorus of critics, faulting Jesus for sharing meals with "tax collectors and sinners" (9:11) and for performing exorcisms by demonic power (9:34). The crowds, to be sure, are impressed (9:8, 33),[5] but when Jesus authorizes his disciples to undertake their mission of healing and preaching (ch. 10), it is the theme of conflict that holds center stage. The disciples will experience opposition and persecution, even to the point of death, precisely because of their connection to him (10:16–25): "If they have called the master of the house Beelzebul, how much more [will they do so to] members of his household!" (v. 25). Verses 24–25, embedded as they are within a mission discourse featuring mortal conflict, clearly foreshadow Jesus' own death.

In this way Matthew indicates what the outcome of Jesus' conflict with his adversaries will be. Subsequent conflict scenes suggest a range of issues[6] on which Jesus and his opponents clash. On the question of Sabbath observance, Jesus' practice incites Pharisees to seek his destruction (12:1–14). For a second time, Pharisees attribute Jesus' exorcistic success to his affiliation with Satan (i.e., Beelzebul, 12:22–37). Interestingly, the label "blasphemy" resurfaces here, but this time in Jesus' reply, where he turns it against his critics (in contrast to 9:3).

---

[3]See Heil, *Death and Resurrection,* 16–17; Jack Dean Kingsbury, *Matthew as Story* (2d ed.; Philadelphia: Fortress, 1988) 72–87; Matera, *Passion Narratives,* 131–35; Senior, *Passion of Jesus in Matthew,* 30–37.

[4]This accusation on the part of "some scribes" prepares for the passion account, where Jesus is condemned by the Sanhedrin for blasphemy (26:65).

[5]And, for the most part, the crowds continue to be positively disposed toward Jesus (see 12:23; 15:30–31; 21:8–11, 46)—that is, until the fateful scene before Pilate (27:11–26).

[6]Mostly concerning questions of *halakah,* appropriate interpretation and application of the Torah.

Herod the tetrarch then confuses Jesus with John the Baptizer, whom he earlier put to death (14:2): "This is John the Baptizer." This sounds an especially ominous warning, for the narrative proceeds to recall Herod's execution of one honored by the people as a prophet (as Jesus will be in 21:11; cf. 16:14; 21:46). While Herod plays no role in the passion drama,[7] the associations between the tetrarch and his father on the one hand, and between Jesus and John on the other, create in readers a strong expectation that Jesus will meet at the hands of civil power the same fate as John.[8]

Matthew 15 returns to halakic disputes between Jesus and the Pharisees and scribes. When Jesus attacks the "traditions of the elders," it is no surprise that his position offends the Pharisees.[9] The ground has been carefully prepared, therefore, for the first prophetic announcement by Jesus that he will suffer at the hands of "the elders, chief priests, and scribes" (16:21).[10] Controversy follows Jesus to Judea (a test from Pharisees on the question of divorce, 19:3-9) and Jerusalem (a series of debates set in the temple, 21:15-22:46). In rapid succession chief priests and elders of the people[11] (21:23-46), Pharisees (22:15-22), Sadducees (22:23-34), and a lawyer affiliated with the Pharisees (22:35-45) all spar with Jesus, only to be vanquished by his words. For his opponents, all that is left at the end is stunned silence (22:46). Jesus, though, has the last word, addressing to the crowds and disciples a barrage of withering criticism aimed at the scribes and Pharisees, and finally at all Jerusalem (23:1-39). Jesus indicts the holy city as a city of murder, and Matthew's reader can only anticipate that Jesus' innocent blood will be mingled with that of so many other prophets before him—righteous martyrs

---

[7]In Luke, of course, he does (23:6-12).

[8]Because Herod is also called "king" in the account (14:9), the reader is inclined to identify him closely with that earlier "Herod the king" who sought Jesus' destruction. There is an intriguing tension between vv. 5 and 9: if Herod was intent on John's death (v. 5), why does he regret that he must execute the Baptizer (v. 9)? This somewhat awkward narrative is evidently the result of Matthean redaction of Mark 6:19. Matthew deflects the death wish from Herodias to Herod, yet the balance of the story, absorbed from Mark, preserves the picture of Herod's wife (and daughter) as the real culprit. Herod's desire to execute John, a desire frustrated by the people's esteem for John as a prophet (14:5)—a uniquely Matthean touch here—prepares for the passion of Jesus, when the authorities' plan to execute Jesus has to take account of the attitude of the people (26:5). For further discussion of Matthew's use of John to prepare for the death of Jesus, see Heil, *Death and Resurrection*, 14-15; Senior, *Passion of Jesus in Matthew*, 23-26.

[9]The word employed for the Pharisees' reaction is ἐσκανδαλίσθησαν, *eskandalisthēsan* (cf. Matt 11:6; 13:57; 26:31, 33).

[10]Presented by the narrator in indirect discourse.

[11]Evidently the "elders of the people" who question Jesus' authority (21:23) are to be identified with the Pharisees who discern that Jesus is targeting them with his parables (21:45).

whose murders are about to come home to roost in the desolate house that was once "God's city." The aftermath of Jesus' death and resurrection will plainly show that the more things change, the more they stay the same. Unable to hold the crucified Jesus in the tomb and unrelenting in their hostility toward him, the chief priests and elders add a conspiracy of deceit to their earlier tokens of antagonism (28:11–15).

Prophetic Announcements of Jesus' Approaching Death

Matthew's story presents the death of Jesus as the inevitable outcome of a life marked by fidelity to God's way of justice,[12] the culmination of bitter conflict between Jesus and the leaders of the people. Jesus also prepares readers for his death by announcing repeatedly that he will face rejection and death (16:21; 17:22–23; 20:17–19; 26:2). The religious authorities may carefully orchestrate his death, but Jesus' prophetic knowledge—and his acceptance—of its necessity instructs the reader in advance that the death of Jesus is not a tragic defeat nor is it an unexpected humiliation that catches him unaware. Rather, even as an event evidently initiated and controlled by Jesus' enemies at Jerusalem, it is an event purposed by God.

The Passion Drama Begins

Like Mark, Matthew clearly signals the beginning of the passion narrative (Mark 14:1–2; Matt 26:1–2). But where Mark has the narrator describe a plot to put Jesus to death, Matthew has Jesus himself predict his death at Passover. Only then (τότε, *tote*) do the religious leaders proceed to hatch the plot to kill him (26:3–5). Once again, it is evident to the reader that despite the scheming of his enemies, Jesus is the one seated in the director's chair. Therefore, faced with a contradiction between Jesus' prediction (death at Passover, 26:2) and the leaders' plot ("not at the feast, lest there be a tumult among the people," 26:5), readers expect Jesus to die at Passover. In fact, as it turns out, the only "tumult among the people" at the feast will be the religious leaders' doing, as they incite the crowd to clamor for the release of Barabbas and the crucifixion of Jesus (27:20–26).[13]

Immediately after the notice of the death plot, the narrator places Jesus in the home of the leper Simon in Bethany. Here Jesus, responding to the strenuous protests of the disciples, interprets a woman's extravagant

---

[12]See Senior, *Passion of Jesus in Matthew*, 26–33.

[13]Note that Pilate perceives that a riot is about to break out (27:24) and for that reason relents, handing Jesus over to death, but only after washing his hands of the affair.

act of devotion as an anointing of his body in preparation for burial (26:6–13). This ritual act lends pathos to the narrative and allows the sober truth to sink in: the death of Jesus is imminent.[14]

This expensive expression of devotion Matthew now deftly juxtaposes to a cheap act of treachery. Judas approaches the elite priests, offering to betray Jesus for a price: "What will you give me to hand him over to you?" (26:15). For the modest sum of thirty silver pieces—blood money that will come back to haunt both parties to the agreement—Judas agrees to betray his master. The narrative is propelling readers swiftly along toward the appointed goal.

The initiative apparently now lies with Jesus' enemies. By shifting the setting to Jesus and his disciples' preparations for, and celebration of, the Passover meal (26:17–29), however, the story restores order. For this scene sharply focuses Jesus' keen awareness of the imminent end. The disciples follow Jesus' directions to prepare the Passover meal, bearing the message of "the Teacher" that "my time [καιρός, kairos] is at hand" (26:18). In the course of the meal "with the twelve disciples,"[15] Jesus tells them that one of them will betray him, and in reply to Judas's ingenuous "Not I, Master?" identifies the traitor: "You have said so" (26:25).[16] The intimate bond of a meal shared by master and disciples throws into sharp relief the treachery of Judas.

More important than the unmasking of the betrayer, though, is the interpretation of Jesus' death with which the meal scene concludes. The bread and wine of the meal are, Jesus avers, tokens of his body and blood. Through the pouring out of his life's blood, he is in fact enacting a covenant that brings forgiveness for the sins of the "many."[17] Matthew's readers begin to appreciate how it is that a grim death that flows from the malevolent designs of Jesus' enemies could fall within the purposes of God. Somehow, in the mystery of the divine action, the death of Jesus fulfills his mission, embodied in his very name, to effect the salvation of the people through the forgiveness of their sins (cf. 1:21). So Jesus

---

[14]Because of this anonymous woman's gesture, after the crucifixion the women at the tomb do not intend to anoint Jesus' body; they only sit and observe (27:61; 28:1; contrast Mark 16:1).

[15]On the importance of Jesus' fellowship "with the disciples" in the Matthean passion narrative, see Senior, *Passion of Jesus in Matthew*, 78; Matera, *Passion Narratives*, 94–96.

[16]The expression σὺ εἶπας, sy eipas, here might be paraphrased, "It is as you have said." The reply tacitly affirms the question, yet returns to the speaker the burden of accepting the truth spoken. The same effect is to be detected in Jesus' responses to the high priest (26:64) and Pilate (27:11).

[17]"Many" (πολλοί, polloi) echoes Isa 53:11, 12 LXX. The sense of the term here is not "some, as opposed to others who are denied the redemptive benefits of the death of Jesus," but "all."

promises his disciples that beyond the grave he will again drink "of this fruit of the vine" with them.[18]

The fragile bond between Jesus and his disciples—fragile because of their weakness, despite his steadfastness—is featured in the next scene, set upon the Mount of Olives. There Jesus predicts the imminent failure of the disciples, although once again Jesus' prophetic word is countered, this time by Peter: "If they all fall away because of you,[19] I will never fall away" (26:33). Scripture, however, is on Jesus' side ("I will strike the shepherd, and the sheep of the shepherd will be scattered," drawn from Zech 13:7), and so for Matthew's readers, guided by the combined testimony of Jesus and Scripture, there is no ambiguity. Peter's protest of undying loyalty and bravery ("I will never fall away"; "Even if I must die with you, I will not deny you") rings hollow. The disciples will surely leave Jesus to his fate; for them, the passion of Jesus will threaten to sever their connection to Jesus.

The wedge between Jesus and the disciples begins to widen in the next scene, at Gethsemane. Unlike Jesus, who through prayer draws strength to accept the critical test about to confront him,[20] the disciples are able only to sleep. So when Judas and the arresting party arrive, the disciples are not ready. Scripture is fulfilled, and with it Jesus' word: they all flee (26:56). The experiment in discipleship seems to have ended in defeat and disgrace. The passion of Jesus has begun.

THE MOTIF OF THE BLOOD OF JESUS

Once Jesus is arrested, he is hauled before the high priest Caiaphas and the Sanhedrin (26:57–68). Although that body unsuccessfully seeks false testimony on the basis of which to condemn Jesus, two credible witnesses lodge against him the charge that he claimed to be able to destroy and then rebuild the temple (26:61). Yet the judgment that he deserves the death sentence (26:66; 27:1) finds its warrant not in that accusation but, rather, in Jesus' own self-incriminating reply to the high priest about his being Messiah and Son of God: "You have said it [i.e.,

---

[18]The "with you" of the future drinking in God's realm is uniquely Matthean (contrast Mark 14:25; Luke 22:18).

[19]This phrase (ἐν σοί, *en soi*), echoing Jesus' prediction (ἐν ἐμοί, *en emoi*, in 26:31), is missing from the Markan parallel (14:29). Matthew accents the bond between Jesus and the disciples, even when their behavior imperils it. See further Matera, *Passion Narratives*, 94–95.

[20]Where Mark draws attention to the threefold failure of the disciples (14:37, 40–41), Matthew throws the spotlight on Jesus' threefold prayer of submission to the divine will. See Senior, *Passion of Jesus in Matthew*, 76–83.

it is as you yourself have said]."[21] Moreover, they themselves will witness his installation in power as the Son of humanity (ὁ υἱὸς τοῦ ἀνθρώπου, *ho huios tou anthrōpou*)—from the very moment when they repudiate him (26:64)!

The reaction is swift: the high priest charges him with blasphemy, and the Sanhedrin judges him to be worthy of death. As Messiah and Son of God, he claims authorization from God for what he does and teaches. But the religious authorities, having already concluded that his authority derives from an evil source (9:34; 10:25; 12:24), now hand him over to death for no other reason than that they refuse to acknowledge him—who is about to be publicly vindicated by God as Son of humanity—as the Messiah, Son of God.[22]

And so they hand him over to Pilate (27:2). Confronted with the Messiah, they have chosen to dismiss him to death. At this point, narrative time grinds to a halt,[23] and the reader listens in fascination while the traitor Judas accosts the chief priests and elders, attempting in vain to undo the damage he has done: "By betraying innocent blood [αἷμα ἀθῷον, *haima athōon*], I have sinned" (27:4). Fresh from their deliberations, buoyed by the satisfaction that must attend a decision to eliminate a blasphemer, the religious authorities are not about to change course now: "What is that to us? You see [to it] yourself." Tacitly, however, they concede that they have a problem. The thirty silver pieces thrown by Judas into the sanctuary (ναός, *naos*, 27:5) represent blood money and may not be placed in the temple treasury. This "price of blood" is, instead, used to purchase a "Field of Blood" (vv. 6–8).

Matthew's readers cannot but recall Jesus' stinging rebuke of scribes and Pharisees who are complicit with their ancestors in the rejection and murder of God's just ones: "that upon you may come all the righteous blood [αἷμα δίκαιον, *haima dikaion*] poured out on the earth. . . . Truly, I tell you, all this will come upon this generation" (23:35). These haunting words reverberate through the temple scene starring a remorseful Judas. He would dissociate himself from the shedding of innocent blood, but he cannot. The religious authorities who have condemned Jesus will have no greater success than Judas in evading responsibility for the death of that Righteous One.

The memorable scene staged before the governor, Pilate, makes that point all too clear. Pilate, urged by his wife to avoid any entanglement

---

[21] Though Jesus, in keeping with his own teaching (5:33–37), refuses to take an oath as the high priest directs (26:63). On the meaning of σὺ εἶπας, "You have said it," see Senior, *Passion of Jesus in Matthew*, 64, 97; Brown, *Death of the Messiah*, 1.489–92.

[22] Cf. the mockery at the cross (27:41–43).

[23] Or even reverses course momentarily, for the religious authorities now speaking with Judas should actually be in the company of Pilate (27:2).

with this just man[24] and aware that Jesus does not deserve to die, washes his hands to disavow any accountability for the execution order he is about to give: "I am innocent of this man's blood. You see [to it] yourselves" (27:24). This is but a reprise of Judas and the chief priests, suggesting that for all Pilate's protests, "innocence" attaches not to him but, rather, to the blood whose stains he would avoid. Then, in a chilling and fateful moment of decision, not just the religious authorities but "all the people," already persuaded by their leaders to press for Jesus' destruction (27:20), accept responsibility for his death: "His blood [be] on us and on our children" (v. 25).

So the haunting image of the (innocent) blood of Jesus prods the reader to explore in its many layers the issue of accountability for the Messiah's death. Judas, the religious authorities, Pilate, all the people of Jerusalem—each has a share of blame. Clearly, this dimension of Matthew's narrative, like the theme of conflict between Jesus and the scribes and Pharisees, reflects the later experiences of Matthew's community within first-century Palestinian Jewish culture.[25] Through these words placed by Matthew on the lips of the chorus at Jerusalem,[26] the author casts light upon the dark episode of the fall of Jerusalem to Roman armies in 70 C.E. What meaning does Matthew assign this catastrophic event at the close of the generation of Jesus?[27] It was divine retribution for the violent death of the Messiah, a judgment that at the same time brings vindication to many other righteous people of God who were likewise victims of violence.[28]

Jerusalem, then, will ultimately pay the price. At least that is the theology of history that shapes this narrative. And yet, the image of Jesus' blood has another, more hopeful meaning even for Jesus' enemies. For the words spoken by Jesus over the cup at his final meal present his death as the making of a covenant, as the pouring out of his blood for the forgiveness of the sins of the many (26:28). If Matthew rivets our attention on the blood of Jesus, therefore, it is not simply to point the

---

[24]She, of course, is the recipient of divine disclosure through the medium of a dream.

[25]The polemical exchanges within the narrative between Jesus and the Pharisees and scribes have been shaped by the later disputes between Matthew's Jewish Christian group and the Jewish community of its environment. On this theme, see J. Andrew Overman, *Matthew's Gospel and Formative Judaism: The Social World of the Matthean Community* (Minneapolis: Fortress, 1990).

[26]Together with such passages as 21:33–41; 22:1–10; and 23:29–39.

[27]Matthew 23:35–36 ("that all the righteous blood shed on earth may come upon you . . . all this will come upon this generation") and 27:25 ("his blood on us and on our children") converge to delimit the retribution to the period of Jesus' contemporaries and the ensuing generation.

[28]For further discussion of the question of responsibility for Jesus' death, see ch. 10 below.

finger at the responsible parties. No, the irony is thick here. The death of Jesus—precisely because it is the shedding of innocent, sacrificial blood—creates the possibility of forgiveness even for the persons who bear responsibility for putting him to death.[29] Tracing the blood of Jesus as it flows through the narrative, therefore, the reader gains insight into the nature of the enmity that brought Jesus to the cross—and experiences something of its tragic effects. But one is also able to perceive in the same events, at a deeper level, the more profound meaning of the passion—and to experience something of its salvific power. Jesus dies so that divine forgiveness may come to the many. The narrative assigns greater prominence, to be sure, to the theme of accountability and retribution. Yet the narrative has another potential reading as well, for it leaves with readers at least the possibility of exploiting an unresolved tension between the awful reality of divine judgment and the mystery of divine mercy.

THE DEATH OF JESUS AS AN APOCALYPTIC EVENT

The apocalyptic fireworks with which Matthew concludes the crucifixion account (27:51–54) lay bare important dimensions of that deep mystery. The "King of the Jews" has been beaten, stripped, crucified alongside two thieves, and treated with contempt. Insult is added to injury, as each of the issues figuring in the Sanhedrin and Roman hearings now forms the basis for mockery (27:40: destroy and rebuild the temple; Son of God; v. 42: King of Israel; v. 43: Son of God). And so in darkness and desolation he dies. Heaven's answer is swift. The death of the Righteous One who "trusted in God" yet could not "save himself" triggers a series of prodigious events signalling the epochal significance of the event.

The narrative strains language as it brings home to the reader the potency of Jesus' death. First, in an image shared with Mark and Luke, the sanctuary veil is split in two, with the direction of the rending ("from above") indicating the divine origin of the sign. Jesus' oracle of judgment has now come true: "Behold, your house [οἶκος, oikos] is desolate" (23:38; cf. 21:12–13; 24:2). The rich symbolism of this occurrence would not be lost on Matthew's first readers, for whom the destruction of the temple in 70 C.E. was still a vivid memory.

---

[29] See Timothy B. Cargal, "'His Blood Be upon Us and upon Our Children': A Matthean Double Entendre?" *NTS* 37 (1991) 101–12; cf. Brown, *Death of the Messiah*, 1.839.

Matthew, though, embellishes the Markan tradition with additional cosmic portents.[30] An earthquake is accompanied by the splitting[31] of rocks, and as a result tombs are opened and "many bodies" of dead saints are raised. The scriptural echoes here are clear and distinct: one recalls especially Ezek 37:12–13, where the graves of the dead are opened and resurrected people are returned to the land of Israel (after a "shaking" [σεισμός, *seismos*], 37:7 LXX); Zech 14:4–5, where the Mount of Olives is "split" and the Lord God comes together with "all the saints"; and Joel 2:10, where the "day of the Lord" brings both extraordinary darkness and earthquakes.

Verse 53 is intriguing.[32] The raised bodies of the saints ventured forth from their tombs "after his resurrection and entered the holy city," where many saw them. Although "his" has no antecedent, clearly Jesus is in view. The narrator (author) has intruded into the story to offer theological commentary. While the death of Jesus is the death-shattering, liberating event of truly apocalyptic import and so serves as the catalyst for this preliminary "resurrection of the righteous," nevertheless the priority of Jesus' own resurrection is acknowledged through the notice "after his resurrection." The awkwardness of the narrative is a clue to its remarkable claim. Pictures race ahead of logic as the story embodies the conviction that Jesus' crucifixion deals death itself the final death blow and inaugurates the resurrection life. The death of Jesus is the pivotal event on which the whole of history turns. Because of Jesus' faithfulness to God, out of his death issues life.[33]

STUDIES IN CHARACTERIZATION

In treating other aspects of Matthew's passion account, we have already crossed the paths of several important actors upon its stage. It will be helpful now, however, to focus more sharply on some of the memorable characters Matthew presents to us. It is appropriate to begin

---

[30]Recall the heavenly sign of the star sighted by the magi (2:2). Note that in Matthew the centurion and the other soldiers with him (who are "keeping" Jesus as they will later "guard" the tomb—a distinctive Matthean touch) are moved to declare Jesus' divine sonship because they have witnessed "the earthquake and the things that happened" (27:54).

[31]The verb here is the same one used to describe the rending of the sanctuary veil (σχίζειν, *schizein*).

[32]For discussion of this difficult verse, see Senior, *Passion of Jesus in Matthew*, 144–47.

[33]John's Gospel, of course, subjects this claim to profound theological reflection. See ch. 5 below.

with the central character, Jesus. We then explore the portrayals of Peter and Judas.[34]

Jesus

Readers of the Matthean passion narrative meet in Jesus (1) a man through whom God extends salvation to the people; (2) one whose death, like his life, fulfills Scripture; (3) a faithful son (of God) who submits to the will of his "Father"; (4) a bona fide king-Messiah who nevertheless wields power as a humble servant; (5) an authoritative figure whose majesty and control are not diminished even in his last fateful days; and (6) a just man who is wrongly put to death.

Jesus and Divine Salvation

Matthew's infancy narrative drew attention to the meaning of Jesus' name and, with it, to his role in Israel's history. He bears the name of one through whom God imparts salvation to the people (1:21). And true to his name, he has brought "salvation" to Israel by offering forgiveness (e.g., 9:2, 5) and healing the sick (e.g., 9:21–22).[35] It is therefore scarcely surprising that Matthew's passion account uses the personal name Jesus far more often than the other Gospels, consistently substituting this name where Mark has the personal pronoun.[36]

Readers consequently appreciate the deep irony of the crucifixion scene, where Jesus' mockers seize, above all, on his inability to "save himself" (27:40, 42–43) and assume that if he were truly king and Son of God, he would remove himself from the cross (v. 40) or God would intervene to rescue him (v. 43). After all, "he saved others," why can he not rescue himself? The reason, known to Jesus but not to those who taunt him, is that it is precisely through his death that he accomplishes the work of salvation, delivering the many from their sins (cf. 1:21 and 26:28). In the hour of his own desperate need, it is by not saving himself that he in fact is able to save others. Right through to the end, Jesus is what he has been advertised to be: he is the one who opens up access to God's salvation.

---

[34]Chapter 10 below develops the role played by Matthew's religious authorities in the death of Jesus, though not with a primary focus on characterization. Helpful sketches are provided by David R. Bauer, "The Major Characters of Matthew's Story: Their Function and Significance," *Int* 46 (1992) 357–67; Kingsbury, *Matthew as Story*, 115–27; Mark Allan Powell, "The Plot to Kill Jesus from Three Different Perspectives: Point of View in Matthew," SBLSP 1990, 603–13.

[35]Also by rescuing disciples from peril (8:25; 14:30).

[36]See Senior, *Passion Narrative*, 25–26.

Jesus and Scripture

Jesus, then, dies as he lived, fulfilling the pattern set for him by Scripture. Matthew's passion narrative continues the motif of Scripture fulfillment that permeates the Gospel as a whole.[37] In a scene set on the Mount of Olives, a setting already reminiscent of King David's ordeals—including betrayal—centuries before (2 Sam 15:30), Jesus, while predicting his disciples' flight, identifies his approaching death with the smiting of the Zecharian shepherd (26:31, quoting Zech 13:7). Then he explains his refusal to resist arrest in terms of submission to Scripture (26:54, 56). The narrator links Judas's betrayal, together with the chief priests' handling of the "price of blood," to the prophecy of Jeremiah (27:9–10).[38]

Although the crucifixion scene lacks any explicit Scripture citations, it is replete with biblical echoes and allusions. There are numerous obvious allusions: the offers of wine mingled with gall (27:34: χολή, *cholē*, an image missing from Mark; cf. Ps 69:21) and, later, of sour wine (27:48: ὄξος, *oxos*); the soldiers' casting of lots for the crucified man's clothing (27:35; cf. Ps 22:18); the "wagging of the head" by passersby (27:39; cf. Ps 22:7); the taunt "He has put his trust in God; let [God] now deliver him if [God] desires him" (27:43; cf. Ps 22:8 and Wis 2:18–20); darkness over the land (27:45; cf. Amos 8:9); Jesus' cry of dereliction (27:46, drawn from Ps 22:1); and the emptying of many tombs (27:52–53; cf. Ezek 37:12).

Many of these allusions Matthew borrows (like Mark before him) from the Righteous Sufferer's psalm of lament (esp. Ps 22). Jesus dies as have so many just people before him, ridiculed and tormented by others who lack his integrity. But some of Matthew's readers will also expect that Jesus will receive the vindication by God anticipated by the lamenting psalmist (Ps 22:22–31)—a hope not articulated by either Jesus or the narrator in this scene. Additional touches reinforce the eschatological import of the moment (imagery from Amos and Ezekiel). In Matthew's theology of history, this is the defining moment for the entire history of Israel, indeed of the world. So it is that in this central episode of the passion, readers hear such a crescendo of intertextual echoes that they can entertain no doubt: Jesus dies no empty death but one full of purpose. In it unfolds the redemptive purpose of God, announced in the

---

[37] See further ch. 11 below.

[38] As others have pointed out, the quotation does not match any known text. We appear to have here a hybrid of materials drawn from both Jeremiah and Zechariah, with the name Jeremiah likely attached to the oracle because of his role as prophet of Jerusalem's demise and because of the established tradition of Jeremiah as the "suffering prophet." For further discussion, see Senior, *Passion of Jesus in Matthew*, 107–8; idem, *Passion Narrative*, 352–62; Brown, *Death of the Messiah*, 1.647–52.

ancient Scriptures, embodied in Jesus' public ministry, and now most effectively realized in his death on the cross.

Jesus, the Faithful Son of God

Matthew's passion narrative highlights the filial relation of Jesus to God and, within that role, the Son's obedience to his Father's will.[39] The Gethsemane scene is paradigmatic. The teacher who had urged his disciples to pray, "Our Father . . . your will be done" (Matt 6:10), now requests that the cup of adversity be removed but then subordinates his own request to his[40] Father's will: "Nevertheless, not as I wish, but as you [do]. . . . [Y]our will be done" (26:39, 42).[41] Recoiling in distress from the ordeal that awaits him, Jesus nevertheless draws strength from his prayer to his Father, and—unlike the sleeping disciples—finds courage to face his passion with serenity.

As we have already seen, the Sanhedrin hearing revolved around the question of Jesus' divine sonship,[42] and it looms large in the crucifixion scene as well. With the very words employed by the devil in his desert testing of Jesus (Matt 4:3, 6), passersby hurl at the man on the cross a challenge, "If you are the Son of God [come down from the cross]" (27:40). The elite priests, scribes, and elders also use the claim "I am Son of God" to good effect when they poke fun at a man clearly estranged from God (27:43). Who could believe that God "desires him"? The disconfirming evidence is there for all to see.

That God's favor does continue to rest with him is the burden of the portents that attend his death and, of course, of his resurrection "on the third day." No less than those early days of testing in the desert, the passion displays Jesus' fidelity to God, his submission—even at cost of his honor and his life—to the purpose of his Father.

Jesus, King and Servant

Jesus' status as Son of God is the pivotal issue in the Sanhedrin session, a fact that the taunts at the cross recall for the reader. What drives the narrative, however, both in the scene before Pilate and during

---

[39] On language of God as "Father" in Matthew, see Robert L. Mowery, "God, Lord and Father: The Theology of the Gospel of Matthew," *BibRes* 33 (1989) 24–36.

[40] The Matthean Jesus' prayer is addressed to "my Father," while in Mark it is "Abba, Father" (14:36) and in Luke simply "Father" (22:42).

[41] A third time, the narrator tells us, Jesus offered the same prayer (26:44). As noted above, Matthew redirects attention from the disciples' failure to Jesus' model prayer.

[42] Evidently the religious authorities did not miss Jesus' implied claim to be Son of God in his vineyard parable (21:33–41). On this point, see Kingsbury, *Matthew as Story*, 83, 87.

the crucifixion itself, is conflict over the claim that Jesus is Christ and "King of the Jews [Israel]." The label "Christ" seems to be synonymous here with "King of Israel."[43] For Pilate twice, in questions addressed to a Jewish audience, refers to Jesus "who is called Christ,"[44] and yet the subsequent mocking by the soldiers (27:29: "Hail, King of the Jews!") and the formal charge against Jesus (27:37: "This is Jesus, the King of the Jews") both concern royal pretensions. Once again on the lips of the religious authorities Jesus is sarcastically named king—though now, in an idiom appropriate to the speakers, he is "King of Israel" (27:42).[45]

The irony of the account is transparent to Matthew's readers. From the very beginning, Matthew's narrative has presented Jesus as Israel's Messiah. Despite the apparently disconfirming experience of repudiation by his own people, culminating in crucifixion, Jesus is exactly what the charge above him on the cross proclaims him to be: "This is Jesus, the King of the Jews."

What kind of king rules in such a way? Matthew's Jesus recasts royalty in a radically different mold, for he exercises kingship as a humble servant. Already the Matthean account of the public ministry prepares for this transmutation. Twice the narrator taps the Isaianic prophecy about the "Servant of the Lord" (8:17, citing Isa 53:4; 12:15–21, citing Isa 42:1–4) to clothe Jesus' ministry of healing in the garb of Isaiah's humble Servant. Even the motif of secrecy attached to Jesus' acts of healing is reframed in terms of the quiet humility of the Servant (12:15–21).[46] Consistent with this portrayal are the numerous references to Jesus' compassion for the people as the motivation underlying his response to their need (9:36; 14:14; 15:32; cf. 20:34). The same is true of the narrator's use of the shepherd metaphor to express concretely Jesus' compassion (that is, a shepherd's compassion for sheep suffering without benefit of a shepherd's care [9:36]) and also to characterize his royal rule (anticipated already in 2:6: "a ruler who will shepherd my people Israel").

The roles of king and shepherd are woven together when the "mother of the sons of Zebedee" asks for her two sons a share in the

---

[43]So also in Mark: "Let the Christ, the king of Israel . . . " (15:32). On the equivalence of "Christ" and "king" in Matthew, see, e.g., 2:2, 4.

[44]In both cases (Matt 27:17, 22) the Markan parallel reads "King of the Jews" rather than "Christ" (Mark 15:9, 12).

[45]So also Mark 15:32.

[46]The silence of Jesus in response to the authorities' accusations in the scene before Pilate (27:12, 14) may be another subtle echo of the Isaianic Servant, who, though afflicted, "opened not his mouth" (53:7). The secrecy motif receives a quite different spin in Mark, where the mystery of Jesus' messiahship pervades the story. For a variety of perspectives on this Markan literary pattern, see Christopher M. Tuckett, ed., *The Messianic Secret* (IRT 1; Philadelphia: Fortress, 1983).

royal power of Jesus (20:20–28).[47] Jesus seizes upon the patterns of lordship exemplified by the "rulers of the gentiles" as a negative model. True greatness (certainly, in this context, including true kingship), he asserts, is a matter of the slave's humble service. Jesus casts himself in the role of such a servant, with the difference that his service means a giving up of his life to procure the freedom of the many.[48]

As we have seen, the Matthean passion narrative portrays the death of Jesus as the death of the "King of the Jews [Israel]." The characterization of Jesus earlier in the story enables the reader to make sense of the enigma of a coronation through crucifixion. Jesus wields his royal rule precisely through the giving up of his life. For like any authentic king, he seeks the well-being (that is, the salvation) of his subjects. But much more, he does so with the compassion and self-sacrifice of a lowly servant.

Jesus' Authority

Since Matthew's Jesus dies as Israel's king, the narrative aptly fits him with the marks of royalty.[49] Especially noteworthy is the sovereign authority with which Jesus goes to his death.[50] Jesus' own passion prediction seems to be the cue for the passion drama to begin. Not until after his announcement of his coming death at Passover (26:1–2) does the plot of the religious authorities "then" (τότε, *tote*) go forward (vv. 3–5). Even here, as we have noted above, it is Jesus' timetable, not theirs, that events honor. Similarly, it is only after Jesus accepts and praises the extravagant gesture of a woman's anointing that Judas "then" (τότε) approaches the elite priests to betray his master. The disciples dutifully follow Jesus' directions to prepare the Passover meal (26:17–19). He then displays his deep knowledge of his disciples, from Judas's act of betrayal (26:20–25) to Peter's denial (26:34) and all the disciples' flight (26:31). Before these flustered and untrustworthy characters, Jesus cuts a magisterial figure. This contrast appears in bold relief again in the Gethsemane prayer scene and yet again at the arrest. Face-to-face with those who would seize him, Jesus—even as he refuses to appeal to the heavenly legions he might command—remains very much in control, allowing events to unfold as purposed by God and as foretold in Scripture.

The contrast between Jesus' courageous affirmation of his identity before the Sanhedrin (26:64) and Peter's cowardly denials (26:69–75) could not be more stark. And Jesus takes this same serenity with him

---

[47] In Mark 10:35 the request comes from James and John directly.
[48] Another text echoing the Servant of Isa 53.
[49] Beyond the symbolism of the mockery in 27:27–31.
[50] Emphasized by Senior, *Passion Narrative*.

to the tribunal of the Roman governor. Pilate cannot but marvel at the majestic silence of the prisoner in the face of the hostile accusations of his enemies (27:14). To the very end, Jesus dictates the character of his death, for he surrenders his own spirit (27:50), with the psalmist's lament on his lips. In terms of the norms of Matthew's narrative, the Roman soldiers get it right: "This is Jesus, the King of the Jews." The remarkable authority that he expressed in his ministry loses none of its luster throughout the grim drama of the passion.

Jesus, the Just One

One of the hallmarks of Jesus' teaching in Matthew is his summons to a life of justice or righteousness (δικαιοσύνη, *dikaiosynē*)—a justice surpassing even that of the Pharisees (5:20).[51] Does Jesus' execution following investigations conducted by the Jewish authorities and the Roman governor expose him as one who fails to practice what he preaches?[52] Not if the history of God's people is any indicator (at least on Jesus' reading of it). Persecution and death are in fact often the badges worn by the righteous (note the threefold use of δίκαιος, *dikaios*, in 23:29, 35–36).

It is no different with Jesus, as Pilate and his wife both attest. The governor discerns that the Jewish leaders have handed him over out of their own envy (27:18), and he washes his hands of Jesus' blood, graphically demonstrating his judgment of the prisoner's innocence. Instructed by a dream, Pilate's wife specifically labels Jesus "just" (δίκαιος, 27:19). It is plain that Matthew's passion account tells of the undeserved death of a righteous man.[53] As he himself taught, however, "Blessed are those persecuted on account of righteousness, for theirs is the realm of heaven" (5:10). The cross of the Just One finds meaning within the larger saving activity of God.

The Matthean passion narrative displays a magisterial Jesus, who never swerves from his commitment to "fulfill all righteousness" (3:15; 5:17–20) yet as king-Messiah accepts a servant's death for the benefit of others. Strengthened through prayer, he summons the courage to face the ordeal of betrayal, arrest, and crucifixion. Certainly Matthew's readers discern in Jesus qualities to be emulated in their own experience of adversity. Yet other characters, whose reactions to crisis contrast sharply with that of Jesus, also guide the reader's reflection on what it means to be brought to a moment of testing in which one's life hangs

---

[51]Note this theme's development in 3:14–15; 5:6, 10, 17–20; 21:28–32; 25:31–46.

[52]This is the focus of Jesus' sharp attack on scribes and Pharisees in 23:2–3.

[53]Cf. Isa 53:11.

in the balance. In the next sections we consider two such figures, Simon Peter and Judas Iscariot.

Peter

Peter, the most prominent of Jesus' disciples in Matthew, is also in many ways a representative disciple, who exemplifies both the best and the worst of discipleship. While this pattern is clear earlier in the narrative, we focus here on the passion account. When Jesus, on the Mount of Olives, forecasts the failure and flight of all the disciples, Peter—the same Peter who so strenuously resisted Jesus' first disclosure of the necessity of his suffering and death (16:21–23)—vows that he will never fall away (26:33). And he responds to Jesus' specific prediction of a threefold denial by Peter with the protest that he would willingly endure death rather than deny Jesus (23:35). The same bravado, the narrator tells us, marked all the disciples (v. 35).

Needless to say, ensuing events put the lie to these confident protests of undying loyalty. Matthew has stressed the bond between Jesus and disciples,[54] but the passion shows how fragile even that bond is. While Jesus finds in prayer the resolve to face adversity, Peter, together with the "sons of Zebedee," sleeps and therefore comes to the time of testing unprepared (26:37–45). So all but Peter flee the arrest scene, and he alone follows Jesus—significantly, though, "at a distance" (26:58).

In the company of the guards within the high priest's courtyard, he awaits "the end," while Jesus, before the Sanhedrin, bravely confronts his enemies with the truth about his divine sonship. Then the narrator shifts the scene back to the courtyard, and in the tense drama that is played out there, Peter finally succumbs. Twice women observe that Peter had been "with Jesus [the Galilean, of Nazareth]," and twice Peter denies the association, the second time with an oath (26:69–72). Finally, a group of bystanders, noting his accent,[55] identifies Peter as "one of them." He calls down a curse upon himself, as he claims that he does not even "know the man" (v. 74). On cue, the cock crows, triggering Peter's memory of Jesus' prediction[56] and eliciting from him bitter tears

---

[54]For discussion of the Matthean emphasis on fellowship of Jesus "with the disciples" and their solidarity "with him," see Senior, *Passion of Jesus in Matthew*, 78.

[55]A distinctively Matthean touch, explaining the Markan bystanders' remark to Peter: "Certainly you are one of them, for you are a Galilean" (14:70). Matthew uses the label "Galilean" of Jesus in the first denial, rather than of Peter in the third denial.

[56]To trigger the hearer's recall, the narrator supplies the text (in abbreviated form) of Jesus' earlier announcement (26:75).

(v. 75). Intent on being with Jesus and on "seeing the end," Peter has instead witnessed the end of his disciple's journey with Jesus. This is the last mention of Peter, although naturally he is present among "the Eleven" who meet the risen Jesus on the mountain and receive from him authorization for their mission to the world (28:16–20). That silent presence as "one of them" at the end of the story indicates that despite the failed discipleship of Peter (and the rest), Jesus has renewed the promises earlier given him (16:18–20; cf. 18:18–20). Matthew's reader suspects that the bravado is gone and the appropriate measure of humility instilled in Peter and, with him, in his codisciples (cf. 18:1–5). But of subsequent tales of fidelity to Jesus' command and of courage in adversity, the narrative, of course, is silent. Enlightened by Peter's example, Matthew's readers may perhaps better assume that role themselves. Their commitment to the disciple's life will be vigilant and faithful, though not self-assured. Even more to the point, one finds in this Gospel no tendency to turn Peter into a heroic ideal. Only Jesus receives acclaim. Only Jesus commands praise.

Judas

If Peter exemplifies the disciple who has genuine faith but whose loyalty wavers in time of crisis, Judas Iscariot is cast in the role of inauthentic disciple. From his very first introduction to the reader, he is the "one who betrayed [Jesus]" (10:4). At the next mention of Judas, the reader finds him face-to-face with the chief priests, offering to hand Jesus over to them—for a price! The fact that Judas asks for payment to betray Jesus (26:15)[57] and the further observation that this scene immediately follows the anonymous woman's anointing of Jesus (a gesture condemned by the disciples as wasteful) prompt Matthew's reader to suspect that Judas's motives include self-interest, specifically self-aggrandizement.

Again at the Last Supper the Matthean narrator gives Judas voice. Mournful disciples have responded, one by one, to Jesus' prediction of betrayal with the earnest question "Not I, Lord?" (26:22).[58] Jesus' reply evokes the intimate bond of meal fellowship (v. 23)—now dissolved by Judas's act of treachery—thus highlighting the incongruity of the betrayal. Although Jesus' death occurs by necessity ("as it has been written of him"), the betrayer is fully culpable ("Woe!"). Judas, "the one who

---

[57]Only in Matthew does Judas ask for money to betray Jesus to the chief priests, although both Mark (14:11) and Luke (22:5) report a promise of payment to Judas. The Matthean version reflects that Gospel's penchant for direct speech by the characters (here, by Judas), and the result is to suggest a financial motive for Judas's act of betrayal.

[58]So far following Mark. Judas's question appears only in Matthew.

betrayed him," then approaches Jesus with the same question asked by the other disciples, though with a significant twist. He calls Jesus "teacher" (rabbi), an address appropriate on the lips of a neutral outsider or an opponent, not a disciple.[59] The distancing of a former disciple from the one he now calls "teacher" is stark. Moreover, since Judas's question expects a negative answer, he implicates himself as a deceiver. Jesus catches him in his lie and throws back to him the truth of the words he would deny: "You have said it" (i.e., "It is as you yourself have said"). Matthew's reader emerges from this charged exchange deeply impressed by Jesus' mastery of the events and by Judas's villainy. The end of Judas's chosen path ("Woe!") will be brought home to the reader in the Gospel's final scene. Judas, "one of the Twelve" (26:14, 47), is missing from the ranks of "the Eleven" when they depart for Galilee (28:16).

Judas's dramatic role in the two remaining scenes allotted to him prepares the reader for his chilling absence from the narrative's triumphant conclusion. The arrest scene (26:47–56) further distances Judas from Jesus, even as it features emblems of intimacy that make the act of betrayal all the more shocking. The narrator explains that Judas, identified as "one of the Twelve" and as "the one who betrayed him," instructed the armed crowd (sent from the chief priests and elders of the people) to arrest the man whom he kissed. Again addressing Jesus as "rabbi," Judas now proceeds to kiss him,[60] but Jesus, aware that this sign of affection has become a device of treachery, responds with measured coolness, "Friend, [do] what you are here [to do]" (v. 50).[61] Permission for the arrest now having been supplied by Jesus, the company immediately seizes him. Judas sought an "opportunity to betray" Jesus (26:16) and capitalized on that moment when it arrived. He has earned his thirty pieces of silver.

Once aware that Jesus has received a capital sentence from the Sanhedrin, however, Judas regrets his action (μεταμεληθείς, *metamelētheis*, 27:3) and attempts to undo it. Seeking to return the silver to the chief priests and elders of the people, he confesses, "I sinned, for I betrayed innocent blood" (v. 4). When he finds them unresponsive, he simply flings the silver pieces into the sanctuary and—the narrative could not be more terse—"he went out and hanged himself" (v. 5). The

---

[59] See Kingsbury, *Matthew as Story*, 143; Heil, *Death and Resurrection*, 33–34; Senior, *Passion of Jesus in Matthew*, 63–64.

[60] Note the intensification from φιλήσω (*philēsō*) "[the one] I kiss" (26:48), to κατεφίλησεν (*katephilēsen*) "he kissed [him]" (v. 49).

[61] The translation of this expression (ἐφ᾽ ὃ πάρει, *eph ho parei*) is exceedingly difficult. Brown (*Death of the Messiah*, 2.1385–88) discusses the various options.

(imminent) death of an innocent man is on his head; he must bear the guilt for his act of betrayal.

Like Simon Peter, Judas surrenders his discipleship at the critical hour, and like Peter he comes to regret his fateful choice. Yet while Peter meant well and discovered in failure a lesson in courage and humility, Judas—out of greed and other motives the reader is left only to ponder—deliberately chose his path. Does that mean that his regret and admission of sin lack the redemptive potential of Peter's bitter tears of remorse?[62] Or does the pouring out of Jesus' innocent blood "for the forgiveness of sins" reach even to Judas? For all the harshness of Jesus' earlier words to Judas,[63] and despite the glaring absence of the betrayer from the circle of disciples privileged to encounter the risen Jesus, it seems to us that the narrative admits of the possibility that for Judas, too, the final word is one of mercy. One has to recall, though, that the norms governing this narrative center on producing good fruit (3:8, 10; 7:15–20) and doing the will of God (7:21–27). Measured against these norms, Judas is found wanting.

---

[62] Senior (*Passion of Jesus in Matthew*, 108) sharply contrasts the fate of Peter, who chose repentance, and Judas, who chose death and so does not escape judgment. Heil (*Death and Resurrection*, 68–69), on the other hand, thinks that according to Matthew Judas repented and therefore may receive forgiveness.

[63] "[W]oe to that man through whom the Son of humanity is betrayed. It would have been better for that man not to be born" (26:24).

 FOUR

"He saved others; let him save himself":
THE DEATH OF JESUS IN THE
GOSPEL ACCORDING TO LUKE

Readers who come to Luke's passion narrative fresh from the study of Mark's (or Matthew's) account are sure to be impressed by the distinctive stamp given the passion by Luke. To be sure, one encounters much that is familiar. Judas betrays Jesus to the Jewish authorities. Jesus interprets his imminent death at a Last Supper scene with his disciples, then, while they sleep, he submits in prayer to the divine will. As Jesus is placed under arrest, a servant of the high priest loses an ear. And while Jesus is in custody, Peter denies Jesus three times. First the Sanhedrin and then Pilate interrogate Jesus, and in the presence of Pilate the people request that he release Barabbas. Simon of Cyrene carries the cross of Jesus to the site of execution, where Jesus is crucified with two other men at "the Skull." Finally, Joseph of Arimathea provides for the burial of Jesus. All these and many other details Luke draws from his predecessor Mark.[1]

Readers of Luke's passion narrative nevertheless journey through uncharted terrain, discovering along the way topographical features noticeably different from those noted on the maps provided by Mark (and Matthew). In a passage signalling the commencement of the passion, the narrator ascribes to Satan Judas's decision to betray Jesus (22:3–4).[2] Jesus seizes upon the occasion of a final meal with his disciples to issue a discourse that has the markings of a last testament

---

[1] Mark was, in our view, among the "many who [had] undertaken to compile a narrative of the things accomplished among us" and upon whose work Luke is able to build in composing his own "orderly account" (Luke 1:1, 3).

[2] Cf. John 13:2, 27, one of the intriguing convergences between Luke and John in the passion.

(22:14–38)[3]—a farewell speech containing sayings unique to this Gospel.[4] The prayer scene on the Mount of Olives[5] provides a single snapshot of Jesus in the posture of prayer, in stark contrast to the threefold sequence of prayer and the disciples' sleep in Mark/Matthew (Luke 22:39–46). At the arrest, Jesus heals the servant whose ear[6] had been struck by a follower of Jesus, and there is no mention of the disciples' flight. Peter's threefold denial of his Lord (22:54–62) is narrated before, rather than after, the Sanhedrin's interrogation of Jesus, and Peter's movement from denial to remorse gains in poignancy as Jesus himself gazes at Peter at the moment of his disgrace (v. 61).

Luke delays until the early morning the Jewish court's examination of Jesus (22:66–71; Mark and Matthew record a late-night Jewish "trial"). Jesus' opponents level specific charges against him in the presence of Pilate (23:2, 5, 14), who three times pronounces Jesus innocent of any wrongdoing. Herod Antipas enjoys a cameo appearance in the passion drama (23:6–12), adding a touch of mockery but also—at least in Pilate's estimation—confirmation of the innocence of Jesus (v. 15). No mockery by Roman soldiers occurs after Pilate hands Jesus over to death (cf. Mark 15:16–20a; Matt 27:27–31a). A comparable mocking scene earlier in the narrative helped fill the time between Jesus' late-night arrest and the convening of the council in the early morning (22:63–65), although in Luke it is evidently Jewish officers who ridicule Jesus (cf. 22:52). En route to the crucifixion site, Jesus pauses to issue an oracle of warning to the "daughters of Jerusalem" (23:27–31). During the crucifixion itself, while taunting is the order of the day,[7] one of the

---

[3]Many scholars have noticed that Jesus' discourse at the Last Supper (Luke 22:14–38) has the features of a farewell speech. For discussion of the genre of this material, see Neyrey, *Passion according to Luke*, 5–48; William S. Kurz, "Luke 22:14–38 and Greco-Roman and Biblical Farewell Addresses," *JBL* 104 (1985) 251–68; Dennis E. Smith, "Table Fellowship as a Literary Motif in the Gospel of Luke," *JBL* 106 (1987) 613–38.

[4]Among the uniquely Lukan materials: Jesus warns Simon (Peter) of Satan's demand to sift the disciples like so much grain, yet also reassures him (Jesus will pray for him and he will "return"; 22:31–32); and Jesus delivers the enigmatic saying concerning the "two swords" (vv. 35–38).

[5]Mark 14:32 and Matt 26:36 locate this scene in a "place called Gethsemane," but Luke mentions only "the place" on the Mount of Olives. This omission of Aramaic terms and expressions is typical of the hellenistic author Luke. Cf. I. Howard Marshall, *Commentary on Luke* (NIGTC 3; Grand Rapids: Eerdmans, 1978) 830.

[6]"Right" ear in Luke (so also in John 18:10). It is characteristic of Luke to enhance the severity of the disorder that Jesus heals. See John T. Carroll, "Jesus as Healer in Luke–Acts," SBLSP 1994, 269–85 (273).

[7]Indeed, Luke preserves Mark's triadic structure of the mockery in this episode. All the more striking, therefore, are the cast changes Luke makes here. In Mark (also Matthew), passersby, Jewish religious leaders, and the other two crucified with Jesus all join in the derision of Jesus. Luke, by contrast, has the

criminals executed alongside Jesus rallies to his defense (23:39–43). And the rending of the temple curtain occurs before the death of Jesus, not after (23:45; contrast Mark 15:38; Matt 27:51).

Until recently, scholars have responded to this impressive array of data primarily by pressing the question of Luke's sources. Did Luke draw this distinctive material from a coherent non-Markan, perhaps even pre-Markan passion narrative?[8] Our concern in this chapter is not to reconstruct the prehistory of Luke's narrative. Rather, granting that Luke tapped available tradition and with considerable literary and theological artistry fashioned it into the narrative we now read, our aim is to explore in that narrative the web of meanings spun for Luke's readers as they ponder the death of one who is Lord, Messiah, and Savior.

No more than in Mark or Matthew does the death of Jesus in Luke come as a surprise to the reader. We begin by considering the way in which Jesus' death receives meaning as a culminating event in a carefully plotted story. We then probe Luke's characterization of Jesus in the passion, focusing on the theme of his innocence and on his role as Savior, before turning to the portrayal of the disciples. A final section treats the way in which the death of Jesus points forward to subsequent developments in Acts.

"This Jesus you killed":
JESUS' DEATH WITHIN LUKE'S NARRATIVE

The opening of Luke's story is charged with expectancy. In the era that dawns with the births of John the Baptizer and Jesus of Nazareth, the hope of Israel is realized on the stage of human history. God's promises to the people rush toward fulfillment.[9] Speeches by angels (1:13–17, 31–33, 35; 2:11), by parents of these two agents of God's redemptive work (Mary, 1:46–55; Zechariah, 1:67–79), and by other human observers (Simeon, 2:29–32, 34–35; Anna, 2:38) celebrate the

---

people standing by observing, while the "rulers" mock Jesus (23:35); then it is soldiers and *one* crucified criminal who add their taunts to the jeering chorus (vv. 36, 39).

[8]See Frank J. Matera, "The Death of Jesus according to Luke: A Question of Sources," *CBQ* 47 (1985) 469–85; Soards, *Passion according to Luke;* and Green, *Death of Jesus,* esp. 102–4.

[9]For further discussion of this theme in Luke–Acts, see Robert C. Tannehill, *The Narrative Unity of Luke–Acts* (2 vols.; FF; Philadelphia/Minneapolis: Fortress, 1986–90) 1.15–44; John T. Carroll, *Response to the End of History: Eschatology and Situation in Luke–Acts* (SBLDS 92; Atlanta: Scholars, 1988) 37–53.

divine benefactions of salvation and peace, of deliverance and forgiveness, that mark the advent of John and Jesus. In language evocative of God's covenantal promises to Abraham (1:54–55, 72–73) and to David (1:32–33, 69), these inspired discourses reveal that Jesus will ascend David's throne and as Lord and Savior offer the forgiveness of sins—the focal point of the experience of salvation.

Yet already these chapters, pervaded by expressions of hope and promise, prepare the reader for the tragic turn this story of salvation must take. Under the inspiration of the Holy Spirit, an old and pious Simeon identifies the infant Jesus as God's σωτήριον (*sōtērion*, "salvation"), a source of revelatory light for Gentiles and glory for Israel (2:29–32). Yet in the very next breath he issues an ominous warning to the child's mother: "Look! This child is set for the fall and rising of many in Israel, and for a sign that will be spoken against—and a sword will also pierce your own soul" (vv. 34–35). The stage has been set, and Luke's audience now knows that the one who ushers in an era of salvation, fulfilling ancient promises to the people, will in the course of the story encounter opposition. There will be sorrow for those who love him.

Even more revealing is the dramatic synagogue scene with which Jesus' public ministry begins (4:16–30). After claiming (by implication) that he represents the fulfillment of Isaiah's promise of a Spirit-anointed herald of peace and liberation (Isa 61:1–2), Jesus antagonizes a hometown crowd by highlighting the way in which, during the careers of Elijah and Elisha, divine benefaction bypassed Israel for the sake of outsiders (vv. 25–27). The reaction is swift: in rage they seek to kill him (vv. 28–30). This confrontation between a prophet and his people is programmatic for the story that ensues. Jesus will embody God's gracious favor for the poor and sick and marginalized—for outsiders.[10] And in doing so, he will make enemies, setting in motion a spiral of conflict that will result in his death. At this point in the story, Luke's reader certainly notices the dark clouds on the horizon of a day so bright with Jubilee promise.[11]

As Jesus carries out his ministry of healing and proclamation, he provokes conflict.[12] Indeed, Luke sketches a picture of mounting

---

[10]Ultimately, of course, for Gentiles, although with few exceptions (7:1–10; 8:26–39), this advance must await the apostolic mission in Acts.

[11]On the connection between Jesus' Nazareth sermon and the proclamation of the Jubilee Year, see Robert B. Sloan, Jr., *The Favorable Year of the Lord: A Study of Jubilary Theology in the Gospel of Luke* (Austin, Tex.: Schola, 1977); Sharon H. Ringe, *Jesus, Liberation, and the Biblical Jubilee: Images for Ethics and Christology* (OBT 19; Philadelphia: Fortress, 1985).

[12]See 5:21, 30 (scribes and Pharisees); 6:2 (some Pharisees); 6:7, 11 (scribes and Pharisees); 7:36–50 (Simon, a Pharisee); 9:53 (Samaritans); 11:15 ("some" in the crowd); 11:37–52 (Pharisees and lawyers); 11:53–54 (scribes and Pharisees);

opposition and escalating hostility.[13] Scribes (or lawyers) and even Pharisees—who are meal partners of Jesus in 7:36-50; 11:37-52; and 14:1-24—are troubled by Jesus' vision and practice of the kingdom of God. Those whom he courts (toll collectors and other notorious "sinners") his critics would exclude from fellowship. Especially during the lengthy journey narrative (9:51-19:44), the parting of the ways becomes clear. The people of God whom Jesus is gathering around himself comes to include just about everyone—except, that is, those who are convinced of their own righteousness. It comes as no surprise, therefore, that when Jesus rides in triumph into Jerusalem, acclaimed king by a "whole multitude of disciples," some Pharisees urge Jesus to distance himself from their praise (19:39). The tension in the air is palpable, drawing its energy from this clash between competing perceptions of Jesus.

Once Jesus is in Jerusalem, the ranks of Jesus' enemies swell, but now opposition centers on the temple institution and its leadership. And no wonder! For through a symbolic gesture of temple purification (19:45-46) and through daily teaching in the temple precincts (19:47), Jesus stakes a king's claim to the holy place. Corresponding to this focus on the temple is the intriguing fact that lawyers and Pharisees—despite their earlier criticism of Jesus—play no role at all in the passion story.[14] In the end, it is the priestly elite (the high priest and other "chief priests"), the temple officers (στρατηγοί, stratēgoi), and "rulers" or "leading men" among the people who oppose Jesus to the death.

Even more striking than the absence of Pharisees from the passion drama is the role of the Jewish populace. While Jesus has not minced words when it comes to "this generation" (7:31-35; 9:41; 11:29-32, 50), the crowds are consistently portrayed as sympathetic to Jesus. Particularly in the passion narrative, Luke drives a wedge between the people and their leaders. The Jewish public stand with Jesus, while the religious authorities plot his demise—thwarted, in fact, only by the esteem in

---

13:14, 17 (synagogue ruler); 14:2 (Pharisees); 15:2 (Pharisees and scribes); 16:14 and 19:39 (Pharisees).

[13]For analysis of the developing conflict in Luke's narrative, see Kingsbury, Conflict in Luke; Frank J. Matera, "Jesus' Journey to Jerusalem (Luke 9.51-19.46): A Conflict with Israel," JSNT 51 (1993) 57-77; John T. Carroll, "Luke's Portrayal of the Pharisees," CBQ 50 (1988) 604-21 (604-16); Tyson, Death of Jesus in Luke-Acts, 48-83; and idem, Images of Judaism in Luke-Acts (Columbia: University of South Carolina, 1992) 56-99.

[14]Observing the Pharisees' absence from the passion drama, Luke's readers will in retrospect refine an initial impression of escalating conflict between Jesus and the Pharisees and will conclude that the Gospel narrative does not, in the end, shut the door on the Pharisees. Of course, the continuation of the story in Acts will reinforce this judgment, for the portrayal of the Pharisees in Acts remains complex, including some positive features (e.g., Gamaliel's "defense" of the apostles in 5:34-39 and Paul's pedigree as Pharisee, openly admitted by him in 23:6; 26:5).

which the crowds hold him.[15] Judas Iscariot finally provides the authorities the opportunity to arrest Jesus in the absence of the crowd (22:2–5), although, ironically, a "crowd" (ὄχλος, *ochlos*) composed of leading priests, temple officers, and elders carries out the arrest (22:47, 52).[16] The entire body of elders, consisting of elite priests and scribes, interrogates Jesus (22:66, 70) and, on the basis of his implied claim to be Son of God,[17] hands him over to Pilate for execution.[18]

Nevertheless, at the pivotal moment the Jewish public align themselves with their leaders against Jesus, a shift in allegiance that leaves Pilate alone as Jesus' defender (23:13–25). The reader has been prepared for such a shift not only by the paradigmatic Nazareth rejection scene (4:16–30) but also by Jesus' parable of a throne claimant who entrusts property to servants while he ventures into a distant country to be confirmed as king (19:11–27). The logic of that parable, within its narrative setting, is that Jesus is going to Jerusalem not to ascend his throne (the expectation of v. 11) but to be rejected by his "citizens" (vv. 14, 27). And true to form, Israel does spurn the prophet par excellence, the one whom God sent as deliverer and ruler (11:49–51; 13:34–35; cf. Acts 7:51–53).[19]

Yet both before and after this fateful decision, the Jewish public are shown to be sympathetic to Jesus. Just moments after the "people" (λαός, *laos*) have joined their leaders in shouting, "Crucify, crucify him" (23:18, 21), the reader listens to the mournful cries of the women of

---

[15] See 19:47–48; 20:19–20; 22:2, 6.

[16] For a closer analysis of Luke's identification of Jesus' adversaries at this point in the story, see ch. 10 below.

[17] "And they all said, 'So you are the Son of God?' And he said to them, 'You yourselves say that I am'" (22:70).

[18] Even though the narrator reports no formal sentence of condemnation (contrast Mark 14:64; Matt 26:66), it is apparent that the Jewish council unanimously approves his transfer to Pilate for execution. Confirmation of this view is supplied by the later characterization of Joseph of Arimathea as a council member who dissented from its action against Jesus (23:50–51) and by the Emmaus disciples' summary of the tragic events: "Our chief priests and rulers handed him over to a judgment of death and crucified him" (24:20).

[19] The Lukan version of the parable of the wicked vineyard tenants (20:9–16) possibly fits this pattern. Jesus addresses the parable to "the people" (v. 9)—not to the religious leaders, as in Mark 12:1—and yet they respond in horror (μὴ γένοιτο, *mē genoito*: "May it not be so!"), perhaps to the images with which Jesus concludes the parable: "He will come and destroy those tenants, and give the vineyard to others." The people's response then prompts Jesus to speak of the builders' rejection of the stone that nevertheless becomes the cornerstone (vv. 17–18, quoting Ps 118:22–23). On the other hand, if the people are reacting to the story as a whole (the narrator simply observes, "when they had heard, they said"), then surely it is also the image of the beloved son brutally murdered by the tenants that provokes the audience's negative response. This reading squares with Luke's characterization of the Jewish public up to this point in the narrative.

Jerusalem (v. 27), and great crowds of people follow Jesus to the place of crucifixion (v. 27), look on as he is crucified (v. 35), and after his death return to their homes beating their chests in remorseful sorrow.[20] Their voices do not merge with the taunting chorus of rulers, soldiers, and one crucified criminal. Luke's reader surmises that there is surely need for repentance for the people's role in the death of Jesus, but at the same time there is room for hope. The mission speeches of Peter in Acts will pick up this thread (e.g., Acts 2:23, 36–41; 3:13–15, 17–21).[21] On one level of the narrative, the reader is guided to interpret Jesus' death as the regrettable outcome of a nation's rejection of its Messiah. Peter's Acts discourses capture well this dimension of the story: "This Jesus you killed, but God raised up" (variously formulated in Acts 2:23–24, 36; 3:15; 4:10; 5:30–31; 10:39–40; cf. 13:27–30). God acts to vindicate as Messiah and Lord the very one whom the nation has refused. Or to use the imagery of Jesus' lament over the holy city, the people proved blind to the divine visitation that greeted them in the person of Jesus (19:41–44).

The Lukan narrative, however, also invites readers to probe deeper layers of meaning in this event. True, actors on the human stage orchestrate the death of Jesus, and Luke carefully sketches their various roles. But their opposition to Jesus is only symptomatic of a larger, more menacing cosmic battle, a contest in which God's archenemy seeks to undermine the work of divine salvation carried on by Jesus. That the malevolent figure of Satan lurks behind the actions of Jesus' opponents is transparent in the arrest scene. There Jesus, after commenting on his enemies' failure to move against him when he taught openly in the temple,[22] has the last word concerning his arrest: "But this is your hour and the power of darkness" (22:53). The forces of darkness will at last have their way with Jesus. Or so it will appear.

As early as the narrative of Jesus' testing in the wilderness (4:1–13), the reader catches a glimpse of the fierce struggle with demonic forces that Jesus must undergo if he is to play the part of Messiah and Savior. Twice the devil invites Jesus to exploit supernatural power with the challenge, "If you are the Son of God . . . " (vv. 3, 9). Sandwiched between these tests is the enticement of earthly rule and glory, promised to Jesus in exchange for his worship of the devil (vv. 5–7). Rebuffed not once but three times, the devil "withdrew from him until an opportune moment

---

[20] For further discussion of the meaning of this gesture, see John T. Carroll, "Luke's Crucifixion Scene," in Sylva, ed., Reimaging the Death of the Lukan Jesus, 108–24, 194–203 (111–13); Senior, Passion of Jesus in Luke, 147–48; Marshall, Luke, 876–77; Tyson, Death of Jesus in Luke–Acts, 46 n. 13.

[21] Cf. William S. Kurz, Reading Luke–Acts: Dynamics of Biblical Narrative (Louisville: Westminster/John Knox, 1993) 66, 198 n. 61.

[22] The reader recalls that this failure to act was an expression of their lack of power, for their designs against Jesus were thwarted by the people's support of him.

[καιρός, *kairos*]." This ominous notice from the narrator (v. 13) prepares readers for Satan's return as the passion drama commences.[23] The narrator marks Satan's return by observing tersely that "Satan entered Judas called Iscariot" (22:3).[24] Judas then immediately enters into his betrayal pact with the religious authorities. If the plot to destroy Jesus lacks only a good strategy, the chief architect of evil is more than happy to oblige.

Clearly, then, the passion represents, on one level, a final, relentless assault upon the faithfulness of Jesus, a last desperate attempt by the forces of evil to undo Jesus' work of salvation. As we will see in the next section of this chapter, Luke leaves no doubt: on each score, Satan fails.

First, though, it is necessary to consider another, more positive meaning assigned to Jesus' death as an event that he himself saw coming and that he embraced within the intention of his mission. Of course, much has been made over the paucity of statements employing atonement or sacrificial imagery to characterize the death of Jesus in Luke's Gospel.[25] But it would be a mistake to conclude that Luke attaches salvific meaning to the resurrection alone and not also to the crucifixion.[26] The death of Jesus is, to be sure, a brutal miscarriage of justice, and it stems, in part, from the malevolent scheming of Satan. It is also, however, purposed by God and embraced by Jesus as the inevitable culmination of his mission.

---

[23] Not that the narrative of Jesus' public ministry is a "Satan-free" period, as Hans Conzelmann contended (*Theology of St. Luke*, 16, 80–81, 132, 156–57, 200). For a recent and telling critique of Conzelmann's view, see Susan R. Garrett, *The Demise of the Devil: Magic and the Demonic in Luke's Writings* (Minneapolis: Fortress, 1989) 41–43. The frequent exorcisms performed by Jesus and by his followers (cf. 10:17) and the portrait he draws of himself in 11:21–22 as a "stronger man" who plunders Satan's goods (that is, heals persons possessed by demons) suggest that Satan has not gone into hiding. One finds a similar picture in Acts when Peter summarizes Jesus' ministry: Jesus, anointed by God with the Holy Spirit and with power, "went about doing good and healing all that were oppressed by the devil" (Acts 10:38). What does resume only with the opening of the passion is the personal attack upon Jesus.

[24] And evidently when he attempts to accomplish similar designs towards Simon Peter and the other apostles (22:31).

[25] Especially striking is the absence of Mark 10:45 in Luke's account. See the discussion in Joel B. Green, "The Death of Jesus, God's Servant," in Sylva, ed., *Reimaging the Death of the Lukan Jesus*, 1–28, 170–73 (esp. 3–7); and idem, "'The Message of Salvation' in Luke–Acts," *Ex Auditu* 5 (1989) 21–34 (esp. 23–26); and cf. ch. 13 below.

[26] Construing Jesus' death as simply the tragic outcome of Israel's rejection of Jesus, to be overcome by the divine act of raising him from the dead. For a constructive statement of the role played by the death of Jesus in Lukan soteriology, see now Joel B. Green, *The Theology of the Gospel of Luke* (NTT 3; Cambridge: Cambridge University, 1995) ch. 3; idem, "'Salvation to the End of the Earth' (Acts 13:47): God as Savior in the Acts of the Apostles," in *The Book of Acts and Its Theology*, ed. I. Howard Marshall and David Peterson (Grand Rapids: Eerdmans, 1995).

Jesus first hints at this destiny in 5:35: in days to come, his disciples will fast, conduct appropriate to the situation of a bridegroom's absence. In the first of a series of passion predictions, Jesus announces in 9:22 that the Son of humanity (ὁ υἱὸς τοῦ ἀνθρώπου, *ho huios tou anthrōpou*) "must" suffer, be rejected by the elders, chief priests, and scribes, be killed, and on the third day be raised. The reader meets similar prophecies in 9:44; 17:25; and 18:31–33 (although there is considerable variety in the identification of the human agents involved). On Easter morning, the angel recalls these prophetic words of Jesus (24:6–7). Moreover, the risen Jesus locates that "must" in sacred Scripture. The inevitability of Jesus' suffering, rejection, and death flows from a divine necessity, from God's redemptive purpose, disclosed long ago in Scripture (24:26–27, 45–46).[27] Jesus dies not simply because Satan contrives it and not simply because Jesus' enemies thereby gain the upper hand. Rather, he also dies because God purposes his death.

And Jesus accepts this destiny. In the transfiguration scene, the Lukan narrator depicts Jesus discussing with Moses and Elijah his coming ἔξοδος, *exodos*, at Jerusalem (9:31). No doubt Luke's reader hears a distinct echo of Moses' exodus liberation of the people from bondage in Egypt, an echo suggesting similar liberating potential for Jesus' destiny in the holy city. That "exodus" likely encompasses the whole sequence of events from crucifixion through ascension.[28] Jesus' embrace of the necessity of his death colors the symbolism of 12:49–50. The "baptism" he somewhat impatiently awaits is the baptism of death.[29] Moreover, when Pharisees alert Jesus to Herod's desire to kill him,[30] Jesus' answer betrays a keen sense of vocation. No prophet can expect any fate other than death in the holy city (13:33–34). For the present, he "must" be about the business of his ministry, healing and performing exorcisms. But soon enough ("on the third day"), Jerusalem

---

[27]Although Luke does not specify which passages of Scripture are involved. See the discussion in John T. Carroll, "The Uses of Scripture in Acts," SBLSP 1990, 512–28.

[28]Cf. also 9:51. For further discussion, see Susan R. Garrett, "Exodus from Bondage: Luke 9:31 and Acts 12:1–24," *CBQ* 52 (1990) 656–80.

[29]The association between baptism and death is even clearer in Mark 10:35–40, a passage not incorporated in Luke's Gospel.

[30]Luke 13:31. It is possible that the Pharisees' warning is insincere (so John A. Darr, *On Character Building: The Reader and the Rhetoric of Characterization in Luke–Acts* [LCBI; Louisville: Westminster/John Knox, 1992] 105–6)—although Jesus does apply the metaphor "fox" to Herod in his reply—or a hostile test (so Luke Timothy Johnson, *The Gospel of Luke* [SP 3; Collegeville, Minn.: Liturgical, 1991] 221). But if the warning has basis in fact, it is curious that there is no indication of this hostility when Jesus meets Herod face-to-face in 23:7–12. The parallel warning in Acts 21:12–14, which rests on both good information and noble motives, suggests that the Pharisees in Luke 13 are likewise sincere. See further Green, *Theology of Luke*, ch. 3.

will have its way with him. This crucial passage reveals the indissoluble link between two seemingly opposed meanings of Jesus' death. It is at one and the same time the act of his enemies and an event purposed by God and intended by Jesus himself.

The words of Jesus at the Last Supper lend poignancy to the theme. For here—in a setting that highlights forces threatening to dissolve the intimate bond of discipleship and meal fellowship—Jesus pictures his imminent death as an intrusive event that interrupts his table fellowship with his disciples (22:15–18):

> And he said to them, "It has been my strong desire to eat this Passover with you before I suffer. For I tell you, I will certainly not eat it until it is fulfilled in the kingdom of God." And he took the cup and gave thanks and said, "Take this and divide it among yourselves. For I tell you, from now on I will certainly not drink of the fruit of the vine until God's kingdom comes."

From this moment on, because Jesus must now "suffer," he can no longer enjoy fellowship at table with his disciples. They, but not he, may eat and drink.[31]

Nevertheless, the sayings that follow develop the positive effect of Jesus' impending death on the band of apostles. Broken bread is a metaphor for Jesus' body, "given for you."[32] The cup after the meal is a metaphor for a new covenant enacted through the blood Jesus spills "on your behalf." Jesus here interprets his death as an event enabling a new covenantal loyalty, a gift creating a new covenantal community (cf. also Acts 20:28). His self-sacrifice is a means of benefaction for the community of his followers.

---

[31]It is significant, therefore, that the risen Jesus eats with his followers (24:30, 41–43; cf. Acts 1:4). The meal fellowship of the eschatological banquet still awaits the era of God's kingdom, but in the meantime there are anticipations of that banquet which also link the church of the present to the public ministry of Jesus.

[32]Luke 22:19. The textual tradition is uncertain at this point. Some Western witnesses, including Codex Bezae, omit vv. 19b–20. A strong argument for the authenticity of the shorter text (omitting vv. 19b–20) has been made by Bart D. Ehrman ("The Cup, the Bread, and the Salvific Effect of Jesus' Death in Luke–Acts," SBLSP 1991, 576–91). Increasingly, however, scholars are preferring the longer text. See, e.g., Bruce M. Metzger, *A Textual Commentary on the Greek New Testament* (New York: United Bible Societies, 1971) 173–77; Joseph A. Fitzmyer, *The Gospel according to Luke: Introduction, Translation, and Notes* (2 vols.; AB 28–28A; Garden City, N.Y.: Doubleday, 1981–85) 2.1387–89; Senior, *Passion of Jesus in Luke*, 59; Marshall, *Luke*, 799–80. We prefer the longer text including vv. 19b–20. This reading enjoys the support of a preponderance of the witnesses. Moreover, because of the unusual sequence of cup-bread-cup, the longer text is likely the source of the other variants, which seek in one way or another to adjust that sequence.

With these sayings of Jesus, we have already begun to consider the characterization of Jesus in Luke's passion account. Luke presents Jesus in his death, as in his life, as the Savior. It is time now to pay closer attention to the development of Jesus' character in the passion narrative.

JESUS, SAVIOR

Luke's Jesus wears many hats. He is Messiah, Son of God—a status validated, not disconfirmed, by his crucifixion. Of this status the resurrection and exaltation of Jesus are decisive proof.[33] He is therefore the legitimate ruler of the nation, and in fact in a penultimate way he exercises that sovereignty through his chosen apostles (22:28–30, a promise of apostolic leadership of Israel fulfilled in the course of Acts). Jesus is also *the* prophet, the "one like Moses" who is the definitive mouthpiece of God (Acts 3:22–23; cf. 7:37), and as such he is also the "Servant of God" who mediates divine blessing through repentance and forgiveness (Acts 3:26).[34] It is part and parcel of Jesus' prophetic vocation that he be rejected and killed by his people (11:49–52; 13:33–34).

Yet at the center of Luke's portrait of Jesus lies his role as σωτήρ (sōtēr, "Savior"). His arrival means that the era of Israel's salvation—indeed, the world's salvation—has dawned.[35] These hopes, awakened by the birth narrative (1:46–55, 68–79; 2:11, 29–32) and their scope broadened by the Baptizer ("all flesh shall see God's salvation," 3:6), are given substance as the ministry of Jesus unfolds. As healer he "saves" (that is, rescues and makes whole) those oppressed by sickness or demonic possession.[36] As proclaimer he "saves" by inviting any and all into God's realm.[37] And as one who summons sick and sinner, poor and rich, to life-giving transformation (μετάνοια, metanoia), he embodies God's salvation of persons beyond the margins of "holy"

---

[33]The angel Gabriel's announcement to Mary celebrates Jesus' status as Son of God, Davidic ruler (1:32–33, 35), and after his birth a heavenly messenger affirms his rank as Messiah and Lord (2:11). With an appeal to Scripture, the risen Jesus claims that his suffering and death do not call into question but, rather, authenticate his role as Messiah (24:26–27, 44–46). Peter's speeches in Acts appeal both to scriptural promise and to the fact of Jesus' resurrection to support the claim that even as one rejected by his nation and crucified, he is Messiah and Lord (e.g., Acts 2:23–32, 36; 3:18; 13:29–33).

[34]On Luke's depiction of Jesus as "Servant," see Green, "Death of Jesus, God's Servant." Johnson (*Luke*) emphasizes Jesus' identity as prophet.

[35]See Tannehill, *Narrative Unity*, 1.15–44. This is the era that king and prophet alike eagerly awaited (10:23–24).

[36]The term σώζειν, sōzein, appears in connection with healing or exorcism in 6:9; 8:36, 48, 50; 17:19; 18:42.

[37]See, e.g., 5:27–32; 7:18–23, 36–50; 14:15–24; 15:1–32.

Israel.[38] If Simeon can identify the infant Jesus, cradled within his arms, as God's σωτήριον (*sōtērion*, "salvation," 2:30), so too Jesus can appropriate the label for himself when he ushers the rich toll collector Zacchaeus into the realm of God's salvation: "*I* must stay at your house today" (19:5); "Today *salvation* has come to this house" (19:9). Jesus embodies God's salvation for the people of God. Above all else, this is Jesus' mission in the world: to save those who are lost, and to do so by offering divine forgiveness (19:10; cf. 5:27–32; 7:47–50; 15:1–32).

The disciples, stunned by the radical demand of Jesus that a rich ruler forsake his wealth to follow him, query, "Who, then, can be saved?" (18:26). Jesus, echoing Gabriel's reassuring word to Mary (1:37, itself echoing Gen 18:14), replies that God is able to accomplish what is humanly impossible. Through the ministry of Jesus, God saves those who open their lives to the change Jesus brings: healing, acceptance symbolized in table fellowship, forgiveness. This is how Jesus plays the part of Savior.

What happens to this pattern when the reader steps into the passion story? If Jesus' mockers are right, the pattern of the public ministry has been broken: "He saved others; let him save himself" (23:35; cf. vv. 37, 39). Since Jesus cannot, or will not, act to save himself, he clearly cannot be God's chosen one, the king-Messiah of Israel. Time has run out on the age of salvation. Luke's reader, however, may recall lines delivered earlier by Jesus: "Whoever wishes to save his life will lose it; but whoever loses his life for my sake, this one will save it" (9:24). And in fact, the invitation to the realm of the saved continues unimpeded even as Jesus goes to his death.[39]

From the cross, Jesus offers a prayer on behalf of his adversaries who are putting him to death: "Father, forgive them, for they do not know what they are doing" (23:34).[40] Jesus continues to offer forgiveness to the very end, extending it even to mortal enemies.[41]

---

[38]See, e.g., 5:27–32; 7:36–50; 8:26–39; 13:23–30; 19:1–10.

[39]See further Carroll, "Crucifixion Scene," 120–23.

[40]This prayer is omitted from some important early manuscripts, including the Bodmer papyrus (𝔓[75]). It is probable, however, that the prayer is original to the Gospel. Intrinsic considerations: The prayer anticipates Stephen's similar petition as he faces martyrdom (Acts 7:60), and since the account of Stephen's death is modeled after that of Jesus, it seems likely that Jesus had earlier offered a prayer for forgiveness. Moreover, it is consistent with an important motif of the speeches in Acts, namely the ignorance out of which both people and leaders acted in putting Jesus to death (Acts 3:17; 13:27). Extrinsic considerations: A motive for the excision of the prayer is not hard to find. Jesus' act of clemency toward his Jewish enemies may well have offended early Christian scribes who lived in a climate pervaded by intense anti-Jewish sentiment (see ch. 10 below). Others who regard the prayer as part of the Lukan text include Senior, *Passion of Jesus in Luke*, 128–29; Brown, *Death of the Messiah*, 2.971–81; Marshall, *Luke*, 867–68; Johnson, *Luke*, 376.

[41]In a similar vein, during the turbulent arrest scene, Jesus stops to heal the ear of the high priest's servant. Throughout the passion drama, Jesus

It is highly ironic that at the very moment when Jesus' incapacity to "save" makes him the target of taunts by Jewish leaders, soldiers, and one of the crucified criminals, he is still pursuing the work of saving others—and not just in this prayer for forgiveness. When one of the evildoers bids him demonstrate his status as Christ by saving himself and them (23:39), the other rallies to Jesus' defense: unlike them, he does not deserve this fate. Beyond this assertion of Jesus' innocence, the penitent criminal also acknowledges that he is truly a king: "Remember me when you come into your royal rule" (v. 42). Jesus, of course, answers this petition with the promise that "today" the evildoer will be with him in "paradise" (v. 43). Jesus, the Righteous One, draws with him into the abode of the righteous this criminal, whose penitent faith is apparently born only in the desperate final hours of his life. Where Jesus is, there the work of God's salvation occurs. This is so no less at the cross than during the public ministry. Jesus is still in the business of reserving a place in the company of the saved for those beyond the pale. He is, indeed, Savior.[42]

Before completing this partial sketch of Luke's characterization of Jesus in the passion, it is important to consider the motif of Jesus' innocence, which figures so prominently in these chapters of the Gospel. Jesus is, in a word, δίκαιος (*dikaios*, "righteous").[43]

Luke's narrative is quite explicit about the charges leveled against Jesus. In the presence of Pilate, the religious leaders ("the whole multi-

---

remains true to his own teaching (6:27–36). His integrity, unshaken to his dying breath, confirms that he dies the death of the "Righteous One" (cf. Acts 3:14). The centurion's declaration ("Truly this man was righteous," 23:47) reinforces a character portrait already impressed upon the reader.

[42]For an attempt to establish the communal and this-worldly character of "salvation" in Luke–Acts, see Luke Timothy Johnson, "The Social Dimensions of *Sōtēria* in Luke–Acts and Paul," SBLSP 1993, 520–36 (524–30). Although somewhat exaggerated, Johnson's study is useful as a corrective against individualistic and strictly eschatological construals of the semantic field of "salvation." The prominence of healings/exorcisms in which Jesus restores persons to community (see, e.g., 5:12–16, 17–26; 7:11–17; 8:26–39, 40–56; 13:10–17; 17:11–19) and of meal scenes in which Jesus invites marginalized persons into a new community suggests that the "salvation" Jesus brings to Israel is thoroughly communal and at least anticipates the ultimate (still future) bestowal of salvation.

[43]Karris (*Luke: Artist and Theologian*, 16–18, 79–119) highlights this dimension of the Lukan passion account, pointing to the influence of the image of the suffering Righteous One in Wis 1–5. Contra Karris, the term δίκαιος encompasses both "righteousness" and "innocence" (see Carroll, "Crucifixion Scene," 116–18, 200 n. 52; cf. Green, "Death of Jesus, God's Servant"). The same motif of innocence pervades the account of Paul in Acts. Like Jesus before him, Paul is wrongly accused and detained; he is innocent of all charges of disloyalty or other crimes, whether religious or political. See further John T. Carroll, "Luke's Apology for Paul," SBLSP 1988, 106–18.

tude of them") enumerate their accusations (23:1–2). It is their determination that Jesus has corrupted the nation, opposed payment of tribute to Caesar, and arrogated to himself the royal position of Christ. Pilate conducts a perfunctory interrogation, asking Jesus if he is indeed "the King of the Jews." After Jesus responds with the ambiguous "You say [so]" (σὺ λέγεις, *sy legeis*, v. 3), Pilate announces his finding: "I find no guilt in this man" (v. 4).

The brevity of Pilate's examination of the prisoner is perhaps surprising. In evaluating these charges, however, Luke's reader is guided by the preceding narrative. Jesus has not opposed but rather upheld—while at the same time relativizing—the obligation to pay tribute to Caesar (20:19–26).[44] And as for corrupting the nation (a charge rehearsed by Pilate in v. 14), Jesus has steadfastly sought to restore it from its corrupt ways to the path of justice. (Of course, Jesus' opponents would beg to differ.) Pilate's judgment is particularly important on the third charge. After all, Jesus *is* the bona fide Messiah and King of Israel. Evidently, Pilate finds no reason to condemn Jesus, whatever truth may inhere in the claim that Jesus is "king." Not satisfied, the Jewish authorities continue to press their case against Jesus, alleging that he has stirred up the people from Galilee to Jerusalem (v. 5) and carrying their accusations also to Herod Antipas (v. 10), once Pilate dispatches the prisoner to the tetrarch for interrogation.

The specificity of the charges is matched by the specificity of the Roman exoneration of Jesus. Pilate repeatedly affirms Jesus' innocence of any and all charges brought against him (vv. 4, 14–15, 22), and the governor reports that Herod the tetrarch reached the same judgment (v. 15). As will also be the case for Paul, Rome's verdict on Jesus is clear: he is not guilty; he does not deserve to die (cf. Acts 26:30–32). The outcome of the case (Jesus' crucifixion) betrays instead the corruption of the proceeding. It is not Roman justice but the desire of the Jewish people—especially their leaders—that prevails.

The narrator corroborates this appraisal of Jesus with the double testimony of a Roman soldier and a condemned criminal at the site of execution. As we have seen, the crucified man (who ought to recognize an evildoer when he sees one!) trumpets Jesus' innocence (23:41). And no doubt more importantly (for Luke's audience), the centurion is moved by the circumstances of Jesus' dying[45] to declare, "Truly, this man was

---

[44]Luke 20:19–20 introduces the exchange about tribute with a blunt description of the motives of those who question Jesus. They are "spies," sent by the religious authorities, who feign sincerity so as to find grounds for accusing Jesus before the governor. Their (false) testimony clearly informs the Jewish leaders' formulation of the charges in 23:2.

[45]Presumably including the darkness over the land (v. 44), the rending of the sanctuary curtain (v. 45), and Jesus' death prayer, "Father, into your hands

righteous" (v. 47). As Luke's readers already have surmised (see 11:47–51; 13:32–34; 19:41–44), the death of Jesus reveals the evil present not in the accused but, rather, in the accuser; ironically, it speaks volumes about the justice and integrity of the one condemned to die in shame.

THE DISCIPLES AND THE DEATH OF JESUS

A striking feature of Luke's passion narrative is its distinctive portrait of the disciples. They are by no means exemplary figures—*Jesus* is the model of righteousness. Nevertheless, the disciples fare much better than in Mark's account.

There is a large crowd of disciples in Luke's Gospel (e.g., 6:17; 19:37). From this multitude of followers, Jesus selects twelve to be his "apostles" (6:13–16). These ἀπόστολοι, *apostoloi*, he sends out to extend his own work of healing and proclamation; buoyed by the "power and authority" he imparts to them, they proclaim good news and heal "everywhere" (9:1–6). Yet the urgent need of laborers for the harvest impels Jesus to dispatch seventy-two others on the same mission of healing the sick and proclaiming the imminence of God's kingdom in "every city and place where he was about to come" (10:1–12). The narrator reports without delay the extraordinary success of the seventy-two's labors (10:17–20).[46] These two missions represent significant anticipations of the apostles' mission "to the end of the earth" in Acts. So the narrative exhibits the continuity between Jesus' activity and that of his followers. In Acts they carry on, in his name and by the same Spirit that empowered him, the work he had begun.

Elsewhere in the Gospel, however, the disciples play the roles of learner and observer. They form a receptive audience for Jesus' teaching and healing, and occasionally individual disciples are singled out:[47] Peter (8:45; 9:20, 32–33; 12:41; 18:28); James and John (9:54); Peter, James, and John (9:28). The fervent request the apostles express to Jesus

---

I commit my spirit" (v. 46). Jesus' fidelity as Son of God—like his commitment to a life of mercy, forgiveness, and nonretaliation—remains unwavering to the bitter end. On the meaning of the torn sanctuary curtain in Luke, see Joel B. Green, "The Demise of the Temple as 'Culture Center' in Luke–Acts: An Exploration of the Rending of the Temple Veil (Luke 23:44–49), *RB* 101 (1994) 495–515.

[46]The disciples earlier were unable to exorcise a demon (9:40), a failure more than matched by the success of the seventy-two: "Lord, even the demons are subject to us in your name!" (10:17).

[47]Although the term μαθητής (*mathētēs*, "disciple") is not used, Luke 8:1–3 gives several women the role of disciple and even patron of Jesus, and 10:38–42 shows Mary in the posture of discipleship, sitting at Jesus' feet.

in 17:5 captures well the disciples' demeanor throughout his public ministry: "Add to our faith!" Not always perceptive, they are nevertheless receptive and diligent inquirers, far removed from the spiritually dull and dense characters Mark portrayed.[48]

How do the disciples measure up in the Lukan passion narrative? The emblems of failure are prominent. Judas betrays his Lord. The apostles dining with Jesus at the Last Supper, undeterred by his announcement that one of them is a traitor, dispute with one another about their relative claims to greatness (22:24). While Jesus prays in submission to the purposes of God, the disciples sleep (22:39–46).[49] Later Peter, who has followed Jesus "at a distance" after his arrest, loses his nerve in the high priest's courtyard and three times denies his association with Jesus (22:54–62).[50] Even on Easter morning, the apostles, confronted with news that is too good to be true, judge the women's report of an empty tomb and an angel's reassuring message to be a tall tale unworthy of belief (24:11).

So far the Lukan disciples might be confused for their Markan counterparts. But in Luke's story, the disciples have redeeming qualities entirely missing from their characterization in Mark. The panic-stricken flight of the disciples from the scene of Jesus' arrest, recorded by both Mark and Matthew, is passed over in silence by Luke. Then, during the account of Jesus' crucifixion, the narrator places "at a distance," standing among Jesus' women followers so as to observe the crucifixion, "all those known to him" (πάντες οἱ γνωστοί, *pantes hoi gnōstoi*, 23:49). Luke's reader has every reason to think that these acquaintances of Jesus include the apostles.[51]

Jesus' farewell discourse at the Last Supper shows that the presence of the apostles (minus Judas) throughout the passion narrative is no accident. Even after correcting their misguided notions about greatness (22:24–27), Jesus praises their steadfastness (vv. 28–30):

---

[48] See the treatments of this theme in ch. 2 above and ch. 12 below.

[49] But notice that the disciples' failure is tempered somewhat in this scene. The narrator attributes their drowsiness to their "grief" (v. 45) and calls attention to their lack of vigilance not three times (Mark/Matthew) but only once.

[50] The denial scene in Luke lacks the dramatic intensification present in both Mark and Matthew, where Peter spices his third denial with the invoking of a curse (Mark 14:71; Matt 26:74; cf. also the solemn oath in the Matthean version of Peter's second denial [v. 72]). In Luke, Peter simply denies (1) knowing Jesus, (2) being "one of them," and (3) knowing what the questioner means.

[51] Cf. Fitzmyer, *Luke*, 2.1364; Senior, *Passion of Jesus in Luke*, 148–49. But if this is the case, why would the Lukan narrator leave the account so ambiguous? Perhaps the established tradition of the disciples' disappearance after the arrest required a muted approach.

> You are the ones who have continued to stand by me in my trials. And [so], just as my Father assigned to me, I assign to you dominion, that you may eat and drink at my table in my royal realm, and that you may be seated on thrones[52] judging the twelve tribes of Israel.

The Lukan disciples do not abandon Jesus in time of crisis; instead, the apostles persevere—though imperfectly—in their loyalty to their Lord.

Luke's readers later discover that the role to be played by the apostles in Acts requires that they "stand by Jesus in his trials." For they are above all else μάρτυρες, *martyres*, "witnesses" of Jesus' ministry and especially of his resurrection (Luke 24:48; Acts 1:21–22). Therefore, although before the arrest the eyes of the disciples were closed in the sleep of grief, they may well be among those standing—at a distance, to be sure, and only as part of a nameless crowd—observing the event of Jesus' death. And although after the resurrection of Jesus their eyes must be opened, both to the presence of Jesus and to the meaning of the Scriptures that pointed to his suffering and death (24:25–27, 31–32, 44–47), they do finally see. They are credible witnesses of Jesus' ministry of healing and proclamation, of his death, of his resurrection, and ultimately of his ascension into glory (Acts 1:9–11).[53]

Thus, Luke's passion account supplies the apostles with the credentials that authenticate their witness to their Lord. In addition, because these are rounded, quite "human" characters,[54] readers are also enabled, by observing the disciples' decisions and struggles, to reflect upon the meaning of their own discipleship.

Luke reframes the disciples' failure in a way that suggests the deeper issues at stake in the passion. This is indeed, for the disciples as for Jesus, a πειρασμός, *peirasmos*, a severe test of fidelity and integrity. To be sure, at the Last Supper Jesus commends them for their steadfastness throughout his time of testing, but when he alerts them to the need for vigilant prayer that they may be spared this ordeal (22:40), they do not pray but sleep. They must rely through prayer upon strength beyond their own strength because this hour belongs to the power of darkness (22:53). Satan stands behind Judas's move to betray Jesus (22:3). Jesus cautions Peter that Satan has also sought to seize control of the others, but Jesus' prayer on behalf of Peter and his perseverance in faith (22:31–32) ultimately proves effectual. Yes, he denies his association with his Lord. But he does later (in the Acts narrative) "return to

---

[52]Not twelve thrones, as in Matt 19:28. Luke here takes account of Judas's apostasy. For symbolic reasons, Matthias will later round out the number of the Twelve (Acts 1:15–26), and presumably the twelfth "throne" is reserved for him.

[53]Notice the heavy accent on the apostles' visual perception in the Acts ascension account.

[54]That is, they possess both positive and negative traits.

strengthen his brothers" (v. 32) and becomes, moreover, a pillar of strength, speaking and acting boldly even in the face of persecution.

Luke also softens the hard blow of Peter's failure by painting a picture of unbroken fellowship with Jesus. Jesus prays for Peter, and then, at the very moment when Peter denies his connection to him, he looks at the apostle, triggering Peter's memory of the denial prediction and eliciting from him tears of remorse and repentance (22:61–62).

Luke's depiction of Peter and the rest of the apostles during the passion ordeal leads readers to attribute the disciples' failure not to their weakness or their lack of faith but to the severity of the crisis that overtakes them. The implication is clear that Luke's readers, too, must in prayer and reliance upon the Spirit seek strength from God if they are to prove faithful in time of peril (cf. 12:4–12; 18:1–8; 21:12–19).

THE STORY CONTINUES

The end of the Gospel does not close the book on the death of Jesus. It casts its shadow far into the story of Christian beginnings narrated in Luke's second book to Theophilus. We focus here on three dimensions of this further elaboration, in Acts, of the meaning of Jesus' death. First, in the mission discourses the crucifixion figures alongside the resurrection in an argument for Jesus' messianic status. Second, these speeches use memory of this event as the basis for an appeal to Judean Jews to repent and believe. Finally, the passion of Jesus sets the pattern for followers like Stephen and Paul who likewise face death at the hands of unscrupulous enemies.

The Death of the Messiah

Already in Luke 24 the risen Jesus makes room for rejection, suffering, and death in the career of the Messiah. For those fitted with the correct hermeneutical lenses, Scripture is quite clear on this point.

> O foolish men, slow in heart to believe in all that the prophets spoke. Was it not necessary for the Christ to suffer these things and [so] enter into his glory? (vv. 25–26)

> Then he opened their minds to understand the Scriptures, and he said to them, "So it is written that the Christ should suffer and on the third day rise from the dead." (vv. 45–46)

Peter develops this line in his Pentecost discourse. "This man [Jesus]," he indicts his audience of Jerusalem and Judean Jews, "you killed by nailing him [to a cross]" (Acts 2:23; cf. v. 36). Yet it was the divine purpose that he be given over through lawless people to such a fate (v. 23). God then confirms his status as Messiah and Lord through his resurrection (vv. 24, 36), realizing the divine plan disclosed in Scripture.[55]

Much the same perspective greets the reader in Peter's second speech. To be sure, Jesus died because he was rejected and handed over by his own people (that is, Peter's audience), who acted without knowing what they were doing (3:13–15, 17). This suffering of the Christ, however, was in fact God's action fulfilling the divine word spoken "by the mouth of all the prophets" (3:18, with some slight hyperbole!). The Messiah's death at the hands of his own people was an event purposed by God. Paul reiterates this claim in his synagogue address at Pisidian Antioch: the people of Jerusalem, in putting Jesus to death, unwittingly (and ironically) fulfilled their own sacred Scriptures (13:27–29). Most specific of all, however, is the apostles' prayer of 4:26–30, which rehearses the events of the passion and in so doing anchors them in Ps 2. The death of the Servant-Messiah resulted from a collusion of hostile parties, each identified in this royal psalm (Gentiles and peoples [of Israel], kings [Herod] and rulers [Pilate]). Yet their actions only accomplished the divine plan (v. 28).[56] The speech material in Acts is emphatic on this score: the Messiah dies in accordance with God's purpose. It is perhaps worth noting in this connection that the treachery of Judas, too, fulfilled scriptural prophecy (Acts 1:16–20).[57]

Luke–Acts redefines the Messiah paradigm in terms of the tragic fate of Jesus. Scripture and divine intention call for his suffering, rejection, and death. Nevertheless, with the resurrection of Jesus God provides the chief attestation of Jesus as Messiah (3:26; 4:10–11; 5:30; 10:39–40; 13:30). Here the recurring picture is of God answering Israel's rejection of the Messiah with the vindication of Easter.

Cross and Repentance

For Jesus, according to Luke, Israel's Scriptures reveal as the divine purpose not only the necessity of the Christ's passion but also the mission of proclamation to the whole world. The offer of forgiveness of sins and the summons to repentance are thus grounded in sacred Scripture (Luke 24:46–47). Peter's early mission speeches in Acts likewise link the death of Jesus and the call to repentance. The temple speech of Acts 3 makes this connection explicit (vv. 13–14, 17, 19):

---

[55]Here, notably, the prophetic testimony of David in Ps 16 (Acts 2:25–31).
[56]See the discussion of this passage in Carroll, "Uses of Scripture," 518–20.
[57]Echoing Pss 69:25; 109:8. See Carroll, "Uses of Scripture," 517–18.

> You denied the holy and just one . . . the author of life you killed. . . . And now, brothers, I know that you acted in ignorance, likewise also your rulers. . . . Repent, therefore, and turn back, so that your sins may be wiped away.

Peter's discourses in Acts 2, 3, and 5 also associate the appeal for repentance with his audience's culpability for the death of Jesus, although in these instances the link is somewhat less direct (2:36–38; 5:30–31). The latter passage suggests that while the Jewish leaders' involvement in the death of Jesus necessitates repentance on their part, it is the exaltation of Jesus that enables repentance and therefore the experience of forgiveness (v. 31). In similar fashion, 3:26 binds together the resurrection of Jesus, the apostles' mission, and the turn away from evil. Clearly, in the speeches of Acts the death *and* the resurrection of Jesus, in tandem, have crucial and distinct roles in the redemptive work of God.

A Paradigmatic Death

In the broad sweep of Luke's narrative, Jesus is not the only person to face the ordeal of arrest, interrogation, and even execution. In fact, the significant parallels between the situation of Jesus and that of his followers indicate that his approach to death serves as the paradigm by which their own experience is to be guided and given meaning.

During his ministry, Jesus on several occasions prepared the disciples for future adversity. Like him, they would be hauled before the religious authorities but would summon strength, aided by the Holy Spirit, to speak appropriately (12:4–12). Like him (and in his name), they would be handed over to prison and required to defend themselves before kings and governors, yet with the assurance of divine support and protection (21:12–19). What Jesus prophesies, Acts narrates. Arrest, hostile interrogation, and bold defense—again and again this cycle is enacted. Into it step Peter and John (Acts 4), the apostles as a group (ch. 5), Stephen (6:8–8:1), James the brother of John and then Peter again (ch. 12), and of course Paul (16:19–40; chs. 21–28).

Only Stephen and James actually complete the pattern by going to death as Jesus had before them, and only Stephen's martyrdom is narrated in any detail. Clearly, though, Luke leaves Paul on the brink of martyrdom,[58] and so to the Jesus-Stephen parallels may also be added

---

[58]The narrative closes on a positive note, with Paul under house arrest in Rome but preaching openly and unhindered to all who come to him. Nevertheless, the episode in which Paul delivers a poignant farewell speech to the Ephesian church's elders (20:17–38) betrays the author's knowledge of Paul's death (see v. 25, echoed in the reaction of Paul's audience, v. 38). The probability that Luke knows of Paul's execution at Rome intensifies the irony of the

Jesus-Paul parallels.[59] In this discussion, however, we concentrate on the person of Stephen.

We noted earlier that in Luke's passion the Jewish public is consistently sympathetic to Jesus, the single exception being the momentous scene before Pilate. It is the Jewish leaders, in particular those connected with the temple institution, who are the principal enemies of Jesus. Much the same pattern reappears in Acts. Peter, John, and the rest of the apostles initially have remarkable rapport with the people of Jerusalem and Judea, who even partially shield the apostles from the wrath of the authorities (2:41, 47; 4:4, 21; 5:13, 26).

The tide turns, however, with Stephen. Now the people (λαός) are drawn into the fray as enemies of "the Way." The triumvirate of "people, elders, and scribes" that hauls Stephen before the Sanhedrin (6:12) resembles the body that opposed Jesus (cf. Luke 22:52, 66; 23:13).[60] The aftermath of Stephen's incendiary speech of "self-defense" impresses readers as a general mob action (7:54–8:1), and by the time Paul is stirring up opposition with his preaching, the narrator can identify his adversaries simply as "the Jews" (9:23). At the close of the Jerusalem mission in Acts, therefore, the people's initial acceptance of the apostles and their message has given way to hostile rejection.[61]

It is noteworthy that at two points where one expects correspondence between the accounts of Stephen and Jesus, the parallel breaks down. First, Stephen's accusers charge him with blasphemy (against Moses and God, 6:11), a charge that forms the basis for the subsequent interrogation in the Sanhedrin (vv. 13–14). Although Pharisees and scribes early in the story label a pronouncement of Jesus blasphemous (Luke 5:21), the language of blasphemy is missing from the passion account (contrast Mark 14:64; Matt 26:65). Second, Stephen's detractors accuse him of speaking against the temple ("this holy place," 6:13), indeed, of asserting that Jesus of Nazareth would destroy "this place" (v. 14). The narrator ascribes this testimony to "false witnesses." All of this is

---

narrative's climactic verdict on Paul's guilt. Herod Agrippa II and the governor Festus agree: "This man is doing nothing deserving of death or imprisonment" (26:31). Then Agrippa adds, "This man could have been released had he not appealed to Caesar" (v. 32). See further Carroll, "Luke's Apology," 112–13.

[59] See Robert F. O'Toole, *The Unity of Luke's Theology: An Analysis of Luke–Acts* (GNS 9; Wilmington, Del.: Michael Glazier, 1984) 67–71; David P. Moessner, "'The Christ Must Suffer': New Light on the Jesus, Stephen, Paul Parallels in Luke–Acts," *NovT* 28 (1986) 220–56.

[60] Although in the account of Stephen's martyrdom the participation by elite priests is muted, the high priest does, naturally, put in an appearance (7:1).

[61] See the analysis by Tyson, *Death of Jesus in Luke–Acts*, 29–42. It would be a mistake, however, to conclude that at this stage the door has been shut on the Jewish people. The ensuing narrative continues the pattern of a divided Jewish response to the proclamation of Paul and his coreligionists.

reminiscent of the Markan passion narrative (Mark 14:55–59), but Luke includes neither a temple charge nor false witnesses in the Sanhedrin's examination of Jesus (Luke 22:66–71). Especially since these two features disrupt a pattern of symmetry between the passion of Jesus and that of Stephen, one suspects that the move to deflect these serious charges from Jesus to Stephen is no accident. The result is a clearer picture of an innocent Jesus, wrongfully accused and condemned, not clouded by somewhat ambiguous details.[62]

Stephen's death, however, echoes that of Jesus in other respects. Like Jesus, Stephen speaks boldly before the council (though at much greater length!), and his testimony provides the basis for condemnation. Like Jesus (Luke 22:69), Stephen (Acts 7:56) speaks of the Son of humanity at the right hand of God, although in the case of Stephen the narrator describes an actual vision, and in that vision the Son of humanity (identified as Jesus) stands rather than sits. Like Jesus (Luke 23:46), Stephen (Acts 7:59) dies in prayer, yielding his spirit (though now to Jesus rather than the "Father"). And like Jesus (Luke 23:34), Stephen (Acts 7:60) prays for the forgiveness of those who put him to death: "Lord, do not hold this sin against them." With the significant difference that the martyrdom of Stephen reflects the postcrucifixion exaltation of Jesus, the death of Stephen conforms closely to the pattern set by Jesus.

While these two figures no doubt play unique, pivotal roles in the redemptive history Luke narrates, the reader is nonetheless able to draw from their stories a lesson on the manner in which one ought to deal with persecution.[63] The examples of Jesus and Stephen cultivate in Luke's readers a commitment to bold witness in the face of opposition, but also to a posture of nonretaliation that goes so far as to seek the forgiveness of one's enemy. As the story goes on, therefore, the manner of Jesus' dying—itself but an illustration of the moral vision he advocated (cf. Luke 6:27–36)—continues to form and reform the life of the Christian disciple.

---

[62]In Luke's account, Jesus does speak against the temple (21:5–6; cf. 19:41–44), but his prophecy of its destruction does not figure in the proceedings issuing in his death. There is accordingly no need to introduce the theme of false testimony. (Notice that unlike Mark, Matt 26:59–61 distinguishes between the ineffectual false testimony and the more successful accusation regarding the temple.) Luke casts the spotlight in this scene not on the status of the temple but on Jesus' own bold self-attestation (Luke 22:71).

[63]The potential of these two approaches to death as models for emulation by Christians who later face persecution is enhanced because the experiences of both martyrs realize concretely the warnings/promises Jesus has given in Luke 12:4–12 and 21:12–19.

# FIVE

"When I am lifted up from the earth . . . ":
THE DEATH OF JESUS IN THE GOSPEL ACCORDING TO JOHN

The Fourth Gospel affords a glimpse of Jesus' passion that is nothing short of breathtaking. The cross, no longer in John a moment of defeat and disgrace, becomes instead Jesus' hour of victory. When arrested by a large company of soldiers, Jesus does not even flinch, and he secures the release of his disciples, while those who would seize him are paralyzed by fear. The accused prisoner becomes the judge, and he summons Pilate, the Jewish nation, indeed the whole world, to appear before the bar of truth. In the Johannine passion narrative Jesus returns in triumph to the Father, who sent him as the embodiment of truth and life into the world. With the achievement of his death, Jesus completes his mission on earth. He has confronted the world created by God with the claim of divine truth, and to those who have responded with genuine belief, he has offered eternal life. In the events surrounding Jesus' death—which, to be sure, still deprive him of honor in the public eye—the author celebrates what only faith can see, the lifting up in glory of the Son of God.

It is a fitting climax to a remarkable Gospel.[1] Some scholars, however, have wondered. Ernst Käsemann, for example, contends that

> in John the glory of Jesus determines his whole presentation so thoroughly from the very outset that the incorporation and position of the passion narrative of necessity becomes problematical. Apart from a few remarks that point ahead to it, the passion comes into view in John only at the very end. One is tempted to regard it as being a mere postscript which had to be included because John could not ignore this tradition nor yet could he fit it organically into his work.[2]

---

[1] See Robert Kysar, *John, the Maverick Gospel* (Atlanta: John Knox, 1976).
[2] Ernst Käsemann, *The Testament of Jesus* (Philadelphia: Fortress, 1968) 7.

John's solution, Käsemann thinks, was "to press the features of Christ's victory upon the passion story."[3] This last observation is exactly right, but the suggestion that the passion account somehow fits only awkwardly in the narrative misses the mark. The first section of this chapter will consider the way in which the death of Jesus in John brings to climax the collision between "word" and "world" that has occurred throughout Jesus' ministry (chs. 1–12). We will then discuss important Johannine literary devices (symbol, misunderstanding, irony) that leave their stamp upon the passion narrative. After a close reading of the encounter between Jesus and Pilate (18:28–19:16), the chapter concludes with a character sketch of Jesus and the disciples in John's passion drama.

"His own people did not receive him":
THE PASSION AND JESUS' CONFLICT WITH THE "WORLD"

One of the striking features of the Johannine passion account is the absence of any substantive trial of Jesus before the religious leaders. To be sure, Annas, father-in-law of the high priest then in office (Caiaphas) and himself a former high priest, conducts a brief interrogation (18:13, 19–24) probing Jesus' teaching and disciples.[4] He then sends the prisoner to Caiaphas, but as far as the reader can tell, nothing happens at the house of the high priest.[5] The Sanhedrin does not convene to examine Jesus.

---

[3]Käsemann, *Testament of Jesus*, 7.

[4]On the historical and literary problems surrounding Annas's role in the narrative, see Raymond E. Brown, *The Gospel according to John* (2 vols.; AB 29–29A; Garden City, N.Y.: Doubleday, 1966–70) 2.828–36; and idem, *Death of the Messiah*, 1.404–11. Discarding rearrangement theories or hypotheses of interpolations into John's source (see, e.g., Rudolf Bultmann, *The Gospel of John: A Commentary* [Philadelphia: Westminster, 1971] 641–45) as counsels in desperation, we ought to consider readers' reactions to the text in its present form. As John's readers overhear the "high priest's" conversation with Jesus, they surely assume initially that it is Caiaphas (previously identified as high priest in 11:49, 51; 18:13) who questions Jesus. The narrator's report that after the inquiry *Annas* dispatched Jesus to Caiaphas the high priest will force readers to revise their initial assumption. Perhaps one effect of this role confusion is to heighten the impression that Jesus is rejected by the elite rulers of the Jewish people. Of course, we cannot reconstruct with any precision this portion of the extratextual repertoire of John's first readers (see Darr, *On Character Building*, 20–23): did they know that Annas, so many of whose sons assumed the office of high priest, was addressed with the honorific title ἀρχιερεύς, *archiereus*, long after he had been deposed?

[5]Brown (*Death of the Messiah*, 1.425 n. 34) suggests that Jesus' appearance

No Jewish trial is necessary in John's passion narrative because it has already occurred. Jesus' public ministry in this Gospel takes the form of one sustained public trial of Jesus by the Jewish authorities.[6] They reach their verdict concerning Jesus in the aftermath of the raising of Lazarus (11:47–53)—the accused is, of course, absent from the deliberations—and therefore the only reason for a Jewish interrogation of Jesus after his arrest is to supply the ammunition for his execution by the Roman governor.[7]

John's reader learns as early as the prologue that Jesus' ministry will provoke conflict and rejection by "his own people" (1:10–11). He steps into the world as the one who makes God known, but the world does not know him (that is, refuses to discern in him the revealer of God). Some, though, will receive life by coming to believe in him (vv. 4, 12–13). Jesus' words and works therefore divide humanity into two camps: those who accept divine disclosure and those who remain in darkness (e.g., 3:16–21).[8]

Conflict between Jesus and his people begins to surface in ch. 3, with the introduction of Nicodemus.[9] Impressed by Jesus' signs (as were others who began to believe on the basis of the signs they had witnessed, 2:23–25; cf. 3:2), this "teacher of Israel" nevertheless comes to Jesus "by night," clearly hinting that he is not yet fully receptive to the truth Jesus has to impart.[10] Of course, the conversation between these two "teach-

---

before Caiaphas serves to show that the same figure who wanted Jesus put to death (11:49–52) handed him over to Pilate. The Johannine narrator does report the second and third of Peter's denials to fill the narrative space between the arrival and departure of Jesus at Caiaphas's house (18:25–27).

[6]Often identified simply as "the Jews." For the view that Jesus' public ministry constitutes his Jewish trial in John, see A. E. Harvey, *Jesus on Trial: A Study in the Fourth Gospel* (London: S.P.C.K., 1976); Frank J. Matera, "Jesus before Annas: John 18,13–14.19–24," *ETL* 66 (1990) 53–54. Raymond E. Brown ("Incidents That Are Units in the Synoptic Gospels but Dispersed in John," *CBQ* 23 [1961] 143–60) identifies materials that resemble the Jewish proceedings in the Synoptic Gospels but that John locates earlier in the narrative (148–52).

[7]Presumably this is the source of Pilate's information about the royal pretensions of Jesus (18:33: "Are you the King of the Jews?"). The narrator does not indicate what prompted Pilate to ask such a question; it is a gap the reader must fill on the basis of other elements of the story. Another gap relates to the figure of Pilate, who is never identified as the prefect or governor of Judea. Evidently the extratextual repertoire of John's readers included some such information about Pilate.

[8]On this point see Josef Blank, *Krisis: Untersuchungen zur johanneischen Christologie und Eschatologie* (Freiburg: Lambertus, 1964).

[9]Even the belief of many in Jerusalem, built on the signs Jesus has performed, foreshadows trouble yet to come, for the narrator discloses Jesus' distrust of faith grounded in signs (2:24–25).

[10]Perhaps also anticipating the "secret disciple" motif associated with Joseph of Arimathea, who with Nicodemus will provide Jesus with a burial in honor (19:38–39). Is Nicodemus on his way to becoming another such "secret

ers" confirms that expectation of the reader. Nicodemus's persistent inability to understand Jesus leaves Jesus exasperated—and elevates the reader to a privileged position of insight from which to view the debates that follow.[11]

After a brief Samaritan interlude (ch. 4), sharp and bitter conflict erupts with Jesus' Sabbath healing of a lame man in ch. 5. From this point on, the disputes in which Jesus is embroiled are deadly, and without fail these disputes are sharply focused on christological claims. The real issue in John 5 concerns Jesus' divine sonship: by naming God his "Father," Jesus has, in the view of his Jewish opponents, sought to "make himself equal to God" (5:18). So for the first time "the Jews" seek to kill Jesus (v. 18). Speaking in his own "defense," Jesus proceeds to claim that God has given to him the prerogatives of judgment and resurrection life. Whether in bestowing eternal life or in pronouncing judgment, Jesus simply enacts the word and work of his Father (5:19-47).

As Jesus' ministry unfolds in chs. 6-12, conflict escalates but remains fixed on Jesus' identity and status. Jesus' assertions grow bolder and bolder and understandably provoke increasingly intense opposition. A feeding miracle leads the crowds to esteem him as the eschatological prophet (6:14), but he withdraws when he realizes that they want to make him king (v. 15).[12] By the next day Jesus' claim to be the bread from heaven that gives life to the world—moreover, that his own flesh must be eaten if one would live—elicits from "the Jews" strenuous objections and even prompts most of his disciples to depart (vv. 25-66). Only the Twelve remain with Jesus, and one of them, in Jesus' own words, is "a devil" (vv. 67-71). The narrator for the first time points forward to Judas's treason.

In John 7 Jesus at first refuses to accompany his brothers to Jerusalem for the feast of Tabernacles (7:1-9), but then later secretly goes to the festival (v. 10). This move is fraught with danger, the reader knows, for at Jerusalem many have previously attempted to kill Jesus, a fact that Jesus recalls when he somewhat surprisingly[13] launches into a public

---

disciple" who conceals his belief "out of fear of the Jews"? That would be more than a little ironic, since the narrator marks Nicodemus in 7:50 as "one of them," that is, the Pharisees. In that episode they upbraid servants/officers (ὑπηρέται, *hypēretai*) who have failed to arrest Jesus, aiming at them the sarcastic barb "Not one of the rulers or of the Pharisees has believed in him, right?" (v. 48). Maybe, maybe not!

[11] See the excellent treatment in R. Alan Culpepper, *Anatomy of the Fourth Gospel* (FF; Philadelphia: Fortress, 1983) 134-36.

[12] Ironically, in the passion account Jesus' Jewish antagonists accuse him of making himself king (19:12).

[13] Jesus is full of surprises in ch. 7. He tells his brothers that he will not attend the festival (v. 8), then does attend. He indicates that he will not go to Jerusalem because it is not yet "my time [καιρός, *kairos*]," and when he does

speech in the temple (v. 14): "Didn't Moses give you the law? Yet not one of you keeps the law. Why are you seeking to kill me?" (v. 19). The reader can only laugh when Jesus' audience ascribes his belief that his life is in danger to demonic influence (v. 20). The reader knows better—and so do some of the people of Jerusalem (v. 25).

The narrator depicts, in fact, a city sharply divided in its perceptions of Jesus (see vv. 12, 25, 31, 40–43; cf. 10:19–21). Now for the first time, Jesus' detractors[14] move to arrest him, but they are unable to do so "because his hour had not yet come" (7:30, 32, 44; 8:20). The narrative juxtaposes a frustrated plot to arrest Jesus and popular support for Jesus in a way that is reminiscent of Luke,[15] but the picture is actually quite different here. The division in John is not between leaders and people; rather, it seems to reach deep into the Jewish public as well. Further (and this has much greater significance), the Johannine narrator attributes the failure of Jesus' opponents to arrest him not to his popular support but to the timing of his "hour" (and, in v. 46, to the persuasive power of Jesus' speech). Jesus—and Jesus alone—dictates the action that will bring him to the cross.

Confusion about Jesus' place of origin feeds the fires of conflict (7:26–29, 40–43, 52) over Jesus' status.[16] The fact that Jesus comes from Galilee gives the Pharisees sufficient reason to dismiss the claim that he is Messiah or prophet and even to jettison appropriate legal procedure. Nicodemus asks, "Does our law judge the man unless it first listens to him and so comes to know what he is doing?" (7:50–51). On one level, this investigation is actually conducted through the series of exchanges in chs. 5–12 and brought to completion by Annas in 18:19–24. And yet the one being judged—who, according to Nicodemus, ought to receive a fair hearing—is conspicuously absent from the pivotal

---

venture to Jerusalem, he does so in secret (v. 10). But before long he is speaking fearlessly in the temple (v. 14). How will John's reader respond to such an unpredictable Jesus? Note that the narrator characterizes the seemingly reasonable challenge by Jesus' brothers as the sentiments of unbelief. ("No one seeking to be out in the open acts in secret. If you do these [works], show yourself to the world.") Jesus does courageously act ἐν παρρησίᾳ (en parrēsia, "in the open") and does through his works show himself to the world. But he will do so on his own terms. The narrative highlights the sovereign freedom of Jesus, following the path he has determined.

[14] Specifically the chief priests and Pharisees, according to 7:32.

[15] See ch. 4 above.

[16] The motif of Jesus' origin is laced with irony. Some in Jerusalem disqualify Jesus as Christ because they know his place of origin (7:26–27), yet Jesus tells Pharisees that they are ignorant of both his origin and his destination (8:14), as they themselves later confirm (see 9:29–30). John's reader, on the other hand, has been given a privileged perspective on Jesus' origin. When Jesus responds to the confusion about his place of origin, speaking of the one from whom he comes, who sent him (7:29), the reader understands (1:1–18).

judgment scene, when the Sanhedrin condemns him to death (11:47–53). In the end, they will judge him without listening to him. So the narrative displays the contempt the Jewish authorities have for their own law.[17]

The disputes of ch. 7 spill over into ch. 8 and by the end of the passage spiral dangerously out of control. Even Jews who had believed in him (8:31) take up stones to put him to death for his blasphemous claim to be not just greater than Abraham but the divine "I am" who existed before Abraham, who can offer eternal life to those who keep his word (8:48–59). Jesus is emphatic that he is not indulging in self-promotion or self-glorification. No, it is the Father who honors him—the God whom they claim to know and worship but in fact do not know at all (vv. 54–55). Their violent rejection of Jesus clearly shows that they are children not of God but of the devil (vv. 39–47).

With Jesus' Sabbath healing of a blind man, the level of hostility drops somewhat, yet the reader soon discovers that the conflict has widened to include any and all who acknowledge Jesus to be the Messiah (9:22).[18] The outcome of this episode is that unlike a blind man who receives both physical and spiritual sight, the Pharisees remain obstinately closed to the truth embodied by Jesus (9:39–41). In John 10 Jesus presents himself as the one authentic shepherd who knows and in turn is known by his sheep. Through him they are assured protection, through him they gain access to life. It is his Father who has given him this flock, and Jesus dares to assert, "I and the Father are one" (10:30). This line[19] precipitates a second attempt to stone Jesus to death (vv. 31, 33) and then yet another foiled arrest attempt (v. 39).

Both the prelude to the raising of Lazarus and its aftermath give hope that faith will spread (see 10:41–42; 11:45; 12:11). Even "Greeks" are

---

[17]The dramatic irony of the passage is therefore similar to that involving another Pharisee, Gamaliel, in Acts 5. The Johannine narrator exposes as superficial, self-serving, and hypocritical the religious authorities' respect for their own law (see also 18:28, 31; 19:7, 31). Because of their scruples about ritual purity, they refuse to enter the praetorium and later press for action to accelerate the death of Jesus before the Sabbath, yet they exhibit little interest in justice and, in the end, put Jesus to death (Pilate hands Jesus over "to them" for crucifixion, 19:16), even though they had previously disavowed the right to do so (18:31).

[18]Notice that the narrator delays the information that Jesus healed the blind man on the Sabbath until 9:14, where it can provide the necessary transition to the ensuing controversy. For John's reader, this literary technique also has the effect of subordinating the Sabbath issue to the question of the meaning of the sign (disclosing Jesus as the "light of the world"). The narrator's observation in 5:18 had a similar effect.

[19]Qualified in Jesus' ensuing defense of his claim: "the Father is in me, and I in the Father" (v. 38). The evidence of this relationship is that Jesus performs the work of the Father.

making an approach to Jesus (12:20–23). But there are also ominous signs. The disciples try without success to dissuade Jesus from going to Bethany by appealing to the climate of hostility toward Jesus in Judea (11:8). Thomas's words of resignation are haunting: "Let us also go to die with him" (v. 16). Although the raising of Lazarus prompts many to believe, it also sends others to the Pharisees (v. 46), a move that leads directly to the decision to have him killed (v. 53). And mortal threat extends also—the irony here is deep—to Lazarus (12:10–11). By the time Jesus has finished speaking in Jerusalem, the crowd's shouts of acclamation have hardened into rejection and unbelief. It is especially noteworthy that in this last round of conflict, dispute centers on his statement "When I am lifted up from the earth, I will draw all to myself" (12:32). It is unthinkable to Jesus' listeners that the Christ should not live forever (v. 34).[20] Their conception of the Christ leaves no room for the event that stands squarely at the center of Jesus' mission. And so the narrator gives the last word to unbelieving rejection (12:37), tempered only by the timid, secret faith of some of the Jewish leaders (vv. 42–43). Therefore, if the approach of interested Greeks signals that Jesus' "hour" has arrived, this can only mean that his death is imminent.

Conflict between Jesus and "the Jews" is the order of the day in chs. 5–12. At issue in this conflict is the belief or unbelief of those who encounter Jesus. And the stakes for them are high indeed: eternal life comes to those who believe and whose belief abides, but there is only self-judgment for those who remain closed to the truth. John's reader meets this pattern over and over again. Jesus' bold declarations about his unique relation to God provoke his hearers. They then seek to kill him or to arrest him, but without success because "his hour has not yet come" (5:18; 7:1, 6, 8, 30, 32; 8:20, 59; 10:34).[21]

Conflict between Jesus and his own people permeates this story, and the death of Jesus is its natural and inevitable culmination. The cast of characters who oppose him and the accusations they lodge against him remain remarkably consistent throughout the narrative. "The Jews," and that means particularly the Jewish authorities, reject Jesus because—they allege—he elevated himself to divine status, because "he made himself Son of God" (19:7). The last charge brought to Pilate by the

---

[20]The reader comes upon a curious gap here. Jesus has said, "When I am lifted up," but his audience counters with the query "How can you say that the Son of humanity [ὁ υἱὸς τοῦ ἀνθρώπου, ho huios tou anthrōpou] must be lifted up? Who is this Son of humanity?" (12:34). Presumably the crowd draws the language of "Son of humanity" from 8:28 (cf. also 3:14). The irony of this statement is not lost on John's reader, who knows that Jesus will, despite being lifted up in crucifixion, "abide forever."

[21]See further Marinus de Jonge, *Jesus: Stranger from Heaven and Son of God* (SBLSBS 11; Missoula, Mont.: Scholars, 1977) 55; Culpepper, *Anatomy,* 89–98.

Jews is an apt summary of the entire Jewish "trial" of Jesus. Far from being a "mere postscript" that "comes into view . . . only at the very end,"[22] therefore, the passion in John encompasses nearly the whole of the Gospel.

LITERARY ARTISTRY IN THE
JOHANNINE PASSION NARRATIVE

We have already had occasion to note elements of John's literary art, especially his skillful use of irony. Before undertaking an analysis of the pivotal encounter between Jesus and Pilate, it will be useful to identify briefly several of the literary techniques employed in the narrative. We focus here on strategies of implicit or indirect communication.[23]

Symbol

The Fourth Gospel's use of symbols is rich and evocative. Light, day, sight, and truth line up as symbols of the divine disclosure through Jesus. They compete with darkness, night, blindness, and falsehood, all of which symbolize a world closed to divine revelation. Thus Nicodemus's choice of night for his visit to Jesus (ch. 3) is not innocent, and Judas's choice of treason has consequences clearly pictured for the reader with the memorable line "So after receiving the piece of bread, that one [Judas] went out at once, and it was night" (13:30).

But Jesus is not only the revealer; he is also the source of life for all who respond in belief to his words and works. He communicates this point directly in persuasive argument (e.g., 3:16–21; 5:19–29). And he deploys an array of symbols expressive of his role as the giver of life. He is an unfailing source of water (4:13–14)[24] and of bread (6:35, 48–51); he is a vine to which branches (disciples) must remain attached if they are to live at all, much less bear fruit (15:1–11). He is a true shepherd who, unlike robbers (λῃσταί, *lēstai*) and even hired workers, cares for his flock (10:7–18), but he is also the gate through which his sheep must pass if they are to find pasture—that is, if they are to live (10:7–10). All these symbols picture Jesus as the source of life for all who turn to him.

John's use of symbolism extends to the passion narrative. As we have seen, Judas's act of betrayal amounts to an embracing of darkness. A cluster of passages play with the imagery of the paschal lamb. Pilate

---

[22]Käsemann, *Testament of Jesus*, 7.
[23]The following discussion of implicit communication draws from Culpepper, *Anatomy*, 151–202. On Johannine irony, see also Paul D. Duke, *Irony in the Fourth Gospel* (Atlanta: John Knox, 1985).
[24]John 7:37–39 links to the Spirit the water Jesus provides.

hands Jesus over to death at the very moment that the slaughter of the Passover lambs commences (19:14–16), recalling the Baptizer's witness to Jesus as the "Lamb of God who takes away the world's sin" (1:29).[25] Two additional details from the crucifixion scene reinforce this paschal-lamb symbolism. First, soldiers use hyssop to lift vinegar to Jesus' lips (19:29). The gesture may be implausible,[26] but it recalls the first Passover, when hyssop was used to sprinkle the slain lamb's blood on the doorposts of Hebrew homes (Exod 12:22). Second, the Johannine narrator reports that Jesus' unexpectedly early death averted the breaking of his legs, thus fulfilling the scriptural promise "Not one of his bones will be broken" (19:36, echoing Exod 12:10 LXX, 12:46; Num 9:12). Jesus, the paschal lamb, dies without a bone being broken.[27]

Most evocative of all in the passion account is the flow—witnessed by the beloved disciple—of blood and water from the side of Jesus after a soldier's spear thrust (19:34–35). It is clear that the event has deep symbolic significance, but the narrator does not explain what its meaning is.[28] Surely, though, John's reader will recall those earlier passages in which Jesus claimed to be the source of an undying spring of water (4:13–14; 7:37–39), water symbolic (according to the narrator) of the Spirit. In all three texts (4:13–14; 7:37–39; 19:28–35), "thirst" and "water" are linked, and in chs. 7 and 19 "Spirit" also appears. Whatever other layers of meaning the imagery may suggest, it certainly scores the point that the death of Jesus imparts life to all who receive the beloved disciple's witness, and the Spirit cannot be far behind (20:22; cf. 16:7).

Misunderstanding

John repeatedly and deftly employs a pattern of misunderstanding in which Jesus makes a statement featuring ambiguity, double meaning, or metaphor and is then misunderstood by his auditor, leading either

---

[25] See Brown, *John* 2.882–83; Senior, *Passion of Jesus in John*, 96–97. John's use of the paschal-lamb symbol also supplies a likely explanation for this Gospel's dating of the crucifixion on the day of preparation for the Passover. For analysis of the problem of chronology, see Brown, *Death of the Messiah*, 2.1350–78. Despite the theological capital the imagery affords John, Brown thinks the Johannine dating of the crucifixion on 14 Nisan is historical.

[26] See Brown, *Death of the Messiah*, 2.1074–77.

[27] The echo of Ps 34:20 suggests that Jesus also dies as the Righteous One delivered by God. See Brown, *Death of the Messiah*, 2.1185–86.

[28] For discussion of the meaning of this symbolism, see Brown, *Death of the Messiah*, 2.1178–82; Senior, *Passion of Jesus in John*, 121–29; Culpepper, *Anatomy*, 195; Rudolf Schnackenburg, *The Gospel according to St. John* (ET; 3 vols; vol. 1, New York: Herder & Herder, 1968; reprint, New York: Crossroad, 1980; vols. 2 and 3, New York: Crossroad, 1980–82) 3.289–94.

Jesus or the narrator to comment on the theme at greater depth.[29] Of particular interest are several passages in which misunderstanding turns on an image pointing to Jesus' death. When Jesus tells his Jewish listeners that he is about to go to a place where they cannot come, they are unable to fathom his meaning (7:33–36; 8:21–22). The disciples, too, struggle to understand this imagery (13:36–38; 14:4–7),[30] although Peter comes close, at least grasping that Jesus is speaking about his coming death (13:36–38). As we have seen earlier, the crowd also misunderstands Jesus' declaration that he must be "lifted up from the earth" (12:32–34)—or, rather, on this occasion they understand that Jesus is speaking about dying yet draw the wrong conclusion from it. They cannot make room for such an event within the career of the Messiah.

While this formal pattern for making further interpretive commentary—misunderstanding—does not appear in the passion account, the conversations between Pilate and Jesus come close. Like Nicodemus in ch. 3, Pilate, when confronted with truth and authentic kingship in the person of Jesus, really does not have a clue.

Irony

Irony pervades John's narrative. We have already pointed to several instances in the first section of this chapter. Irony is built upon a contrast between appearance and reality or between two levels of meaning. While the victim of irony (in John's story, one of the characters who interact with Jesus) remains oblivious to the reality or deeper meaning, the (implied) reader[31] understands in other words, the author communicates indirectly, over the heads of the undiscerning characters, to the (implied) reader.

The third denial by Peter contains a note of irony. Only the reader—who remembers the arrest scene, in which Peter struck the ear of the high priest's slave Malchus—can appreciate the humor in Peter's refusal to admit to a relative of Malchus that he was in the garden with Jesus (18:26–27). For readers who share the point of view of the author, the trial before Pilate and the crucifixion scene constitute the enthronement

---

[29] This extension of the conversation is primarily addressed to the reader. Culpepper (*Anatomy*, 161–62) provides a convenient table listing eighteen misunderstandings in the Fourth Gospel.

[30] Cf. 16:16–19, where the disciples are confused by Jesus' remark that "in a little while" they will not see him. Eventually Jesus says clearly that he is departing the world to return to the Father (16:28). On the importance of this motif in John's gospel, see Nicholson, *Death as Departure*.

[31] That is, a reader equipped to make the sorts of interpretive moves that optimize the reading potential of the narrative.

of a king.[32] He stands accused of royal pretensions, and the soldiers have adorned him in the garb of royalty and mockingly acclaimed him "King of the Jews" (19:1–3). Pilate later presents Jesus to the Jews with the words "Behold, your king!" (19:14), and he himself writes the title to be placed above Jesus' head on the cross, "Jesus of Nazareth, the King of the Jews." John's readers are quite sure that the soldiers do not intend to honor Jesus as king, and they are less convinced of the sincerity of the belief expressed in Pilate's words than they are of the truth of that belief. Nevertheless, the reader hears loud and clear the message hidden in the words and gestures of Jesus' adversaries: he is king.[33]

Probably the most striking instance of Johannine irony occurs in the Sanhedrin session, in which the high priest Caiaphas plays the prophet, urging the death of Jesus on behalf of (ὑπέρ, hyper) the people, to save the nation from destruction. The deeper truth in this advice, which is naturally concealed from the speaker Caiaphas, is no doubt clear to the reader even without the narrator's comment (vv. 51–52). Jesus' death will indeed "save" the nation, though not in the manner envisaged by the high priest, and benefit will accrue not to the nation alone but to all the dispersed children of God. Jesus' mortal enemy here unwittingly articulates for the benefit of believers the true meaning of the death of Jesus.

THE TRIAL OF JESUS BEFORE PILATE

The trial before Pilate dominates the Johannine passion narrative and merits detailed analysis. Ostensibly, the Roman governor sits in judgment upon Jesus. In truth, though, John's reader witnesses a stunning role reversal in which Jesus becomes the judge—and not of Pilate alone. By the end of this scene, "the Jews" have not only rejected Jesus but also denied their own heritage.[34]

The structure of the episode reflects effective dramatic staging.[35] Scenes inside the praetorium, featuring Jesus and Pilate, alternate with

---

[32]See Josef Blank, "Die Verhandlung vor Pilatus Joh 18,28–19,16 im Lichte johanneischer Theologie," *BZ* 3 (1958–59) 60–81.

[33]A king of a peculiar pedigree, to be sure, but a king nonetheless. Jesus' royal reign is constituted by his commitment to speak the truth. Wayne A. Meeks (*The Prophet-King: Moses Traditions and the Johannine Christology* [NovTSup 14; Leiden: E. J. Brill, 1967] 67) argues that John radically redefines Jesus' kingship in terms of his prophetic role.

[34]On this role reversal, see the especially perceptive analysis by Blank, "Verhandlung," 60–62; cf. J. Terence Forestell, *The Word of the Cross: Salvation as Revelation in the Fourth Gospel* (AnBib 57; Rome: Biblical Institute, 1974) 85–86.

[35]See, e.g., Blank, "Verhandlung," 61; Brown, *John*, 2:857–59; Bart D. Ehrman, "Jesus' Trial before Pilate: John 18:28–19:16," *BTB* 13 (1983) 124–31; Senior, *Passion of Jesus in John*, 68–71.

scenes outside, featuring Pilate and "the Jews" (meaning, in this connection, principally the Jewish leaders).[36] This two-stage drama is set
up by the Jewish leaders' refusal to enter the praetorium so that they
may remain ritually pure for observance of the Passover (18:28). Pilate
must therefore move back and forth between Jesus and his accusers,
now interrogating Jesus—or, rather, undergoing interrogation himself—
about matters of kingship and truth, now defending Jesus against his
detractors and attempting to release him.[37]

Scene 1: Pilate and the Jews (18:28–32)

Early in the morning of 14 Nisan "they" (identified a few verses later
as "the Jews") lead Jesus to Pilate. Since they desire to observe the
Passover, they refuse to defile themselves by entering the praetorium,
and Pilate must therefore come out to them. This first exchange between Pilate and the Jewish leaders is strained. They refuse to give a
direct answer to Pilate's request for a statement of the charges against
Jesus: "If this man were not an evildoer, we would not have handed him
over to you" (v. 30). Eventually in the course of the trial, the accusations
will come out into the open ("he made himself Son of God," 19:7;
"everyone who makes himself king opposes Caesar," 19:12), but in this
first scene it is the Jewish opponents of Jesus who are being evaluated.

Pilate would turn the matter back to Jesus' accusers: "You take him
and judge him in accordance with your law." They protest, "We are not
permitted to kill anyone" (v. 30). In the light of the earlier attempts to
put Jesus to death by stoning (8:59; 10:31; cf. 5:18), this protest strikes
the reader as disingenuous. Moreover, John's reader may recall Nicodemus's statement that "the law does not judge the man unless it first
listens to him and so comes to know what he is doing" (7:51). Judging
Jesus in accordance with their law is precisely what the Jews cannot and
will not do.[38] Furthermore, when they claim that they are not permitted

---

[36]The labels John uses for Jesus' Jewish opponents in the passion narrative
are fluid. See our discussion, ch. 10 below. On John's portrayal of "the Jews" as
enemies of Jesus, see further Culpepper, *Anatomy*, 125–32; Senior, *Passion of
Jesus in John*, 155–57; Reginald H. Fuller, "The 'Jews' in the Fourth Gospel,"
Dialog 16 (1977) 31–37; D. Moody Smith, "Judaism and the Gospel of John," in
Jews and Christians, ed. James H. Charlesworth (New York: Crossroad, 1990)
76–99; and U. C. von Walde, "The Johannine Jews: A Critical Survey," *NTS* 28
(1982) 33–60.

[37]Culpepper (*Anatomy*, 142–43) exploits this dramatic staging in his
sketch of John's characterization of Pilate, who embodies "the futility of
attempted compromise."

[38]We focus here on the function of this statement within the narrative. For
discussion of the problem of historicity, see Brown, *Death of the Messiah*,
1.363–72.

to kill him, a deeper truth lies beneath the surface.[39] They cannot kill him because they do not control the events of Jesus' passion, a point the narrator scores in the next verse: "so that the word of Jesus, which he said signifying by what death he was about to die, would be fulfilled." Jesus, the narrator explains, must die at the hands of the Romans, not the Jews, because he has announced that he must die by being lifted up from the earth (12:32–33; cf. 3:14; 8:28). Behind the helplessness of the Jews to put Jesus to death stands his sovereign freedom.[40]

Scene 2: Pilate and Jesus (18:33–38a)

The scene shifts with Pilate's movement into the praetorium. The interrogation begins abruptly: "Are you the King of the Jews?" (v. 33). The prisoner counters with a question of his own: "Do you say this yourself, or did others tell you about me?" (v. 34). On one level this question appears to aid the reader in filling the gap in the narrative (noted earlier): how did Pilate get this information? Jesus' question implies—and Pilate's reply corroborates—that Pilate has derived this language from the Jews.

More to the point, however, is the way Jesus' question begins to press Pilate to voice his own belief about Jesus. The trial of the Roman governor has begun. Pilate's answer continues the pattern of countering a question with another question: "Am I a Jew?" (v. 35). But he goes on to say, "Your own nation and the chief priests handed you over [παρέδωκαν, paredōkan] to me. What have you done?" Pilate here picks up the language used by the Jewish accusers of Jesus (v. 30: "if he were not doing evil, we would not have handed him over [παρεδώκαμεν, paredōkamen] to you").

Now that Jesus has begun his interrogation of Pilate, he can respond, though somewhat obliquely, to the question about kingship. The kingship of Jesus does not have its origin in—and therefore does not receive its character from—this world; otherwise his servants would have fought to prevent his being handed over to the Jews.[41] Pilate distills from Jesus' declaration the relevant testimony: "So then, you are a king?" (v. 37). Setting aside the language of kingship, Jesus responds by

---

[39] Accessible only to John's reader: another instance of dramatic irony.

[40] A sovereignty vividly displayed in the earlier arrest scene (cf. Brown, *Death of the Messiah*, 1.259, 278–79, 290).

[41] A third use of παραδίδωμι (*paradidōmi*, "hand over") in the trial. The parallel in v. 36 between the phrase οὐκ ἔστιν ἐκ τοῦ κόσμου τούτου (*ouk estin ek tou kosmou toutou*, "is not of this world") and οὐκ ἔστιν ἐντεῦθεν (*ouk estin enteuthen*, "is not from here") indicates that this is a genitive of origin. It is not that Jesus' royal rule is otherworldly, located in some other world. Rather, the source of Jesus' royal rule is "from above." Cf. Meeks, *Prophet-King*, 63.

defining his royal role in terms of the fundamental purpose of his coming into the world—his mission to bear witness to the truth. "Everyone who is from the truth," he asserts, "hears my voice." This line echoes Jesus' earlier characterization of himself as the "good shepherd," whose sheep hear his (and only his) voice (10:3–5, 16, 27),[42] and with this line Jesus again presses Pilate to take a stand. The governor, however, refuses to do so; he dismisses Jesus' implicit appeal with a rhetorical question, "What is truth?" He does not belong to the truth.[43]

Scene 3: Pilate and the Jews (18:38b–40)

Again, Pilate's movement signals the start of the next scene. Coming out to the Jews, he declares Jesus' innocence (v. 38b) and then proposes that he honor their Passover custom of setting free one prisoner by releasing the "King of the Jews" for them.[44] They clamor instead for the release of Barabbas. At this point the narrator intrudes with a brief but revealing notice: "Now Barabbas was a robber [λῃστής, *lēstēs*]" (v. 40). Jesus had drawn a stark contrast between his life-giving work as the faithful shepherd[45] and the destructive behavior of "all who came before me," whom he labels "robbers" (λῃσταί, 10:8, 10). How fitting it is (and how tragic) that John's Jewish leaders should show their true colors by siding with a robber against Jesus.[46]

Scene 4: Pilate, the Soldiers, and Jesus (19:1–3)

The level of intensity and violence in the narrative rises dramatically after Jesus' opponents cry out for the release of a robber. Pilate has Jesus scourged (ἐμαστίγωσεν, *emastigōsen*), and to the brutality of that physical abuse the soldiers add mockery. Each detail in the scene contributes to the picture of royalty. Jesus wears a purple robe and a

---

[42]A hearing of his voice that issues in eternal life (10:28). Face-to-face with Jesus, Pilate confronts a momentous decision, one that he will try unsuccessfully to evade as the trial progresses.

[43]If the question were intended as a serious question, Pilate would have remained to hear an answer, but he does not.

[44]Or "to them." Ironically, while Pilate is unable to release Jesus to the Jews, he will in the end hand him over to them—for crucifixion. The historical basis of the release of Barabbas has, of course, been much discussed. See Brown, *Death of the Messiah*, 1.814–20.

[45]And, in a shift of metaphors, as the sheep gate.

[46]It is significant that although in John's narrative two other men (19:18) are crucified along with Jesus, the narrator does not identify them as robbers (Mark 15:27; Matt 27:38) or evildoers (Luke 23:32). As Senior observes, the men on Jesus' right and left become in John part of the "royal retinue" of Jesus during his coronation on the cross (*Passion of Jesus in John*, 103).

crown made of thorns, both emblematic of royal power, and then is acclaimed king by soldiers who proceed to beat him. He will continue to wear the symbols of his royal status, as the narrator makes clear in the next scene (v. 5). These soldiers may be mocking Jesus, but Pilate misses no opportunity to display his contempt for the Jewish authorities.[47] The scene, of course, drips with irony. The soldiers aim to humiliate a prisoner accused of royal aspirations by ridiculing those aspirations. In the eyes of John and John's readers, however, the enemies of Jesus unwittingly bear witness to his true dignity and authority.

Scene 5: Pilate and the Jews (19:4–8)

Pilate again emerges from the praetorium, for a second time pronouncing Jesus' innocence (v. 4). But this time Jesus, dressed in royal garb, accompanies him. Pilate presents Jesus in impressively solemn fashion: "Behold, the man!"[48] The sight of Jesus incites the "chief priests and officers" to cry out, "Crucify! Crucify!" prompting Pilate to repeat his pronouncement of Jesus' innocence and to attempt once again to turn the prisoner back to his Jewish enemies (v. 6).

As in 18:31, Pilate's endeavor to dissociate himself from the case, forcing the Jews to act against one of their own, is coupled with a reference to the Jewish law. The Jews again appeal to their law in order to convince Pilate that Jesus must die, and in so doing they state for the first time in the trial their real charges against Jesus: "We have a law, and in accordance with that law he ought to die, because he made himself Son of God" (v. 7). The continuity between the trial before Pilate and Jesus' earlier controversies with his people is transparent. In John's

---

[47] In v. 15 Pilate presents Jesus to the Jews: "Behold, your king!" And in vv. 19–22, to the chagrin of the chief priests, he announces Jesus' kingship to the world (in Latin, Greek, and Hebrew). Gestures and words that express Pilate's disdain for the Jewish leaders communicate at the same time to the reader the truth about Jesus: more Johannine irony.

[48] Meeks (*Prophet-King*, 70) argues that the dramatic structure of the two scenes in which Pilate presents Jesus to the Jews makes sense only if "the man" in v. 5 is a "throne name"; cf. Senior, *Passion of Jesus in John*, 86–88. Brown (*Death of the Messiah*, 1.827–28), on the other hand, thinks that Pilate intends to portray Jesus as a pathetic figure who poses no threat either to the Jewish people or to Rome. The royal and messianic potential of the acclamation, "Behold, the man," is evident in its echo of Zech 6:11–12, where the prophet is instructed to place a crown on the head of the high priest Joshua with the words "Here is a man whose name is the Branch." Cf. Senior, *Passion of Jesus in John*, 88; C. K. Barrett, *The Gospel according to St. John* (2d ed.; Philadelphia: Westminster, 1978) 541. Does John's reader also connect the title ὁ ἄνθρωπος, *ho anthrōpos*, to the fuller expression ὁ υἱὸς τοῦ ἀνθρώπου, *ho huios tou anthrōpou*, "the Son of humanity" who must be lifted up from the earth (3:14; 8:28)?

Gospel Jesus goes to his death precisely because his own people do not receive him as the Son of God.[49]

With the injection of the issue of divine sonship, the stakes clearly rise for Pilate. The narrator depicts his reaction in terms of growing fear (v. 8).[50] So he beats a hasty retreat back into the safety of the praetorium, where he may get to the real truth about Jesus.

Scene 6: Pilate and Jesus (19:9–11)

The question Pilate now puts to Jesus is the most fundamental christological question in the Fourth Gospel: "Where are you from?" (v. 9).[51] There is no mystery here for the reader, who has long known that Jesus comes "from above," from the Father, to whom he is also returning. Apparently Jesus has drawn from his first conversation with Pilate the conclusion that the official is closed to the truth; he responds to the question with chilling silence.

Pilate attempts to cajole Jesus into an answer: "Don't you realize that I have power [ἐξουσίαν, *exousian*] to release you and that I have power to crucify you?" (v. 10). At this, Jesus breaks his silence. True, Pilate does possess this power, but only because it is an authority given to him "from above" (ἄνωθεν, *anōthen*)—by which Jesus means not Caesar but God (v. 11). Pilate's guilt is not negligible—like all others, he is susceptible to judgment if he refuses to hear the voice of the revealer—but the greater measure of guilt belongs to "the one who handed me over [παραδούς, *paradous*] to you." Who is in view here?[52] Judas, the betrayer? Certainly he handed Jesus over (6:64, 71; 12:4; 13:2), but he handed him to the Jewish leaders, not to Pilate. Pilate, echoing the language used by Jesus' accusers (18:30), has told him that "your own

---

[49]John's readers are able to see the distortion in the charge that Jesus "made himself" Son of God. Jesus has that role because the Father has given it to him. Jesus does not act on his own but does what God has assigned to him (e.g., 5:19–20, 30; 7:16–18; 8:28). He does not honor himself but receives the honor that God bestows upon him (7:18; 8:50).

[50]Readers may recall the reaction of the large crowd of soldiers and officers to Jesus' "I am" at the arrest (18:6).

[51]See Nicholson, *Death as Departure*, 51–57.

[52]Barrett (*John*, 543) is aware of the ambiguity but favors Judas as the one to whom Jesus points. On the other hand, Bultmann (*John*, 662 n. 6), Brown (*John*, 2.878–79; and *Death of the Messiah*, 1.842), Ernst Haenchen (*John* [2 vols.; Hermeneia; Philadelphia: Fortress, 1984] 182–83), and Forestell (*Word of the Cross*, 86 n. 114) have all argued that the referent of ὁ παραδούς, *ho paradous*, is the Jewish leaders—perhaps as represented by or under the leadership of Caiaphas. Senior (*Passion of Jesus in John*, 93) thinks that the precise referent remains unclear, and Schnackenburg (*John*, 3.261–62) suggests that the singular participle expresses a "general meaning: All those who have done it," including Judas, Caiaphas, and the chief priests.

nation and the chief priests handed you over to me" (18:35). Behind the singular ὁ παραδούς stand above all others the high priest and his coterie. So there is plenty of guilt to spread around. Judas must accept his share, and so too must the religious leaders. Through the voice of Jesus, the narrative assigns much of the burden of responsibility for the death of Jesus to the Jewish leaders.[53] Yet Pilate, too, cannot evade responsibility for his choice.

Scene 7: Pilate, the Jews, and Jesus (19:12–16)

Inspired by Jesus' words, Pilate tries yet again to release Jesus, only to be boxed into a corner by the Jews: "If you release this man, you are not Caesar's friend; everyone who makes himself king opposes Caesar" (v. 12). Pilate has called Jesus the "King of the Jews" (18:39), and his detractors pressure Pilate to put two and two together. There is no room in Caesar's realm for pretenders to kingship, and if Pilate sets free such a man, he will betray his allegiance to the emperor and forfeit his status as friend of Caesar.[54]

Pilate's hands are now tied, and he summons the prisoner for judgment. There is no doubt that in this scene's thick irony Jesus, not Pilate, is truly playing the part of judge here. If the verb ἐκάθισεν, *ekathisen* in v. 13 is used transitively, so that Pilate seats Jesus on the βῆμα (*bēma*, the judgment seat or platform), the role reversal of judge and prisoner becomes even more dramatic. But John's readers likely read the verb as intransitive; they see Pilate sitting down for the formal pronouncement of judgment.[55]

The narrator gives precise details of place and time (vv. 13–14), lending added solemnity to the occasion.[56] This is obviously the deci-

---

[53]On this theme, see further ch. 10 below.

[54]For analysis of this label and the probable historical background, see Barrett, *John*, 543; Brown, *John*, 2.893–94.

[55]Meeks (*Prophet-King*, 73–76), following Ignace de la Potterie ("Jesus, King and Judge according to John 19:13," *Scripture* 13 [1961] 97–111), argues for the transitive meaning: Jesus sat on the seat of judgment. Bultmann (*John*, 664 n. 2), Schnackenburg (*John*, 3:263–64), Senior (*Passion of Jesus in John*, 94–95), and Brown (*Death of the Messiah*, 1.844–45) all opt for the intransitive: Pilate sat down on the judgment seat. Barrett (*John*, 544) waffles, suggesting that while it is actually Pilate who sits down, the believing reader can see Jesus occupying that place instead (a case of Johannine double meaning, but using grammatical ambiguity). The comparable usage of ἐκάθισεν in 12:14 tips the balance toward the intransitive meaning, despite the theological advantages that would accrue to John if Jesus were the one seated as judge.

[56]As noted above, the temporal reference also supports the narrative's paschal-lamb symbolism. Jesus receives his sentence at the very moment when the priests begin to slaughter the Passover lambs. Of course, to appreciate that facet of the paschal symbolism, John's readers would have to possess in their

sive and climactic moment in the entire passion drama. Pilate presents Jesus to the Jews: "Behold, your king!" (v. 14). Their "acclamation" of their king takes the subversive form of shouts demanding his crucifixion (v. 15). And the last words of the chief priests amount to a shocking surrender of a conviction that forms the very foundation of their religious identity: "We have no king but Caesar" (v. 15).[57]

Now that the Jewish leaders have aligned themselves with Rome rather than with Jesus their king, Pilate can hand Jesus over to them for crucifixion (v. 16a).[58] We have already had occasion to point out the deep irony of this plot twist. The judgment scene is over, and Jesus alone emerges unscathed. Pilate has shown himself to be closed to the truth staring him in the face, and against his own judicial instincts he has succumbed to the unrelenting pressure of the Jewish leaders and is sending Jesus to death. For their part, in their zeal to be rid of Jesus, they have abandoned core values and commitments of their Jewish identity and heritage. As for Jesus, the reader has seen him wear the emblems of royalty, listened to him courageously proclaim the truth, and heard his royal authority and his innocence publicly affirmed by Roman authority. This is indeed his hour, the moment of his glory.

JOHN'S PASSION NARRATIVE: CHARACTER STUDIES

As we have explored the development of conflict in the narrative and probed in considerable detail the climactic trial before Pilate, crucial elements of the Johannine characterization of Jesus, his disciples, and his opponents have already caught our eye. We conclude our discussion of the Fourth Gospel by giving more focused attention to John's presentation of Jesus and the disciples in the passion drama.

Jesus

The majestic figure of Jesus dominates the Johannine passion account, as it has the whole Gospel.[59] Jesus remains in the director's

---

extratextual repertoire some knowledge of the Passover observance.

[57] Meeks (*Prophet-King*, 76) spells out the implications of this declaration of loyalty to the Roman emperor: rejecting their king, "the Jews cease to be 'Israel,' the special people of God, and become only one of the ἔθνη [*ethnē*, 'peoples'] subject to Caesar."

[58] Roman soldiers do carry out the execution (v. 23), although the antecedent of "they" in v. 18 ("they crucified him") must be the chief priests from v. 15. The ambiguity of John's narrative throws the spotlight on the actions of Jesus' Jewish antagonists, who finally have their way at the cross.

[59] On the characterization of Jesus in the Fourth Gospel and especially in

chair throughout, even as a bound prisoner who is mocked, beaten, and crucified. In these events he completes the mission for which he was sent into the world; this is the hour of his glory.

Jesus and His "Hour"

The motif of Jesus' hour weaves its way throughout John's story, building suspense and creating in the reader the expectation of decisive events still to come. The refrain runs, "My [his] hour has not yet come,"[60] until, that is, a group of Greeks make their approach to Jesus in Jerusalem (12:23). Now, he proclaims, the hour has come for the Son of humanity to be glorified (cf. 17:1). And with the approach of this last Passover, the narrator reports, Jesus knows that the hour of his departure to the Father has arrived (13:1). This motif accents not only Jesus' knowledge of the divine plan but also his control of the course of events leading to the cross. His death comes as a surprise neither to himself nor to John's reader.

A Shepherd's Sacrifice

In the course of his controversies with the Jewish people, Jesus casts himself in the role of a shepherd who freely lays down his life for the sake of his sheep (10:7–18). This metaphor highlights from another direction Jesus' sovereign action in going to his death. In contrast both to robbers and to hired sheepherders, the true shepherd can be counted on to protect his flock, even at great personal risk. So too Jesus chooses self-sacrifice to ensure the well-being (namely, eternal life) of his people. Interpreted in this light, the death of Jesus is not something imposed upon him but, rather, a destiny he willingly embraces. It realizes the purpose of his coming into the world: the gift of life to all who hear and heed his voice.

Not long after making these comments, Jesus hazards a journey to Bethany to restore Lazarus to life (ch. 11). This climactic sign presents Jesus as the author of resurrection, of eternal life. For those who believe, death has been vanquished. Nevertheless, this episode, framed as it is by Jesus' reflections on his role as shepherd (ch. 10) and by the plot to put him to death (11:47–53), reinforces the point of the shepherd image. Jesus is willing to die in order to ensure life for those whom he loves.[61]

---

the passion narrative, see Culpepper, *Anatomy*, 106–12; Senior, *Passion of Jesus in John*, 144–55.

[60] This refrain, placed on Jesus' lips in 2:4, is echoed by the narrator in 7:30; 8:20 (cf. also the formulation with καιρός, *kairos*, in 7:6, 8).

[61] The irony of the raising of Lazarus is profound. Jesus risks death in order to restore Lazarus to life. This very act of bestowing life then sets in motion a chain of events issuing in his own death, but that death is itself the means by

Jesus later turns to yet another metaphor, drawn from the world of the farmer, to bring out the life-giving effects of his death. The message that Greeks desire to see him prompts Jesus to speak of the arrival of the hour of his glorification (12:23). He then seizes upon the image of a grain of wheat, which is fruitful only if it falls into the ground and (as it were) dies (v. 24). Jesus extends the gift of life to others through his own death, and others, too, must surrender life in order to bear fruit (v. 25). It would appear that the path to the inclusion of Greeks within the people of God is about to be opened up by the event of Jesus' glorification— that is to say, by his death, his departure to the Father.

The Son's Return to the Father

Again and again Jesus pictures his approaching death as a return to the Father, who sent him into the world (7:33; 8:21–27; 13:3; 14:2–6, 12, 28; 16:5, 10, 17, 28; 17:11, 13; 20:17; cf. 3:13; 6:62; 8:14; 13:33). Jesus descended from above and now returns there.[62] When the Fourth Gospel subsumes the death of Jesus under this descent-ascent pattern, it places the event in a cosmic, transhistorical frame. Jesus' whole earthly career—including his crucifixion—has its origin and its destination in God. Clearly, his departure from this world and return to God are not confined to the crucifixion alone but are part of his glorification, encompassing death, resurrection, and ascension.

With his last breath, Jesus affirms, "It is finished [or accomplished]" (19:30). The purpose of his coming into the world from above has been achieved (cf. 12:27; 17:4); he has confronted the world with the claim of God's truth and now may return to the Father. The death of Jesus, then, is a real event within human history, and a politically charged one at that, but to readers who adopt the divine perspective encoded within the narrative, it is but a point (though a crucial one) on Jesus' journey back home.

"The Son of Humanity Must Be Lifted Up"

Closely linked to the motif of Jesus' death as his departure and return to God is a series of sayings describing that death and return in terms of being lifted up from the earth. As Moses effected healing by raising up a serpent during the wilderness wanderings, so Jesus, the Son of humanity, must be lifted up to give life to all who believe (3:14–15, echoing Num 21:9). Jesus' identity as the "I am" who has received

---

which life comes to the world. John's reader is placed in a privileged position to discern this deeper meaning in the events of the passion.

[62]Hence Jesus' origin and destiny are crucial elements of the Johannine christological portrait. For detailed treatment of this descent-ascent pattern in John, see Nicholson, *Death as Departure*.

authorization from God will become transparent to the Jews when they have lifted up the Son of humanity (8:28). Finally, when he has been lifted up from the earth, he will draw all to himself (12:32). The narrator appends to this last saying by Jesus an explanatory comment that explicitly ties the lifting up to the mode of Jesus' death—a lifting up on the cross is obviously in view (12:33).

"Lifting up" (or "being exalted," ὑψωθῆναι, hypsōthēnai) is an apt image for the death of Jesus in the Fourth Gospel. Not only does the word suggest to the reader the elevation of the crucified one on the cross, and not only does it express the exaltation that the death of Jesus, as his hour of glory, entails. It also points beyond the cross to Jesus' return to the world above.

The lifting-up motif builds upon a complex pattern of intratextual and intertextual echoes—both of Scripture (Moses and the serpent, 3:14) and of Jesus' own words (threefold repetition of the imagery, and then the narrator's reminder in 18:32). The Johannine passion account makes liberal use of scriptural echoes and explicit quotations, yet another way in which the narrative presses home the conviction that the death of Jesus was divinely purposed. (We discuss the role played by Scripture in John's passion narrative in ch. 11 below.) Moreover, the fact that Jesus' sayings are raised to the same level of prophetic authority as Scripture reinforces both the narrative's close alignment of Jesus and God and its characterization of Jesus as controlling the events surrounding his death.

Judgment of the World

The accent in the Fourth Gospel surely falls upon the death of Jesus as divinely purposed, as an event freely chosen by the Son of God in order to extend life to the world and then return to the Father. But as we have seen, Jesus' death represents, at the same time, the culmination of his bitter conflict with the Jews; it is in fact the outcome desired by his enemies. And lurking beneath the surface of their enmity can be detected the menacing activity of the "ruler of this world," namely, Satan. Jesus attributes the hostility of his Jewish auditors to their being children of the devil (8:44). This architect of evil impels Judas to betray Jesus.[63] Moreover, Jesus points the disciples to the approach of "the ruler of the world" (14:30) shortly before his arrest.

---

[63]Note, however, that Satan enters Judas only after Jesus has assigned him the role of traitor by handing him a piece of bread (13:26). This is so despite 13:2, where the narrator indicates that the devil had made up his mind (literally, "put it into his heart") that Judas should betray Jesus. (For defense of this reading, see James V. Brownson, "Neutralizing the Intimate Enemy: The Portrayal of Judas in the Fourth Gospel," SBLSP 1992, 52 n. 5.) The malevolent activity of Satan notwithstanding, Jesus continues to direct the play. The

Even here, though, the rays of Jesus' triumphant glory shine through the dark clouds of Jewish antagonism and demonic interference. Anticipating his being lifted up from the earth, Jesus exclaims, "Now is the judgment of this world; now will the ruler of this world be cast out" (12:31). Moreover, in his farewell discourses, Jesus reassures the disciples that "the ruler of the world has nothing in me" (14:30), that "the ruler of this world has been judged" (16:11), and that he (Jesus) has "conquered the world" (16:33).

Jesus' death entails, therefore, the decisive judgment of the world—a world created by God, a world to which Jesus came to reveal God, a world it has been his aim to save. The words and works of Jesus offer life to those who believe, but those who refuse to believe judge themselves and remain in the domain of death. So in one sense Jesus did not come for the purpose of judging (8:15; 12:47), yet in another he does exercise judgment on unbelief (3:17–21; 5:26–27, 30; 8:16; 9:39; 12:48). And the repudiation of Jesus expressed in his death is the epitome of unbelief.

This close inner connection between judgment and (un)belief[64] shapes the way in which the reader understands, in retrospect, the Baptizer's claim that Jesus is "the Lamb of God who takes away the sin of the world" (1:29). True, the fourth evangelist exploits the paschal-lamb symbol, as we have seen. Yet Jesus does not lift up the world's sin through a sacrificial offering of his lifeblood. His self-surrender mediates life instead, through its supreme offer of love for friends.[65] And so in his death-exaltation he draws all to himself—all, that is, who believe (12:32). Sin in this Gospel means primarily unbelief (8:24; 16:9; cf. 15:22). The removal of sin, therefore, happens not through observance of a sacrificial rite but through the movement from unbelief to belief, from darkness to light, from falsehood to the truth, as one encounters Jesus' word (cf. 8:28). After his death, the disciples, guided by the Spirit-Paraclete, will continue to confront the world with this revelatory word (14:16–17, 25; 15:26–27; 16:7–15).

Disciples and the Death of Jesus

So far in this chapter we have attended primarily to the interactions between Jesus and his opponents. In drawing the discussion to a close,

---

Johannine narrator does not (as in the Synoptics) show Judas conferring with the chief priests. It is enough to relate, "he went out at once, and it was night" (v. 30). John sharply accents the demonic affiliation of Judas.

[64]Clearly expressed in 3:18: "The one who believes in him is not judged, but the one who does not believe has already been judged, because [this one] did not believe in the name of God's only begotten Son."

[65]Cf. Forestell, *Word of the Cross*, 74–76, 82, 91–92.

it is appropriate to consider briefly the depiction of Jesus' disciples in John's passion narrative.[66] To be a disciple of Jesus in the Fourth Gospel means that while one is in the world, one no longer derives one's identity or character "from the world" (see, e.g., 17:6–19). By responding in belief to Jesus' disclosure of truth, the disciple has moved from the sphere of darkness and death to the sphere of light and life (e.g., 3:16–21). Discipleship in John's story, then, is a matter of believing in Jesus as the one sent from God and returning to God, the revealer of God.

In this story, however, beliefs come and go. The test of genuine discipleship is abiding faith. To remain a disciple, one must continue to believe. Jesus makes this point emphatically in 15:1–11 with his allegory of the vine (Jesus) and the branches (disciples). If they would continue to receive that life which only he can impart, the disciples must remain connected to him by an enduring commitment to faith and to the expression of that faith in love for one another. At this stage of the narrative, Jesus' words provide a retrospective commentary on a pattern that the reader has seen enacted more than once. With his bread-of-life discourse, Jesus so provokes his auditors—including most of his disciples—that all but a few abandon him (6:60–66). Later, when he urges "Jews who had believed in him" (8:31) to continue in his word so as to experience true freedom, he offends these proud descendants of Abraham. By the end of the scene, the epithets are flying, with each party assigning the other to the demonic realm. As if that were not enough, Jesus' audacious claim, "Before Abraham was, I am" (8:58), leads these people who had entered the conversation as believing disciples to try to kill Jesus.

To be a disciple means to persevere in faith, and within the plot of the Gospel story, only the Twelve and a few women[67] exhibit faith that abides (see 6:67–71). Granted, disciples like Philip and Thomas misunderstand Jesus almost as often as outsiders do.[68] And in a farewell scene thick with pathos, Jesus counters their confident expression of belief with the sober prediction that they will scatter, forsaking Jesus (16:30–32).[69] Then Peter three times denies being a disciple of Jesus (18:17–18, 25–27).[70] Nevertheless, these are true disciples whose faith does abide, an impression confirmed by Jesus' prayer in ch. 17:

---

[66]On the characterization of the disciples, see Culpepper, *Anatomy*, 115–25; Senior, *Passion of Jesus in John*, 159–66.

[67]Like Mary and Martha (11:1–44; 12:1–8), Mary Magdalene (19:25–27; 20:1–2, 11–18), and Jesus' own mother (19:25–27).

[68]Misunderstanding by disciples occurs primarily during the discourses and dialogue at the Last Supper: 13:6–10, 36–38 (Peter); 14:5–7 (Thomas); 14:8–11 (Philip).

[69]Although in John's account of the arrest no flight of the disciples is mentioned; rather, Jesus negotiates the release of the disciples (19:8).

[70]In the appendix to the Gospel (ch. 21), Jesus restores Peter to discipleship,

I have manifested your name to those persons whom you gave me out of the world . . . and they have kept your word. Now they have come to know that everything you have given me is from you. For the words you gave me I have given to them, and they have received them and come to know truly that I proceeded from you; and they have come to believe that you sent me. . . . I have guarded them, and not one of them has been lost except the son of destruction, that the Scripture might be fulfilled. (vv. 6–8, 12)

The disciples continue in faith and so remain connected to the source of their life.[71]

Judas, the Betrayer

The same cannot be said for Judas. Even as Peter and the rest of the Twelve demonstrate fierce loyalty to Jesus when his "hard saying" results in the departure of most of the disciples (6:67–69), Jesus identifies one of the Twelve as a "devil" (v. 70). The narrator points the finger at Judas, "one of the Twelve, who was about to betray him [or hand him over, παραδιδόναι, *paradidonai*]."[72] Commenting on Jesus' knowledge of those who stand against him, the narrator in 6:64 associates persons who do not believe and the one who betrays. This link suggests that in Judas, unlike the rest of the Twelve, faith does not abide. Reflection on Jesus' vine-and-branch allegory (15:1–11) leads John's reader to the same evaluation of Judas's failure. In that passage Jesus merges the disciple's abiding in him (and his word) with an abiding in love. But Judas, far from demonstrating his love by laying down his life for his friends (15:12–14), betrays an intimate friend. The narrator does not hesitate to mark other character flaws in Judas. He is greedy and dishonest: his objection to Mary's extravagant anointing of Jesus stems not from any concern for the poor but from the greed of a dishonest thief (he is the "treasurer" for Jesus' band, 12:4–6).

Nevertheless, it is Judas's violation of the intimate bond of friendship that is most contemptible. Whatever else motivates Judas to turn against Jesus in this manner, the narrative hints that betrayal is possible because faith does not abide. But there is more. The narrator relates that Satan

---

allowing him to match his three denials with three expressions of devotion to Jesus (vv. 15–19) and then reissuing the call to discipleship: "Follow me!"

[71]This picture resembles that painted by Luke (e.g., 22:28–30). See ch. 4 above.

[72]Note the emphatic final position given to "one of the Twelve." Judas's treachery is all the more disconcerting because it is the act of an intimate companion of Jesus. The supper scene makes the same point, for it is the very act of eating bread dipped in a shared vessel that propels Judas out into the dark night of betrayal (13:26–30). For an illuminating study of John's presentation of Judas, see Brownson, "Neutralizing the Intimate Enemy."

enters Judas as soon as Jesus hands him the piece of moist bread that marks him as the traitor. When he leaves the supper, he ventures out into "the night" (13:30). Judas, in abandoning the posture of belief, has allied himself with the darkness, with the forces of evil. Small wonder, then, that when Judas plays the part of tribune, leading an immense company of soldiers and officials out to arrest Jesus, he must light his path with "lanterns and torches" (18:3). Having surrendered his place by the side of one who is the "light of the world," he is now lost to the darkness.

The Disciple Whom Jesus Loved

If Peter embodies discipleship that succumbs to fear and must be renewed by Jesus and if Judas exemplifies discipleship dissolved by defection and apostasy, the beloved disciple shows John's reader what genuine discipleship looks like.[73] First introduced at the Last Supper (13:23–26), this anonymous disciple remains closely bound to Jesus to the very end of the narrative. Each time the beloved disciple is mentioned, the narrator pairs him with Peter, invariably in a way that privileges the unnamed disciple at Peter's expense (in addition to 13:23–26, see also 20:2–10; 21:7, 20–23). The singular exception, the appearance of the beloved disciple at the foot of the cross, is telling (19:25–27). When Jesus transfers his mother to the care of this disciple, thereby constituting a new family of faith, Peter is conspicuous by his absence. He has denied his association with Jesus not once but three times; now it is the beloved disciple, not Peter, who remains with Jesus to the end. This puts the lie to Peter's confident assertion of loyalty: "I will lay down my life for you" (13:37). Not Peter but the beloved disciple (presumably—cf. 21:24) finds himself in a position to witness the sign of blood and water issuing from the dead Jesus' side. He is the reliable witness on whose testimony the Gospel rests.

Within the passion narrative itself, the reader also encounters an anonymous "other disciple" (ἄλλος μαθητής, *allos mathētēs*), an acquaintance of the high priest, who sees to it that Peter is admitted to the high priest's courtyard (18:15–16). Is this the same character? Four times in John 20 the narrator refers to the beloved disciple as "the other disciple" (ὁ ἄλλος μαθητής), that is, the other disciple along with Peter (vv. 2, 3, 4, 8). In each case, though, the narrator uses the definite article, whereas in 18:15–16 the noun is anarthrous ("another disciple"). If the reader is to assume it is the beloved disciple who appears in the high priest's home, why is the narrator not more precise, as in the other passages?[74] Moreover, would John's reader expect an associate of the

---

[73]For a sketch of John's characterization of this figure, see Culpepper, *Anatomy*, 121–23.

[74]John 13:23: "one of his disciples, whom Jesus loved"; 20:2: "the other

high priest to be an intimate, trusted companion of Jesus? Is he perhaps one of the "secret disciples" among the "rulers" who out of fear conceal their affiliation with Jesus? (Such is the case with Joseph of Arimathea, introduced in 19:38.) But this figure does not act like a fearful "secret disciple": he intercedes on behalf of Peter, and he accompanies Jesus into the high priest's home; indeed, the young woman attending the door may know him as a disciple of Jesus.[75]

From the other side, this nameless disciple possesses some qualities that square with the portrait of the beloved disciple. He remains close to Jesus, even after the arrest (18:15), and as in the other passages featuring the beloved disciple, this character appears in tandem with Peter—and not to Peter's advantage. Some ambiguity remains; the evidence is not conclusive. Nonetheless, John's readers may be inclined to fill this gap in the narrative by identifying "another disciple" of 18:15–16 with the beloved disciple. In this way, the narrative is seen to present a continuity of disciples' witness throughout the events of the passion (see esp. 19:25–27).[76] With or without this passage, the beloved disciple is an exemplary figure, one who embodies enduring commitment to Jesus and provides authentic testimony to the truth about his Lord.

"Secret Disciples": Nicodemus and Joseph of Arimathea

Immediately after the death of Jesus, two men step forward to claim his body and give him a burial with honor. Joseph of Arimathea the narrator characterizes as a "secret disciple," evidently one of the timid disciples in the ranks of the elite whose fear prevented public declaration of support for Jesus (12:42–43). He is moving in the right direction, for when he summons the courage to ask Pilate for the dead body, he is making a bold public expression of his devotion to Jesus.

Nicodemus, too, seems to be making some progress.[77] He entered his first nocturnal conversation with Jesus deeply impressed by the signs

---

disciple, whom Jesus loved"; 21:7: "that disciple whom Jesus loved"; and esp. 21:20: "the disciple whom Jesus loved, who during the supper had reclined at his breast and said, 'Lord, who is it that is going to betray you?' "

[75] As this other disciple escorts Peter into the high priest's courtyard, she asks Peter, "It isn't the case that you *too* are among the disciples of this man, is it?" (18:17). The adverbial καί (*kai*, "too" or "also") here may indicate that the woman already knows the anonymous disciple's tie to Jesus.

[76] Bultmann (*John*, 645 n. 4) and Schnackenburg (*John*, 3.234–35) argue that the disciple of 18:15–16 is *not* the beloved disciple. Frans Neirynck ("The 'Other Disciple' in Jn 18:15–16," *ETL* 51 [1975] 113–41), Brown (*Death of the Messiah*, 1.596–98, 623), and Senior (*Passion of Jesus in John*, 63–64) conclude that the "other disciple" of ch. 18 *is* the beloved disciple. Barrett (*John*, 525) thinks that identification possible but not definite.

[77] For further discussion of Nicodemus, see Culpepper, *Anatomy*, 134–36;

Jesus was performing, but he emerged from this exchange confused and bewildered (ch. 3). As the conflict between Jesus and his people heats up, Nicodemus becomes a moderating voice, urging his fellow Pharisees to honor their law by giving Jesus a hearing before condemning him (7:50–51). For that advice he wins the label "Galilean"—not a compliment on the lips of these Jewish leaders.[78] While Nicodemus's comment addresses correct legal procedure and does not directly defend Jesus and while the narrator describes him as "one of them" (that is, the Pharisees), he clearly now occupies a middle position between Jesus and his enemies.

Therefore, Nicodemus's final gesture in the story—joining forces with Joseph to honor Jesus—leads the reader to think that he is advancing closer to the circle of disciples. True, readers may find amusing all this attention to the body of one who is returning through death and resurrection to the Father. In particular, the narrator may well be seen winking and the reader heard laughing as Nicodemus brings such an immense quantity of spices (100 Roman pounds!) to prepare the body for burial. On the other hand, burial was necessary,[79] and the extravagant spices recall for the reader another excessive display of affection for Jesus, one that earned Mary no criticism from Jesus (12:3–8). Moreover, such a lavish burial rite is a fitting tribute to a king, and John has narrated the trial and crucifixion of Jesus in a way that underscores his royal status. Nicodemus and Joseph may not (yet) bear all the marks of genuine discipleship (namely, faith that abides), but the direction in which their characters are developing is promising.

If this is so, then the dominant, sharply dualistic pattern of the Gospel is tempered somewhat. To be sure, Jesus confronts the world

---

Jouette M. Bassler, "Mixed Signals: Nicodemus in the Fourth Gospel," *JBL* 108 (1989) 635–46; Senior, *Passion of Jesus in John*, 130–33.

[78] Note that the narrator introduces Nicodemus this second time with a reminder to the reader of his first meeting with Jesus ("who had gone to him before," 7:50). When Nicodemus appears for the third and final time in the story, the narrator expands this reminder: "Nicodemus, too, who at first had come to him by night" (19:39). While the repeated association of Nicodemus and the night might lead John's reader to view Nicodemus negatively, there is created at the same time a contrast between his previous coming by night and his present public action as the evening approaches. He is not a static character in the story. See further ch. 12 below.

[79] One might contend that the spices are no longer needed because of Mary's anointing of Jesus at Bethany, an action interpreted by Jesus in relation to burial (12:7). The formulation, however, is unusual. "Let her be," Jesus directs the disciples, "so that she may keep it for the day of my burial." Yet she has already used the expensive ointment to anoint Jesus, filling the house with the aroma. Where Mark's Jesus interprets the act as an anointing of Jesus' body for burial (14:8), it is not clear from Jesus' interpretive comment in John that his body is now ready for burial.

with divine truth and invites people to life-giving belief in him, and their response yields a picture that is black and white. Either one believes and lives, or one persists in unbelief and so remains in the realm of death. For the most part, wherever John's narrative evidences movement, it is movement away from genuine discipleship, away from belief to disbelieving rejection of Jesus. Yet at the close of the passion drama, Nicodemus and Joseph provide much-needed relief, softening at least slightly the stridently sectarian character of this Gospel. It is possible, after all, to move into rather than out of the community of disciples.[80]

Jesus' Death as Model for the Disciples

We draw this discussion of the disciples to a close by considering briefly the way in which John presents Jesus' death as exemplary. Jesus' washing of the disciples' feet dramatically enacts one meaning of his death. By giving up himself for their sake, he makes them wholly clean (13:1–11). But his act of abasement also presents a model of self-giving service to be emulated by the disciples (vv. 14–15). They ought to show the same love for one another that Jesus offered them (v. 34), and that means being willing to surrender life out of love for one's friends (15:12–13).

The death of Jesus in the Fourth Gospel is paradigmatic also because the disciples, like Jesus, must inevitably meet hostility in the world. As they testify to the truth, they can be sure that those who do not know God will hate them (15:18–21). At the hands of such adversaries, the disciples may expect to be driven out of synagogues and even put to death (16:2–3). They will be hated[81] because they share Jesus' heavenly origin (17:14–18). They are not "from this world." Yet Jesus leaves them in the world (v. 15); indeed, he dispatches them into that hostile world in the same way that he himself was sent by the Father (v. 18). Guided and strengthened by the Paraclete, whose arrival coincides with Jesus' departure (16:7), the disciples will continue Jesus' mission. They may expect to be accorded the same hostile reception that greeted him. Yet they will face that destiny secure in the knowledge that the malevolent ruler of this world is powerless before the one who reigns from the cross, the one they call Lord. For those whose faith abides, the only reality is life.

---

[80]Provided, of course, that God has drawn one into Jesus' fold (see 10:29; 17:6–19). An influential essay advancing the view that the Fourth Gospel is a sectarian document is that of Wayne A. Meeks, "The Man from Heaven in Johannine Sectarianism," *JBL* 91 (1972) 44–72.

[81]Jesus actually declares (17:14), "the world has hated them" (aorist tense). Here, where one would expect a future tense verb, the temporal perspective of the author and the community of readers breaks into the narrative. They have already experienced the hostility envisaged by Jesus.

Part Two

*Other Early Christian
Views of the Death of Jesus*

 SIX

"Nothing but Christ and him crucified"
PAUL'S THEOLOGY OF THE CROSS

INTRODUCTION

Paul is widely recognized as the quintessential theologian of the cross.[1] The aptness of the description is suggested not only by the sheer quantity of references to the cross in his correspondence[2] but also by the multitudinous ways in which Jesus' suffering and death are woven into the fabric of Paul's letters.[3] Indeed, the passion of Christ is related to all aspects of Paul's apostolic message—especially his soteriology, Christology, eschatology, and ethics—and is pivotal to his self-characterization as an apostle and servant of Christ.

Although it is difficult to overstate the importance of the cross for Paul, neglect of the many ways in which the cross registers its importance in Paul has not been uncommon. This is in part a consequence of the ascendancy of interest in the doctrine of the atonement in Christian

---

[1]The phrase "theology of the cross" *(theologia crucis)* was used by Martin Luther in contrast to a "theology of glory" that minimized the import of the cross (cf. the Heidelberg Theses [1518]); it denotes an understanding of the cross as the centerpoint of God's self-revelation and thus as the foundation and hub of all theology. On Paul's *theologia crucis*, see Peter Stuhlmacher, "Eighteen Theses on Paul's Theology of the Cross," in *Reconciliation, Law, and Righteousness: Essays in Biblical Theology* (Philadelphia: Fortress, 1986) 155–68.

[2]E.g., outside the Gospels and Acts, Paul is responsible for all but one use of the verb σταυρόω *(stauroō,* "crucify," 1 Cor 1:13, 23; 2:2, 8; 2 Cor 13:4; Gal 3:1; 5:24; 6:14) and the noun σταυρός *(stauros,* "cross," 1 Cor 1:17, 18; Gal 5:11; 6:12, 14; Phil 2:8; 3:18; Col 1:20; 2:14; cf. Eph 2:16) in the NT. Cf. also συσταυρόω *(systauroō,* "crucify with"), which appears outside the Gospels only in Rom 6:6; Gal 2:19.

[3]This chapter relies on the article "Death of Christ," by Joel B. Green, in *DPL,* 201–9.

soteriology.[4] Interpreters of Paul's understanding of the death of Jesus have not always appreciated the dazzling array of colors in the mural of Paul's theology of the cross, often reducing those images to a one-dimensional, monochromatic rendition that brings into sharp focus only the Pauline emphasis on the crucifixion as the definitive soteriological event. But this emphasis, too, has suffered from a lack of perception of the contours of Paul's atonement theology. Paul has dozens of ways of explicating the meaning of the cross, many of which can be construed along more narrow soteriological lines, but even these have repeatedly served as invitations for reading into the myriad references to the cross in Paul only abstract and often lackluster statements about the problem of sin and the divine solution.[5]

If this failure to interpret Paul on a larger canvass is a consequence of centuries of speculation on the nature or mechanics of the atonement, it is also a corollary of especially eighteenth- and nineteenth-century attempts to arrange the Pauline material about the cross in a manner governed by systematic concerns. Study of Pauline "theology" today has repeatedly underscored two realities that undermine these more traditional renderings.[6] First, as is increasingly recognized, the "theology of Paul" is in some ways unattainable, for the primary sources with which we have to work are *occasional* documents. Letters addressing specific questions and concerns cannot be assumed to reveal the full theology of their author. Second, and as a corollary, as occasional documents, the letters of Paul may be expected to employ theological metaphors and argumentation appropriate to the context of Paul's audience. On the one hand, this means that we might expect Paul's theology of the cross, were he to have worked it out and written it down, to be even richer and fuller than his letters evidence. On the other, this means that Paul's understanding of the cross in any given letter is itself being formed in critical discourse with a particular people at a particular time in the midst of particular sociohistorical and communal circumstances.

Our understanding of Paul's theology of the cross, then, would be significantly advanced if we were able to consider first the theology of

---

[4]See ch. 13 below.

[5]Cf. the similar complaint registered against traditional readings of Gal 3:10–14 in N. T. Wright, *The Climax of the Covenant: Christ and the Law in Pauline Theology* (Minneapolis: Fortress, 1991) 138. See also John Driver, *Understanding the Atonement for the Mission of the Church* (Scottdale, Pa.: Herald, 1986).

[6]Cf. the programmatic thoughts in James D. G. Dunn, "Prolegomena to a Theology of Paul," *NTS* 40 (1994) 407–32 (esp. 415–23). For the work of the Society of Biblical Literature group concerned with such issues, cf. Jouette M. Bassler, ed., *Pauline Theology*, vol. 1, *Thessalonians, Philippians, Galatians, Philemon* (Minneapolis: Fortress, 1991); David M. Hay, ed., *Pauline Theology*, vol. 2, *1 and 2 Corinthians* (Minneapolis: Fortress, 1993).

the cross in each of Paul's letters. An approach of this nature would as a matter of course situate Paul's thought within a wider stream of influence. This would include, e.g., the literature of ancient Israel, Second Temple Judaism, and the wider Greco-Roman world, as well as other thinking about Jesus' passion among Christians before and alongside Paul. It would also examine the wider marketplace of ideas and language providing substance for Paul's discursive engagement with his respective audiences as he works to bring them into formative and transformative encounters with the expansive relevance of the cross for faith and practice. Such an agenda is unfortunately far beyond the perimeters of this chapter, and we must content ourselves with a somewhat more modest agenda. We will be able to provide only hints of the richness of Paul's thought—a richness recognized especially when we read Paul's letters primarily as theological units rather than as components of a theological library—as we explore the centrality of Jesus' death for Paul, the relation of the death of Christ to salvation in Pauline thought, and Paul's understanding of the cross as it relates particularly to his apostleship and to Christian life more generally.

THE CENTRALITY OF THE DEATH OF JESUS

For Paul the cross of Christ was critical for Christian reflection and life, especially as the means by which God has provided for salvation and as the instrument and measure of new life in Christ.

The Story of Salvation

One way of assessing the prominence of the cross for Paul is to grapple with the location of the cross in Pauline discourse. It is true that in Paul the cross is often set in tandem with the resurrection of Jesus. As J. Paul Sampley has observed: "The death and resurrection of Jesus Christ is [*sic*] the primary reference point in Paul's thought world. Paul sees past, present, and future in light of that pivotal event. For Paul, believers relate to the death and resurrection of Christ as the formative event in their past."[7] But for Paul it is especially the cross, located at the midpoint of salvation history in Paul's discourse, that should determine one's understanding of God and of reconciliation with God on the one hand and of the nature of faithful Christian existence on the other. While the resurrection has inaugurated the new order and grounds

---

[7]J. Paul Sampley, *Walking between the Times: Paul's Moral Reasoning* (Minneapolis: Fortress, 1991) 7.

eschatological hope, the period between "first fruits" (Jesus' resurrection) and the full harvest (the general resurrection) is marked fundamentally by the cross of Christ. Thus, Paul can assert that while among the Corinthians, he had "resolved to know nothing . . . other than Jesus Christ and him crucified" (1 Cor 2:2).

Our earlier reference to Pauline discourse has a particular, focused meaning, related to one way of exploring how Paul portrays the great drama of salvation. Literary theorists make a basic distinction between *story* and *discourse*, and it is this distinction that we want to pursue here. Story refers to the content, the "what" of discourse; it has to do with a series of events and characters without reference to causality or plot. Discourse, on the other hand, refers to the communication of that content, now construed so as to reveal purpose and plot. If story refers to the "what," discourse refers to the "how," the way a medium is used to present that "what."[8] At the level of discourse (or "performance"), the elements of story are construed in relation to each other, with a variety of literary devices (e.g., the ordering or even repetition of events) employed to mark the relative emphasis of the parts and the overall significance of the whole. In asserting the centrality of the cross in Pauline discourse, then, we are claiming that Paul has repeatedly orchestrated his representation of the divine-human story so as to bring to the foreground the immediate relevance and determinative influence of the crucifixion of Jesus Christ.

According to the Pauline correspondence, the story of redemption has a number of key components, including, but not limited to:

the creation of the world and of humanity

the transgression of Adam, which marks the invasion of sin and death

the communication of God's purpose in covenant with Abraham

the election of Israel and the revelation of the Law

---

[8]Cf. Michael J. Toolan, *Narrative: A Critical Linguistic Introduction* (Interface; London/New York: Routledge, 1988) 9–145; Seymour Chatman, *Story and Discourse: Narrative Structure in Fiction and Film* (Ithaca, N.Y./London: Cornell University, 1978). In the use of the more neutral term "discourse," over against "narrative," we are distancing ourselves somewhat from recent attempts to examine Paul's "narrative" (cf., e.g., Richard B. Hays, *The Faith of Jesus Christ: An Investigation of the Narrative Substructure of Galatians 3:1–4:11* [SBLDS 56; Chico, Calif.: Scholars, 1983]; Norman R. Petersen, *Rediscovering Paul: Philemon and the Sociology of Paul's Narrative World* [Philadelphia: Fortress, 1985]). By "narrative," such interpreters typically mean something like what we have referred to as the way the story is presented, but they introduce important ambiguities on issues of *genre*. Although epistolary literature might contain narrative sections (e.g., Phil 2:6–11) and although an epistle itself participates in an ongoing story (say, the story of Paul's interaction with the Corinthians), epistles may be distinguished from, say, Acts on generic grounds.

God's sending his Son, Jesus Christ, to redeem humanity and usher in the new epoch

the achievement of God's purpose in the death and resurrection of Jesus

the life of the church in the temporally anomalous present—cruciform, hopeful, Spirit-empowered, mission-oriented

the final transformation, the new creation, marked by Jesus' Parousia.[9]

In his correspondence with various churches, Paul arranges elements of the story, relating some in temporal and causal ways while omitting others altogether. The Thessalonians, for example, have upset the temporal logic of the story as Paul understands it and so misconstrue their present vocation. Concern about those who have "died in Christ" is addressed by a reminder that the time of the Parousia is still future. What is more, concern with "the times and seasons" ought to give way to sobriety and faithfulness rooted in the recollection that Jesus' death "for us" has made possible ongoing life "with him" (1 Thess 4:13–5:11). Indeed, by the *inclusio* provided by the dual references to Jesus' death in 4:14 and 5:9–10, Paul urges his Thessalonian audience to comprehend the enduring efficacy of Jesus' salvific death so as to embrace, first, the hope of salvation that differentiates them from the rest of humanity and, second, the behaviors appropriate to those called to cruciform existence (cf. 1 Thess 1:6; 3:1–5).

To illustrate further, in his dealings with the Corinthians, Paul repeatedly attempts to situate the Corinthians temporally back at the proper place in the ongoing story of redemption. Particularly in 1 Corinthians, he reflects on the meaning of the crucified Christ in large part to counter competing ideas. The word of the cross opposes wrongheaded thinking about the nature of present existence, as though this were the time for triumphalism following the consummation of the new age. Apparently, Paul must remind the Corinthians that the Lord has *not* yet returned and that the present is reserved for proclaiming the Lord's death "until he comes" (1 Cor 11:26). This "proclamation" is not only or necessarily the public voice of the gifted preacher or teacher (cf. 1 Cor 12) but is, above all else, the representation of Jesus' self-sacrifice within the diaconal and cruciform life of the community of his followers. Against the "wisdom of the world" and the status-seeking orientation of the believers at Corinth, Paul posits the scandalous cross of Christ as the "power of God" "to us who are being saved." Paul foregrounds "what is weak in the world," "what is low and despised in the

---

[9]Cf. Richard B. Hays, "Crucified with Christ: A Synthesis of the Theology of 1 and 2 Thessalonians, Philemon, Philippians, and Galatians," in Bassler, *Pauline Theology*, 1.227–46 (231–33).

world"—i.e., "Christ crucified" and the community oriented around the crucified Christ (1 Cor 1:18–31).

An example of a different sort is provided in Paul's letter to the Galatians. There, already in the opening verses, Paul expresses shock that the brothers and sisters in Galatia have abandoned the gospel of Jesus Christ in favor of "another gospel." In terms relevant to our distinction between story and discourse, Paul is vitally concerned that the Galatians have regressed to a former moment in the continuing story. They have begun to be persuaded of the importance of circumcision—the hallmark of Jewish identity appropriate to an earlier period. Paul, on the other hand, insists on the centrality of the cross of Christ, which the apostle juxtaposes with circumcision as its antithesis:[10]

Circumcision	*Cross*
It is those who want to make a fair showing in the flesh that are trying to compel you to be circumcised,	but only that they might not be persecuted for the cross of Christ.
Even the circumcised do not themselves keep the law, but want you to be circumcised in order that they might boast in your flesh.	May I never boast of anything except the cross of our Lord Jesus Christ, through whom the whole world has been crucified to me and I to the world. For neither circumcision nor uncircumcision counts for anything; what counts is a new creation.
And as many as will follow this rule, peace be on them and mercy, as also on the Israel of God. From now on let no one cause me trouble,	for I bear the marks of Jesus on my body. (Gal 6:12–17)

In Paul's mind, the distinction between the circumcised and the uncircumcised, so crucial in former times, had been radically relativized for the present and future by Jesus' crucifixion. The significance of the cross of Christ thus achieves in Paul's thought epochal proportions.[11]

---

[10] See Charles B. Cousar, *A Theology of the Cross: The Death of Jesus in the Pauline Letters* (OBT; Minneapolis: Fortress, 1990) 137–48; James D. G. Dunn, *The Theology of Paul's Letter to the Galatians* (NTT; Cambridge: Cambridge University, 1993) 28–33 (29).

[11] See further Anthony Tyrrell Hanson, *The Paradox of the Cross in the Thought of St. Paul* (JSNTSup 17; Sheffield: JSOT, 1987).

Kerygmatic and Formulaic Expressions

The centrality of the cross for Paul is manifest in other ways, too. Thus, its gravity is implied by the phrases he utilizes to denote the kerygma. In 1 Cor 1:18 we find the expression "the message of the cross" used as a virtual synonym for "gospel." In 2 Cor 5:19 "the message of reconciliation" appears in a context wherein the salvific event is presented in the parallelism: "And he died for all, so that those who live might live no longer for themselves, but for him who on their behalf died and was raised." In other texts, too, Paul represents the content of the Christian message by metonymy through references to Jesus' death and the cross (e.g., 1 Cor 1:13, 17–18, 23; 2:2, 8; 2 Cor 13:4; Gal 3:1; 5:11; 6:12; Phil 2:8; 3:18; Col 1:20; 2:14–15).[12]

Two stereotypical expressions appear regularly in Paul, both denoting the atoning significance of the cross.[13] The first presents the "giving up" of Jesus for the salvation of humankind—either as a divine act (e.g., Rom 4:25: "who was given up on account of our trespasses"; 8:32: "who did not spare his own son, but gave him up on behalf of us all") or as Jesus' act of self-giving (e.g., Gal 1:4: "who gave himself up for our sins"; 2:20: "gave himself up for me"). The second expression, the "dying formula," is found frequently—e.g., in the celebrated tradition represented in 1 Cor 15:3: "Christ died for our sins" (cf. further Rom 5:6, 8; 14:9; 1 Cor 8:11; 2 Cor 5:14, 15; Gal 2:21; 1 Thess 5:10). Paul's phrase "Christ died for us," according to Martin Hengel, "is the most frequent and most important confessional statement in the Pauline epistles and at the same time in the primitive Christian tradition in the Greek language which underlies them."[14]

The traditional foundation to which Hengel points is portentous, for it suggests the degree to which Paul inscribes himself in the common faith of the early church. His letters draw on the common vocabulary of the Christian communities before and alongside him. Even where his innovations in theological formulation are most apparent, he is building on the foundation of the shared faith. What is more, when faced with hostility, as in his relations with the Christian communities at Corinth and Galatia, Paul's deployment of traditional materials related to the cross serves to legitimize his authority in the face of opposition. The cross of Christ is crucial to the message of the whole church, Paul may be heard to say, and not only for his own thought.

---

[12]Cf. Karl Kertelge, "Das Verständnis des Todes Jesu bei Paulus," in Kertelge, ed., *Der Tod Jesu*, 114–36 (124–27).

[13]Cf. Martin Hengel, *The Atonement: The Origins of the Doctrine in the New Testament* (Philadelphia: Fortress, 1981) 34–39.

[14]Martin Hengel, *Crucifixion in the Ancient World and the Folly of the Message of the Cross* (Philadelphia: Fortress, 1977) 37.

Paul and the Passion Tradition

Finally, there are hints that Paul was aware of the drama of Jesus' suffering and death, accounts of which would have circulated in earliest Christianity and thus been available to him.[15] A reference to the narrative tradition of Jesus' death may lie behind Gal 3:1, where Paul writes, "Before your eyes Jesus Christ was publicly portrayed as crucified." Certainly, this is a way of underscoring that it was precisely as the crucified one that Paul presented Jesus as the Christ to the Galatians, presumably in direct contrast to the preaching of Paul's opponents. The language he employs, especially the phrases "before your eyes" and "publicly portrayed" (προεγράφη, proegraphē), suggests further the graphic quality of his proclamation. Paul insists that he painted a picture with his words, and this opens the possibility that his missionary preaching made use of some form of a narrative of Jesus' passion.[16] Additionally, his introduction to the tradition of the Last Supper, "in the night when he was delivered up (παρεδίδετο, paredideto)" (1 Cor 11:23–25), presumes that Paul shares with his readers at Corinth some intimacy with a narrative context for the eucharistic tradition.

Equally evocative are the themes with which Paul describes his own suffering, especially in 2 Corinthians. In 2 Cor 6:3–10, e.g., he lists the sufferings, grace, and paradoxical aspects of his service in a way that reverberates with themes familiar to us from the Gospel accounts of Jesus' suffering and death. Not unlike what one finds in the Gospel of Mark, then, Paul has his own understanding of the "way of the cross," the way of suffering through which one identifies with the manner of Christ's suffering.[17] Finally, while Pauline only in the broad sense, 1 Tim 6:13 alludes to Jesus' trial before Pontius Pilate in a way that presupposes at least rudimentary knowledge of the passion story. Although Paul shows little interest in recounting the historical details of Jesus' passion qua historical data, he seems to have been aware of them and was concerned with their significance for Christian faith and life.

---

[15]Cf. Green, Death of Jesus; Stuhlmacher, "Eighteen Theses," 164.

[16]Cf. Hans Dieter Betz, Galatians: A Commentary on Paul's Letter to the Churches in Galatia (Hermeneia; Philadelphia: Fortress, 1979) 131: "One of the goals of the ancient orator was to deliver his speech so vividly and impressively that his listeners imagined the matter to have happened right before their eyes. All kinds of techniques were recommended to achieve this effect, including impersonations and even holding up painted pictures."

[17]Cf. Ralph P. Martin, Mark: Evangelist and Theologian (CEP; Grand Rapids: Zondervan, 1972) 156–62.

THE DEATH OF CHRIST AND SALVATION

In the foregoing we have suggested that the death of Jesus has for Paul epoch-making significance both as the decisive salvific event and as the fundamental criterion for measuring faithful Christian life. Although these two are inseparable in Paul's theology of the cross, for purposes of discussion we will first address the former, then turn to the latter.

The Purpose of God

Paul's theology of the cross is first and foremost *theo*logy, for Paul's message is theocentric in its essentials. Questions about the nature of humanity (theological anthropology) and about salvation (soteriology) are for Paul first and foremost questions about God. His theology of the cross is rooted in his understanding of the divine purpose and of God as the primary actor in the drama of salvation. Although he affirms that Christ "gave himself for our sins in order to set us free from the present evil age," he goes on to affirm that Christ does so "according to the will of our God and Father" (Gal 1:4). That is, Christ's self-giving signifies his identification and solidarity with God's salvific aim. By this affirmation, any attribution to Paul of a view of the atonement that segregates the activity of God from that of God's Son is disallowed. Nevertheless, at center stage stands God's initiative: "God was in Christ reconciling the world to himself" (1 Cor 5:19); "God . . . sent his own son" (Rom 8:3).

God's Integrity and Justice

The precedence Paul gives to God in his theology of the cross is perhaps underscored best in the tightly packed passage Rom 3:21–26. Two questions related to the character of God are raised in the verses leading up to this passage: (1) What are we to make of God's faithfulness vis-à-vis the covenantal promises to the Jewish people? If, as Paul has earlier argued, both Jew and Gentile stand side by side before God as implicated in sin, what are we to make of God's covenantal history with Israel? "Will their faithlessness nullify the faithfulness of God?" (Rom 3:3). (2) If salvation is available outside the law, should we not engage in evil so that God's goodness may abound all the more (Rom 3:8)? Or to raise the question in a way more oriented around the character of God, if God's goodness is available to sinners, how can God judge the world? The first is a question about the reliability of God, the second about the moral integrity of God.[18]

---

[18] See Cousar, *Theology of the Cross*, 37–41.

These questions place the righteousness of God in the dock, for in the OT "the righteousness of God" is a central conviction, affirming God's faithful orientation toward the covenant and setting the pattern for the character of Israel's comportment and behavior before God. Paul is not unaware of this. First, he grounds his treatment of these two questions in the prior disclosure of the righteousness of God ("attested by the law and the prophets," Rom 3:21). Then he develops his present perspective on God's faithfulness with clear echoes of occasions of covenant making and covenant keeping in Israel's past (cf. "redemption," Rom 3:24; "sacrifice of atonement," Rom 3:25). Moreover, he does so via a traditional Jewish-Christian formula, demonstrating even more the rootedness of this representation of God's character in the history of God's interaction with the community of God's people.

In this context, Christ's salvific death, as it were, "proves" the reliability and integrity of God. To put it differently, the righteousness of God is manifest in this intervention to bring salvation to a humanity mired in sin. And God's righteousness is manifest precisely in the revelation of God in the cross as one who keeps promises; who does not wink at sin but, through the faithful obedience and sacrificial death of Jesus Christ, redeems all who believe, whether Jew or Gentile; and who thus does not introduce a way of salvation that nullifies the law but actually upholds it (cf. Rom 3:31). Consequently, Paul affirms that the righteousness of God is revealed in Christ not merely as a description of God in the role of judge but also and especially as the activity of God oriented around covenant making and covenant keeping; in the death of Christ the righteousness of God is exhibited in God's delivering people from sin.

The Wrath and Love of God

How is this divine justice related to Paul's notion of divine wrath? God's wrath stands as a corollary to his righteousness: "Since God's fidelity to covenant demands human response and responsibility, wrath is what one experiences when one rejects God's offer of justice."[19] It is imperative to recognize, however, that for Paul divine wrath is not a divine property, or essential attribute, but the active presence of God's judgment toward "all ungodliness and wickedness" (Rom 1:18). The wrath of God is not vindictive indignation or the anger of divine retribution but the divine response to human unfaithfulness. God's wrath may be future, eschatological (Rom 2:5, 8; 1 Thess 1:10; 5:9; Col

---

[19]Anthony J. Tambasco, *A Theology of Atonement and Paul's Vision of Christianity* (ZSNT; Collegeville, Minn.: Liturgical, 1991) 33. Cf. Stephen H. Travis, "Christ as Bearer of Divine Judgment in Paul's Thought about the Atonement," in Green and Turner, *Jesus of Nazareth*, 332–45.

3:6), but it is also already present, for God is now handing people over to experience the consequences of the sin they choose (Rom 1:18, 24, 26, 28; cf. Wis 11:15–16; 12:23).

Paul does not portray an angry God requiring mollification. For him, divine wrath is a means of underscoring how seriously God takes sin, but it is not an affective quality, or "feeling," on God's part. The righteousness of God is effective in the present to save, but as men and women resist it, they experience God's righteousness as condemnation.

All of this suggests that Paul does not regard the death of Jesus as a vicarious punishment. His theology of the cross lacks a developed sense of divine retribution. Quite the contrary, according to such texts as Rom 5:6–8, the death of Christ is the ultimate expression of the boundless love of God: "But God demonstrates his love for us in that while we were still sinners Christ died for us" (Rom 5:8).

Within its cotext, this affirmation brings to the fore three crucial declarations. First, the love of God for humanity is immeasurable, for there are no anthropomorphic analogues by which to plumb its depths. Even though someone might dare to die on behalf of a righteous person (Rom 5:7), Christ died for "the ungodly" (Rom 5:6), for "sinners" (Rom 5:8), for "enemies" of God (Rom 5:10). Second, Paul's audience can be certain that their suffering (cf. Rom 5:1–5) has significance because the suffering of Christ has proven to be so meaningful. Through his death "we have been justified," "saved from the wrath of God," "reconciled to God" (Rom 5:9–11). In the midst of our impotence, Christ took on the measure of our powerlessness and died in our place; as a result of his death, we share in his life, and we find that our own suffering has significance.

Third, in a perhaps unexpected turn of phrase (Rom 5:8), we are told that *God* demonstrates his love by means of what *Christ* did. We might have anticipated that God's love would be manifest best in God's own deed. This way of putting things certifies that "Christ's death does not merely express his own sentiment, . . . but God's; or to put it another way, God's stance toward the world is quintessentially demonstrated in the action of Christ."[20] In the end we find in Pauline discourse the unrelenting affirmation of the oneness of purpose and activity of God and God's Son in the cross.

Of course, the theocentricity of Paul's thought does not completely overshadow his understanding of the need for atonement from the human side of the equation. Quite the contrary, it is meant to introduce the sharp contrast Paul sees between God and humanity—that is, between the faithfulness of God and human unfaithfulness (e.g., cf. Rom 1:17–18). Paul's portrait of humanity "before Christ" is that of

---

[20]Cousar, *Theology of the Cross*, 45.

persons, collectively and individually, ensnared in sin, enslaved to powers from which they are impotent to escape.

Paul's anthropology comes into special focus in Rom 1:18–32. Here sin (in the broad sense; the language Paul uses in 1:18 is "ungodliness" and "unrighteousness") is identified not with individual acts of wickedness but with a general disposition to refuse to honor God as God and to render him thanks, to substitute things created for the Creator. To sin, then, is to turn away from authentic human existence by turning away from God.

Four aspects of Paul's reflections in this passage are of particular significance here. First, Paul is not giving the autobiography of individual persons; he is not bent on outlining how each person in his or her own experience comes to be implicated in sin. Instead, his is a universalistic presentation, a diagnosis of the condition of the human family taken as a whole (cf. Rom 3:9). Second, the acts of wickedness that Paul goes on to enumerate by way of illustration are not themselves the problem. Lust, gossip, envy, deceit, same-sex relations, rebelliousness toward parents, and the rest—these are *expressions* of sin. Third, within the fabric of Paul's argument, these activities are themselves expressions of the wrath of God. They evidence the moral integrity of a God who takes sin seriously. It is this, God's moral character, that Paul is defending here, and he does so by showing the progression from (1) the human refusal to honor God with its consequent denial of the human vocation to live in relation to God; to (2) God's giving humanity over to its own desires, giving humanity, as it were, the life it sought apart from God; and from this to (3) human acts of wickedness—which, then, do not arouse the wrath of God but are themselves already the consequences of its active presence.

Finally, it is remarkable that for Paul sin marks a rupture in the divine-human relationship but also manifests itself in human relations and in relations between humanity and the material creation. Sin, in this broad sense, then, can never be understood as something private or individualistic, for it always manifests itself in relation to others and to the cosmos (see Rom 1:26–32). Clearly, then, the soteriological effects of Jesus' death must be understood in relational, communal, and cosmological terms.

What is more, Paul recognizes that ungodliness and unrighteousness have as their object their own self-legitimation: humanity embraces a lie (Rom 1:25) and receives a corrupt mind (Rom 1:28), with the consequence that it defines its unjust ways as just. Consequently, it is small wonder that Paul's preaching of, and identification with, the cross would excite opposition and misunderstanding. A humanity that has turned against itself as it turned against God will not easily sanction so revolutionary a reordering of the world as would be required by this accentuation of the crucified Christ. This would call for an apparently topsy-turvy way of understanding what it means to be human, for an inversion of the social system. Power rooted in powerlessness? This emphasizes the profound role the word of the cross would have in Paul's conception and experience of the Christian life, but also the severity and magnitude of the predicament to which God's saving activity would have to address itself.

A Plurality of Metaphors

In explicating the significance of Jesus' crucifixion, Paul seems never to tire of adding new images to his interpretive vocabulary. Although the crucified Christ lies at the center of his theology, this central truth is manifestly capable of multiple interpretations. In fact, Paul seems capable of tailoring his representation of the significance of the death of Jesus to the needs of his audience in particular, contextualized circumstances.[21] Of the several dozen metaphors Paul employs to lay bare the benefits of the death of Christ, only a handful can be mentioned here. These are conveniently aggregated in two Pauline texts—2 Cor 5:14–6:2 and Gal 3:10–14.

An examination of the presentation of the effects of Jesus' death in 2 Cor 5:14–6:2 underscores the degree to which the many categories by which Paul drew out the significance of the cross overlap one another. Even though *reconciliation* stands at the center of this passage (2 Cor 5:18, 19, 20), other categories are in the foreground: *vicarious substitution* ("for us," 2 Cor 5:14, 15), *representation* (2 Cor 5:14, 21) or *interchange*,[22] *sacrifice* (2 Cor 5:21),[23] *justification* (implicitly, 2 Cor 5:19, 21), *forgiveness* (2 Cor 5:19), and *new creation* (2 Cor 5:16–17). Moreover, the cross and the resurrection of Christ appear in tandem as salvific events (2 Cor 5:15).

"Reconciliation" as a term is not found very often in the Pauline corpus. Apart from this passage, it appears in Rom 5:10–11 referring to the reconciliation of humanity to God; in Col 1:20 referring to the reconciliation of the cosmos to God; and in (the probably post-Pauline) Eph 2:16 referring to the reconciliation of both Jew and Gentile to God and one another. Whether Ephesians is judged to be Pauline or not, its

---

[21] See Driver, *Understanding the Atonement*; Leonardo Boff, *Passion of Christ, Passion of the World: The Facts, Their Interpretation, and Their Meaning Yesterday and Today* (Maryknoll, N.Y.: Orbis, 1987) 78–84; Cousar, *Theology of the Cross*, 82–87.

[22] Cf. Morna D. Hooker, "Interchange and Atonement," *BJRL* 60 (1978) 462–81; and idem, "Interchange in Christ," *JTS* 22 (1974) 349–61.

[23] Cf. James D. G. Dunn, "Paul's Understanding of the Death of Jesus as Sacrifice," in *Sacrifice and Redemption: Durham Essays in Theology*, ed. S. W. Sykes (Cambridge: Cambridge University, 1991) 35–56.

message here is clearly Pauline, for this notion of "restored relationship" in Paul consistently embraces the dynamic presence of love, active not only to restore the divine-human relationship but also to call for and to enable persons to exhibit toward one another this same restoration. Moreover, especially in 2 Corinthians and Colossians, the work of reconciliation is extended to the entire creation.

In 2 Cor 5 Paul's choice of terminology and logic of argumentation is context-specific, for here Paul needs not only to counter the triumphalistic boasting of his opponents at Corinth but also to overcome the disharmony between himself and his "children" at Corinth. By rooting the message of reconciliation fundamentally in the sacrificial death of Jesus and asserting that reconciliation entails living no longer for oneself but for Christ (and thus for others), he addresses his first aim. His impassioned appeal to the Corinthians to be reconciled to God (2 Cor 5:20; 6:1–2), followed by an affirmation of his own openhandedness to the Corinthians (2 Cor 6:11–13; 7:2), deals with the second.

Similarly, Gal 3:10–14 consists of a conglomeration of images or theological categories by which Paul expounds the salvific character of the cross of Christ. The larger unit, Gal 3:1–14, contends that the Galatians' experience of receiving the Spirit by faith signified the fulfillment of God's promise to bless the Gentiles through Abraham and that this fulfillment was made possible through the death of Christ. The benefits of the death of Christ are presented in Gal 3:10–14 through an amalgamation of images: Christ as the *representative* of Israel in whose death the *covenant* reaches its climax;[24] *justification* (Gal 3:11); *redemption* (Gal 3:13), evoking exodus and exilic themes (cf. the corollary of *adoption* in Gal 3:26–29); *substitution* ("for us," Gal 3:13); *sacrifice* (implicitly, Gal 3:13); the *promise of the Spirit* (Gal 3:14); and the *triumph over the powers*.

In these representative passages, we have specimens of Paul's ongoing reflection on Israel, particularly his inclusion of believing Gentiles in the "Israel of God" (Gal 6:10). For Paul, believers share in the benefits of the new creation and thus of their identity as the people of God because of their inclusion in the salvific work of Christ. As Paul acknowledges: "I have been crucified with Christ. It is no longer I who live, but Christ who lives in me" (Gal 2:19b–20a). Even if the eschatological role of Israel in Pauline thought is not thus settled, it is nonetheless apparent that the death of Christ marks the new aeon in which Gentiles may be embraced, in Christ, as children of Abraham.

Many other interpretive categories or images might be mentioned from the Pauline letters, for he makes use of a rich variety of metaphors to comprehend the cross and encourage both understanding and re-

---

[24]Cf. Wright, *Climax of the Covenant*, 137–56.

sponse among his varied audiences. This multiplicity raises a caution against moving too quickly to posit for Paul a single (or one central) theory of the atonement or interpretation of Jesus' passion.

The Cross and Apocalyptic

Reflection on these two representative texts, 2 Cor 5:14–6:2 and Gal 3:10–14, raises another issue of importance in Paul's theology of the cross—namely, Paul's apocalyptic horizon. The cross has cosmic repercussions. This is the importance of such language as "new creation" in 2 Cor 5:17 and Gal 6:15, for these texts must be understood not, as in some modern translations, as individual-focused (e.g., NIV, NAS) but as signifying the role of Jesus' death in the termination of the old epoch and the presentation of the new (e.g., NRSV, NCV). Galatians 3:10–14 analogously points to the death of Jesus as the defeat of the powers—a motif that emerges also in Eph 2:14–15. In this deutero-Pauline writing, the law appears as a barrier separating Jew and Gentile, and the death of Christ abolishes this "dividing wall." In Galatians, however, the law is characterized more as a force, like the elemental spirits of this world, holding the Jewish people captive (Gal 4:1, 3). In a context-specific way, then, Paul insists that the death of Christ has triumphed not by denying the law but by demonstrating its validity and executing the blessing of the covenant.

Elsewhere in Paul we continue to read that the death of Christ marks the end of the rule of the apocalyptic powers (e.g., Col 2:15) and deliverance "from the present evil age" (Gal 1:4).[25] In Colossians, this is the result not of the annihilation of the powers but of their restoration to their purpose in creation; stripped of the garments of their dominion (Col 2:15), they have been reconciled by the instrumentality of Jesus' death on the cross (1:20). Moreover, Dale Allison has detected in the Pauline corpus evidence of an early interpretation of Jesus' sufferings as the beginning of the messianic woes by which the eschaton is introduced (cf., e.g., 1 Cor 10:11; 2 Cor 5:17; Col 1:24).[26] The intrusion of the new world into contemporary life has for Paul far-reaching consequences for those who would follow the crucified Christ and embody in their lives together the new creation revealed in the cross. Old ways of relating to one another (e.g., boasting in a continuous game of one-upmanship in the service of status seeking) and of drawing lines between Jew and Gentile, slave and free, male and female, are shown to be just that—old, out of date, and thus condemned (cf., e.g., Gal 3:26–29; Philemon).

---

[25] See J. Christiaan Beker, *Paul the Apostle: The Triumph of God in Life and Thought* (Edinburgh: T. & T. Clark, 1980) 189–92.

[26] Allison, *End of the Ages*, 62–69; cf. John S. Pobee, *Persecution and Martyrdom in the Theology of Paul* (JSNTSup 6; Sheffield: JSOT, 1985).

The Scandal of the Cross

Paul summarizes his proclamation of the cross as the central tenet of Christian faith: "For Jews demand signs and Greeks desire wisdom, but we proclaim Christ crucified—a stumbling block to Jews and foolishness to Gentiles" (1 Cor 1:22–23). The reasons for opposition to the "word of the cross" are many but revolve especially around the shameful and heinous connotations attached to this form of execution. As John Pobee remarks, "The crucifixion of Jesus ruled him out of court for any serious consideration as a man of God and the turning point of history."[27] It is all the more remarkable, then, that Paul locates the cross as the centerpiece of his kerygma. We have observed a variety of strategies adopted by Paul to grapple with the scandal of the cross. First and foremost, he positions the cross of Christ deeply in the heart of God's purpose. Jesus' execution came through his deep-seated commitment to God's will, his obedience to God (e.g., Phil 2:6–11). He died "according to the Scriptures" (e.g., 1 Cor 15:3), as an outworking of the divine plan (e.g., Rom 8:32). Closely related to this important theme is Paul's unyielding affirmation that in the cross we see the character of God; the crucifixion of Jesus is the gauge of God's immeasurable love just as it is the ultimate object lesson for God's unorthodox notion of the exercise of power. In the cross, God defines power and wisdom in ways otherwise regarded as weak and foolish. Further, Paul imbues the cross with more specifically soteriological meaning. Jesus' death was an outworking of God's redemptive design.

How does Paul understand the redemptive role of Jesus' death? He borrows metaphors from within the history of the covenant of God with Israel. Thus, Paul does not think of Christ as having been punished by execution on the cross to satisfy the justice of God.[28] The cross of Christ can be understood as substitutionary, but within the matrix of the OT conception of sacrifice. The rationale for the sacrificial system in Israel is not worked out fully in the OT; nevertheless, James Dunn has argued that the notion of "identification" or "representation" is basic. That is, the sin offering in some way came to represent the sinners in their sin. Thus, by laying hands on the beast's head in the ritual of sacrifice, sinners identified themselves with the beast, indicating that the beast now represented the sinner *in his or her sin* (i.e., qua sinner). As a consequence, the sinner's sin was identified with the beast, and its life became forfeit—"just as Christ, taking the initiative from the other side,

---

[27] Pobee, *Persecution and Martyrdom*, 47. See further ch. 9 below.
[28] See further Travis, "Christ as Bearer of Divine Judgment."

identified himself with [human beings] in their fallenness (Rom. 8:3), and was made sin (2 Cor. 5:21)."[29]

This logic introduces Christ's dual role in his death—his substitution *for humanity* before God and in the face of God's justice but also his substitution *for God* in the face of human sin. The language of representation to assist our understanding of substitution is not designed to deny the sense of Christ's having achieved something objective in his death. Indeed, according to Paul, Christ gave himself up for us so that we might live in him (cf. 1 Thess 5:9–10; Rom 8:3–4; 14:9; 2 Cor 5:15, 21). As significant as the theme of participation in Christ's death (and resurrection) is for Paul (cf., e.g., Phil 3:10), the possibility of such participation is grounded in his first dying "for us."

The death of Jesus has meaning for Paul beyond what we have discussed heretofore, however. As a direct corollary to the theological, christological, and soteriological significance of Jesus' death on a cross, Paul goes on to posit the cross as a central revelation of the nature of Christian existence.

THE DEATH OF CHRIST AND THE LIFE OF GOD'S PEOPLE

The Death of Christ and the Suffering of the Apostle

According to the Lukan narrative, Paul's divine vocation as an apostle to the Gentiles was intimately tied to opposition and rejection. Regarding Paul, the Lord says to Ananias, "I myself will show him how much he must suffer for the sake of my name" (Acts 9:16). Luke goes on to portray Paul as the object of numerous incidents of opposition and persecution, and this parallels closely Paul's revelations of his experience as an apostle and servant of Christ. He outlines his ordeals in a series of catalogs—Rom 8:35; 1 Cor 4:9–13; 2 Cor 4:8–9; 6:4–5; 11:23–29; 12:10—as well as in numerous autobiographical statements: "I die everyday!" (1 Cor 15:31); "For while we live, we are always being given up to death for Jesus' sake" (2 Cor 4:11); "I make up in my flesh what is lacking in the suffering of Christ" (Col 1:24). Even his decision to work with his hands, as a tentmaker, resulted in his further acquaintance with suffering (1 Cor 4:12).[30] Apostles, accordingly, are likened to those condemned to death in the amphitheater or led to death in the Roman victory procession (1 Cor 4:9; 2 Cor 1:9; 2:14; 4:11).

---

[29]Dunn, "Paul's Understanding of the Death of Jesus," 44.

[30]Cf. Ronald F. Hock, *The Social Context of Paul's Ministry: Tentmaking and Apostleship* (Philadelphia: Fortress, 1980) 35. Pobee (*Persecution and Martyrdom*, 1–12) outlines various forms of persecution to which Paul alludes or to which Paul might have been subjected.

Amazingly, Paul seems anything but reticent to mention the hostility he has encountered in the mission. Instead, his suffering provides the arena for the outworking of his theology of the cross. Rather than a source of shame or evidence of his lack of faithfulness before God, his suffering is presented as proof of his apostleship. So closely intertwined are his views of Jesus' death and of his own suffering that he says of those who degrade him because of his suffering that they preach "another Jesus" (2 Cor 11:4). God's purpose is served in his suffering, he insists. In his weakness God's power is manifest, and in his persecution Paul serves as a living exemplar of the faithfulness of Jesus (cf. Phil 3:10–11). After all, Jesus' faithfulness was most evident in his acceptance of the way of the cross, and as we have seen, Paul's discourse foregrounds the cross as the standard of faithfulness prior to the Parousia of Christ.

In other words, most important in Paul's understanding of his own suffering is his capacity to become thus like Christ and so express his essential unity with Christ. In his experiences of hostility and opposition, Paul insists, the effective power of the crucified Messiah is worked out in Paul's ministry. Moreover, as Col 1:24 implies, Paul regards his suffering as a way in which he participates in the messianic woes by which the reign of God is given birth into the world.[31]

The Identity and Practices of God's People

According to Paul, the death and resurrection of Christ mark the beginning of a new epoch, and this fundamentally changes the way one understands life in the present. First, awareness that Christ's death and resurrection have instituted a new epoch allows believers to envision new life in contrast to old ways of living and to embrace the power of God requisite for new life. Moreover, considering the present in light of the past motivates believers to act in gratitude for deliverance from the slavery of sin. Finally, recognition of this new time encourages believers' further recognition that life in the present is determined by the cross. Thus one effect of the cross is the possibility of restored humanity, restored in its relationships to God, to itself, and to all creation. It also means that the definition of existence put forward by sinful humanity has been radically altered, so that those who follow Christ must look to Christ for the expression of restored humanity. "The church whose

---

[31]Cf. esp. Pobee, *Persecution and Martyrdom*, 102–6. On Paul's suffering more generally, see Scott J. Hafemann, "Suffering," *DPL*, 919–21; Karl A. Plank, *Paul and the Irony of Affliction* (SBLSS; Atlanta: Scholars, 1987); John T. Fitzgerald, *Cracks in an Earthen Vessel: An Examination of the Catalogues of Hardships in the Corinthian Correspondence* (SBLDS 99; Atlanta: Scholars, 1988).

theology is shaped by the message of the cross must itself take on a cruciform life if its theology is to carry credibility."[32]

In practice this entails above all that believers take on themselves the form of obedience to God represented in Christ's life, expressed ultimately in his death. This thought lies behind Paul's use of the hymn to Christ in Phil 2:6–11. As we have seen, it also lies behind his defense of his own apostolic ministry, his sense that in his weakness and suffering he is engaged in the imitation of Christ and participates in the suffering of the Messiah. Paul does not regard himself as unique in this regard. Philippians 2 urges practices of humility and selflessness (2:1–5) following the examples of Christ Jesus (2:6–11), Paul (2:17–18), Timothy (2:19–24), and Epaphroditus (2:25–30).

Paul's emphasis on lives of humility and power in weakness is rooted in the cross; as such, it radically crosses the grain of the dominant ethos informing practices in the Roman world. The cross was an instrument of shame; how could it serve positively and paradigmatically for any Roman? The empire, symbolically constructed as one great household, was governed generally by a well-known ethos based on the values of honor and shame and the practices of patronal friendship. (Patronal friendships included, on the one hand, persons who provided goods and services to others and, on the other hand, those who received those goods and services and concomitantly the debt of loyalty and homage to those giving those gifts.) Paul subverts the patronage-based Roman order through his theology of the cross. He does so by not having God assume the role of the patron who has been dishonored and stands in need of mollification. God has been dishonored by a sinful humanity yet refuses to act according to the Roman script. Instead, God gives without placing the recipients of his benefaction in his debt; moreover, he gives not to those already bound to him in a patronal friendship but to his enemies, those who oppose his ways. Rather than respond as a bruised Roman patron, with retribution or withdrawal of friendship, God acts to restore the relationship. He sends his Son, the Messiah, who so completely identifies with God's purpose that his crucifixion can be interpreted as an expression of God's own love. In this way, God repeatedly steps out of the model of patronal friendship propagated in the Roman world, then calls upon humanity to do the same. The cross is thus positioned both as the means of reconciliation and as the exemplar of a way of life lived for others. In this way Paul commends a politics, an ordering of power, a way of living, distinct from, and indeed opposed to, the politics of Rome.

The cross of Christ has as its effect the transformation of humanity in another sense, too. The cross is understood by Paul as a boundary-

---

[32]Cousar, *Theology of the Cross*, 186.

shattering event.[33] Thus, Paul can assert in 1 Corinthians that those who follow the example of Christ in his selfless death will not nurture their status-based divisions within the Christian community but will gain a fuller understanding and appreciation of the body of Christ (1 Cor 11:17–12:31). This, after all, is a manifestation of the new covenant in Christ's blood (1 Cor 11:25). But Paul can also assert that faithful identification with Christ in his salvific work opposes even more fundamental ethnic, social, and sexual boundaries, "for in Christ Jesus you are all children of God through faith" (Gal 3:26 [3:27–29]; cf. Eph 2:11–22). In this way, then, the cross not only enables new life; it also points beyond itself to disclose the norms of that life, and thus it inaugurates the new era wherein the salvific will of God will be realized.

---

[33] See esp. Driver, *Understanding the Atonement*, ch. 13.

SEVEN

THE DEATH OF JESUS IN HEBREWS, 1 PETER, AND REVELATION

Reflection upon the meaning and significance of the death of Jesus is by no means confined to the Gospels and the letters of Paul. We turn in this chapter to three other NT writings in which Jesus' death figures prominently: Hebrews, 1 Peter, and Revelation. In the next chapter we explore several early extracanonical treatments of the theme.

"He has appeared once for all at the end of the Age to remove sin by the sacrifice of himself ":
THE DEATH OF JESUS IN HEBREWS

The death of Jesus is a pervasive concern in Hebrews. The reader encounters sustained theological reflection upon the meaning and significance of Jesus' death, in tandem with urgent moral appeals grounded in this event (so interpreted). This homily, or "message of exhortation" (13:22), appealing for Christian faithfulness[1] deploys an impressive array of images, all drawing out the saving significance of the cross. Certainly the spotlight falls on the remarkable portrayal of Jesus as both perfect sacrificial victim and high priest offering this sacrifice. Accordingly, we focus the discussion on these related themes.

---

[1]Hebrews does contain epistolary features in its concluding section (13:22–25) but otherwise assumes the form of a homily. On the problems of genre, authorship, setting, and dating, see Harold Attridge, *Hebrews* (Hermeneia; Philadelphia: Fortress, 1989) 1–14; Barnabas Lindars, *The Theology of the Letter to the Hebrews* (NTT; Cambridge: Cambridge University, 1991) 4–21.

Jesus' Death as Sacrifice

"Without the shedding of blood, there is no forgiveness" (Heb 9:22): for the writer of Hebrews this bold claim is axiomatic, and he builds upon it a theological argument stressing the sole sufficiency of Christ's sacrificial death as the means of forgiveness and of access to God's presence.

Hebrews relates the death of Jesus to the theme of *covenant*. His is the sacrifice that enables the enacting of a new and superior covenant between God and the people.[2] Jesus is the "mediator" (μεσίτης, *mesitēs*) of a new and improved covenant (8:6; cf. 7:22). Hebrews 9:15–22 draws the language of redemption (ἀπολύτρωσις, *apolytrōsis*, v. 15) into the orbit of expiatory sacrifice ("redemption from transgressions [committed] under the first covenant") in order to show how it is that Jesus became the guarantor[3] (7:22) or mediator (8:6; 9:15; 12:24) of a new covenantal relationship between God and the people. It was not simply as a covenant sacrifice that Jesus died. Rather, precisely because he frees the sinner from the domain of sin (transgression) and thereby enables genuine worship with a purified conscience (9:14; cf. 10:2), he can be said to have inaugurated a new covenant. So it is that the covenant inaugurated through the sacrificial offering of Jesus' life is an *eternal* covenant (13:20), one in which the people are *sanctified* (10:29)—that is, their lives reshaped so as to reflect the divine holiness.

The act of redemption that supplies the foundation for this new covenant is the death of Jesus. In forging a close link between covenant and death, Heb 9:16–18 plays with the dual meaning of διαθήκη (*diathēkē*) as "covenant" and "testament" or "will."[4] A will takes effect only at the death of the one who issued it. In the same way, Jesus mediates a covenant with the people that becomes effective only with his death. (Verses 18–21 show that the same principle governed the enacting of the Mosaic covenant, and v. 22 again ties the theme of covenant making to release from guilt.)

Hebrews, then, presents the death of Jesus as a covenant sacrifice, but a covenant sacrifice of a special kind. By liberating from the destructive grasp of sin and so enabling the faithful to enter into the sphere of the divine holiness, Jesus through his death makes a covenant for eternity.

A more prevalent sacrificial image in Hebrews, therefore, is that of expiatory sacrifice. Jesus dies a representative death on behalf of the

---

[2]Reflecting on the relationship between the themes of covenant and atonement in Hebrews, Lindars suggests (*Theology of Hebrews*, 95) that while the expiatory sacrifice deals with past sins, the covenant sacrifice establishes a permanent new arrangement.

[3]Jesus is guarantor of the covenant in the sense that he gives assurance of the fulfillment of the promises of God (cf. 8:6); cf. also Attridge, *Hebrews*, 208–9.

[4]Cf. Attridge, *Hebrews*, 253–54; Lindars, *Theology of Hebrews*, 95–96.

many, bearing their sins for them (9:28; cf. 2:9). Through this offering of himself, he achieves cleansing or purification for sins (1:3). Invariably, however, the passages that develop Jesus' death as expiatory sacrifice do so by accenting even more sharply his dual role as sacrificial victim and priest (this is implicit already in 1:3). It is therefore appropriate to consider together these two aspects of the portrayal of Jesus in Hebrews.

Jesus the High Priest

As early as 1:3, Jesus' priestly function comes into view: "having made purification [καθαρισμόν, *katharismon*] for sins, he sat down at the right hand of the Majesty on high."[5] At the center of this letter's portrayal of Jesus, however, stands the figure of the high priest. The high priest in Israel's cultus (1) is appointed to office by God (5:4); (2) offers sacrifice for human sins (v. 1); (3) is able, because of his own weakness, to sympathize with those on whose behalf he offers sacrifice (v. 2); and (4) as a sinner himself must offer sacrifice not only for the people's sins but also for his own (v. 3). The high priest's sinfulness means necessarily that the liturgy of expiatory sacrifice must be perpetual. Day after day he must offer sacrifice for his own sins and for those of the people (7:27; 10:11), and year after year he must enter the holy of holies in the Day of Atonement ritual (9:7, 25). Yet that is not the true holy place but only a copy, fashioned by human hands, of the heavenly sanctuary that is the locus of the divine presence (8:5; 9:24; cf. 8:2; 9:11).

Hebrews presents Jesus as high priest, but as a high priest with a difference: (1) Although not born into a family of priests (7:13–14; cf. 8:4), he too is appointed to office by God—as the Messiah, he is eternal priest of the order of Melchizedek (5:5–6, quoting Ps 110:4). (2) As high priest, Jesus offers expiatory sacrifice on behalf of sinners (2:17; 9:11–14, 25–28; cf. 8:3). (3) Moreover, Jesus is able to assume the mediatorial role of the priest, standing in solidarity with the people and showing sympathy for their condition since he shares that condition (2:17–18; 4:14–15). (4) Unlike temple priests, however, Jesus is not a sinner and therefore has no need to offer expiatory sacrifices for his own sins (4:15; 7:26; 9:14). His is a perfect sacrifice, effective for all time, obviating the need for daily and yearly sacrifices of atonement (9:25–28; 10:10, 12–14; cf. 7:27). The ritual of the Day of Atonement, in particular, finds fulfillment in Jesus' entry into the (heavenly) holy place.[6]

---

[5]For the LXX usage of καθαρισμός to refer to cultic purification, see, e.g., Exod 29:36; Lev 15:13; and esp. Exod 30:10 (the Day of Atonement ritual).

[6]Though with considerable reduction in detail; the scapegoat ritual is noteworthy for its absence in Hebrews. Lindars (*Theology of Hebrews*, 92–93) points out that in the Day of Atonement observance the scapegoat did not figure in the rituals of expiatory sacrifice and entry into the holy of holies, which are

It is crucial to see that the death of Jesus is a "once for all" expiatory sacrifice not simply because he is free of sin but above all because, as high priest, he sprinkles the atoning blood—his own—in the authentic, heavenly sanctuary, thus truly giving access to the throne of grace, that is, to the presence of the holy God (4:16; 8:1–2; 9:11–12, 24). The outcome of this sacrificial offering, eternally effective, once for all time and all persons, is therefore true forgiveness (10:18) and a sound conscience (9:14; 10:22; cf. 10:2; 13:18)—neither of which, the author contends, resulted from the temple worship (9:9–10; 10:1–4).[7]

As we have already discovered, the "perfection" of Jesus—a high priest untainted by sin, a sacrificial victim without blemish—is a matter of considerable emphasis in Hebrews.[8] This perfection is not static but dynamic (the author uses the verb τελειόω, teleioō) and is not to be confused with the simple absence of any flaw or defect. Quite the contrary, this "perfection" embraces the human condition with its ambiguity and struggle. It entails testing, learning, and showing fidelity through adversity. God "perfects" Jesus through his experience of suffering (2:10); he "learned obedience" through that suffering and so was "made perfect" (5:8–9) with the eternal perfection of the Son of God (7:28). Only such perfection can enter the authentic sanctuary in the heavenly realm, but only because it is grounded in the human condition is it able to draw also the believer into that realm. The Christian, too, is "made perfect" in a faithfulness that is the outcome of the divine

---

the focus of Jesus' priestly activity in Hebrews. John Dunnill likewise observes (Covenant and Sacrifice in the Letter to the Hebrews [SNTSMS 75; Cambridge: Cambridge University, 1992] 140, 233) that interest centers on the priest's entry into the holy of holies rather than on the high priest's manipulation of the blood or on the "disjunctive symbol" of the scapegoat. The argument, at bottom, concerns access to the sphere of the holy, not separation from it. Functioning as high priest at his exaltation, Jesus brings the atoning blood of his own sacrificed life into the heavenly sanctuary, thus opening up access to the divine presence.

[7] The underlying argument seems to be that since the sacrificial cultus of the temple does not issue in a transformed life free of corruption from sin, participation in that worship, instead of delivering from sin ("cleansing the conscience"), serves only to remind the worshipper of his or her sinfulness (esp. 10:2–3). Clearly, for the argument of Hebrews to work, the atoning sacrifice offered by Jesus must be seen to reorder life so that it truly is "sanctified." Marie E. Isaacs (Sacred Space: An Approach to the Theology of the Epistle to the Hebrews [JSNTSup 73; Sheffield: JSOT, 1992] 98–99) stresses that the efficacy of Christ's blood stems from its capacity to cleanse the interior of a person (i.e., a guilty conscience).

[8] See the excursus on language of "perfection" in Attridge, Hebrews, 83–87. David Peterson (Hebrews and Perfection: An Examination of the Concept of Perfection in the "Epistle to the Hebrews" [SNTSMS 47; Cambridge: Cambridge University, 1982] 66–73) opposes one-sided moral and cultic interpretations of "perfection," arguing instead for a "vocational" meaning: suffering is the process through which Jesus realizes and fulfills his vocation as Son of God.

mercy (10:1, 14; 11:40; 12:23; cf. 7:19). So Jesus becomes in Hebrews a "pioneer" who charts the course of salvation that others will follow.

Other Images

Jesus as Pioneer of Salvation

Jesus is the ἀρχηγός, *archēgos*, the pioneer of salvation (2:10) and of faith(fulness) (12:2) whose path the Christian is to follow.[9] He is also the πρόδρομος, *prodromos*, the one who "runs ahead" into the holy place and opens up access to the divine presence (6:20; cf. 10:19–22). These images point to the uniqueness of Jesus' role in the saving activity of God: he is the source of salvation, he is the one who gains access to the heavenly sanctuary. At the same time, though, these terms forge a close link between the one who through his faithfulness blazes the trail and those who in trust and fidelity follow him.

Jesus Effects the Destruction of Forces That Impose Death

Hebrews also sets the death of Jesus over against the life-destroying activity of the forces of evil (2:14–15). By wielding the menacing power of death, the devil has held humanity in slavery to fear—the fear of death. But since the death of Jesus nullifies the death-dealing power of the devil, it liberates the faithful from their bondage to fear and therefore to death. That is, Jesus' death strikes a blow for life! The rich interpretive potential of this image remains unexploited in Hebrews, largely because of the author's preoccupation with the cultic models of expiatory sacrifice and high-priestly service. Its presence in 2:14–15, however, reassures the reader that God wills life for the people—and also serves to remind the interpreter that the challenge of making sense of, and responding to, the event of Jesus' death has always elicited a variety of models and images.

The Suffering of Jesus

The Christology of Hebrews is simultaneously "high" and "low":[10] Jesus is the eternal Son of God, who participates in the glory and being of God (1:2–3); yet the one who is installed in the position of power at God's right hand (1:3, 13; 8:1; 10:12; 12:2; quoting Ps 110:1) was "for a little while lower than the angels" (2:7, 9; citing Ps 8:5)—that is, he fully entered the human condition, with its challenges, its sufferings, and its finitude. The author sharply accents the humanity of Jesus, for, as we

---

[9]Jesus is called ἀρχηγός also in Acts 3:15; 5:31.
[10]See the discussion in Attridge, *Hebrews*, 25–26.

have seen, only as one who stands in solidarity with humankind can he exercise his priestly function. And at the heart of that experience of the human condition lies the suffering of Jesus. Vivid imagery characterizes that suffering for the reader of Hebrews. Jesus' suffering imposed on him a test of his faithfulness to God (2:18; cf. 4:15). Face-to-face with death, he prayed "with loud cries and tears," and his prayers were heard (5:7).[11] He endured the shameful death of a cross (12:2), suffering abuse "outside the city gate" (13:12–13). Such fidelity, displayed through the severest of sufferings, provides readers of Hebrews a model to be emulated in their own experience of adversity (cf. 10:32–36; 13:13).[12]

Implications for Christian Living: The Death of Jesus and the Parenetic Appeals of Hebrews

As an exemplar of faithfulness to God through the stringent test of persecution, Jesus' death undergirds the author's exhortation to Christian faithfulness. Inspired by his example of perseverance, Christians may find new determination for their own struggle to achieve a life of integrity, no longer dominated by sin (12:1–2). But of course, the death of Jesus understood as atoning sacrifice for sins does not need to be replicated. For the parenetic sections of Hebrews primarily call for a transformed life that honors the divine act of grace expressed in the cross.

The author of Hebrews is no advocate of cheap grace. To claim the divine gift of forgiveness communicated through the sacrificial offering of Jesus' life and then to persist in rebellion or sin means to crucify Jesus contemptuously all over again (6:4–6). Having spurned the gift of forgiveness, one cannot hope to find refuge in another offering for sins, another opportunity to repent. All that remains is the prospect of judgment (10:26–31). Through such stern warnings, Hebrews aims to

---

[11] This verse (Heb 5:7) is riddled with interpretive difficulties. Among the significant questions: (1) Does the author allude here to the Gethsemane scene? (2) If so, is the content of Jesus' prayer that he be delivered from death? (3) If Jesus prayed to the one (God) who could save him from death, then what does it mean that he was "heard because of [ἀπό, apo] his reverence" (since he was not "saved from death")? Whether or not one agrees with Attridge's claim that the language of the verse is only "vaguely reminiscent" of the Gospel accounts of Gethsemane (*Hebrews*, 148), one should not press the details of that scene into Hebrews. The author presents Jesus as praying to God, who has the power to save him from the realm of death, and as being heard—and the divine response takes the form of resurrection and exaltation to God's right hand. See further Attridge, *Hebrews*, 148–52.

[12] The spatial metaphor in Heb 13:11–14 inverts the earlier image of "drawing near to the throne of grace" (4:16): "Let us then go to him outside the camp, bearing his [i.e., the same] reproach" (13:13); cf. Dunnill, *Covenant and Sacrifice*, 148; Attridge, *Hebrews*, 398–99.

impress upon the reader how much is at stake in the character of Christian living. One honors the Son of God, and so honors God, through a life of fidelity and enduring commitment.

For all its emphasis on the past accomplishment of atonement, therefore, Hebrews situates the reader squarely in the creative tension and uncertainty of the eschatological "not yet," when faith is defined above all else by its capacity to hope.[13] Faith in such a context means an enduring fidelity, a holding firm to one's commitment to God, even against all the empirical evidence (ch. 11). So the picture of Jesus behind the inner curtain of the holy place is for the believer not a reason for self-assurance but the basis of hope (6:19) for all who await salvation at Christ's return (9:28).

The argument of Hebrews that God has called the people into a new covenantal relationship that transcends the first covenant and renders it obsolete (8:8–13) hinges on the moral transformation of the Christian's life, even though that is always also a matter of eschatological hope. The sacrifice offered by the high priest of Melchizedek's order is effectual because through it knowledge of the divine will and the capacity to obey it are now, as Jeremiah promised (31:31–34), written on the human heart. The death of Jesus in Hebrews is, then, inextricably tied to the moral life of the Christian community. This connection is an even more central concern of 1 Peter.

"Christ also suffered for you, leaving you an example": THE DEATH OF JESUS IN 1 PETER

First Peter underscores the manner of Jesus' dying. To be sure, the method of his execution receives scant attention, apart from a single reference to a "tree" (ξύλον, *xylon*) as the mode of Jesus' death or, rather, as the instrument of his sacrificial offering for "our sins" (2:24). What is of interest is the way in which Jesus approached and experienced death, the integrity with which he endured undeserved "suffering." First Peter presents Jesus as the paradigm guiding the Christian community's response to its own experience of suffering in the world. The author's claim to have witnessed Jesus' suffering (5:1) undergirds the moral appeal of the letter.[14]

---

[13]As Dunnill observes, the imagery of drawing near to a personal God "places the whole community permanently in the liminal zone," cast adrift from all human sources of security (*Covenant and Sacrifice*, 242). Finally, the author of Hebrews is interested not in cultic affairs but in "eschatological peril and hope" (237).

[14]The author claims to be the apostle Peter (1:1). For discussion of the

The Purpose of God and the Suffering of Jesus

The letter's opening already ties the fortunes—and conduct—of the recipients (Christians in Asia Minor addressed metaphorically as "exiles of the Dispersion")[15] to the death of Jesus. By divine providence, they have been chosen to receive benefit from the "sprinkling of Jesus Christ's blood" and summoned to obedient lives in response (1:2). The divine purpose, in fact, embraces both the suffering of Jesus and that of his followers. Long ago the prophets had announced the suffering that awaited Christ (1:11). In accordance with scriptural testimony, he was rejected but became, for the benefit of those who believe, the chief cornerstone of a new sanctuary, a new holy people (2:4–10, drawing upon Ps 118:22; Isa 8:14).

Yet God's sovereign purpose is to be seen not in Christ's suffering alone but also and especially in his subsequent entrance into glory. Raised to life "in the spirit," he brought his life-giving message even to the domain of the dead (3:19–21; 4:6) and now is installed in the seat of power (3:18–22).[16] Since Jesus' ordeal of suffering and death derives meaning, within God's providential ordering of human history, as a preparation for his ultimate glory, the Christian community facing adversity in a hostile environment is reassured that for it too the last word will be not suffering and shame but honor and life.

Jesus' Death as Exemplary Suffering

Clearly, the preoccupation with Christ's suffering in 1 Peter is no accident, for it reflects the difficult circumstance of the communities addressed by the letter.[17] Because they bear the stigma of the name "Christian," they are victimized by various forms of abuse within their social world. So it is above all this dimension of Jesus' death that commands interest.

---

problem of authorship, see John H. Elliott, *A Home for the Homeless: A Sociological Exegesis of 1 Peter, Its Situation and Strategy* (Philadelphia: Fortress, 1981) 270–80; Leonhard Goppelt, *A Commentary on 1 Peter*, ed. Ferdinand Hahn, trans. John E. Alsup (Grand Rapids: Eerdmans, 1993) 7–15, 48–53.

[15] For discussion of the letter's audience and social setting, see Goppelt, *Commentary on 1 Peter*, 3–7, 36–45; Elliott, *Home for the Homeless*, esp. 59–100; and the exchange between Elliott ("1 Peter, Its Situation and Strategy: A Discussion with David Balch" [61–78]) and David Balch ("Hellenization/Acculturation in 1 Peter" [79–101]) in *Perspectives on First Peter*, ed. Charles H. Talbert (SSS 9; Macon, Ga.: Mercer University, 1986) 61–101.

[16] Though the full revelation of Christ's glory and the Christian's participation in it will come only with the Parousia (1:7; 4:13).

[17] See Earl Richard, "The Functional Christology of 1 Peter," in Talbert, *Perspectives on First Peter*, 121–39 (133).

The formulation in 3:18 is revealing: "For Christ too suffered for sins once for all, the just for the unjust, to bring you to God." The death of Jesus deals effectively with human sin, opening up access to the holy God, yet in a typically Petrine turn of phrase, Jesus is said to have "suffered" (ἔπαθεν, *epathen*) for sin, not "died" (ἀπέθανεν, *apethanen*),[18] and to have suffered as a just man—that is, as a victim of injustice. This intense interest in the undeserved suffering endured by Jesus (2:21–23; 3:18; 4:1) speaks directly to the situation of the letter's first readers. Like Christ, they too may suffer even though they are innocent of wrongdoing (2:19–21; 3:14, 17; 4:1, 12–19; 5:10). Indeed, to endure abuse for doing what is right is a badge not of shame but of honor.[19]

In such a setting, then, 1 Peter presents Jesus as a model of innocent suffering. He refused to retaliate against his adversaries; the treachery and deceit of his enemies served only to place in bold relief his own unfailing integrity and truthfulness (2:21–23). He is a model of faithful obedience and trust in God to be emulated by the Christian. Appropriately, the author colors this portrait with the help of the scriptural image of the Suffering Servant of Isa 52:13–53:12—a paradigm of undeserved suffering through which a righteous man confers benefit upon the unrighteous (several lines from this passage are woven into the fabric of the argument in 2:22–24).[20] Viewed through the lens supplied by this passage from Isaiah, the undeserved suffering of Jesus is seen to be redemptive, offering healing and delivering from the sphere of sin to a life of righteousness.

Christ's redemptive suffering and the Christian community's experience of adversity in the world are in 1 Peter bound indissolubly together. The Christian life, for this author, is cruciform in shape and character. To live as a "Christian" in a world that mocks that affiliation means to share in the suffering undergone by Christ (4:13), and to do so after his example—that is, remaining true to one's commitments, refusing to return evil for evil (2:18–23).[21]

---

[18]Although some manuscripts betray a scribal tendency to conform the text to the Pauline idiom by replacing ἔπαθεν with ἀπέθανεν (a phenomenon occurring also in 2:21); see further Goppelt, *Commentary on 1 Peter*, 202.

[19]On the interpretation given by the author of 1 Peter to the suffering of his readers, see Elliott, *Home for the Homeless*, esp. 142–43; Charles H. Talbert, *Learning through Suffering: The Educational Value of Suffering in the New Testament and in Its Milieu* (ZSNT; Collegeville, Minn.: Liturgical, 1991) 42–57.

[20]As Paul J. Achtemeier observes, however ("Suffering Servant and Suffering Christ in 1 Peter," in *The Future of Christology: Essays in Honor of Leander E. Keck*, ed. Abraham J. Malherbe and Wayne A. Meeks [Minneapolis: Fortress, 1993] 176–88), the explicit development in 1 Pet 2:21–25 of the connection between the suffering of Christ and the Servant of Isa 52:13–53:12 is highly unusual in the NT (see esp. pp. 177, 187). For detailed analysis of the role played by this passage in the Gospel passion narratives, see ch. 11 below.

[21]This passage explicitly addresses household slaves, but the tenor of the

Other Images

While the exemplary character of Jesus' suffering takes center stage in 1 Peter, the author also interprets the death of Jesus through the images of *ransom* and *sacrifice*.[22] Economic metaphor converges with language drawn from the arena of worship in 1:18–19. The death of Christ has "ransomed" the letter's hearers (ἐλυτρώθητε, *elytrōthēte*) from the spiritual bondage of their pagan past, and the price of that redemption was not a precious metal but the blood of Christ, like that of a sacrificial lamb, free of blemish or defect. Out of this act of redemption a new people of God is summoned into existence, a people who have known God's mercy (2:9–10, with clear echoes of Hos 1:6, 9).

Sacrificial metaphors for the death of Jesus appear with some regularity in the letter, although the author never elaborates upon them (1:2; 2:21, 24; 3:18). Jesus is the decisive[23] sacrificial offering—representing the sinner, the just for the unjust—and through the sprinkling of his blood he procures freedom from sin and access to the holy God. First Peter shares this understanding of Jesus' death as sacrifice with the letters of Paul, Hebrews, and many other early Christian writings but does not subject it to sustained reflection. First Peter focuses sharply, instead, upon the exemplary suffering of Jesus.

"Worthy is the lamb that was slaughtered":
THE DEATH OF JESUS IN THE BOOK OF REVELATION

Within the framework of a pastoral letter and using the vehicle of a series of visions cast in apocalyptic idiom, the author of Revelation conveys his prophetic message to the Christian communities of Asia (western Asia Minor) toward the end of the first century C.E.[24] Writing

---

letter's moral appeals suggests that all Christians, not just slaves, should emulate Christ's example of endurance. Cf. further Achtemeier, "Suffering Servant," 177. In the social world known to this author, every Christian's life is cruciform.

[22] For theological reflection on the uses to which the NT puts these images, see ch. 13 below. In considering the nature of the *imitatio* theme in 1 Peter, Goppelt (*Commentary on 1 Peter*, 206) develops the relationship in the letter between Jesus' redemptive suffering ὑπέρ (*hyper*, "for" or "on behalf of") the Christian and the exemplary character of that suffering: Christ leads the Christian into proper conduct through his suffering "for us," thereby leading the Christian, too, into suffering.

[23] See 1 Pet 3:18: "once for all" (ἅπαξ, *hapax*)—a prominent theme in Hebrews, as we have already seen.

[24] On issues of authorship and dating, see Adela Yarbro Collins, *Crisis and*

from exile in the shadow of imperial Rome, and all too aware of its claims to religious and political supremacy, John issues a bold appeal for uncompromising loyalty to the one true God. To those who persevere in faithfulness—even at the cost of their lives—he holds out the promise of a share in the victory of God, a place in the eternal realm of God. In the prophet's vision of the critical times in which he lived, the death of Jesus appears as the pivotal event on which the whole of human history turns.

Death, Resurrection, and Parousia

For John the seer, Jesus' death is not a closure event but one moment in a life that is unending: "I am . . . the one who lives and was dead; and behold, I am alive forever" (1:17). The message to the church in Smyrna echoes this designation of Jesus, "the first and the last, who was dead and came to life" (2:8). The letter opening also characterizes Jesus as the "first born from the dead" (1:5). So John can speak of Jesus' death and his resurrection life in the same breath. He "was" and "is"—but he is also "coming." Especially at the close of Revelation, and in the seven messages to the churches in Asia, the author highlights the imminent return of Jesus (2:16, 25; 3:11; 22:7, 12, 20; cf. also 1:7).[25]

Already the fact that death could not keep Jesus in its grip suggests a basis of hope for Christians called to bear faithful witness to their religious commitment in precarious times. To those who remain faithful even to the point of death, John holds out the promise of a "crown of life" (2:10). One who "conquers" through faithful witness to God will be untouched by the second, i.e., eternal, death (2:11). In the experience of the Christian as in Jesus' own life, the themes of death, witness, and conquest are closely intertwined.

Jesus' Death as Faithful Witness

The first description of Jesus in Revelation affirms (1:5) that Jesus is "first born from the dead" precisely as "the faithful witness" (ὁ μάρτυς ὁ πιστός, *ho martys ho pistos*), an epithet echoed in the message to Laodicea (3:14). The example of Antipas (2:13) suggests that one who faithfully gives testimony to the truth pays with his life, a pattern repeated in the visionary account of the two witnesses in ch. 11 (see vv. 7–10). Yet again here, the last word is vindication and life (11:11–12).

Catharsis: The Power of the Apocalypse (Philadelphia: Westminster, 1984) 25–83; Leonard Thompson, *The Book of Revelation: Apocalypse and Empire* (Oxford: Oxford University, 1990) 11–24.

[25] See the discussion of this theme in M. Eugene Boring, *Revelation* (IBC; Louisville: John Knox, 1989) 68–74.

Clearly, the author is presenting the death of Jesus in terms reflecting the circumstance of the Christian communities known to him. In a vivid image that highlights the connection between the faithful witness of Jesus and the contemporary situation of the church, John has the bodies of the two slain witnesses lie in the streets of "the great city that is figuratively called Sodom and Egypt, where their Lord, too, was crucified" (11:8).[26] Jesus' faithful testimony resulted in his death, to be sure, but death was not the final word, any more than it will be for Antipas and other Christians who dare to speak the truth at risk of their lives.

Jesus' Death as Victory

Conquest is a central image in the Book of Revelation, one that John uses to subvert conventional notions of war and military triumph. The church at Laodicea receives this word of consolation:

> To the one who conquers [ὁ νικῶν, *ho nikōn*][27] I will grant to sit with me on my throne, just as I conquered and sat down with my Father on his throne. (3:21)

How does Jesus conquer, and how do his followers conquer? Through the apparent defeat of an ignominious death.

This stunning "rebirth of images"[28] relating to political power (θρόνος, *thronos*, "throne") and military victory comes to most forceful expression in ch. 5. The vision of ch. 4 transports John's readers into the throne room of heaven, where they hear the glory and power of the Creator God celebrated in song. But there is a problem. The lengthy scroll in the right hand of the one seated on the throne (God)—the scroll the reading of which will draw history to its appointed goal—is sealed with seven seals, and none can open it (5:1–4). John is reassured that "the Lion of the tribe of Judah, the Root of David, has conquered" and is worthy to open the sealed scroll. These stock messianic metaphors awaken in the reader the expectation that a mighty Davidic ruler will

---

[26]Presumably a cipher for Jerusalem, boldly characterizing the "holy city" as a place of oppression, desolation, and judgment. Jürgen Roloff (*The Revelation of John: A Continental Commentary* [Minneapolis: Fortress, 1993] 133) suggests that the picture of Jerusalem in 11:8 blends with that of Rome and becomes emblematic of the world's hostility to God.

[27]This substantival participle should be placed in the dative case but appears in the nominative, a common grammatical solecism in Revelation. Collins (*Crisis and Catharsis*, 47) interprets these grammatical irregularities as the product of a "Semitizing Greek" that is a deliberate expression of cultural protest on the part of the author.

[28]To borrow the apt expression of Austin M. Farrer, *A Rebirth of Images* (Westminster: Dacre, 1949).

ascend the throne (see Gen 49:8–10; Isa 11:1; *T. Judah* 24.5; 4 Ezra 12:31–32).

What the seer discovers instead is a "Lamb standing, as though slaughtered" (5:6). The heavenly court acclaims the Lamb with a "new song" that credits to his redemptive death his authority to open the scroll (v. 9). He receives the same dominion and honor that are due God (vv. 12–14).[29] To be sure, this is no ordinary lamb. Its limitless strength and discernment, for example, are symbolized in its seven horns and seven eyes (v. 6). Nevertheless, the shift from lion to slaughtered Lamb entails an astonishing transformation of images. Power is being radically redefined before John's eyes. Conquest and sovereign rule belong not to the mighty but to the one who is faithful unto death. The centrality of the image of the Lamb in Revelation assures that the reader never loses sight of this conviction.[30]

Jesus, then, conquers through his death. The cosmic triumph of heaven over the forces of evil is assured by that death (12:11). And this means the triumph of life over the domain of death, for Jesus, as the one who died but lives forever, now holds the keys of death and Hades (1:18; cf. 2:10–11) and will ultimately put death itself to death forever (20:14). Empowered by this vision—which completely redraws the world's political and military maps—John's readers find the courage to seek victory through the same costly commitment to the truth.[31] In the end, they will share in God's sovereign rule over the nations (e.g., 20:4–6).

Jesus' Death as Redemption

The Lamb and those who are loyal to him conquer through their persevering witness to God despite grave personal risk. The visions of Revelation, however, picture two colliding systems of power, allegiance, and worship. Imperial Rome, especially as symbolized through the image of the beast, appears in the guise of a lamb (a "parody" of the Lamb).[32] The beast achieves conquest, dominion, and even worship

---

[29]Note that in the vision of the eschatological, heavenly Jerusalem, both God and the Lamb occupy the throne (22:3)!

[30]See Sophie Laws, *In the Light of the Lamb: Imagery, Parody, and Theology in the Apocalypse of John* (Wilmington, Del.: Michael Glazier, 1988) 24; Boring, *Revelation*, 108–11.

[31]The Christian martyrs who cry out for vindication in 6:9–10 were, like Jesus, "slaughtered" for their testimony. This scene ties the deaths of faithful Christians closely to the death of Jesus. Cf. Laws, *Light of the Lamb*, 57–58.

[32]Like the Lamb, the beast receives a mortal wound but still lives (13:3, 12, 14), conquers (v. 7), is the object of worship (vv. 4, 8), and is given authority over "every tribe and people and language and nation" (v. 7; cf. 5:9; 7:9). Significantly, while the beast has the two horns of a lamb, its voice betrays its true character—and the source of its authority. It sounds like a dragon (v. 11).

through the exercise of coercive power. The Lamb, by contrast, through his death has "purchased" for God a people drawn from every tribe and language and people and nation and has made them "a kingdom and priests"—a holy people worthy of participating in God's rule over the earth (5:9–10).

The root image here is that of redemption; John uses the verb ἠγόρασας (*ēgorasas*, "purchased").[33] The death of Jesus is the means through which a people faithful to God is constituted (a people "purchased by his blood"). John underscores the universal scope of this holy kingdom, for it is built upon the acts of worship and loyal service of people from every nation on the earth. This universal dominion comes into being not through coercive force but through the Lamb's faithful witness unto death.

In another visionary scene linking the "blood of the Lamb" and a multitude drawn "from every nation and from all tribes and peoples and languages," John provides a new image of the meaning of Jesus' redemptive death (7:9–17). The 144,000—to be construed not as a limiting number but as a figure for an innumerable multitude (cf. 7:9)—appear before the throne, wearing white robes, robes made white (symbolizing both victory and purity)[34] by the blood of the Lamb (7:14; cf. 19:11–14). Not their own deaths as faithful witnesses (implied in 7:14) but the death of Jesus gives them victory and sanctifies them. And in yet another transformation of images, the Lamb who reigns from the throne with God becomes "shepherd" to God's people (7:17). Formerly they have known adversity and oppression; now the Lamb-shepherd will guide them in safety to living waters. Their suffering will be but a distant memory.

The death of Jesus, an act of faithful witness from which springs a new people of God, is in John's Apocalypse the pivotal event in human history. In a turbulent world in which right and privilege appear to belong to the mighty, the death of the Lamb testifies to another way. The transcendent power of the sovereign God refuses to coerce expressions of allegiance and worship; vulnerable to violent rejection, it speaks the truth. Ultimately, this is the power that sways the future. In the light of this vision of power, John summons his readers to embrace the risk of uncompromising loyalty to the ways of God. John's stirring prophetic vision of a world reclaimed by the Creator God, liberated from

---

[33] Elisabeth Schüssler Fiorenza (*The Book of Revelation: Justice and Judgment* [Philadelphia: Fortress, 1985] 74) suggests that the commercial transaction in view is the ransom of prisoners of war at the slave market and, further, that the image alludes to the exodus tradition and the redemption from slavery in Egypt. See further ch. 13 below.

[34] See George B. Caird, *The Revelation of St. John the Divine* (BNTC 19; Peabody, Mass.: Hendrickson, 1966) 101.

oppression and injustice, and restored to the joyful worship of God is, in such a world as John's—or ours—a daring act of hope (some might say, of folly). Nevertheless, John writes to inspire Christians, living in a world where Caesar claims dominion and worship, to commit themselves to the cause of the Crucified One, the one who was dead but lives and reigns forever, "King of kings and Lord of lords" (19:16; cf. 1:5; 11:15; 15:3–4).

A REFLECTION

In our study of the interpretation of Jesus' death in Hebrews, 1 Peter, and Revelation, we have confined ourselves to the task of elucidating the perspectives expressed in these documents—each communicating its message in a specific setting to a specific audience confronting particular challenges in the Roman world of the latter part of the first century C.E. We have not pressed the question of contemporary appropriation of these perspectives.[35]

Especially in the case of 1 Peter and Revelation, however, a word of caution is in order. These documents can be—and have been—read as providing a warrant for the passive embrace of victimization in the face of even the most brutal forms of oppression and injustice, and even as an invitation to masochism. To live as a Christian, in this view, means in every circumstance to accept silently the abuse inflicted by others or perhaps even to seek out suffering, the "badge" of one's Christian identity.

Such approaches fail to reckon, however, with the quite specific social milieu of both these writings. When the open, active pursuit of social and political change is not a viable option in society, the virtue of endurance, or perseverance, in the face of oppressive evil is itself a courageous act of resistance. Yet to adopt the same strategy in another day and in a different social reality may mean not fidelity to God but capitulation to evil. We need first to let John (or the author of 1 Peter) speak to his own time and place and to resist the temptation to collapse the horizons of that world and our own. Then we may address the challenge of discerning what forms that persevering faithfulness to God ought properly to assume in our own time and place—and of embodying that commitment in praxis.

---

[35]For more extensive discussion of the contemporary relevance of NT interpretations of Jesus' death, see ch. 13 below.

EIGHT

EXTRACANONICAL PASSION NARRATIVES

Robert E. Van Voorst
Associate Professor of Religion
Lycoming College, Williamsport, Pa.

This chapter will examine narratives of the passion of Jesus[1] found in religious literature outside the NT surviving from the second and third centuries C.E. This is a large collection of literature, many times that of the entire NT, with a rapidly growing body of scholarship.[2] Therefore, we will be able to examine here with some depth only certain crucial texts and a few issues important in recent study.

For our purposes, this literature following (and in its early stages sometimes overlapping) the documents that now form the NT can be divided into four main types: writings of the emerging Great (Catholic) Church,[3] gnostic gospels, Jewish-Christian literature, and Jewish Mishnaic-talmudic traditions. We will offer a brief introduction to how each of these types treats the passion of Jesus, give one sample text important in recent historical study, and examine the issues under study in

---

[1]I assume "passion narratives" to mean accounts of Jesus from his arrest to his burial.

[2]One wag has even suggested that in view of the strong attention being paid to extrabiblical literature in biblical studies, the Society of Biblical Literature should be renamed the "Society of Extrabiblical Literature." See Ray L. Hart, "Religious and Theological Studies in American Higher Education: A Pilot Study," *JAAR* 59 (1991) 715–827 (765 n. 67). To be fair, research into early Christianity needs a full examination of all the evidence, canonical and non-canonical, even though the attention currently given to the latter might seem extreme to some.

[3]In this chapter the term "Great Church" is used to refer to the "orthodox" Christianity that emerged in the second and third centuries as ecclesial identity was shaped over against various heterodox movements.

scholarship related to that text. The discussion itself will give a general historical analysis; readers who wish to delve more fully into the details and nuances are urged to consult the footnotes.

A PASSION NARRATIVE OF THE GREAT CHURCH

In 1886 a French archaeological team excavating the cemetery of an ancient Pachomian monastery about 250 miles south of Cairo found a small book in a monk's grave. Pages 2–10 of this book, which was dated to the seventh to ninth centuries, contain an account of the death and resurrection of Jesus that scholars soon concluded was part of the *Gospel of Peter*, mentioned by early church fathers from the beginning of the third century. Scholarship at first paid close attention to the *Gospel of Peter*, but when the consensus developed that it was a popularizing and docetic adaptation of the canonical Gospels, especially Matthew, disinterest soon enveloped it. In the last few years, scholars have renewed their interest in this book, with some researchers claiming that a source of the passion narrative of the *Gospel of Peter* is a source of the passion narratives of the canonical Gospels.[4]

We will begin by offering a rather literal translation of this document's passion narrative.[5]

> (1.1) But none of the Jews washed their hands, neither Herod nor one of his judges. (2) And because they did not want to wash, Pilate arose. Then Herod the king ordered that the Lord be handed over, saying to them, "Do what I ordered you to do to him."

> (2.3) Joseph was standing there, the friend of Pilate and the Lord; and knowing that they were about to crucify him, he came to Pilate and asked for the body of the Lord for burial. (4) Pilate sent to Herod

---

[4]The literature on the *Gospel of Peter* is large and growing. For some of the more important titles on issues of source criticism, see Raymond E. Brown, "The Gospel of Peter and Canonical Gospel Priority," *NTS* 33 (1987) 321–43; and idem, "The Gospel of Peter—A Noncanonical Passion Narrative," an appendix in *Death of the Messiah*, 2.1317–49; Crossan, *Cross That Spoke*; Albert Fuchs, *Das Petrusevangelium* (SNTU 2; Linz, Austria; Freistadt: Plöchl, 1978); Green, *"Gospel of Peter,"* 293–301; Helmut Koester, "Apocryphal and Canonical Gospels," *HTR* 73 (1980) 105–30; Meier, *A Marginal Jew*, vol 1.; Susan E. Schaeffer, "The 'Gospel of Peter,' the Canonical Gospels, and Oral Tradition" (Ph.D. diss., Union Theological Seminary, 1990); David Wenham, ed., *The Jesus Tradition outside the Gospels* (GP 5; Sheffield: JSOT, 1985).

[5]The Greek version relied on here is from Frans Neirynck, "The Apocryphal Gospels and the Gospel of Mark," in *The New Testament in Early Christianity*, ed. Jean-Marie Sevrin (BETL 86; Louvain: Leuven University, 1989) 123–75 (171–75).

and asked for his body. (5) Herod said, "Brother Pilate, even if no one asked for him, we [should] bury him, since the Sabbath is approaching. For it is written in the law that the sun should not [set] upon one put to death."

He delivered him to the people before the first day of Unleavened Bread, their feast. (3.6) Taking the Lord, they pushed him hurriedly and said, "Let us hail the Son of God, since we have power over him." (7) And they wrapped him in purple and sat him upon a judgment seat, saying, "Judge rightly, King of Israel!" (8) And one of them, taking a crown of thorns, put it on the head of the Lord. (9) Some standing [there] spat on his face, and others struck his cheeks, and others struck him with a reed, and some whipped him, saying, "With this honor let us honor the Son of God."

(4.10) And they took two evildoers and crucified the Lord between them. But he was silent as if having no pain. (11) And when they set up the cross, they wrote upon it, "This is the King of Israel." (12) And when they put his garments before him, they divided them, and they cast a lot upon them. (13) But a certain one of those evildoers reviled them, saying, "We are suffering this way because of the evils we have done, but what wrong has this one who has become the Savior of humankind done to you?" (14) And as they were angry with him, they ordered that his legs not be broken, so that he would die in torment.

(5.15) Now it was midday, and darkness covered all Judea. They were anxious and troubled that the sun had set while he was still alive, for it is written for them that the sun should not [set] upon one put to death. (16) And one of them said, "Give him gall with vinegar to drink"; and when they had mixed it, they gave it to him to drink. (17) And they fulfilled all things and completed their sins upon their heads.

(18) Many of them walked about with lamps, supposing that it was night, and they went to bed [or: they stumbled]. (19) And the Lord cried out, saying, "My power, O power, you have forsaken me." Having said [this], he was taken up. (20) And at that hour the curtain of the temple of Jerusalem was torn in two.

(6.21) Then they removed the nails from the hands of the Lord and placed him upon the earth; and all the earth shook, and there was a great fear. (22) Then the sun shone out, and it was found to be the ninth hour. (23) The Jews rejoiced and gave his body to Joseph so that he might bury it, since he had seen all the good things he [Jesus] had done. (24) Taking the Lord, he washed [him] and wrapped [him] in linen, and buried him in his own tomb, called the Garden of Joseph. (trans. Robert E. Van Voorst)

As mentioned above, at first scholarship branded this document docetic and gnostic. Recent study has seen it as more at home in the Great Church than in Gnosticism. The *Gospel of Peter* does indeed share several characteristics of Great Church literature of this time. It popularizes the gospel traditions with which it works; this popularizing can be seen in both style (the somewhat crude parataxis) and content. The *Gospel of Peter* emphasizes the miraculous more than do the canonical-Gospel traditions and makes miracles into seemingly obvious proofs of the faith. It has some strong connections (either oral or written) with the canonical Gospels. Like the *Acts of Pilate*, the other main passion narrative to come from the Great Church at this time, the *Gospel of Peter* features a strong anti-Jewish polemic, which may be connected with its popular origins, where anti-Judaism probably was stronger than in official circles. Finally, the *Gospel of Peter* has a pronounced devotional element, especially seen in its consistent use of "the Lord" rather than "Jesus." All these features of the *Gospel of Peter* indicate that it is a Great Church document.

Yet the *Gospel of Peter* can also be read as at least incipiently gnostic and might therefore have had an appeal to gnostic Christians. The phrase "as if having no pain" (4.10) would appeal to gnostic Christians who downplayed or denied the suffering of Christ. The cry of dereliction, "My power, O power, you have forsaken me" (5.19), would also appeal to Gnostics who held that the divine element of Jesus left him shortly before the crucifixion or in some other way was not fully involved in suffering and death.[6] That the *Gospel of Peter* could appeal to, and be used by, both orthodox and gnostic Christians should not surprise us—after all, both groups also used the Gospel of John and the letters of Paul.[7]

The dual appeal of the *Gospel of Peter* is illustrated by the well-known story of Serapion, bishop of Antioch, and his encounter with this book. The church historian Eusebius quotes a passage from Serapion's volume, "Concerning What Is Known as the Gospel of Peter":

> For I myself, when I came among you [the church at Rhossus], imagined that all of you clung to the true faith; and, without going through the Gospel put forward by them in the name of Peter, I said: If this is the only thing that seemingly causes captious feelings among you, let it be read. But since I have now learnt, from what has been told me, that their mind was lurking in some hole of heresy, I shall give diligence to come again to you; . . . Those who began [this Gospel] we call

---

[6]See, for example, the *Acts of John* 97: "And when he was hung on Friday, at the sixth hour of the day there came a darkness over the whole earth. And my Lord stood in the middle of the cave [on the Mount of Olives, to which John had fled] and gave light to it and said, 'John, for the people below in Jerusalem I am being crucified and pierced with lances and reeds and given vinegar and gall to drink. But to you I am speaking, and listen to what I speak.'" Jesus then goes on to reveal to John the true meaning of the crucifixion, concluding, "So then I have suffered none of those things which they will say of me" (101).

[7]See, for example, the treatment given the gnostic exegesis of the Pauline letters in Elaine H. Pagels, *The Gnostic Paul* (Philadelphia: Fortress, 1975).

Docetae (for most of the ideas [in the book] belong to their teaching) (*Hist. Eccl.* 6.12.3–6).[8]

To judge from this passage and its context, Bishop Serapion had visited his congregation at Rhossus and heard some unknown portion of the *Gospel of Peter* read in the service. He had no objection to it at the time, concluding that its influence was somewhat negative but not serious enough to prohibit its reading. Upon returning to Antioch, however, he learned that this church had hidden leanings toward what was known as Docetism, and surmised that the *Gospel of Peter* had some connection to that heresy. Therefore, he prohibited its use in his important diocese. This was perhaps the deathblow to the fortunes of the *Gospel of Peter*; as it could not be read in divine worship, it was no longer widely copied among the orthodox. (Scholarship is fortunate, though, that it continued to be copied in Egypt and was esteemed highly enough to be placed in a monk's grave.) For our purposes, the interesting point is that Serapion recognized heresy in this document not when he heard it but only when he later learned that people he considered heretics were using it for their own ends.

The most controverted—and controversial—issue in current scholarship on the *Gospel of Peter* is its place in early Christian tradition.[9] Is a source of the passion narrative of the *Gospel of Peter* also a source of the passion narratives in the canonical Gospels? Helmut Koester and John Dominic Crossan, among others, have strongly argued for such a position.[10] The kind of source-critical analysis that is necessary to contribute significantly to this argument is far beyond the bounds of this chapter. Here I offer one rather general comment on the current state of the question. Those who advocate such a source-critical position must do a much more careful job of establishing their hypothesis and defending it against criticism. For example, Crossan's major statement of his hypothesis, *The Cross That Spoke*, features no sustained, detailed display of his source-critical efforts. He asserts his hypothesis and explains it, but the documentation is missing. Until those who promote such a source hypothesis for the *Gospel of Peter* match the source-critical scope, detail, and precision of those who oppose it (e.g., Green, Brown, Schaeffer), this fascinating hypothesis will continue to hold a minority position.[11]

---

[8]Quoted, with minor adaptation, from Eusebius, *The Ecclesiastical History*, trans. John Ernest Leonard Oulton (2 vols.; LCL; Cambridge: Harvard University, 1932) 2.41, 43.

[9]A measure of the controversial, even at times bitter, nature of this debate is seen in the pointed comments of Helmut Koester, *Ancient Christian Gospels: Their History and Development* (Philadelphia: Trinity, 1990) xxx.

[10]See the literature in n. 4 above.

[11]For further discussion of the composition and theological perspective of

THE PASSION OF JESUS IN THE GNOSTIC GOSPELS

Our knowledge of Gnosticism has been greatly enhanced by the discovery in 1945 of the Nag Hammadi library of gnostic literature. Now scholars can read what some Gnostics had to say for themselves about their view of Jesus and their form of Christianity, and not depend on the limited and polemical witness about them from leaders in the Great Church. Given that Gnostics themselves called most of their writings "gospels" and composed them to some extent as counterpoints to the Gospels of their opponents in the Great Church, these gospels contain remarkably little narrative. Most are "sayings gospels"; their purpose is to convey the secret knowledge (γνῶσις, *gnōsis*) of the risen Christ, not to narrate the life and death of Jesus and place his teaching in that narrative context.[12] For the most part, Gnostics saw salvation as outside history, so one looks in vain for any passion narrative in the surviving gnostic gospels.

Does this absence of a passion narrative mean that Gnostics always ignored the death of Jesus and discounted its value for their faith? Leaders of the Great Church might well be expected to level such a charge at their heterodox opponents. For the orthodox, the passion of Jesus was at the center of Christianity; their Gospels narrated it quite fully, and a shorter version of its story was recounted in the developing creeds and at the celebration of the Eucharist. Yet recent scholarship has shown significant variety within Gnosticism's view of the death of Jesus.[13] While most gnostic documents indeed do not see any salvific purpose in the death of Jesus, interpreting it docetically when not totally ignoring or downplaying it, a few gnostic writings have a rather positive view of the passion. Perhaps the most remarkable is the second- or

---

the *Gospel of Peter*, see Brown, *Death of the Messiah*, 2.1317–49. On the anti-Jewish tenor of this account of Jesus' death, see ch. 10 below.

[12]When Gnostics placed their teachings in the mouth of Jesus, it was the risen Jesus who spoke, even if those sayings are attested in other gospel traditions as belonging to the earthly Jesus. In the Great Church, most of Jesus' gospel teaching is from before his death and resurrection. Some recent scholarship has argued that the gospel tradition that culminated in the canonical Gospels even had a tendency to place the words of the risen Christ speaking through prophets back into the earthly life of Jesus—the exact opposite of the gnostic tendency.

[13]The most extensive analysis is by Karl-Wolfgang Tröger, "Die Passion Jesu Christi in der Gnosis nach den Schriften von Nag Hammadi" (diss., University of Berlin, 1978). See also Elaine H. Pagels, "Gnostic and Orthodox Views of Christ's Passion: Paradigms for the Christian's Response to Persecution?" in *The Rediscovery of Gnosticism*, ed. Bentley Layton (Leiden: E. J. Brill, 1980) 1.262–83. A more popular version of this article can be found as a chapter in her book *The Gnostic Gospels* (New York: Vintage, 1979).

third-century *Apocryphon of James* 4.37–5.35, where the risen Jesus teaches James:

> If you are oppressed by Satan and persecuted and you do his [the Father's] will, I say that he will love you and make you equal with me. ... So will you not cease loving the flesh and being afraid of sufferings? Do you not know that you have yet to be mistreated and accused unjustly, and shut up in prison, and condemned unlawfully, and crucified without reason, and buried as I was myself, by the evil one? Do you dare to spare the flesh, you for whom the spirit is an encircling wall? Truly I say to you, none will be saved unless they believe in my cross. ... Scorn death, therefore, and think of life! Remember my cross and my death, and you will live.[14]

This teaching links the suffering and death of Jesus with the suffering and death of the (gnostic) disciples. It affirms the reality of the passion of Jesus and holds it up as a pattern for persecuted disciples. The salvific power of the cross lies not in Jesus' sacrifice for sin but in his example as one who, in accordance with gnostic religion, uses death to destroy the "flesh" and liberate the spirit.[15] The appearance of this rather positive gnostic view of martyrdom in a secret book addressed to James is not coincidental. This is James the Just, Jesus' kin, who was a leader in the early Jerusalem church and known in later centuries as a prominent martyr (although his martyrdom is not made explicit in this book).

Elaine Pagels has carefully examined the relationship between the view of Jesus' passion and martyrdom in the Great Church and that in gnostic circles and concluded that the passion accounts provide "paradigms for the Christian's response to persecution." Orthodox Christians, she argues, approved of martyrdom and linked it to the salvific death of Jesus; gnostic Christians typically discounted martyrdom and the death of Jesus. Her main conclusion has been found convincing by subsequent scholarship. But her analysis is confined to the second and third centuries and implies that the orthodox understanding of the imitation of Jesus' death appears de novo in the second century as a response to Gnosticism.

So the question arises: does this later debate reflect first-century Christian concerns about the connection between the death of Jesus and the persecution to death of Christians? The first document of the NT to be written, 1 Thessalonians, links imitation "of us and the Lord" with suffering (1:6; see also 2:14–16;[16] 3:3–5). The first canonical Gospel, Mark, draws a strong connection between the two, as, for example, in

---

[14]Quoted from *The Nag Hammadi Library in English*, ed. James M. Robinson (New York: Harper & Row, 1977) 31.

[15]This could arguably be called an ancient form of the "moral influence" theory of the atonement.

[16]Of contested authenticity; see ch. 10 below.

Jesus' saying to pick up one's cross and follow him (8:34 and parallels). First Peter links the righteous suffering of the believer with the suffering of Christ: "For to this [suffering] you have been called, because Christ also suffered for you, leaving you an example" (2:21). Many other such examples could be adduced.

This cursory glance at the NT shows that already in the first century, Christians were drawing strong connections between the death of Jesus and the suffering and death of Christians under persecution, affirming the significance (and, implicitly, the reality) of both. (No explicit evidence from the NT relates what early Gnostics may have thought about martyrdom; their side of the debate does not appear until the second century.) Analysis of this topic in the second and third centuries cannot be complete without tracing its antecedents in earlier Christian literature. These antecedents are of special importance if one seeks to use this issue of the death of Jesus to answer the important, wider question whether second-century, fully developed Christian Gnosticism was a legitimate successor of first-century types of Christianity.

THE DEATH OF JESUS IN JEWISH CHRISTIANITY

Among those second- and third-century Christians who combined Christianity and Judaism, seeking the best of both,[17] gospel literature was quite common.[18] Unfortunately, very little of it has survived, aside from occasional quotations by Great Church writers and sections of Jewish-Christian writings taken up into Great Church literature. In the latter category is a mid-second-century book attested by Epiphanius, the *Ascents of James*.[19] The *Ascents of James* is now incorporated into a large amalgamation of literary material called the *Pseudo-Clementine Recognitions*, purportedly the story of Clement, the early bishop of

---

[17]We cannot enter here into the controversial issue of the definition of "Jewish Christianity." For our purposes, we can understand it informally as that part of early Christianity that was predominantly Jewish in membership (birth or conversion), practice (especially observance of the Mosaic law), and belief (the attempt to express Christianity in Jewish vocabulary). For two of the several recent attempts at definition, see A. Frederik J. Klijn, "The Study of Jewish Christianity," *NTS* 20 (1974) 419–31; Raymond E. Brown, "Not Jewish Christianity and Gentile Christianity but Types of Jewish/Gentile Christianity," *CBQ* 45 (1983) 74–79.

[18]See, most recently, A. Frederik J. Klijn, *Jewish-Christian Gospel Tradition* (Supplements to *Vigiliae Christianae* 17; Leiden: E. J. Brill, 1992).

[19]See Robert E. Van Voorst, *The Ascents of James* (SBLDS 112; Atlanta: Scholars, 1989). For the fullest account of recent scholarship on the entire Pseudo-Clementine literature, see F. Stanley Jones, "The Pseudo-Clementines: A History of Research," *SecCent* 2 (1982) 1–33, 63–96.

Rome and missionary partner of Peter. Originally written in Greek, it now survives in Latin and Syriac versions. The *Ascents of James* is a Jewish-Christian document that tells the story of the people of God from Abraham to the early church. It depicts Jesus as the prophet like Moses and therefore Messiah. Its title, *Anabathmoi Iakōbou*, comes from the ascents of James the brother of Jesus to the temple to debate with the high priest about Jesus, a debate that would have won over the whole Jewish nation to Christianity had not "the enemy" (a thinly disguised Paul) intervened.

A part of the *Ascents of James* is a short narrative of the passion of Jesus.[20] We can present its Latin version (against which the Syriac version varies little) as follows:

> (1.41.2) This prophet like Moses, whose rise he himself predicted, although he healed every weakness and every infirmity in the common people, worked innumerable wonders and preached the good news of eternal life, was driven to the cross by wicked men. This deed, however, was turned into good by his power. (3) Finally, when he suffered the whole world suffered with him. The sun was darkened and the stars were disturbed; the sea was shaken and the mountains moved, and the graves opened. The veil of the temple was split, as if lamenting the destruction hanging over the place. (4) Nevertheless, although the whole world was moved, they themselves are still not yet moved to the consideration of such great things. . . . [There follows a four-sentence discussion of a mission to the Gentiles to "satisfy the number" shown to Abraham.] (43.3) In the meantime, after he had suffered, and darkness had overcome the world from the sixth hour to the ninth, when the sun returned things came back to normal. Wicked people once more went back to themselves and to their old customs, because their fear had ended. (4) Some of them, after guarding the place with all diligence, called him a magician, whom they could not prevent from rising; others pretended that he was stolen.[21]

This passion narrative is considerably shorter than those of the canonical Gospels. Yet even this short narrative has three notable dependencies upon the passion narrative material that is peculiar to

---

[20]Current scholarship is divided on whether the passion narrative in book 1 of the *Recognitions* does in fact belong to the *Ascents of James*. Hans-Joachim Schoeps assigns it to another source document, an Ebionite *Acts of the Apostles* (*Theologie und Geschichte des Judenchristentums* [Tübingen: J. C. B. Mohr (Paul Siebeck), 1949] 383, 406). More recently and influentially, Gerd Lüdemann has argued that it belongs to an "R 1 Source" (*Paulus, der Heidenapostel* [FRLANT 130; Göttingen: Vandenhoeck & Ruprecht, 1983] 2.228–57). Perhaps it is safe to conclude that although scholars assign this passion narrative to various sources, all would see this as a second- or third-century Jewish-Christian narrative.

[21]The translation is from Van Voorst, *The Ascents of James*, 56–58.

Matthew. (Because we lack the original Greek of the *Ascents of James*, it is impossible to tell with certainty whether this dependence is literary or oral.) The *Ascents of James* takes Matthew's "shaking of the earth" (27:51) and expands it by adding "the sea was shaken" (*Rec.* 1.41.3). It does this to include the whole physical world in the portents attending Jesus' death; as *Rec.* 1.41.3 emphasizes, "When he suffered the whole world suffered with him." Second, the *Ascents of James* links the shaking of the mountains (Matt 27:51 has "the rocks were split") to the opening of the tombs, which it moves from its Matthean position at Jesus' resurrection to his death. Third, the *Ascents of James* draws on the Matthean tradition of the guard at the tomb of Jesus (Matt 27:62–66; 28:11–15). In general, the *Ascents of James* follows the Matthean order of the portents and develops for its own purposes the special Matthean passion material.

Another characteristic of the passion narrative in the *Ascents of James* is its nonsoteriological view of the passion. For the community of this document, the crucifixion of Jesus did not bring salvation. Jesus' death is not portrayed as a sacrifice for sin (his innocence is not emphasized, there is no mention of Jesus as the lamb, etc.), and his death is not said to have atoning power. Rather, salvation in the *Ascents of James* comes through baptism in the name of Jesus, a baptism Jesus brought to replace the temple sacrifices (*Rec.* 1.39.1–2; 1.55.3–4; 1.69.8–1.70.1). Salvation is in the baptism Jesus taught, not in his death. This lack of emphasis on the soteriological meaning of the cross agrees with much of early Jewish Christianity. It also explains why so much attention is given in the *Ascents of James*'s passion narrative to the portents surrounding Jesus' death; they are impressive while they last, but their impression wears off as soon as they end. The portents surrounding the crucifixion of Jesus are arguably the real theme of this section of the *Ascents of James*; it is just as much a portent narrative as a passion narrative, but the portents ultimately fail. Only James the brother of Jesus will be able to convince the Jewish people that Jesus is Messiah. This lack of permanent persuasion in the portents is also the reason for the long digression in the *Ascents of James*'s passion narrative. The digression explains that the whole people of the Jews is not converted at the crucifixion of Jesus, so a mission to the Gentiles must be undertaken to fulfill the complete number of the people of God shown to Abraham.

Scholarship on Jewish Christianity has been hampered by ambiguous and controverted definitions of this term and, more important, by a lack of extant documents. But in the *Ascents of James* we get a fascinating glimpse of Jewish Christianity and one of its views of Jesus' passion. The passion of Jesus in the *Ascents of James* is not nearly as significant as his teaching. Perhaps the prophet-like-Moses Christology contributed to this downplaying of the passion, as it seems to have little room for a suffering Messiah.

THE DEATH OF JESUS NARRATED IN JUDAISM

Much scholarship in our generation, from both the Christian and Jewish sides, has analyzed the intricate relationships of early Christianity and Judaism.[22] The surviving literature on this topic largely comes from Christianity. The rabbis who laid the foundation of talmudic Judaism seemed to have much less to say about Christianity than Christianity about Judaism. Perhaps they spoke of it only when necessary, and then in sparing language, attempting to oppose it with silence. (A case in point is their use of the term *minim*, "sectaries"; even today debate occurs on whether it refers especially to Christians or to lapsed/sectarian Jews in general.) This makes "the most famous 'Jesus reference' in all of rabbinic literature,"[23] from *Sanh.* 43a of the Babylonian Talmud, all the more remarkable:

> It was taught: On the eve of the Passover they hanged Yeshu. And a herald went before him for forty days (saying), "He will be stoned, because he practiced magic and enticed and led Israel astray. Anyone who knows anything in his favor, let him come forward and plead on his behalf." But when nothing was found in his favor, they hanged him on the eve of the Passover.[24]

This short narrative is the only surviving rabbinic treatment of the death of Jesus. Its many problems are probed extensively in several treatments.[25] Here we will address only its value as a passion narrative.

First, the content and context of this passage indicate that its main topic is the legal practice of sending a herald out to announce charges against a person accused of a serious crime. The person so accused usually went behind the herald, and this passage implies that Yeshu (Aramaic for "Jesus") followed such a herald for forty days. This forty-day activity came between Jesus' arrest and his trial. The contrast between this passage and both the canonical and Great Church noncanonical gospels' portrayal of the speed and secrecy of Jesus' trial could hardly be more pronounced. In the Talmud Jesus is held for forty

---

[22]For the most up-to-date treatment of this topic, especially its formative stages, see Claudia J. Setzer, *Jewish Responses to Early Christians: History and Polemics, 30–150 C.E.* (Minneapolis: Fortress, 1994).

[23]J. Louis Martyn, *History and Theology in the Fourth Gospel* (2d ed.; Nashville: Abingdon, 1979) 78.

[24]Quoted from Martyn, *History and Theology*, 79.

[25]Besides J. Louis Martyn, who is especially concerned to relate it to the Fourth Gospel, see also R. Travers Herford, *Christianity in Talmud and Midrash* (London: Williams & Norgate, 1903) 344–60; Johann Maier, *Jesus von Nazareth in der talmudischen Überlieferung* (Darmstadt: Wissenschaftliche Buchgesellschaft, 1978) 216–29; and Jacob Zallel Lauterbach, *Rabbinic Essays* (Cincinnati: Hebrew Union College, 1951) 473–96.

days—a time period with ancient biblical associations of fullness of length—not overnight. Seemingly all the public knows of his impending death. Moreover, the whole public knows of his guilt, because no one comes forward to defend Jesus. The speed and secrecy that the canonical Gospels portray have been debated recently, but no one has argued that this passage from the Talmud is historically accurate.

The charges against Jesus are threefold: by magic (probably his miracles) Jesus enticed Israel to go astray from the one true God to the worship of other gods. These are technical Jewish religious charges not at all connected here with Roman rule, and this passage envisions the Sanhedrin itself carrying out this whole process from trial to execution. "They" at the beginning and end refers in context to the Sanhedrin. The "stoning" referred to by the herald is the prescribed biblical punishment. But the rabbis knew that Jesus was crucified, not actually stoned, and so the passage refers at its beginning and end to "hanging," the Hebrew-Aramaic equivalent of crucifixion.[26] This passage is remarkable: a Jewish writing in which Jews, not Romans, execute Jesus on solely religious charges after a solely Jewish trial. We can safely deduce that the rabbis responsible for this tradition (and it is an old one for the Babylonian Talmud, perhaps from the second century, as it is identified at its beginning as a *baraita*) probably did not feel significant polemical pressure from Christians about responsibility for the death of Jesus, else they would not have been so bold in this oral and then written tradition. The passage seems to have no contact, literary or oral, with gospel tradition, with the notable exception of the expression "on the eve of the Passover," which agrees with the Johannine dating of the crucifixion. In sum, this short narrative does not seem to be a direct polemical attack on Christian understandings of the passion of Jesus. Rather, it is more probably an inner-Jewish explanation of the fully legal, routine way in which one famous criminal, Jesus of Nazareth, was put to death.

CONCLUSIONS

This sketch of extracanonical treatments of the death of Jesus suggests a number of important issues deserving further reflection. First, do the passion narratives of the second and third centuries possess historical value for our understanding of the death of Jesus? Put another way, does this literature tell us anything we do not already know with

---

[26]In ancient practice as prescribed by Jewish law, the criminal would be stoned first to induce death, and then his body would be hung until the end of the day. Here, death itself is by hanging, and the references to stoning seem to be in deference to the biblical mandates.

some confidence from the canonical Gospels? Probably not. In fact, most of these later narratives lead us away from what certainties we do have from the admittedly difficult first-century accounts. The passage of one to two hundred years since the death of Jesus has blunted the historical significance of these narratives; they now are used for different purposes than those of the canonical Gospels. Later passion narratives are characteristically more popularizing and tendentious than accounts from the first century.

Second, are any hypothetical sources of second- and third-century passion narratives also the source for canonical narratives? Once again, probably not. Most current scholarship points the other way, and our analysis suggests that this view is correct. Nevertheless, we can expect the debate to continue. If those arguing for such a source in the *Gospel of Peter* offer more detailed, careful analyses, the argument will become even more lively and interesting.

Third, the primary historical value of later passion narratives is rooted in their own time and space. (The same is true, of course, of the canonical passion narratives, but they stand much closer to the event and were perhaps subject to some criticism and correction by people who stood near these events.) The writings considered above give us a rich perspective on the variety of Christianity after the NT era. They show some variety of approach within gnostic circles to the value of the death of Jesus. Moreover, they demonstrate the depth of popularizing tendencies in the Great Church and also point to the distinctive witness of Jewish Christianity. For recent scholarship in general, the value of second- and third-century Christian works lies primarily in the witness they give to their own time. Their relationship to the NT, although an important and enduring question, is now being given less attention, while their role in reconstructing the religious and social history of second- and third-century Christianity receives much more attention. This trend in scholarship can especially be seen in the new edition of such an influential reference work as Schneemelcher's *New Testament Apocrypha*.[27]

Finally, important questions arise when one considers the implications for contemporary Christianity of research into the variety of early Christianity. For example, Robert J. Miller has stated, "Insights gleaned from such effort [to understand noncanonical gospels] are useful in our own age because contemporary Christianity is even more diverse than it was in its formative years, despite centuries of effort (and even violent

---

[27]Edgar Hennecke, Wilhelm Schneemelcher, and R. McL. Wilson, eds., *New Testament Apocrypha* (ET; 2 vols.; Philadelphia: Westminster, 1963–65; 2d ed., Louisville: Westminster/John Knox; Cambridge: James Clarke, 1991–92). See the comments by Robert F. Stoops, Jr., "Apostolic Apocrypha: Where Do We Stand with Schneemelcher's Fifth Edition?" in SBLA 1993, 170.

attempts) to homogenize it."[28] While this comparative claim is open to question, it is undeniable that Christianity—in its first three centuries and today—is indeed diverse. But historians may overstep their bounds by implying that diversity in itself is always desirable, or that all forms of diversity are typically good and efforts (usually by the orthodox) to reduce unacceptable diversity are typically bad.[29] Much less should the descriptive study of matters like the passion traditions be skewed by issues of contemporary relevance.

---

[28] Robert J. Miller, "The Gospels That Didn't Make the Cut," *BibRev* 9, no. 4 (1993) 14–25, 56 (16).

[29] Brown (*Death of the Messiah*, 2.1347) speaks of "a simplistic tendency to regard extracanonical works as the key to true Christianity as contrasted with a narrow-minded censorship represented by the canonical NT."

Part Three

*Historical and
Theological Issues*

# NINE

WHY CRUCIFIXION?
THE HISTORICAL MEANING
OF THE CROSS

INTRODUCTION: WHY DID JESUS HAVE TO DIE?

For those who follow Jesus as Messiah, the cross has always occupied the center of the Christian message. The same may be said for those, past and present, who have found in Jesus' crucifixion, as Paul put it, "a stumbling block," "foolishness" (1 Cor 1:23). Whether as eschatological turning point or as irreconcilable ignominy, the execution of Jesus on a Roman cross occupies a prominent place on the horizon of Christian faith and practice. As such it begs for elucidation. Why did Jesus have to die?

As a theological problematic, the cross was not self-interpreting,[1] and the quandary of the crucified Messiah demanded scrutiny from the earliest days of the fledgling Christian movement. The NT itself bears witness to the variety of interpretive paths taken and resolutions commended.[2] Before it is a puzzle for the theologian, however, the crucifixion of Jesus presents itself as the object of historical inquiry.

---

[1] Cf. Wolfhart Pannenberg, *Jesus—God and Man* (London: SCM, 1968) 246.
[2] The modern classic is James Denney, *The Death of Christ: Its Place and Interpretation in the New Testament* (3d ed.; New York: A. C. Armstrong & Sons, 1903); also Vincent Taylor, *The Atonement in New Testament Teaching* (2d ed.; London: Epworth, 1945). More recently, e.g., Boff, *Passion of Christ*; Gerhard Delling, *Der Kreuzestod in der urchristlichen Verkündigung* (Göttingen: Vandenhoeck & Ruprecht, 1972); Driver, *Understanding the Atonement*; Gerhard Friedrich, *Die Verkündigung des Todes Jesu im Neuen Testament* (BTS 6; Neukirchen-Vluyn: Neukirchener, 1982); Joseph A. Grassi, *Rediscovering the Impact of Jesus' Death: Clues from the Gospel Accounts* (Kansas City, Mo.: Sheed & Ward, 1987); Karl Kertelge, *Der Tod Jesu*; Eduard Lohse, *Märtyrer und*

The historian's interest is piqued, first, by the certainty of the claim that Jesus of Nazareth was crucified in human history. In fact, on the continuum of historical probability, Jesus' crucifixion "under Pontius Pilate" is the most certain of all claims related to Jesus. This event is recounted in extraordinary detail in the passion narratives of the NT Gospels and mentioned repeatedly as a historical event by the various authors of the NT writings. It is noted in passing by the Latin historian Tacitus in *Ann.* 15.44 and perhaps attested in the historical accounts of Josephus (*Ant.* 18.3.3 §§63–64).[3] What is more, it is apparent from both Christian and non-Christian sources of the first centuries C.E. that it was the offense of the abhorrent death of Jesus that opponents of the Christian message seized upon to discredit the claims made by Christians on behalf of Jesus and that Christians had to overcome in order to render their faith intelligible within the wider world. As the early Christian apologist Justin Martyr remarks, "They say that our madness consists in the fact that we put a crucified man in second place after the unchangeable and eternal God, the creator of the world" (*First Apology* 13.4).[4]

What is most pressing for the historian, however, lies elsewhere than in data of this nature. Given that Jesus was executed by the method

---

Gottesknecht: Untersuchungen zur urchristlichen Verkündigung vom Sühntod Jesu Christi (2d ed.; FRLANT n.s. 46; Göttingen: Vandenhoeck & Ruprecht, 1963); Leon Morris, *The Apostolic Preaching of the Cross* (3d ed.; Leicester: Inter-Varsity, 1965); and idem, *The Cross in the New Testament* (Grand Rapids: Eerdmans, 1965); Hans-Ruedi Weber, *The Cross: Tradition and Interpretation* (London: S.P.C.K., 1979).

[3] The text from Josephus reads:

> About this time there lived Jesus, a wise man, if indeed one ought to call him a human. For he was one who wrought surprising feats and was a teacher of such people as accept the truth gladly. He won over many Jews and many of the Greeks. He was the Messiah. When Pilate, upon hearing him accused by the people of the highest standing among us, had condemned him to be crucified, those who had in the first place come to love him did not give up their affection for him. On the third day he appeared to them restored to life, for the prophets of God had prophesied these and countless other marvelous things about him. And the tribe of Christians, so called after him, has still to this day not disappeared. (*Ant.* 18.3.3 §§63–64)

The authenticity of this passage as a whole is seriously doubted, particularly given its unabashed affirmation of Jesus' messiahship. Many scholars now believe, though, that the original form of this section of Josephus's *Antiquities of the Jews* contained some statement regarding Jesus, probably negative and probably related to a messianic claim, subsequently altered by Christian hands. See the summary in Craig A. Evans, "Jesus in Non-Christian Sources," *DJG*, 364–68 (364–65).

[4] Cf. further Hengel, *Crucifixion*, esp. 1–21, 84–85; Green, *Death of Jesus*, 157–69.

of crucifixion, and given further that in the first-century Roman world, death by crucifixion was a mode of capital punishment reserved for those who threatened imperial rule, we are more immediately interested in how Jesus came to be viewed in this way. As A. E. Harvey has put it:

> Jesus was crucified as an actual or potential enemy of the Roman authority. But if we turn to the gospels, there is virtually nothing which gives any colour to such a charge. Indeed we can go further. *The portrait of Jesus, as it is presented to us not only in the gospels but throughout the New Testament, is utterly irreconcilable with this explanation of his death.*[5]

The enigma to which Harvey directs us provides an agenda for this chapter and, to a lesser degree, for the chapters that immediately follow. Here our inquiry will follow more narrowly defined *historical* lines as we seek, first, to establish the perimeters within which crucifixion in general might have been understood in the Greco-Roman world. Following this, we will be in a position to return to the NT documents in a more focused way, inquiring into how they present the motivation(s) for Jesus' execution and how they grapple with the heinous reality of Jesus' death on a cross. Finally, we must ask: If Jesus' execution brands him as a political threat—say, a pretender to the throne—how does this shed light backward on the nature of his ministry and message? Given what we may know of his mission, why did Jesus have to die? To put the question differently, in what sense might we regard Jesus, as we know him via the Gospels, as a political risk?

CRUCIFIXION AND THE ANCIENT WORLD

Despite the claims of innumerable popular accounts in sermons and books oriented to the general public, we actually know very little about the techniques used in crucifixion.[6] Martin Hengel describes the passion narratives of the canonical Gospels as the most detailed reports of crucifixion available to us from the ancient world.[7] Yet, when it comes to describing the act of crucifying Jesus itself, these reports are singularly reserved. They report simply, "They crucified him" (Mark 15:24; Luke 23:33; John 19:18), or anticipate his crucifixion, only to pick up the story line again after the deed is done (Matt 27:31, 35). How was it carried out? What did a crucifixion "look like"? The Gospels give us very little

---

[5]Harvey, *Jesus and the Constraints of History*, 14; emphasis added.
[6]On what follows, see esp. Hengel, *Crucifixion*; also Green, "Death of Jesus," 146–63 (147–48); and idem, "Crucifixion," *DPL*, 197–99.
[7]Hengel, *Crucifixion*, 25.

information indeed, nor do we find much help outside the NT, with the result that our understanding of how this sentence was executed must be pieced together from disparate sources.

What is evident from this dearth of testimony is that literate Roman society had no desire to dwell on the details of crucifixion. So brutal and shameful a mode of capital punishment worked against the literary-aesthetic sensibilities of the Roman world.

To what can we attribute the particularly heinous character of this mode of execution? It had to do in part with the public humiliation accompanying crucifixion and in part with the act itself. Bound or nailed to a stake, tree, or cross, the victim faced death with all organs intact and with relatively little blood loss. As a consequence, death came slowly, sometimes over several days, as the body surrendered to shock or to the painful process of asphyxiation as the muscles used in breathing experienced paralysis brought on by fatigue.

Even where descriptions of the method of crucifixion are available, it is clear that no standard form was universally practiced. Were the victims of crucifixion fixed to the stake in order to die or only after death, as a public display? The evidence suggests both. Nor is it clear whether those crucified were bound or nailed to the cross—though in the case of Jesus multiple witnesses intimate the latter (John 20:25; Acts 2:23; Col 2:14; *Gos. Pet.* 6.21; Justin *Dial.* 97; cf. Luke 24:39).

Archaeological evidence on the practice of crucifixion from first-century Palestine is both sparse and ambiguous. In 1968 an ossuary containing the bones of an adult male was discovered in northern Jerusalem. This man had apparently been executed by crucifixion at some time in the first sixty years of the Common Era. Initial examination of this find suggested that a single iron nail had been driven through both of the victim's heel bones. Wood fragments found at both ends of the nail indicated that the nail passed through a small wooden plaque, through the victim's feet, and finally into a vertical beam. In addition, it was thought that a nail had been driven through each of his forearms and that his shins had been deliberately broken. Subsequent reexamination recommended a quite different picture, however. Rather than having the victim's feet crisscross so as to be attached by a single nail through the heels to the front of the stake, this reevaluation found that the victim straddled the upright beam, with a nail attaching each foot to its respective side of the stake. Further questions were raised about whether his shin bones had been broken at all prior to death. Moreover, finding no clear evidence of trauma to the bones of the forearm, this later investigation led to the proposal that the victim had been tied, not nailed, to the crossbeam.[8] Although any anthropological testimony of

---

[8]Joseph Zias and Eliezer Sekeles, "The Crucified Man from Giv'at ha-

this nature is a welcome addition to the sparse literary data, it is obvious that more evidence is needed if we are to acquire more certainty in interpretation.[9]

From the available evidence, crucifixions by the Romans seem to have followed a relatively uniform procedure, and a summary outline is possible.[10] Crucifixion included a flogging beforehand, with victims often required to carry their own crossbeams to the site of execution, where they were nailed or bound to the cross with arms extended, raised up, and perhaps seated on a *sedicula*, or small wooden peg. But even among the Romans this procedure was subject to variation. Thus, in his eyewitness account of the siege of Jerusalem by the Romans, Josephus observes how hundreds of Jews were "scourged and subjected to torture of every description . . . and then crucified opposite the city walls." Free to fulfill their whims in the hope of persuading those Jews remaining in the city to surrender their positions, "the soldiers out of rage and hatred amused themselves by nailing their prisoners in different positions" (Josephus *J.W.* 5.11.1 §§449–51).

Josephus's account brings to the foreground two other important issues. First, crucifixion was a characteristically public affair. Second, and closely related, crucifixion was reserved by the Romans especially for those who resisted the authority of Roman occupation. Naked and fastened to a tree, stake, or cross, usually located at major crossroads, the victim was subjected both to a particularly heinous form of capital punishment and to optimum, savage ridicule. To add shame upon shame, the crucified person was often denied burial[11]—and this in a culture where proper burial was of immense social and religious significance. In the case of the Roman public, funeral societies were formed to guarantee the proper burial of deceased members; in Jewish tradition, the exposure of one's corpse was tantamount to a curse from God.[12] But the

---

Mivtar: A Reappraisal," *IEJ* 35 (1985) 22–27.

[9] It is not surprising that we have access to such sparse physical evidence. Those crucified were generally left on their crosses as carrion for birds and beasts; even if they were granted burial, as executed criminals they typically would have been denied proper burial (cf. Josephus *Ant.* 5.1.14 §44; 4.8.6 §202).

[10] Hengel, *Crucifixion*, 22–32.

[11] Tacitus (*Ann.* 6.29) observes that legally condemned criminals were precluded from burial. Philo (*Flacc.* 10.83–84) notes how, on the eve of a festive occasion, the crucified were removed from their crosses and handed over to relatives for burial.

[12] Cf., e.g., Deut 28:26; Jer 8:1–2; 16:1–4; Ezek 29:5. On the import of burial in the world of Jesus, cf. Tob 1:16–2:10; Josephus *Ag. Ap.* 2.29 §211; *J.W.* 3.8.5 §377; 4.5.2 §317. Note also the subtle contribution to the narration of the status disjunction between Lazarus and the rich man in Luke 16:19–31: "The poor man died and was carried away by the angels to be with Abraham. The rich man also died *and was buried*" (v. 22). For the Roman world, cf. J. M. C. Toynbee, *Death and Burial in the Roman World* (London: Thames & Hudson, 1971).

corpse of the crucified was normally left on the tree to rot or as food for scavenging birds. In this way the general populace was granted a somber reminder of the fate of those daring to assert themselves against Rome.

CRUCIFIXION AND THE NEW TESTAMENT

It is no surprise that the NT is far more concerned with making theological sense of the execution of Jesus than in investigating its historical cause(s). In a society where the values of honor and shame have been identified as "pivotal,"[13] the public spectacle of being subjected to naked humiliation and public crucifixion as a criminal serving a rebellious objective is a shame the magnitude of which resists measure. How could this thoroughly disgraced man from Galilee be hailed as Messiah, God's Anointed One?

As we will see, early Christians were not oblivious to the social meaning of crucifixion. In fact, as readers of the Scriptures of Israel, they would, and clearly did, experience the infamy of Jesus' mode of execution in greater depth than is possible for a modern reader. At the same time, the Gospel records do provide some evidence on the nature of the charges Jesus faced. But first we will consider how some NT writers seem quite openly to have grappled with the dimension of Jesus' disgrace in light of contemporary readings of the OT.

"Hung on a Tree"

Speculation on the so-called pierced-Messiah fragment among the Qumran texts notwithstanding,[14] the notion of a suffering Messiah runs counter to everything we know of the varieties of messianic expectation in Second Temple Judaism. (In the Scriptures, the righteous were to be rescued from death—cf., e.g., Dan 3 and 6; also Wis 2:17–20.) Clearly it was easy enough to read Messiah Jesus back into the songs of the Suffering Servant in Isaiah—as the Gospels make clear, not least in their passion narratives.[15] It is quite another thing, though, to find evidence of the identification of the Messiah with the Suffering Servant (or with

---

[13] See Bruce J. Malina, *The New Testament World: Insights from Cultural Anthropology* (Atlanta: John Knox, 1981) 25–50.

[14] For this discussion, see, e.g., James D. Tabor, "A Pierced or Piercing Messiah? The Verdict Is Still Out," *BAR* 18, no. 6 (1992) 58–59.

[15] Cf., e.g., the following Servant motifs in the passion narratives of the four Gospels: the willingness of the chosen one to complete his mission via suffering; his innocence; his silence before his accusers; his death "for many"; his being "handed over"; his suffering abuse; his being "numbered with transgressors"; and anticipation of his vindication.

suffering more generally) in contemporary Jewish writing. Such testimony is lacking, and this serves only to underscore all the more the enigma of Jesus' crucifixion.[16] Indeed, given the more dominant strands of messianism current in Jesus' day, the Pauline proclamation of "Christ crucified" (e.g., 1 Cor 1:23; 2:2) and the Markan narration of the crucifixion of the Messiah, King of the Jews (e.g., 15:12–14, 18, 20, 24–26, 32), seem strange indeed—incongruous, oxymoronic. The hoped-for Davidic or royal Messiah, the priest Messiah, the eschatological prophet like Moses—these figures, each with its own history of significance in Israel's past, are attested in the literature of Second Temple Judaism,[17] but the motif of suffering is integral to none of them.

The scandal of a crucified Messiah runs even deeper still. Three NT writers—Luke, Paul, and the author of 1 Peter—take a step further by describing the act of crucifixion as Jesus' being "hung on a tree." Their language echoes the words of Deut 21:22–23:

Acts 5:30	"The God of our ancestors raised up Jesus, whom you had killed by hanging him on a tree."
Acts 10:39	"The Jewish leaders in Jerusalem had Jesus put to death by hanging him on a tree."
Acts 13:29	"They took him down from the tree."
Gal 3:13	"Cursed is everyone who hangs on a tree."
1 Pet 2:24	"He himself bore our sins in his body on the tree."
Deut 21:22–23	"When someone is convicted of a crime punishable by death and is executed, and you hang him on a tree, his corpse must not remain all night upon the tree;

[16] The attempt, above all by Joachim Jeremias ("παῖς θεοῦ," *TDNT*, 5.654–717), to find analogues to the messianic interpretation of the Isaianic Suffering Servant in Second Temple Jewish writings has not been convincing. Most of the texts to which Jeremias points are irrelevant to the question. Of more immediate interest is the Targum on Isa 52:13–53:12, which makes an undeniable identification of Messiah and Servant but radically transforms the role of the Servant away from any note of suffering!

[17] See the helpful assemblage of the evidence in James D. G. Dunn, "Messianic Ideas and Their Influence on the Jesus of History," in Charlesworth, *Messiah*, 365–81 (367–69). Dunn makes the helpful distinction between "messianic ideas" current in Jesus' day and "potentially messianic ideas" "which might within the constraints of the Jewish history of revelation, tradition, and hermeneutics be candidates for application to a putative messiah" (369). In this latter category might be included, e.g., the Isaianic Suffering Servant, even though the identification of Servant and Messiah apparently did not figure prominently, if at all, in the discourse of eschatological anticipation prior to the advent of Jesus.

you shall bury him that same day, for anyone hung
on a tree is under God's curse."

These NT texts, together with Luke 23:39, account for every use of the
Greek term κρεμάννυμι (kremannymi, "hang"), also employed in the
Deuteronomic text; this suggests the formative influence of the LXX text
of Deut 21:22–23 on this aspect of the NT understanding of the cross.
Of course, this passage from Deuteronomy does not envision crucifixion per se but, rather, impalement of the body of the executed after
death. Nevertheless, in pre-Christian times it was already being applied
to the victims of crucifixion.[18]

These references provide insight into the early Christian use of
Deut 21:22–23 in the interpretation of the cross of Jesus: (1) They
indicate that Jesus' followers were aware of the passage's contemporary
association with victims of crucifixion. Early Christians knew of the
disgrace this identification would have signalled for their Lord, yet they
did not attempt to disavow the ensuing predicament they faced. (2)
Instead, they worked to interpret this troublesome declaration of divine
curse. That is, following a course often used in instances of intertextuality, Jesus' followers not only used the earlier text to help interpret their
present understanding of Jesus' demise but also, in the process, transformed that ancient text. In Gal 3, for example, Paul actually quotes
Deut 21:23 not to repudiate its denunciation of Jesus as one "cursed by
God" but to acknowledge it. In doing so, though, Paul goes on to show
that even this divine curse had redemptive effect: it was "for us."
Likewise, 1 Peter states that Jesus, hung on a tree, bore our sins in his
body. Luke does not develop the salvific meaning of Jesus' death in the
way Paul does, but his allusions to Deut 21:22–23 serve to locate Jesus'
death firmly in the necessity of God's purpose. The ultimate disgrace,
the curse from God, is antecedent to divine exaltation—i.e., to Jesus'
resurrection and ascension. The Deuteronomic text is thus used in
parodic ways, registering dissimilarity in the midst of similarity, transforming the earlier passage beyond what one might regard as its original
intention by applying it to God's Anointed One.

The execution of Jesus on a cross, then, was shameful in every way,
from both Roman and Jewish points of view. Disgrace of this nature was
premeditated, at least on the Roman part, for it helped to secure the
effectiveness of crucifixion as a deterrent to others who might be

---

[18]See, e.g., Philo Spec. Leg. 3.152; Post. C. 61; and Somn. 2.213; 4QpNah
3–4.1.7–8; 11QTemple 64.6–13; cf. Johannes Schneider, "ξύλον," TDNT,
5.37–41; Joseph A. Fitzmyer, "Crucifixion in Ancient Palestine, Qumran Literature, and the New Testament," in To Advance the Gospel (New York: Crossroad,
1981) 125–46. Cf. Max Wilcox, "'Upon the Tree'—Deuteronomy 21:22–23 in
the New Testament," JBL 96 (1977) 85–99.

contemplating crimes against the state. Having established the extent of disgrace associated with crucifixion, especially for his Jewish disciples, we may now inquire more pointedly into the historical forces leading to his execution.

Religious and Political Motivations for Jesus' Execution

Why did Jesus have to die? According to the Gospels of Matthew and Mark, the Jewish council found Jesus guilty of blasphemy and pronounced on him the death sentence (Matt 26:59–65; Mark 14:55–64; cf. John 19:7). On this matter, Luke is not so clear (Luke 22:66–71). First, Luke portrays this scene as less a trial, more an informal hearing prior to a trial. Second, although those assembled seem shocked by Jesus' words, they are not reported by Luke to have reached a verdict, nor does their meeting conclude with the pronouncement of a sentence. This squares well with the later report in Acts 13:28, where Paul declares to his synagogue audience at Pisidian Antioch that the Jerusalem leaders "found no cause for a sentence of death, but nevertheless asked Pilate to have Jesus killed."[19]

Hence, when Francis Watson complains that the Gospels inappropriately answer the question, Why was Jesus crucified? by claiming only a religious crime, we may complain that perhaps Watson has not read the evidence closely enough.[20] The actual charges brought against Jesus before Pilate in Luke 23:1–5 are political in nature; indeed, the third evangelist attests an alternative tradition in which the alleged crime of Jesus was not defined as blasphemy.[21]

What are we to make of the Markan and Matthean trial accounts? E. P. Sanders has argued that the trial scene envisioned by these evangelists cannot be accurate. His strongest allegation is that of missed opportunity. Speaking and acting against the temple might have garnered the charge of blasphemy, but it does not; rather, the charge of blasphemy follows Jesus' statement,

(From now on) you will see the Son of humanity[22]
seated at the right hand of Power
and coming with/on the clouds of heaven.
(Matt 26:64; Mark 14:62; cf. Luke 22:69)

---

[19]According to Acts 13:27, the Jewish leaders "made a decision" regarding Jesus, but in this case κρίναντες, *krinantes*, need not imply "condemn" (NRSV); cf. Acts 25:25.

[20]Watson, "Why Was Jesus Crucified?" 105–12.

[21]Cf. Harvey, *Jesus and the Constraints of History*, 11–35.

[22]Here, as elsewhere in this book, we are using the expression "Son of humanity" to render the Greek ὁ υἱὸς τοῦ ἀνθρώπου, *ho huios tou anthrōpou*.

But this statement is, for Sanders, clearly "unblasphemous."[23] In a recent essay, Darrell Bock has addressed this question in a fresh way. He observes that blasphemy in Second Temple Judaism might involve either word or deed and that special sensitivity existed where the temple was concerned. Moreover, he insists that Jesus' statement about the Son of humanity seated at the right hand of God could have been heard as Jesus' claim that he was able to enter directly into God's presence and share in God's rule. Such an assertion would have been taken as blasphemous.[24]

This is not to suggest that Jesus died on account of blasphemy, however. It might suggest at least one reason the Jewish leadership were motivated to hand Jesus over to Pilate, but would not explain adequately why Jesus had to die *by crucifixion*.[25] Whether or not the Jewish leadership had formal authority over life and death (cf. John 18:31), according to Luke 4:29–30 and Acts 7:54–60 execution by Jewish mob action, even in Jerusalem—quite apart from the involvement of the Roman legal system—was not unknown. A blasphemer might have met death in this way, but this is not how Jesus died. He was crucified, and this demands something more than his alleged transgression of even deeply rooted Jewish sensibilities.

In fact, more can be said, including what might be regarded at least initially as a more narrowly defined religious foundation for Jesus' execution. Fundamental to the history of Jesus' passion is his execution as a messianic pretender who claimed to be the King of the Jews. This is the content of the inscription on the cross in all four Gospel accounts (Matt 27:37; Mark 15:26; Luke 23:38; John 19:19–22). How could such a crime have been attributed to Jesus? One approach to this question has been to note, first, the interchangeability of the titles "King of the Jews" (befitting a Roman setting) and "Messiah" (more germane in a Jewish setting) and, second, in Jesus' trial before the Sanhedrin, the association of destroying and rebuilding the temple with the question of Jesus' messiahship (Matt 26:61–63; Mark 14:57–61). The historicity of the temple statement is well established (cf. Matt 26:61; Mark 14:58; 15:29; John 2:19; Acts 6:14; *Gos. Thom.* 71), so it is of further interest that eschatological speculation grounded in 2 Sam 7:13–14 led in some sectors to the expectation of a royal Messiah, God's Son, who would rebuild the temple.[26] In other words, Jesus' claim to rebuild the temple,

---

[23] Sanders, *Jesus and Judaism*, 297–98 (298).

[24] Bock, "Son of Man," 181–91.

[25] Hengel (*Atonement*, 43) suggests, though, that the Jewish leaders pressed for Jesus' death by crucifixion since this would have provided a clear denial of his status as God's Anointed One.

[26] Cf. 2 Sam 7:5–16; Zech 6:12–13; *Tg. Neb.* Zech 6:12–13; *Tg. Neb.* Isa 53:5; *1 Enoch* 90:28–29; 4 Ezra 10:27; 4QFlor 1.1–13; Green, *Death of Jesus*, 277–81; Otto Betz, *What Do We Know about Jesus?* (London: SCM, 1968) 88–91; Sanders, *Jesus and Judaism*, 77–90.

the import of which is heightened by his prophetic action against the temple upon arriving in Jerusalem (cf. Matt 21:12–13; Mark 11:15–17; Luke 19:45–46; John 2:13–16), would have had obvious political ramifications. Such a claim would be tantamount to the assumption of the messianic role, leading to the Jewish question, Are you the Messiah? and to the Roman question, Are you the King of the Jews? Clearly, at this juncture Jewish/religious and Roman/political issues have become closely intertwined.

The political implications of Jesus' mission are, in fact, faced squarely and explicitly in several key passages. We have seen that we are led to infer from the mode of his execution that Jesus died as a threat to Rome. The one passage in which we read explicitly of the charges brought against Jesus by the Jewish leadership, Luke 23:1–5, reports how he was accused of "subverting our nation, opposing the payment of taxes to Caesar, and saying of himself that he is the Christ. . . . He stirs up the people throughout Judea by his teaching." This language, together with the parallel allegation against Jesus that he is a deceiver in Matt 27:63, discredits Jesus as a false prophet who turns God's people away from the ways of the Lord (Deut 13).[27] This implies, on the one hand, a motivation for Jesus' condemnation by the Jewish council. We may note, on the other, how easily these concerns are parlayed into explicitly political terms—Jesus' threat to the Roman empire. Indeed, in Luke's account these accusations are brought against Jesus during his hearing before Rome's representative, Pontius Pilate. Other texts add to this portrait. According to John 11:47–53, for example, the potential of Jesus' popularity to jeopardize Rome-Jerusalem relations is recognized. This problem comes to the fore in a different way in John 19:12, 15, where the dominion of Caesar is juxtaposed with that of Jesus. And Jesus is executed between two insurrectionists, underneath an inscription describing this as his crime.

The Problematic of the Cross

Earlier we noted the apparent incongruity between the manner of Jesus' demise and the Gospel portrayals of him and cited A. E. Harvey to the effect that the portrait of Jesus in the NT is irreconcilable with his death as a political criminal. We have now begun to see that Harvey's assertion was exaggerated, for there are a number of passages containing both under- and overtones that Jesus died because he jeopardized the political order. Nevertheless, it is true that the fact of Jesus' crucifixion

---

[27] See Stanton, "Jesus of Nazareth," 164–80; August Strobel, *Die Stunde der Wahrheit: Untersuchungen zum Strafverfahren gegen Jesu* (WUNT 21; Tübingen: J. C. B. Mohr [Paul Siebeck], 1980).

by the Romans marks him as a political risk in ways not commonly discerned in the Gospel portraits of his ministry. And this is the problematic to which we must finally turn.

JESUS: A POLITICAL RISK?

Why did Jesus have to die? Peter Stuhlmacher suggests that from the very beginning, diverse answers would have been given to this query. According to Jesus' most influential Jewish opponents, "this man had to die because a religious deceiver and false prophet must be eliminated from the context of the people of Israel, according to the law of Moses (cf. Deut 13; 17:1–7; 18:20)." Pilate, on behalf of Rome, had a different view: "This Jesus of Nazareth had to be crucified to serve as a shock treatment, so that henceforth no one else will dare to assert himself as the messianic king of Israel in the purview of the Romans, and incite the Jewish people to rebellion."[28] This way of putting things is helpful as a reminder of the possibility that diverse motives were at work in bringing Jesus to Golgotha and of the inseparable and, as we will see more fully shortly, highly consequential interweaving of religious and political motifs in Roman antiquity.

Before we develop the political risk of Jesus in more detail, it will be helpful to outline an important assumption behind the discussion that follows. Recent work, especially in the sociology of knowledge but also, more broadly, in cultural anthropology, has underscored the degree to which a people's experience of the world is socially determined, communicated, and conserved. Institutions, like the Roman Empire or the Jewish leadership in Jerusalem, are not only built on, and belong to, that socially constructed understanding of the world but actively work to perpetuate that understanding or worldview. What is more, institutions at the center of this world come to believe and, indeed, to foster the idea that the way things are is the way they are supposed to be, the way they were created to be. God (or the gods) made them this way. They are divinely legitimated.[29] Hence, anyone who works against the way things are not only trespasses conventional wisdom but also, and more importantly, commits an infraction against the divine. Political violations are by definition religious, then, just as religious transgressions are political, for they upset the moral order, they disturb the proper and regular distribution of power, and they operate according to an alternative and

---

[28] Stuhlmacher, *Jesus of Nazareth—Christ of Faith*, 39–57 (42, 43).
[29] Peter L. Berger and Thomas Luckmann, *The Social Construction of Reality: A Treatise in the Sociology of Knowledge* (New York: Doubleday, 1966); Douglas, *How Institutions Think.*

competing understanding of the world. This is perhaps more obvious in the case of, say, the temple cult in Jerusalem or legislation on Sabbath keeping in Second Temple Judaism; after all, could one not appeal to the Scriptures to certify that current practices were determined by God? But as we shall see, this is also true in the wider Roman world—a world whose shape (it would be assumed) had been set in place by the gods.

Undoubtedly, the immediate cause of the judgment against Jesus was his action against the Jerusalem temple.[30] This marked him as a threat to public order and, in the high-strung atmosphere of a Passover feast in Palestine under Roman occupation, could easily have precipitated Jesus' deliverance by the Jewish authorities over to Roman jurisdiction.[31] It would be a mistake, however, to imagine that this prophetic deed on Jesus' part was an isolated event in Jesus' ministry, as though this alone were responsible for his sentence to crucifixion. Much more was at stake.

Jesus and Jewish Politics

The now recognized variety within Second Temple Judaism complicates how we understand what about Jesus would have been taken as scandalous by his Jewish contemporaries. On some matters he resembles a Pharisee, for example, on others a revolutionary, and so on. Dunn's work on Second Temple Judaism assists our efforts, however, by identifying key symbols of Jewish identity in this period: circumcision, Sabbath keeping, and matters related to the table—what one eats and with whom one eats.[32] With these in mind, we can briefly outline three scenarios wherein Jesus shows himself to be troublesome.

(1) The Synoptic Gospels, especially Luke, agree that Jesus was notorious for his manners at the table. In particular, he flaunted the normal protocol of meals by parodying it. Fellowship at the table generally signified extension of friendship and the sharing of religious experience, in some circles a foretaste of the heavenly banquet. One thus ate with one's own kin group and the wider circle of friends who could be counted upon to maintain one's purity and bolster one's status. Jesus did not ignore these conventions but took advantage of them. He ate with toll collectors and sinners, becoming a friend to them and

---

[30] See further ch. 10 below.

[31] Cf. Josephus *Ant.* 18.5.2 §§117–18; and *J.W.* 6.5.3 §§300–305; Geza Vermes, *Jesus and the World of Judaism* (London: SCM, 1983) viii.

[32] James D. G. Dunn, *Jesus, Paul, and the Law: Studies in Mark and Galatians* (Louisville: Westminster/John Knox, 1990); on table fellowship, see also Philip Francis Esler, *Community and Gospel in Luke–Acts: The Social and Political Motivations of Lucan Theology* (SNTSMS 57; Cambridge: Cambridge University, 1987) 71–109.

communicating to them the grace of God's presence. What is more, in providing food for the multitudes, he overturned concerns with ritual purity and status by having apparent strangers, the masses, sit in company and break bread together.

(2) In Second Temple Judaism, keeping the Sabbath had become a kind of litmus test for faithfulness to God. Although the Hebrew Scriptures had not devoted much detail to explicating how one might keep this day holy, contemporary interpretations had more than made up for this lack by spelling out the limits of appropriate Sabbath day behavior. Jesus' behavior repeatedly transgressed those boundaries—e.g., he allowed his disciples to harvest on the Sabbath, and he himself engaged in healing on this special day.

(3) Although not directly related to Dunn's list of the three "badges" that designate one as Jewish, the centrality of the temple to Judaism in Jesus' day is axiomatic. Even those Jews who had separated themselves from Judaism as a whole, joining sectarian communities like that at Qumran, ordered their understanding of human purity and divine holiness in ways embodied in the architecture of the temple. The Jerusalem temple maintained in the configuration of its structures the fundamental separation between clean and unclean, Jew and Gentile, Jewish male and Jewish female, priest and nonpriest. From this configuration emanated a way of life, a separateness from what was unclean, for all who wished to draw as near as possible to the holiness of God.

Priests, especially chief priests centered in Jerusalem and the high priest together with his entourage, were thus established at the center of the Jewish world. They possessed the divine, exclusive right to handle holy paraphernalia, to make pronouncements on ritual cleanness, to perform sacrifices on behalf of the people, to collect tithes and maintain the temple treasury, and so on, and so occupied positions of prominence on the sociopolitical stage of Jesus' world. Pharisees, for their part, took this view of the world with such seriousness that in their daily interactions at the dining table, they emulated a separateness that was more at home in the temple. Jesus, on the other hand, disparaged this system and censured the temple and its associated practices. He habitually crossed the boundaries between clean and unclean, even to the point of touching lepers and handling corpses. And through word and deed, he prophesied the temple's destruction.

To these scenarios others could be added. It must be remembered, though, that these activities of Jesus were not directed simply against, say, contemporary Sabbath legislation per se but reached further to call into serious question the way the world works. The moral order and distribution of power represented by the temple was at stake in Jesus' behavior. And these possessed (as it was generally supposed) the imprimatur of God, so that for many, and especially for those most invested in this system—the Jewish leadership—Jesus' activity was not simply countercultural but was deliberately set in opposition to God.

Jesus and Roman Politics

As with the Judaism of Jesus' day, so with the wider Roman world, it is difficult to address how Jesus might have been taken as a political risk without our bogging down in the quagmire of generalities. An approach deserving closer scrutiny, however, situates Jesus' message over against the political order upon which Rome carried out day-to-day affairs.[33]

After the final victory of Octavian in the civil wars (27 B.C.E.), Rome was unified not simply under one emperor but also by a political order based on the ethic of patronage. Octavian took for himself the name Augustus (cf. Luke 2:1) as well as other titles—including *princeps,* the patron of the Roman people. He also received the title *pater patriae* (i.e., father of the land of fathers), thus conceptualizing the empire as a household indebted to him as its head. Note, for example, the Myrian inscription "Divine Augustus Caesar, son of a god, imperator of land and sea, the benefactor and savior of the whole world."[34]

Thus Augustus assumed for himself the role of benefactor, patron, a role that during this period was pervasive throughout the empire. Slaves were indebted to their master, the *paterfamilias* (i.e., the patriarch of an extended family). Sons were under the rule of their fathers, awaiting the death of their fathers so that they might ascend to the status of patriarch. Clients were bound to their patrons and often had clients of their own. Patrons shared clients. And so on. The network of overlapping obligation spread throughout the empire, ultimately with everyone indebted to the emperor as benefactor—either as a result of his direct patronage throughout the empire or indirectly, through the levels and webs of obligation that found their way back to him.

But even the emperor had client status of a sort, for the hierarchy of patronal relations extended beyond the sphere of humans to include the gods. The gods had shown favor to Rome, and especially to the *princeps,* the patron, the emperor. He was not himself divine, but he was the recipient of the gods' patronage and served as their special agent. Thus the reciprocity of patronal relations obligated slaves to masters, sons to fathers, the elite to the emperor, and the emperor, together with all of Rome, to the gods.

---

[33] The following discussion is borrowed from Green, *Theology of Luke,* ch. 5.

[34] David C. Braund, *Augustus to Nero: A Sourcebook on Roman History, 31 BC–AD 68* (London: Crook Helm, 1985) §66.

In this way, the political order, the binding ethic of patronage, was rooted in the divine. The ethic of obligation found its legitimation in the gods themselves. It was sacred. To deviate from the sacred order, then, was not simply to involve oneself in a social embarrassment but was a violation of the sacred order. Against such a world order Jesus' message stands in stark contrast, as the following two scenarios intimate.

(1) Jesus' disciples are said to have struggled repeatedly with the question of who among them was the greatest. Jesus' response to such posturing was to pull the rug from under all such maneuvering, asserting that the kingdom of God belonged to little children. He further insisted that status in the new community being established around him must be measured by one's role as a servant. Service, of course, was expected when directed to people of higher status, but Jesus, even while acknowledging his own superior status when measured in the company of his followers, communicated by word and deed that service was to be given to those of lower status, including little children.

(2) Jesus further undermined the patronal ethics upon which the empire existed by insisting that people give without expectation of return. Within the normally expected social roles, gifts, whether banquet invitations or goods, brought with them expectations of reciprocity: this was the way of the Roman household whose father was Caesar. Jesus set forth for his listeners an alternative household, one not run by relations of debt and obligation. The household he imagined was one in which people would be treated as family, with services performed and goods shared freely, without the attachment of reciprocal obligation. As Luke summarizes in his version of the Lord's Prayer, "Forgive us our sins, for we also release from their obligations those indebted to us" (11:4).

Undoubtedly, Jesus' message thus crossed the grain of the Roman political order. As we have seen, however, this too was fundamentally a religious infraction, for the character of the Roman household (i.e., Rome portrayed as one large household) was instituted and validated by the gods. Jesus ran afoul of this religio-political order and taught others to do the same; therefore, he must have been regarded as a political risk.

CONCLUSION

This discussion of crucifixion has ranged over a wide array of issues bound together by one question: why did Jesus have to die? We have observed that the mode of his death, by execution on a cross, places certain constraints on any historical answer we might entertain. In particular, that Jesus was "crucified under Pontius Pilate" indicates that Jesus was understood to be a political risk, an indictment perfectly consonant with the inscription on the cross, "The King of the Jews."

Even if Jesus' first followers might have seen in this charge an ironic affirmation of Jesus' messiahship, it functions well, too, to identify the impetus for the hearings against Jesus and his final sentencing.

The Gospel accounts, whether in the passion narratives or in prior material, are not strangers to political charges of this kind. In fact, we have observed that the probable immediate cause of the proceedings against Jesus—his prophetic action against the temple—should be counted as only one among many of his practices that would lead those in power to regard Jesus as an irritant needing to be silenced. Moreover, Jesus' activities that worked against the worldview of those in power, such as those we have enumerated, were not themselves ancillary to his mission. Quite the contrary, the very message conveyed by Jesus in word and deed and leading to his arrest, conviction, and execution was integral to his public mission. Jesus had to die because too many people, leaders both Roman and Jewish, opposed the nature of his ministry.

TEN

Who was responsible for the death of Jesus?
THE CROSS AND "ANTI-JUDAISM" IN EARLY CHRISTIANITY

At this stage of the study, it is crucial to address an age-old historical question: who actually put Jesus to death? The importance of this historical issue is already clear from our discussion of each Gospel passion narrative. It is all the more important because of the implications of the question for current interfaith relations, particularly between Jews and Christians. Indeed, largely because of interfaith concerns in the aftermath of the Holocaust, many scholars—both Jewish and Christian—have revisited this topic.[1]

We need to be clear that this is a *historical* question, though admittedly one in which there has been an immense religious, theological, moral, and cultural investment. Because it is a historical question (who was, not who is, responsible for putting Jesus to death?), it can only be answered through careful critical evaluation of the available evidence, taking into account the biases operative in ancient sources and also setting aside, for the moment, the possible relevance of one or another answer for contemporary dialogue. It is to this task that we now turn.

---

[1]Of special interest is the series of articles in *Judaism* 20 (1971) 10–74. Among the classic treatments of this topic is that of Paul Winter, *On the Trial of Jesus* (2d ed.; SJ 1; Berlin: Walter de Gruyter, 1974). See also Solomon Zeitlin, *Who Crucified Jesus?* (4th ed.; New York: Bloch, 1964); Dominic M. Crossan, "Anti-Semitism and the Gospel," *TS* 26 (1965) 189–214; Haim Cohn, *The Trial and Death of Jesus* (New York: Harper & Row, 1971); Rivkin, *What Crucified Jesus?*; and most recently Brown, *Death of the Messiah*, 1.383–97.

THE QUESTION IN EARLY CHRISTIAN RETROSPECTIVE

It is useful to begin by observing the direction of movement on this question in early Christianity. Whom (that is, what historical agents) did Christians of the second through fourth centuries hold accountable for the death of Jesus? A sampling of early Christian sources is revealing: consistently, and often with vehemence, Christian authors of this period lay blame for Jesus' death at the doorstep of the Jewish people. Roman involvement in the event is occasionally noted, but even then it is invariably overshadowed by the charge of Jewish complicity.

Early Christian Views

Gospel of Peter

Whatever earlier traditions may underlie the *Gospel of Peter*,[2] this extracanonical passion narrative in its present form may be dated to the mid–second century C.E.[3] Our manuscript picks the story up midsentence, with the Jews—both Herod and his judges—refusing to wash their hands, evidently after Pilate has done so (as in Matt 27:24; an echo of this tradition is heard later in the story, at 11.46). It is "Herod the king" who commands that Jesus be marched off to his crucifixion (1.2), and when Joseph requests the body of Jesus (in advance of the execution), Pilate must obtain Herod's permission. Pilate therefore plays essentially no role in the death of Jesus; his part is given over to Herod, identified as king of the Jews. "They" mock and crucify Jesus, and it remains ambiguous just who "they" are (3.6–6.22)—that is, until 6.23–7.25, where it becomes clear that the responsible party is "the Jews and the elders and the priests." In the aftermath of Jesus' death (and the cosmic portents attending it), they confess their guilt and mourn the judgment that will now come upon them. And "the Jews," rather than Pilate, surrender the body to Joseph (6.23).[4]

Clearly the Jewish people have orchestrated the execution of Jesus, according to the *Gospel of Peter*. The section beginning at 8.28, however, drives a sharp wedge between the people (λαός, *laos*) and their leaders

---

[2]Crossan, *Cross That Spoke*, vigorously advances the theory that the core of the *Gospel of Peter* is the earliest passion narrative, which also became a source of the canonical passion accounts. For criticism of the view that the *Gospel of Peter* is substantially a precanonical gospel, see Green, "Gospel of Peter." See further ch. 8 above.

[3]For the text of the *Gospel of Peter*, see above, pp. 149–50.

[4]Cf. the statement in Acts 13:29 that the people of Jerusalem buried Jesus. See Green, "Burial of Jesus."

(scribes, Pharisees, and elders). The elders request that Pilate set a guard at the tomb; their motive is a desire to keep from being harmed by the people in the event they should come to believe that Jesus has been raised from the dead. This stratagem is foiled by angelic visitors, who lead Jesus out of the tomb, a spectacle witnessed by both elders and soldiers. Pilate then accedes to their (presumably the elders') desperate plea to order the soldiers to keep silent. Again they fear the retaliation of "the people of the Jews" (11.48), preferring instead the wrath of God.

While there is some ambiguity in this narrative about the involvement of the Jewish public, the basic picture is clear. Jesus is killed not by the Romans but by the Jewish people and their leaders. What separates the Jewish people and the authorities is not complicity in the death of Jesus but contrasting responses to the signs of divine disfavor that accompany the event. The treachery of the Jewish leaders continues unabated to the very end.

What the *Gospel of Peter* does through the vehicle of narrative, other early Christian authors accomplish through homily and treatise. A cursory sampling of this material will be sufficient to demonstrate the wide dispersal of the belief that the Jews were responsible for Jesus' death.[5]

Justin Martyr (ca. 100–165 C.E.)

Writing in the mid–second century, the apologist Justin rehearses a tradition that assigns blame in an evenhanded way to Jewish and Roman opponents of Jesus. He demonstrates that David's prophecy (Ps 2:1–2, cited also in Acts 4:25–28) was fulfilled in the conspiracy of Herod, "king of the Jews," the Jews themselves, and Pilate the governor (together with his soldiers) against the Christ (*First Apology* 40). Elsewhere, however, Justin speaks simply of the Jewish role: the Jews rejected the Christ, treating him shamefully (*First Apology* 49); they failed to recognize Christ when he came, and so murdered him (*Dial.* 14, 16, 17, 93); and now they direct their hatred at Christians, "who declare that he has come and show that he was crucified by them as had been predicted" (*First Apology* 36).[6]

---

[5]For broader treatments of the characterization of Jews in early Christian literature, see Jeffrey S. Siker, *Disinheriting the Jews: Abraham in Early Christian Controversy* (Louisville: Westminster/John Knox, 1991); Robert S. MacLennan, *Early Christian Texts on Jews and Judaism* (BJS 194; Atlanta: Scholars, 1990); Robert Wilken, *John Chrysostom and the Jews* (Berkeley: University of California, 1983); and idem, *Judaism and the Early Christian Mind: A Study of Cyril of Alexandria's Exegesis and Theology* (New Haven: Yale University, 1971); Robert Wilde, *The Treatment of the Jews in the Greek Christian Writers of the First Three Centuries* (Washington: Catholic University of America, 1949).

[6]The translation is from *Early Christian Fathers*, ed. Cyril Richardson

Melito of Sardis (died ca. 190 C.E.)

A few years later, the bishop of Sardis, a city with a significant Jewish community, uses the occasion of the paschal homily to castigate Israel for its rejection of Jesus. The rhetoric is inflammatory:

> For him whom the Gentiles worshipped and uncircumcised people admired and foreigners glorified, over whom even Pilate washed his hands, you killed at the great feast. Bitter therefore for you is the feast of unleavened bread. . . . Bitter for you are the nails you sharpened, bitter for you the tongue you incited, bitter for you the false witnesses you instructed . . . bitter for you Judas whom you hired, bitter for you Herod whom you followed, bitter for you Caiaphas whom you trusted, . . . bitter for you the hands you bloodied; you killed your Lord in the middle of Jerusalem.
> . . . the King of Israel has been put to death by an Israelite right hand. O unprecedented murder! Unprecedented crime![7]

Commentary is scarcely necessary. Pilate recedes from view, and the Jewish people take center stage, in Melito's polemical reframing of the feast of Passover.

Irenaeus (ca. 130–200 C.E.)

To Irenaeus, bishop of Lyons and a contemporary of Melito, the Jews' killing of Jesus is analogous to Cain's murder of Abel (*Haer.* 4.18.3). Even though this event was divinely purposed for the salvation of Christians, the Jewish people remained culpable, as shown by the consequent national disasters (4.28.3; 4.33.12). Irenaeus does not excuse Pilate altogether, but he credits Jesus' arrest and crucifixion to the Jews, who forced Pilate against his will to deliver him to death (*Demonstratio* 74, 82).

Origen (ca. 185–254 C.E.)

Like Irenaeus, Origen of Alexandria contends that the Jews were punished by God because they killed Christ (*Against Celsus* 4.73).[8] He refuses to accept the excuse that since Jesus' death was determined by God, the Jews were neither free nor responsible agents, nor does he think their guilt diminished because Jesus went to death willingly and

---

(Philadelphia: Westminster, 1953) 265. For further discussion of the anti-Jewish theme in Justin, see Siker, *Disinheriting*, 163–84.

[7]*Homily on Pascha*, 91–93, 96–97, adapted from the translation by Stuart George Hall (Oxford Early Christian Texts; Oxford: Clarendon, 1979).

[8]For further references to this theme in Origen's writings, see Wilde, *Treatment of the Jews*, 189–91; Brown, *Death of the Messiah*, 1.832.

suffered no real pain (*Against Celsus* 2.23–24) or because they acted at the direction of the devil (*Comm. Matt.* 13.9). Pilate, a passive and cowardly instrument in the passion drama, was less at fault than the Jews (*Against Celsus* 2.34; *Comm. Matt.* 12.1). And among the Jews, the rulers, chief priests, scribes, and Pharisees bear the greatest responsibility.[9] Yet through their persistent failure to listen to Scripture, the Jews of Origen's day remain guilty of the murder of Christ, though ultimately they will be saved by divine mercy (*Hom. Jer.* 12.13). Origen draws from Matt 27:23–25 the conclusion that the blood of Jesus falls upon all generations of Jews to the end of time (*Comm. Matt.* 27.22–26).

Didascalia Apostolorum (Apostolic Constitutions)

This document from third-century Syria is replete with intriguing details on the passion.[10] Of interest here is the view that Herod issued the crucifixion order (5.19). Pilate too cuts an uncomplimentary figure, for while he recognizes and declares Jesus' innocence, he dishonors himself by acceding to the demands of the multitude, illegally sending to the cross an innocent man (5.14). Nevertheless, prime movers behind the trial and crucifixion are the leaders of the people, who play the roles of accuser, witness, judge, and author of the sentence (5.14).

John Chrysostom (ca. 347–407 c.e.)

John Chrysostom, bishop of Antioch, was, like Melito, forced to come to terms with an active local Jewish congregation, one whose religious life (rituals, festivals, etc.) evidently attracted many Christians. In response, he delivered a series of homilies "against Judaizing Christians,"[11] discourses marked by a vehemence surpassing even that

---

[9]*Comm. Matt.* 16.3; *Comm. John* 28.18; *Hom. Jer.* 15.2.

[10]E.g., an explanation (5.14) is provided for the shift to the charge of treason: false witnesses appear in the trial before *Pilate*, and because of the discrepancies in their testimony, they alter the nature of their accusations.

[11]Perhaps these "Judaizing Christians" included nominal Christians of Jewish origins who continued to observe Jewish customs after Theodosius II decreed Christianity to be the official religion of the Roman Empire (381 c.e.). Wayne A. Meeks and Robert L. Wilken (*Jews and Christians in Antioch in the First Four Centuries of the Common Era* [SBLSBS 13; Missoula, Mont.: Scholars, 1978] 31) suggest, however, that "far from representing a popular hostility toward Judaism among Christians in Antioch, Chrysostom's imprecations reveal the exact opposite: a widespread Christian infatuation with Judaism." For the full text of the homilies, see St. John Chrysostom, *Discourses against Judaizing Christians* (*Fathers of the Church* 68; Washington: Catholic University of America, 1979). The preface by translator Paul Harkins contains this statement: "Chrysostom held the position, which was common for centuries, that all Jews are responsible for Christ's passion and death, that they have been repudiated and cursed by God, and that they stand condemned out of the

of Melito. In these discourses, he characterizes the Jews as "pitiable and miserable," people who from childhood read the prophets yet "crucified him whom the prophets had foretold" (1.2.1). A synagogue composed of persons who do not know God and crucified the Son of God can only be termed a "dwelling of demons" (1.3.3). The target of Chrysostom's barbs is those Christians who are drawn toward the worship of the synagogue. People with this "disease" share the feast with those who crucified the one they worship (1.5.1), for the synagogue is the place where the "slayers of Christ" gather (1.6.3). Chrysostom memorializes this "crime of crimes" (1.7.2), which provides ample cause for the policy that the Christian and Jewish religions cannot be mixed: "They crucified the Christ whom you adore as God. . . . How is it, then, that you keep running to those who slew Christ when you say that you worship him whom they crucified?" (4.3.6). His final warning for those who would rush off to the synagogue is ominous. At the final judgment, they should expect to hear the words "Depart, I know you not. You made common cause with those who crucified me" (6.7.4).

The calculated rhetorical effect of these homilies—vilifying the synagogue, and especially Christians drawn toward its liturgy, by associating even contemporary Jews with the murder of Jesus—is chilling. Yet this is only an episode in a continuing story.

We have focused attention on various early Christian attempts to fix blame for Jesus' death on the Jews. Certainly, we might have traced more closely the progressive rehabilitation of Pilate.[12] An important early credal formulation may tie the death of Jesus to the Roman prefect who ordered it ("crucified under Pontius Pilate"), but the prevalent view, enshrined in writings of diverse genres, times, and places, appears to have been that the Jewish leaders—or even the Jewish people generally—were responsible for Jesus' execution. Increasingly, Roman involvement in the death of Jesus was diminished, and the Jewish role expanded. Why?

---

mouths of their own prophets" (x). Harkins sets this position against the October 28, 1965, decree of Vatican II, which rejected the belief that the Jewish people were collectively guilty of the death of Jesus. On John Chrysostom and Judaism, see further Wilken, *John Chrysostom.*

[12]A fabricated letter from Pilate to the Roman emperor—mentioned by Tertullian as addressed to Tiberius in *Apology* 21.24 (cf. ch. 5) and likely the same letter inserted, much later, in the *Acts of Peter and Paul* as a letter to Claudius—locates the transformation within Pilate's own experience. He admits to having been deceived by the chief priests into allowing the Jews to crucify Jesus but now writes to make the record straight. The text is available in Johannes Quasten, *Patrology* (3 vols.; Westminster, Md.: Newman, 1950–60) 1.117. Of course, in some Christian circles, Pilate was believed to have converted to Christianity and was canonized as a saint. See Brown, *Death of the Messiah,* 1.696.

Early Christian Motives

The emergence of "Christian" groups (i.e., messianist Jews who believed that in Jesus the Messiah had come) within the multiform world of first-century Judaism was attended by considerable controversy. Even a casual reading of such NT writings as the letters of Paul, the Gospels of Matthew and John, Luke–Acts, and Revelation discloses as much. Once Christian religion became divorced from Judaism, a process that occurred during the late first and early second centuries,[13] conflict between "Christians" and "Jews" continued, though in new settings. One finds occasional echoes of this conflict in the rabbinic literature but frequent and often acrimonious evidence of it in early Christian literature. Beyond the obvious competition for adherents, the polemics betray an acute need, particularly in the case of Christians, for legitimation: this community sought to establish itself as a legitimate heir to the rich Jewish heritage; even though it was increasingly composed of Gentiles (who did not observe the Mosaic laws) and its claims were for the most part rejected by Jews, the Christian community contended it could rightly appropriate to itself the Scriptures, the hopes, and the promises of the Jewish people. This polemical setting shaped early Christian memory of the public ministry of Jesus. It left its stamp as well on the memory of his death. In that memory Jesus himself, like his later followers, would necessarily wage the battle with Jews.

Once Christians were recognizable as distinct religious groups separate from Jewish communities in their cities, they faced a crisis of legitimation within Roman society. Given the prevalent bias against novel religious movements, this task of legitimation could prove exceedingly difficult.[14] It did not help this cause that the founder of the movement had been crucified by order of the Roman prefect of Judea. What better way to give legitimacy to Christians and to defend them against charges that they were disloyal, dangerous, and immoral than to show that legitimate Roman authority, after examining

---

[13] The pace of this development varied considerably from one region to the next. See the discussion in James D. G. Dunn, *The Partings of the Ways between Christianity and Judaism and Their Significance for the Character of Christianity* (London: SCM; Philadelphia: Trinity, 1991) 230–43.

[14] To cite only two examples: (1) an exchange of letters (112–13 C.E.) between Pliny the Younger, governor of Pontus and Bithynia, and the emperor Trajan over the proper handling of accused Christians reveals both the precariousness of public Christian identity and the bewilderment and ignorance of Roman officials about Christian religion; (2) the Roman historian Tacitus voices a common misapprehension of Christians when he terms them "superstitious" and "haters of the human race" (*Ann.* 15.44; cf. Suetonius *Lives of the Caesars* 6.16).

similar charges against Jesus, publicly avowed his innocence of any and all crimes?[15]

Both the ongoing conflict with Jewish communities and the need to be seen as good citizens in Roman society point early Christian traditions about Jesus' death in the same direction: it was Jewish leaders at Jerusalem, not Roman officials, who put Jesus to death. But there is another dimension to the conflict with Jewish communities. After the separation of Jewish and Christian groups, Jewish culture and Jewish institutions did not disappear. Indeed, even in the post-Constantinian era, synagogues seem to have had magnetic appeal for some Christians, to a degree that has probably been downplayed in the history of Christian scholarship.[16] Jewish liturgy, its rituals and festivals, remained attractive, so that, as we have seen, Melito, John Chrysostom, and other Christian leaders (e.g., Ignatius of Antioch) had to contend with the phenomenon of Judaizing. We need to consider the possibility that the emphasis upon Jews as "killers of Christ" did not reflect a consensus opinion among Christians but, rather, was, at least in part, a boundary-maintenance measure, necessary precisely because many Christians continued to be drawn toward aspects of the Jewish way.

ASSESSING THE CANONICAL EVIDENCE

Now that we have approached the question from the vantage point of later Christians and observed the pressures and motives that shaped their views, we are in a position to evaluate critically the accounts contained within the NT writings. We will begin with Paul's sharp indictment of the Jews in his Thessalonian correspondence (1 Thess 2:13–16) and then consider each of the four Gospels in turn.

1 Thessalonians 2:13–16

In what is probably Paul's earliest extant letter, the apostle commends his Thessalonian converts for persisting in their new commitment despite the suffering caused by the antagonism of others in their community. In this way the Thessalonian Christians became imitators of their coreligionists in Judea, who likewise suffered at the hands of the Jews ('Ιουδαῖοι, *Ioudaioi*), and it was these Jews who also had killed Jesus and the prophets (v. 15) and hindered the mission to Gentiles. To

---

[15]Of course, Luke provides the same defense for Paul. See Carroll, "Luke's Apology," 106–18.

[16]See Meeks and Wilken, *Jews and Christians*, 30–36; Wilken, *John Chrysostom*, 66–94.

be sure, the interpretation of this passage is difficult, and many have argued that it does not come from Paul but is a later interpolation.[17] Even if it is a gloss, it must be quite early, since no extant manuscripts exclude the pericope. But as the passage plays an important role in the rhetorical structure and design of the letter, it is probably original. If so, then we have from Paul—fifteen to twenty years after the crucifixion—the earliest indictment of Jesus' fellow Jews in Judea as agents of his death.

There is no mention in this passage, or anywhere else in the undisputed letters of Paul, of any Roman role in the death of Jesus.[18] In the light of Romans 13:1–7, with its picture of rulers ordained by God to punish evildoers, one wonders how Paul might have explained Pilate's participation in the event. Paul does credit the crucifixion of Jesus to "the rulers of this age," who were acting in ignorance (1 Cor 2:8), but he appears to have not human but spiritual powers in mind.[19] More frequently in Paul's letters, of course, we encounter the claim that God was the author of the death of Jesus,[20] but evidently the apostle also knew a tradition that assigned responsibility to (Judean) Jews.

Gospel according to Mark

In Mark's narrative the enemies of Jesus contemplate his death while his public ministry is still in its earliest phase. At the close of the series of conflict stories in 2:1–3:6, the Pharisees initiate a conference with the Herodians, intending to effect his destruction (3:6). Jesus later warns the disciples of the dangerous "leaven" of the Pharisees and of Herod (8:15). Then, during the debates in Jerusalem before Jesus' arrest, "some of the Pharisees and Herodians" surface one last time, sent (evidently by "the chief priests and the scribes and the elders," 11:27) to entrap Jesus with a question on the legitimacy of the tribute to Caesar (12:13). Nevertheless, the Pharisees and the coterie of Herod play no role in the Markan passion narrative. Rather, the "chief priests, scribes, and elders" form a united front in Jerusalem that finally succeeds in orchestrating his death. In fact, the narrator's

---

[17]Recent advocates of the passage's authenticity include Brown, *Death of the Messiah*, 1.378–81; and Karl P. Donfried, "Paul and Judaism: 1 Thessalonians 2:13–16 as a Test Case," *Int* 38 (1984) 242–53. The opposite conclusion is reached by Daryl Schmidt, "1 Thess 2:13–16: Linguistic Evidence for an Interpolation," *JBL* 102 (1983) 269–79.

[18]Though note the clear reference to the "testimony of Christ Jesus before Pontius Pilate" in (the deuteropauline) 1 Tim 6:13.

[19]See Cousar, *Theology of the Cross*, 26.

[20]See, e.g., Rom 3:25; 5:8; 8:32; cf. further Cousar, *Theology of the Cross*, 25–51.

brief mention of the plot of the chief priests and the scribes signals the beginning of the passion account (14:1).

Already Jesus' three passion predictions (8:31; 9:31; 10:33–34) indict, proleptically, the chief priests, scribes, and elders as the responsible agents of his death. All three groups are named in 8:31, and 10:33–34 announces that chief priests and scribes "will condemn [κατα-κρινοῦσιν, *katakrinousin*] him to death."[21] When Mark reports the hostile reception given to Jesus' dramatic act in the temple (11:18), the language echoes 3:6, but now the chief priests and the scribes have replaced Pharisees and Herodians as antagonists of Jesus. The elders join the chief priests and scribes in issuing a sharp challenge to Jesus' authority (11:27) and later seek to arrest him (12:12). Once the passion narrative itself begins, the action is clearly dictated by this Jerusalem triumvirate of leading priests, scribes, and elders. They appear again and again in ch. 14, in various combinations (vv. 1, 10, 43, 53, 55). The culmination of their opposition to Jesus comes with the late-night judgment of "all" (identified in 14:55 as the chief priests and the whole Sanhedrin, that is, the chief priests, elders, and scribes [v. 53]) to condemn (κατέκριναν, *katekrinan*) him as deserving (ἔνοχον, *enochon*) death (14:64) and with the early-morning decision of the same parties to hand him over to Pilate (15:1). From this point on, apart from a cameo appearance by the scribes in 15:31 (they join the leading priests in taunting Jesus), it is the chief priests who continue to hold the narrator's interest: they accuse Jesus before Pilate (15:3), turn the crowd against Jesus (15:11), and finally mock him as "king" (15:31).

It is clear that Mark attributes the death of Jesus to his rejection and condemnation by Jewish leaders in Jerusalem. Yet he also presents the Roman governor and soldiers as the instruments of that death. From the third and most detailed of Jesus' passion predictions (10:33–34), the reader expects that the Jewish leaders, after condemning Jesus, will deliver him to Gentiles who will mistreat him and kill him. And that is exactly what later occurs. Although Pilate can see through the leading priests' hostility to Jesus (it is prompted by "envy," 15:10) and although he tries to arrange the release of a "King of the Jews" who has obviously done nothing wrong (15:9, 14), in the end the prefect hands Jesus over to be crucified (v. 15). The narrator explains Pilate's motivation: he wanted to do the crowd, convened to press for Barabbas's release, a favor. Roman soldiers then mock Jesus, beat him, and crucify him (vv. 21–25). Although these Gentile soldiers are conscripted to serve as instruments of Jesus' crucifixion in Mark's account, the last word on them is a favorable one: having seen the manner of Jesus' dying, the centurion is

---

[21] Mark 9:31 contains only a general reference to "persons."

prompted to affirm his divine sonship (15:39). The Markan picture of the Roman part in Jesus' death is markedly ambivalent.

Who put Jesus to death? According to Mark's account, Roman soldiers crucified Jesus, implementing a death sentence pronounced by the Roman prefect, but Jesus went to death only because of the implacable hostility of the Jewish leaders at Jerusalem, whose power was threatened, above all, by Jesus' activity in "their" temple.

Gospel according to Matthew

Matthew reports mortal danger to Jesus as early as his infancy. Disturbed by the magi's quest for one "born King of the Jews" (Matt 2:2), King Herod the Great—consistently identified as "the king" (vv. 1, 3, 9)—attempts to kill the young child. "All Jerusalem" shares his distress (v. 3), if not his murderous rage. The leading priests and scribes of the people supply Herod with precise information concerning the place of the Messiah's birth (vv. 4-6), and there is no indication that they dissociate themselves from Herod's pogrom. Matthew's reader now knows Jerusalem as the city of threat to Jesus, is led to expect that royal authority will be at stake in his life (and death), and wonders just how far the alliance of the religious authorities with Herod—over against Jesus—will go.

In these and other ways,[22] the Matthean infancy narrative anticipates the account of Jesus' death. In the central sections of Matthew's story, it is Pharisees and scribes who regularly spar with Jesus—primarily over issues of legal interpretation and observance (e.g., 9:3, 11, 34; 12:2, 14, 24, 38; 15:1, 12; 19:3). On one occasion, however, conflict with the Pharisees widens to include Sadducees as well (16:1, with Jesus' evaluation in vv. 6, 11–12). Once Jesus reaches Jerusalem, the Jewish public (the ὄχλοι, ochloi) may be favorably disposed to him, esteeming him as a prophet (21:11, 46), but religious authorities of every pedigree oppose him (chief priests and scribes, 21:15; chief priests and elders of the people, 21:23; chief priests and Pharisees, 21:45–46; Pharisees, 22:15, 34; Sadducees, 22:23). In his address to the crowds and the disciples (ch. 23), Jesus focuses his criticism on the scribes and Pharisees, but the whole city has been rocked by his dramatic entry into Jerusalem (21:10, echoing 2:3), and in reaction to his temple demonstration, the leading priests and the elders of the people repudiate his implicit claim to divine authorization (21:23). Matthew's reader, therefore, experiences with greater clarity and intensity even than Mark's a

---

[22]Note, e.g., the sympathetic role given to Gentiles both in the infancy narrative (the magi) and in the passion narrative (Pilate and his wife).

Jesus who is opposed and repudiated by all the Jewish leadership groups of his day.

It is perhaps no surprise, then, that the Pharisees do not completely disappear from the passion account in Matthew (as they do in Mark), for in the aftermath of the crucifixion they accompany the leading priests to Pilate to request that Jesus' tomb be secured with a guard of soldiers (27:62). Nevertheless, as in Mark, the mortal enemies of Jesus throughout the passion drama are the chief priests, scribes, and elders. Leading priests and elders of the people[23] plot to kill Jesus (26:3), a large crowd "from the chief priests and elders of the people" arrests him (26:47), and the assembly of chief priests, elders, and scribes (26:57; or chief priests and the whole Sanhedrin, v. 59) finds him deserving (ἔνοχος, *enochos*) of death (v. 66). The Matthean narrator tells us that all the leading priests and elders of the people decided that he should be put to death and (to that end) handed him over (παρέδωκαν, *paredōkan*) to Pilate (27:1–2). The Roman governor (regularly identified in Matthew by that title), though convinced of Jesus' innocence, handed him over (παρέδωκεν, *paredōken*) to crucifixion (27:26).

Fundamentally, therefore, Matthew follows the Markan pattern. Yet at two crucial points the Matthean account intensifies Jewish involvement in the events surrounding Jesus' death. First, in the decisive scene before Pilate, after the governor has washed his hands of Jesus' blood, "all the people" assume responsibility for the death of Jesus (27:25): "His blood [be] on us and on our children." Pilate, cautioned by his wife after her dreams about "that righteous man," had conducted his own interrogation of the prisoner and then unambiguously and publicly asserted Jesus' innocence. By contrast, the Jewish authorities succeed in swaying the "people" to their side at the key moment, and all these Jews are to be held accountable—according to Matthew—for the death of Jesus. So, from the vantage point of Matthew's community, after the fall of Jerusalem and the destruction of the second temple near the close of the rebellion against Rome (70 C.E.), the narrative informs the reader's attempt to make sense of the recent national catastrophe: it was the working out of divine judgment for the evil done to the Messiah by his Jewish contemporaries.[24] This view is reflected also in the climactic section of the discourse against scribes and Pharisees (ch. 23), where Jesus characterizes Jerusalem as the perennial slayer of God's commissioned agents (v. 37) and announces that "this generation" will be called to account for the spilling of "all righteous [δίκαιον, *dikaion*] blood" throughout history (vv. 35–36)—including, of course, his own.

---

[23]Matthew twice characterizes the elders as elders of the "people" (λαός, *laos*). This redactional touch perhaps prepares the reader for the decisive rejection of Jesus by "all the people" (πᾶς ὁ λαός, *pas ho laos*) in 27:25.

[24]See further Senior, *Passion of Jesus in Matthew*, 119–22.

After the burial of Jesus, Matthew inserts a second scene deepening the complicity of the Jewish leaders. Foiled in their attempt to keep Jesus in the tomb, the leading priests and elders bribe the soldiers to spread the false report that the disciples of Jesus have stolen his body from the tomb, a rumor still in circulation "among Jews" to Matthew's own day (28:11–15). This Gospel not only indicts the Jewish authorities for their part in bringing Jesus to death but also exposes their entanglement in a web of deception that, even in the author's time, continued to mislead Jews about the facts of Jesus' death and resurrection.

Luke–Acts

We have seen that although Matthew, for the most part, follows the Markan passion account, the Matthean narrative accents the Jewish role more sharply than does Mark. On the other hand, Roman characters (Pilate, his wife, the soldiers) attest, more pointedly than in Mark, to Jesus' innocence. The author of Luke–Acts pushes even further in this direction. In Luke's narrative, Pilate emphatically asserts Jesus' innocence and does not, in fact, pronounce the death sentence. The Jewish leaders at Jerusalem have their way with Jesus and are joined by the Jewish people (λαός, laos) at the moment of decision. It is apparently the Jewish authorities who carry out the crucifixion,[25] although soldiers are present to mock Jesus (23:36–37) and, in the person of the centurion, to respond to his death with the declaration "Truly this man was righteous!" (23:47). Both the Lukan resurrection narrative (Luke 24) and a series of speeches by Peter and Paul in Acts explicitly assign responsibility for the death of Jesus to the Jewish people of Jerusalem, especially their leaders.

And yet careful reading of Luke–Acts discloses a more complex picture. Luke's distinctive handling of the death of Jesus is already evident in his version of Jesus' passion predictions (Luke 9:22, 44; 17:25; 18:31–32), but in a way that seems to run counter to the sketch given in the previous paragraph.[26] The last prediction is particularly surprising, for here Jesus does not, as in Mark and Matthew, speak of a handing

---

[25]With the omission of the Roman soldiers' mockery of Jesus after the death sentence (cf. Mark 15:16–20), the "they" (cf. Mark 15:21) who lead Jesus out to the place of the skull and crucify him there are no longer the soldiers but (at least syntactically) the same "they" who have been demanding that Pilate condemn Jesus—namely, the Jewish leaders and people last specifically identified in Luke 23:13. For a different analysis, see Brown, *Death of the Messiah*, 1.856–59.

[26]The third of these predictions (17:25) is unique to Luke; embedded in an eschatological discourse, it envisages the rejection of the "Son of humanity" (ὁ υἱὸς τοῦ ἀνθρώπου, ho huios tou anthrōpou) by "this generation" (cf. Matt 23:36).

over to the leading priests and scribes or of their condemning him to death (Mark 10:33; Matt 20:18). Rather, Jesus simply prophesies his surrender to the Gentiles, who will abuse and kill him (18:32). Moreover, where the Gospel passion narrative portrays a Pilate who is sympathetic to Jesus, repeatedly protests his innocence, and finally surrenders him to the desires and devices of the Jewish leaders, a prayer of the nascent apostolic community, drawing upon Ps 2, numbers Pilate (and Herod Antipas) among the enemies gathered against the Messiah Jesus (Acts 4:25–28). Within the narrative world of Luke–Acts, did the Jewish leaders (and people) actually kill Jesus? How is Pilate's role to be understood? A closer reading of Luke's account of the death of Jesus is necessary.

As in Mark and Matthew, Jesus' principal critics during the course of his public ministry are the scribes and Pharisees, although Luke often substitutes the term νομικοί (*nomikoi*, "lawyers") for γραμματεῖς (*grammateis*, "scribes").[27] Even though the Pharisees on three occasions share meals with Jesus (7:36–50; 11:37–54; 14:1–24), they appear to stand at some distance from his vision and praxis of God's reign (e.g., 15:2; 16:14), and in the final appearance of Pharisees in the Gospel, some of their ranks vehemently deny the messianic implications of Jesus' triumphal entry into Jerusalem (19:39– 40). Yet no Pharisee is mentioned in the passion narrative itself, even as the Pharisees in Acts do not—apart from the temporary involvement of Saul—oppose the community of the apostles to the death.[28] Once Jesus has completed the fateful journey to Jerusalem, his enemies are not Pharisees but temple functionaries— leading priests, scribes allied with them, officers of the temple (στρατηγοί, *stratēgoi*)—and a group of elite persons variously labelled "elders" (or "elders of the people"), persons of high status (πρῶτοι, *prōtoi*), and "rulers." In Acts it is again the circle of powerful priests in Jerusalem that are the chief enemies of the apostolic community, although with

---

[27] Luke retains the Markan γραμματεύς (*grammateus*, "scribe") in 5:21, 30; 6:7; 11:53–54; 15:2; 19:47; 20:1, 19, 45–47. He employs νομικός (*nomikos*, "lawyer") in 7:30; 10:25; 11:37–52; 14:3. The juxtaposition of Jesus' criticism of "lawyers" (11:37–52) with the hostile reaction of "scribes" (11:53–54) indicates that the terms are interchangeable in Luke.

[28] For a variety of approaches to Luke's intriguing and complex characterization of the Pharisees, see Jack T. Sanders, *The Jews in Luke–Acts* (Philadelphia: Fortress, 1987) 84–131; Robert L. Brawley, *Luke–Acts and the Jews: Conflict, Apology, and Conciliation* (SBLMS 33; Atlanta: Scholars, 1987); Carroll, "Luke's Portrayal of the Pharisees," 604–21; Joseph B. Tyson, ed., *Luke–Acts and the Jewish People: Eight Critical Perspectives* (Minneapolis: Augsburg, 1988); David B. Gowler, *Host, Guest, Enemy, and Friend: Portraits of the Pharisees in Luke and Acts* (New York: Peter Lang, 1991); and Darr, *On Character Building*, 85–126.

the shift to Paul's Diaspora mission the label "the Jews" ultimately becomes the blanket term for antagonists of the "Way."

The Jerusalem narrative of Luke's Gospel drives a sharp wedge between the response of the Jewish leaders to Jesus and that of the Jewish public (the λαός). The leaders (chief priests and elders, or chief priests and rulers) seek to arrest Jesus and have him killed, while the people hang on his every word (e.g., 19:47–48; 20:1, 19, 26; 21:38; 22:2, 6; 23:5).[29] And it is in precisely these terms that Cleopas and an unnamed disciple summarize recent events for the risen Jesus: "[Jesus] was a prophet, mighty in deed and word before God and all the people, [but] our chief priests and rulers handed him over [παρέδωκαν, paredōkan] to a judgment [κρίμα, krima] of death and crucified him" (24:19–20).[30]

There can be no doubt that Luke pictures the Jewish leaders in Jerusalem as bearing primary responsibility for the death of Jesus. This view is reinforced in Acts: Peter and the other apostles, hauled before the Sanhedrin, mince no words: "God . . . raised Jesus, whom you killed by hanging him on a tree" (Acts 5:30). The rulers of the people and the elders are those builders who despised the stone that became the cornerstone (Acts 4:8, 11).[31] Therefore, one should not place too much weight on Jesus' silence about Jewish authorities in the third passion prediction (Luke 18:31–32). That passage focuses on the Gentile role in Jesus' death and simply does not address Jewish involvement (already established in the first passion prediction, 9:22). Luke's reader cannot miss the presence of the Jewish leaders in the passion drama, despite their absence from 18:31–32.

Luke does not, however, present a formal Jewish trial, complete with witnesses, judgment, and sentence.[32] Rather, we find what amounts to

---

[29] To be sure, Luke has reported conflict between Jesus and the crowds over the course of his ministry (e.g., 4:28–30; 19:5–7; cf. 19:39), and Jesus could deliver sweeping criticisms of his Jewish contemporaries (e.g., 7:31–35; 9:41; 10:13–15; 11:29–32; 12:54–56). This feature of the Gospel has been emphasized—and, in our judgment, exaggerated—especially by David P. Moessner (*Lord of the Banquet: The Literary and Theological Significance of the Lukan Travel Narrative* [Minneapolis: Fortress, 1989]) and by Kingsbury (*Conflict in Luke*). See further the analyses by Tyson, "Conflict as a Literary Theme"; and Matera, "Journey to Jerusalem," 57–77. Nevertheless, the passion narrative consistently distances the λαός from the Jewish leaders' rejection of Jesus.

[30] One might wish to argue that the two disciples are unreliable spokespersons (Jesus must open their eyes to the meaning of the Scriptures and of the crucifixion, not to mention to his presence with them!) and therefore this assessment of the passion events should be viewed with suspicion. The view expressed by these disciples, however, conforms too closely to the Lukan passion account, as well as to the speeches in Acts, to be considered unreliable.

[31] Luke adds "you [builders]" to the citation from Ps 118:22.

[32] See Frank J. Matera, "The Trial of Jesus: Problems and Proposals," *Int* 45

a preliminary hearing before the elders (πρεσβυτέριον, *presbyterion*) of the people, both chief priests and scribes, in their Sanhedrin (22:66–71). Not the high priest alone but the whole assembly interrogate Jesus, lead him to Pilate for the real trial, and there accuse him before the governor (23:1–5). The session before Jewish authorities, convened in the early morning,[33] includes neither testimony from witnesses (other than Jesus himself) nor any verdict or sentence.

Luke does not thereby let the Jewish authorities off the hook; rather, he shifts the scene in which they express their decisive, public rejection of Jesus from the Jewish court to the Roman tribunal. Before Pilate, the chief priests (joined, at 23:4, by crowds [ὄχλοι, *ochloi*]—evidently drawn from the ranks of the Sanhedrin and temple leadership) accuse Jesus of crimes with clear political overtones (vv. 2, 5): corrupting the nation; opposing payment of tribute to the emperor; calling himself Christ, a king; and agitating the people (λαός).[34] Pilate repeatedly asserts Jesus' innocence, but in the end the Jewish leaders carry the day. The narrator informs us that "their voices prevailed," that Pilate decided to grant "their demand," that he released to them the one (Barabbas) for whom "they were asking," and that he handed Jesus over "to their will" (23:23–25). Having heard all the charges brought against Jesus, Pilate judged him to be innocent, yet he allowed a blatant miscarriage of justice, caving in to the unrelenting pressure of the Jewish leaders. That portrait of Pilate is unflattering enough: Luke is not rewriting the trial of Jesus to construct a pro-Roman apology.[35] No, Luke is using the Roman Pilate to vindicate Jesus.

(1991) 7–8. For a different view, see Brown, *Death of the Messiah*, 1.389 n. 142; 1.423–24.

[33]Rather than in the late night, as in Mark and Matthew.

[34]The mention of "crowds" in 23:4 does not yet place the Jewish public (the λαός) at the trial. This ὄχλος corresponds to the group that was present for the arrest of Jesus (22:47). The fact that the narrator has these crowds, with the chief priests, accuse Jesus of agitating the people (λαός) clearly differentiates the two "crowds"—one associated with the temple leadership, the other (the λαός) the Jewish public, until now firmly in Jesus' camp. Having heard Jesus accused of stirring up the people, Pilate then summons them for the final phase of the trial (v. 13). Only now do they side with their "rulers" against Jesus. Cf. the analyses by J. Bradley Chance, "The Jewish People and the Death of Jesus in Luke–Acts: Some Implications of an Inconsistent Narrative Role," SBLSP 1991, 50–81 (51–60); Johnson, *Luke*, 370–75; and Tannehill, *Narrative Unity*, 1.164–66. For a different reading, see Tyson, *Death of Jesus in Luke–Acts*, 37–38, 48, 120–21; Brown, *Death of the Messiah*, 1.790–91. Tyson finds in Luke–Acts a consistent pattern of initial acceptance by the people, followed by final rejection, and thinks that already at the arrest of Jesus the Jewish public (i.e., the "crowd") has joined the opposition.

[35]So also Brown, *Death of the Messiah*, 1.389–90.

We should not be surprised, therefore, when in the community prayer of Acts 4 Pilate appears alongside Herod, and the Gentiles and the peoples of Israel, as an enemy of Jesus (fulfilling Ps 2:1–2). In that context, the more "realistic" depiction of Pilate—consistent with Jesus' own characterization of him (Luke 13:1)—suits the situation of the apostolic community. If the Lukan passion account assigns blame primarily to the Jewish leaders, it is not to excuse Pilate. On the contrary, Pilate's role is to excuse Jesus. The part played by the Jewish leaders, on the other hand, belongs to the unfolding of the history of salvation, in which God's agents of deliverance are rejected by the nation and a door is thus opened to the Gentile world.

Yet it is not the leaders alone who play the part of villains. We have noted that the Jewish public (the λαός) are on Jesus' side until the Roman trial. Immediately after the decision of Pilate to surrender Jesus to the Jewish leaders, they resume a posture sympathetic to Jesus: a multitude of the people and of women mourn his fate (23:27); while the "rulers" mock the crucified "Savior," the people simply stand observing (v. 35); and after Jesus has died, all the crowds gathered to witness the event leave the scene shaken and remorseful (v. 48). The solitary exception to this pattern, within the Gospel passion narrative, is the people's rejection of Jesus in the pivotal scene before Pilate. They appear to be among the assembly who, all together (παμπληθεί, pamplēthei), demand that Jesus be crucified (v. 18).

The speeches of Acts reinforce this impression, for repeatedly Peter and Paul hold the Jewish people in Jerusalem responsible for the death of Jesus (Acts 2:22–23, 36; 3:12–13; 4:10; 10:39; 13:27–28). It is important to observe, of course, that they lay this blame at the doorstep of the Jewish people of Jerusalem not to shut the door on them but to summon the people to repentance and a place in the company of the saved. And according to Luke, many thousands of them responded positively to that summons. For the most part, however, the power brokers at Jerusalem—the leading priests, the rulers, and those allied with them—continue to play the part of villain in Acts, as in the Gospel.[36] Luke's narrative faults Judas, the Jewish people, and Pilate (in his own way) for their roles in the death of Jesus. But it is the leaders of the Jewish people who must shoulder most of that burden in Luke's telling of the story.

---

[36] The narrator does include many priests among those joining the community of disciples (Acts 6:7), but for the most part the leaders at Jerusalem are, in Gamaliel's own description, θεομάχοι (theomachoi, "enemies of God") (5:39), or, in the terms of Stephen's indictment, those who "resist the Holy Spirit," "murderers of the Righteous One" (7:51–52).

Gospel according to John

We have seen that Matthew and Luke, each in its own way, expands the involvement of Jewish authorities in Jesus' death, with a correspondingly diminished role for the Roman actors. The Fourth Gospel is yet another witness to this tendency in early Christian literature. In John, as in Luke, Pilate again and again asserts Jesus' innocence and seeks to release him, only to be thwarted by Jesus' enemies, "the Jews" ('Ιουδαῖοι, *Ioudaioi*). Not that John paints a pretty picture of the Roman prefect! He is weak, vacillating, unable either to discern the truth (Jesus) or to act on the basis of what he knows is right.[37] But the real villains of the piece are "the Jews," and the true "trial" of Jesus before a Jewish tribunal is the whole of Jesus' public ministry (chs. 2–12).[38] The case is closed and the fate of Jesus sealed long before the passion narrative begins, so that no formal process other than a Roman trial is needed after Jesus' arrest. The irony is that while the Roman trial is necessary because the Jews cannot put anyone to death (18:31), at the close of the trial Pilate hands Jesus over (παρέδωκεν, *paredōken*) to them for crucifixion. In the capacity of executioners, they now "receive" (παρέλαβον, *parelabon*) him for the first time, having failed to receive him throughout the narrative (as already anticipated in 1:11; and see 3:11, 32; 5:43).

Concerted efforts to put Jesus to death begin as early as ch. 5. The Jews ('Ιουδαῖοι, *Ioudaioi*), unimpressed by Jesus' defense of his Sabbath healing of the lame man, are incited by his claim of divine sonship to seek to kill him (5:18). The basic complaint, here and elsewhere in the story, is that Jesus "makes himself" equal to God by claiming to be the Son of God.[39] After the feeding of the crowd, their immediate reaction may be to crown a new king, but by the time Jesus has finished interpreting his sign, all but a few have been scandalized, and the Jews in Judea are seeking to kill him (7:1). The fact that people in Judea are looking to put him to death becomes a matter for some debate (7:19–20, 25), and then the first attempts to arrest Jesus are frustrated (7:30, 32, 44).[40] In a dispute with "Jewish believers" (!), Jesus chal-

---

[37]Cf. Culpepper, *Anatomy*, 142–43; Brown, *Death of the Messiah*, 1.390–91.

[38]For the view that John's whole narrative constitutes the trial of Jesus, see ch. 5 above; cf. Harvey, *Jesus on Trial*; Matera, "Trial of Jesus," 10–11.

[39]The charge that Jesus "makes himself" out to be what he cannot be recurs in 8:53; 10:33; and 19:7, 12. Of course, for John Jesus *is*, as Son of God, "equal to God," greater than Abraham, and king, but the charge itself is false because what Jesus has he is given by God. See ch. 5 above.

[40]John 7:32 is quite specific: leading priests and Pharisees send officers to arrest Jesus. The notices in vv. 30 and 44 are general; some of Jesus' audience (of Jews) are angered by his speech and so want him arrested. In another context (8:20), no move is made to arrest Jesus, the narrator explains, because "his hour had not yet come."

lenges their claim to be children of Abraham, a claim invalidated, in part, by their attempts to kill him (8:37, 40). Conflict escalates to the point that Jesus' auditors try to stone him to death for blasphemy (8:59).

Later, addressing "the Jews" in Jerusalem, Jesus speaks of his oneness with God and, not surprisingly, encounters the same hostile reception (10:31–33).[41] Another unsuccessful attempt to arrest him ensues (10:39). When the disciples acknowledge this menacing threat in Judea (11:8, 16), they unwittingly introduce Jesus' journey to give life to Lazarus as a journey to death. And their premonition is realized with the council's final resolution to put Jesus to death (11:53). In a sense, this decision is anticlimactic, but it does put official and formal touches on the Jewish enmity toward Jesus, for, prompted by the high priest Caiaphas, the Sanhedrin convened by chief priests and Pharisees commits itself to his destruction. Once this step has been taken, there is no further need for deliberation after Jesus is arrested. To be sure, he is brought to Annas's home and questioned by the high priest[42] about his followers and his teaching (18:19), but that inquiry appears to have no other purpose than to gather information for the trial Pilate will hold.

Typically, Jesus' mortal enemies are "the Jews" ('Ιουδαῖοι). It is they who seek his demise, and in the end, it is they who effect his death (note 'Ιουδαῖοι in 18:31, 36, 38; 19:7, 12, 14).[43] Who are these Jews? Sometimes John uses the term 'Ιουδαῖοι in a general and neutral way (e.g., for Jewish observances). Far more often, however, the label is applied to Jesus' own people who reject him. Within the trial narrative, the narrator oscillates between the generic term "the Jews" and much more specific names designating the Jewish leadership groups. So, for example, Pilate tells Jesus, "Your nation [ἔθνος, ethnos] and the chief priests handed you over to me" (18:35). Jesus replies that if his were an earthly realm, his servants would have prevented his being handed over to "the Jews" (v. 36). In 19:6 the chief priests and officers (ὑπηρέται, hypēretai) clamor for Jesus' crucifixion, and when Pilate tries to place the ball back in their court, it is "the Jews" who reply (v. 7). When Pilate presents a scourged Jesus to "the Jews" as their king, they (ἐκεῖνοι, ekeinoi) again call for his crucifixion (vv. 14–15a); then it is the chief priests who answer Pilate's question, "Shall I crucify your king?" (v. 15b).

---

[41] Intriguing echoes of the synoptic "Jewish trial" can be heard in this passage. The Jews surround Jesus and ask, "Are you the Christ?" (10:24; cf. Luke 22:67). His evasive reply, couched in terms of his listeners' unbelief (vv. 25–26), is also reminiscent of Luke 22:67. Moreover, the charge of blasphemy here (v. 33) is placed by Mark and Matthew at the Sanhedrin session (Mark 14:64; Matt 26:65).

[42] Presumably Annas, formerly high priest (6–15 C.E.) and distinguished by John from the current high priest "that year" (11:51), Annas's son-in-law Caiaphas. Annas then transfers the prisoner to Caiaphas, who sends him on to Pilate.

[43] Note, too, the refrain "out of fear of the Jews" (7:13; 9:22; 19:38; 20:19).

In a similar way, earlier passages associate "the Jews" with the Pharisees (1:19, 24; 3:1; 9:13–22), and yet the narrator can also clearly distinguish between the two (11:45). Likewise, the Pharisees are both linked to the "rulers" (3:1; 7:48) and distinguished from them (12:42). A number of passages characterize the Pharisees as a ruling group, in partnership with the chief priests (e.g., 7:32, 45, 48; 11:47, 57; 18:3). There is a marked fluidity to John's usage; depending upon the context, he can identify Jesus' antagonists as "Jews," "Pharisees," or "chief priests." He does appear, however, to portray the Pharisees and the leading priests as the "rulers" among the Jews who finally succeed in putting Jesus to death after so many foiled attempts.

The trial by Pilate may be a carefully staged and highly dramatic scene,[44] but as far as Jesus' death is concerned, it is of relatively minor importance. A Roman trial and typically Roman mode of execution seem necessary if Jesus' word (about his "being lifted up") is to be realized (18:32), yet, as we have already observed, Pilate gives Jesus back to the Jewish leaders to be crucified (19:15–16). The Roman trial does afford the narrator a canvas on which to paint in vivid colors the majesty of Jesus, attested to by the Roman governor, and the apostasy of the rulers of the Jews. For in their zeal to be rid of Jesus, they deny not only him but the sovereign rule of God, preferring instead to acknowledge the supremacy of Caesar ("We have no king but Caesar" [19:15]).

WHO KILLED JESUS? A PROPOSAL AND A REFLECTION

We have sifted through the relevant source material and proceed now to propose a sketch of the events that brought Jesus to the cross. Early Christian sources, as we have discovered, make the task exceedingly difficult, if not impossible. They preserve traditions that lack unanimity at some critical points, and they increasingly reflect the apologetic and polemical concerns of the nascent Christian movement in relation both to its Jewish rivals and to Roman society. Because of the nature of the sources at our disposal, we can claim no more than plausibility for this reconstruction.

Proposal

Jesus had participated in his share of conflicts with other Jewish teachers during his public career. No doubt, that history of controversy

---

[44]See the analysis in ch. 5 above.

shaped the course of events in Jerusalem, though it is difficult to draw the connections with any precision.[45] But after all, he was a charismatic figure who had strongly challenged the religious and social norms of his day,[46] and he had a following. And now he had come to Jerusalem at the time of the Passover festival, when conditions were ripe for popular disturbance.

It is probable that because of words and actions critical of the temple, Jesus was perceived by the high priest and other custodians of the temple as a threat to the public order.[47] So they had Jesus arrested and, after interrogation, handed him over to the Roman prefect, who examined him and found him guilty of the crime of treason. He therefore had this disturber of the provincial peace executed. What else would Caesar expect him to do with a would-be "King of the Jews"?[48]

It seems likely, then, that certain power brokers, both Jewish and Roman—acting, no doubt, in what they perceived to be the best interest of the Jewish people, but also their own—moved swiftly against an apparent threat to the tenuous Roman peace in Judea.

---

[45] Brown provides a helpful discussion (*Death of the Messiah*, 1.391–93).

[46] See our discussion in ch. 9 above.

[47] On the historical argument sketched in this section, cf. the analysis by Harvey, *Jesus and the Constraints of History*, ch. 2. Naturally, some have contested the historicity of these materials. Jesus' stance toward the temple, however, was clearly problematic from the beginning of the Christian movement and was subjected to considerable reinterpretation. Luke postpones all charges about the temple from the trial of Jesus to the interrogation of Stephen (Acts 6:13–14). John reports controversy centering on a saying of Jesus about the destruction and rebuilding of the temple (2:19–22) but makes clear that the saying has to do with the true temple of Jesus' own body. The Markan narrator evaluates the temple charge against Jesus as false testimony (Mark 14:56–57; contrast Matt 26:59–61), yet there is at the same time a measure of truth to it (Jesus did prophesy the temple's demise). Like the disruptive act in the temple, this tradition probably preserves a solid historical core. Public knowledge of Jesus' critical discourse against the temple institution, together with his dramatic act against the money changers in the temple (whatever the precise meaning of the gesture), would have been sufficient to provoke his arrest, as the later example of the antitemple preacher Jesus ben Ananias confirms (Josephus *J.W.* 6.5.3). On the historicity of the temple materials, see further Brown, *Death of the Messiah*, 1.454–60.

[48] Of course, as Gerard S. Sloyan points out (*Jesus on Trial* [Philadelphia: Fortress, 1973] 128, 131), it is possible that Pilate regarded the charges against Jesus as baseless, that he perceived in Jesus no threat to Roman power. In that case the historical facts would square rather well with the Gospel accounts of the proceeding before Pilate—and with the apologetic motives we have found present in early Christian treatments of the topic. While the possibility cannot be ruled out, the nature of our extracanonical evidence for Pilate's style of governance (Philo, Josephus) tips the balance of probability toward the view that the Roman prefect needed little persuasion to move against Jesus. Note Brown's critical analysis of these accounts of Pilate in *Death of the Messiah*, 1.698–705.

The long-debated issue of the competency of the Jewish court is relevant but not of decisive importance here.[49] Was the Sanhedrin authorized to implement the death sentence, or does John 18:31—"It is not permitted us to kill anyone"—accurately summarize the situation at the time of Jesus? Whether or not the Jewish court could, in certain circumstances, sentence an offender to death and carry out the sentence, in the case of Jesus we have every reason to think that a Roman capital sentence was in effect. Once the case came under Pilate's jurisdiction, the Roman prefect, invested with the Roman *imperium*, would not have relinquished jurisdiction over the case. And while we have some evidence of the Jewish practice of crucifixion, it remained a predominantly Roman mode of execution in Judea.[50]

It is perhaps significant that two non-Christian sources, one Jewish and the other Roman, corroborate this brief sketch. The Jewish historian Josephus, writing in the second-to-last decade of the first century, reports that Pilate, on the basis of accusations from the "leading men among us" (τῶν πρώτων ἀνδρῶν παρ' ἡμῖν, *tōn prōtōn andrōn par hēmin*), condemned Jesus to the cross (*Ant.* 18.64).[51] The Roman historian Tacitus presents a similar account, though mentioning only the Roman involvement: "Christus . . . had undergone the death penalty in the reign of Tiberius, by sentence of the procurator Pontius Pilate" (*Ann.* 15.44; LCL translation).

Reflection

In the interest of interfaith harmony, it would have been convenient if the results of our historical investigation had come out differently—if,

---

[49]For a good sketch of the problem, see Brown, *Death of the Messiah*, 1.363–72. David R. Catchpole (*The Trial of Jesus: A Study in the Gospels and Jewish Historiography from 1770 to the Present Day* [SPB 18; Leiden: E. J. Brill, 1971] 254) thinks that the Sanhedrin had authority in Jesus' day to pass capital sentences but that execution of the sentence was restricted by and to the Romans. Catchpole argues, then, that there was a Jewish proceeding against Jesus issuing in his condemnation.

[50]See ch. 9 above. For appraisal of the evidence, see Hengel, *Crucifixion*; cf. Fitzmyer, "Crucifixion in Ancient Palestine," 125–46.

[51]Of course, this section of the *Antiquities of the Jews* has been embellished by Christian scribes, but the reference to Jesus' condemnation by Pilate on the basis of accusations by leading Jews lacks the inflation of the clear interpolations surrounding it (e.g.: "if indeed one ought to call him a man"; "he was the Messiah"; "he appeared to them alive on the third day"). If this line originally stood in Josephus's text—independent of early Christian tradition—it would represent important early testimony pointing in the direction of our historical proposal. One must, however, be extremely cautious. See n. 3 in ch. 9 above; and Brown, *Death of the Messiah*, 1.373–76.

with some other recent scholars, we had been able to erase any and all Jewish complicity in the death of Jesus.[52] It has, of course, become painfully clear that early Christians, for a variety of motives, enhanced the Jewish role and diminished the Roman role in these events. Yet the earliest Christians did not invent the story of the Jerusalem leadership's antagonism to Jesus.

None of this amounts to any monolithic rejection of Jesus by his own people back then and there, or even by all their religious and political elite.[53] And certainly it has nothing to do with moral responsibility on the part of generations of Jews since. We must challenge and repudiate all forms of anti-Jewish slander, even if they are grounded in the canonical accounts of Matthew ("And all the people answered, 'His blood be on us and on our children'" [27:25]), of John ("You are of your father the devil" [8:44]), of Luke ("This Jesus whom you crucified, God raised up" [Acts 2:36]), or of Paul ("the Jews who killed the Lord Jesus" [1 Thess 2:14–15]). The historical reality—however elusive its details—possessed a complexity that belies the sweeping indictments that through much of Christian history have sprung up from such soil in sacred Scripture.

---

[52]Notable among the authors who deny any real involvement by Jewish leaders in Jesus' death is Rivkin (What Crucified Jesus?). Perhaps the most extreme position is that of Cohn (The Trial and Death of Jesus), who contends that the Jewish leadership met with Jesus to prepare a case in his *defense* before the Roman governor. For a sanguine view of the practical effects on contemporary religious attitudes of any revised history produced by modern scholarship, see Samuel Sandmel, "The Trial of Jesus: Reservations," Judaism 20 (1971) 69–74. Catchpole (Trial of Jesus) surveys Jewish historiography on the trial of Jesus from 1770 to the modern era.

[53]See our discussion in ch. 9 above. There is something to be said for Rivkin's reframing the question to, What killed Jesus? (What Crucified Jesus?). Dahl, too, has termed this a more fruitful question ("Messianic Ideas," 402). Rivkin's own reconstruction, however—that no legitimate Jewish institution had anything to do with Jesus' trial and death, which is to be blamed on the "Roman imperial system"—relies on an untenable division of Jewish life into distinct religious and political spheres.

⊕ ELEVEN

The Old Testament and the death of Jesus:
THE ROLE OF SCRIPTURE IN THE GOSPEL PASSION NARRATIVES

Joel Marcus
Lecturer in Biblical Studies
University of Glasgow

THE OLD TESTAMENT AND THE GENESIS OF THE PASSION NARRATIVES

From a very early stage of its existence, the church would have required an explanation for the fact that Jesus, whom it proclaimed to be the Messiah, the expected King of Israel, had finished his life on a Roman cross, abandoned by his followers. Messiahs were not supposed to end up like this—though several would-be messiahs did—but were to overthrow the yoke of pagan oppression through the power of God and to lead Israel to national liberation and world rulership as well as spiritual rejuvenation. Even some Gentiles knew that Jesus did not fit the standard messianic pattern; the pagan writer Celsus, for example, quotes a Jew who confutes Christian claims by saying that Jesus fulfilled none of his promises, was led away as a prisoner, and was abandoned by his associates (Origen *Against Celsus* 2.9).

We can see the germ of the Christian response to this sort of challenge, and indeed the germ of the passion narratives of the Gospels, in Paul's statement in 1 Cor 15:3 that "Christ died for our sins in accordance with the Scriptures."[1] It is significant that Paul himself does

---

[1] NRSV; unless otherwise noted, all biblical quotations in this chapter are either directly from this translation or altered from it, in which case they are marked "alt." Chapter and verse numbers also follow the NRSV.

not here or elsewhere refer to specific OT passages that were fulfilled by the manner of Christ's death; apparently the conviction of scriptural necessity is all that is important to him. Our earliest written Gospel, Mark, which was composed about twenty years later than Paul's letter, still contains remnants of this way of thinking; in two passages, for example, Jesus says that his approaching maltreatment and death must happen in order to fulfill the Scriptures, but he does not specify what scriptures he has in mind (Mark 9:12; 14:49; cf. Matt 26:54, 56).

Perhaps already in Paul's time, however, a connected narrative of the events of Jesus' last days on earth was beginning to be formed. Bald assertions that Jesus' death fulfilled the Scriptures would very soon need to be backed up by a demonstration that it did so. The best way of doing this would have been to compose a narrative showing that Jesus' suffering and death were in line with the hints that God had squirreled away in the only scriptures that the earliest church possessed, namely the sacred writings of Israel, or what modern-day Christians call the Old Testament. Many scholars accept the hypothesis that such a narrative developed at a fairly early stage, before the Gospels were written.

The Gospel accounts of Jesus' suffering and death, probably in dependence upon this pre-Gospel passion narrative, are more strongly marked with OT references than any other section of the Gospels, with the possible exception of the birth narratives in Matthew and Luke. In the Synoptics, very few of these references are direct quotations introduced by citation formulas (see Mark 14:27 par. Matt 26:31; Matt 27:9; Luke 22:37). On the contrary, most are allusions embedded in the narrative, the recognition of which depends upon the assumed biblical literacy of the reader rather than on editorial elbow jabbing from the author. Mark, for example, does not in ch. 15 (as he does in 13:14) step out of his role as objective narrator to direct his readers' attention to the fact that the division of Jesus' garments, the mockery of the bystanders, the jibe that Jesus should save himself, and Jesus' own cry of dereliction are features drawn from Ps 22 (Mark 15:24, 29, 30–32, 34; cf. Ps 22:1, 6–9, 18). He seems, rather, to presuppose that at least some of his readers will pick up these allusions on their own and thus penetrate to the deeper level of the story, where what is being done to Jesus is the fulfillment of a biblical pattern.

OLD TESTAMENT PASSAGES USED IN THE PASSION NARRATIVES

The Psalms of the Righteous Sufferer

The psalm just mentioned, Ps 22, is one of a series of texts, scattered throughout the Psalter, in which the speaker laments the persecution that he suffers from his enemies, protests his innocence, and calls upon God to deliver him. These "Psalms of the Righteous Sufferer" are the most pervasive scriptural resource utilized in the Gospel passion narratives. Their usage may be summed up in the following chart:[2]

Gospels		*Psalms*
Matt 26:3–4	gathered together and took counsel to kill	31:14 LXX
Mark 14:1 par. Matt 26:4	to kill by cunning	10:7–8
Mark 14:18 par. John 13:18	the one eating with me	41:9 LXX (Mark)
John 15:25	hated me without cause	35:19; 69:4 LXX
Mark 14:34 par. Matt 26:38	very sad	42:5, 11; 43:5 LXX
John 12:27	soul troubled	6:3–4 LXX
Mark 14:41 par. Matt 26:45	delivered to hands of sinners	140:8 LXX
Mark 14:45 par. Matt 26:49 par. Luke 22:47–48	deceitful kiss	38:12; 41:6

---

[2]This and the following charts and references to OT allusions rely on the work of Howard Clark Kee ("The Function of Scriptural Quotations and Allusions in Mark 11–16," in *Jesus und Paulus: Festschrift für Werner Georg Kümmel zum 70. Geburtstag,* ed. E. Earle Ellis and Erich Grässer [Göttingen: Vandenhoeck & Ruprecht, 1975] 165–88) and Moo *(Old Testament)* which I followed and expanded in *Way of the Lord.* The charts have now been further expanded with references from Green, *Death of Jesus.* See now also the magisterial work by Brown, *Death of the Messiah,* which appeared after this essay was substantially written; the appendix in vol. 2 on "The Old Testament Background of the Passion Narratives" is worth careful scrutiny. Most of the OT texts in this and the subsequent charts are marked "LXX." This indicates that there are vocabulary overlaps with the Septuagint, the early Greek translation of the OT. Since, however, most of the OT references are allusions rather than actual quotations and since the LXX usually chooses logical Greek words to translate the Hebrew, this notation does not necessarily mean that the NT author is basing his allusion on the LXX—only that he might be doing so. In a few cases the reference seems definitely to depend on the Hebrew text (or a Greek translation independent of the LXX) rather than the LXX; in these cases the chart is marked "MT" (= Masoretic Text).

Mark 14:54 par. Matt 26:58 par. Luke 22:54	following at a distance	38:11 LXX
Mark 14:57	false witnesses rising up	27:12 LXX; 35:11 LXX
Mark 14:61 par. Matt 26:63; Mark 15:5 par. Matt 27:14; Luke 23:9	silence before accusers	38:13–14
Luke 22:71	we have heard it ourselves	35:21
Mark 15:3 par. Luke 23:10	vehement verbal attack	109:3
Matt 27:34	offered gall	69:21 LXX
Mark 15:24 par. Matt 27:35 par. Luke 23:34 par. John 19:24	division of garments	22:18 LXX
Mark 15:29 par. Matt 27:39	mockery, head wagging	22:7 LXX
Mark 15:30–31 par. Matt 27:40, 42	"Save yourself!"	22:8 LXX
Matt 27:43	"He trusts in God; let God deliver him!"	22:8 LXX? (πέποιθεν, pepoithen; ἤλπισεν, ēlpisen)
Mark 15:32 par. Matt 27:44	reviling	22:6 LXX
Mark 15:34 par. Matt 27:46	cry of dereliction	22:1 LXX
Luke 23:46	"Into your hands I commit my spirit!"	31:5 LXX
John 19:28	"I am thirsty"	22:15? 69:21?
Mark 15:36 par. Matt 27:48	offered vinegar to drink	69:21 LXX
Mark 15:39 par. Matt 27:54	worshipped by Gentiles	22:27

Luke 23:47	just, innocent (δίκαιος, *dikaios*)	34:15, 17, 19, 21; 37:12; etc. LXX
Mark 15:40 par. Matt 27:55 par. Luke 23:49	looking on from a distance	38:11 LXX
John 19:36	no bone broken	34:20 LXX
Mark 15:43 par. Luke 23:51	kingdom of God	22:28

Not all of these allusions are as explicitly related to OT texts as the others, but most are fairly obvious; this majority creates a presumption that the others may be present as well.[3] This is especially so in the case of the suggested allusions to Ps 22, since that psalm so dominates its immediate Gospel context.

As we have already remarked, most of these allusions, at least those in the Synoptics, are embedded rather than explicit, and for them to "work," they would have to be familiar to the earliest readers of these Gospels. Such familiarity may well have arisen through early Christian communities' use of the Psalms in worship, which is a priori likely given the usage of the Psalms in the temple worship and later in the synagogue and the church.[4] This presumed familiarity would have had important consequences for the response of the Gospel readers to the passion narratives. First, anyone who recognized the biblical echoes would have drawn the inference that Jesus' death was a divine necessity, since it was foretold in the Scriptures. These same echoes, moreover, would reinforce the hearers' conviction that Jesus was innocent, since the speaker in these laments is a person who is unjustly harassed or physically harmed by his neighbors. John clearly brings out this aspect of innocent suffering when he narrates Jesus' allusion to Ps 35:19 par. 69:4: "It is to fulfill the word that is written in their law, 'they hated me without a cause'" (John 15:25).

Another consequence of the Gospel readers' presumed familiarity with the Psalms of the Righteous Sufferer is that they would have known that while these psalms begin with complaint, they almost invariably

---

[3]Cf. Richard J. Dillon, "The Psalms of the Suffering Just in the Accounts of Jesus' Passion," *Worship* 61 (1987) 430–40 (431).

[4]On the usage of the Psalms in temple and synagogue, see Stefan C. Reif, *Judaism and Hebrew Prayer: New Perspectives on Jewish Liturgical History* (Cambridge: Cambridge University, 1993), index under "Psalms"; on their usage in the early church, see Everett Ferguson, "Psalms," in *Encyclopedia of Early Christianity*, ed. Everett Ferguson et al. (Garland Reference Library of the Humanities 846; New York/London: Garland, 1990) 763–65.

end with praise of God; despite his terrible experiences, the psalmist trusts that God will ultimately deliver a faithful people. For example, the same Ps 22 that begins with the anguished accusation of divine betrayal, "My God, my God, why have you forsaken me?" (alt.), ends with the affirmation that

> all the ends of the earth shall remember and turn to the Lord; and all the families of the nations shall worship before him. For dominion belongs to the Lord, and he rules over the nations. (Ps 22:27–28)

As our chart suggests, this conclusion may be reflected in the way that, in Mark and Matthew, the Gentile centurion (along with his companions in Matthew) ends up acknowledging Jesus' divine sonship,[5] as well as in the way that, in Mark and Luke, Joseph of Arimathea is described as one looking for the kingdom of God. On the basis of their knowledge of these psalms, then, some Gospel readers may have detected in the passion narratives' allusions to the Psalms of the Righteous Sufferer not only a mirror of Jesus' torment but also a hint of his ultimate vindication and the arrival of the kingdom of God in his death.

This putative awareness of context on the part of the Gospel writers and some of their readers, by the way, needs to be distinguished from the suggestion sometimes made that Jesus himself, when he echoed the despairing first verse of Ps 22 on the cross, really had in mind the rest of it, particularly its triumphant conclusion. This theory neatly eliminates the problem posed by Jesus' complaint that God has abandoned him, but for that very reason one suspects it of being Christian apologetic rather than historical reconstruction. It is a bit much, moreover, to expect a man on the point of death to keep in mind the larger context of the psalm verse he cites; if Jesus had really wanted to allude to the triumphant ending of the psalm, he probably would have quoted it directly.[6]

To return to our main point, which is not Jesus' awareness of the OT but the Gospel writers' awareness of it, Matthew's and Luke's editing of Mark supports this point. In his account of Jesus' crucifixion, for example, Matthew usually follows his source, Mark, rather closely, but occasionally he fills out the narrative with details of his own, and one of these additions reveals his awareness of the background of Mark's story in Ps 22. Matthew 27:43 adds to the scribes' and elders' words of

---

[5]Brown (*Death of the Messiah*, 2.1461 and n. 55) pronounces this allusion "very dubious." It is certainly not as obvious as some of the others in the crucifixion scene, but the strong imprint of Ps 22 on the rest of that scene creates the presumption that the Gospel readers knew the psalm well and would have recognized even a relatively obscure allusion.

[6]See Gerard Rossé, *The Cry of Jesus on the Cross: A Biblical and Theological Study* (Mahwah, N.J.: Paulist, 1987) 103–7.

mockery of the crucified Jesus a passage, not found in Mark, that begins, "He trusts in God; let God deliver him now, if he desires him." This addition, as our chart shows, reproduces almost exactly the phrasing of Ps 22:8—which is alluded to but not quoted in the Markan source. Matthew, then, apparently realizing the background of the story in Ps 22, works a more exact echo of that psalm into his own account, "creating" history out of the OT text. In the transition from Mark to Matthew, therefore, we can see the narrative growing right before our eyes out of OT soil.

Even more radical is Luke's reworking of Jesus' cry of dereliction, again on the basis of his knowledge of the OT source for the cry and of the larger biblical context of that source. In Mark, as we have seen, Jesus' last words are a quotation of the first verse of Ps 22. This anguished cry of complaint, however, is intolerable for Luke, who elsewhere in his passion narrative tones down a Markan passage in which Jesus is distressed (Luke 22:40–42 par. Mark 14:33–36) and who emphasizes Jesus' sovereign transcendence over the maltreatment he undergoes (Luke 23:28, 34, 42–43). So Luke substitutes a cry of affirmation for the Markan cry of dereliction; now Jesus' last words express not abandonment but trust in God, willingness to die, and a sense of divine sonship even in extremis: "Father, into your hands I commit my spirit!" (Luke 23:46, alt.). This more affirmative death cry is a quotation from another Righteous Sufferer psalm, Ps 31:5. Like Matthew, then, Luke seems to realize the scriptural background of Mark's story, but since he is unhappy with the implications of the particular psalm verse that Mark places on Jesus' lips, he chooses a more palatable verse from another Righteous Sufferer psalm to represent Jesus' last words.

The synoptic evangelists, then, are at least sometimes aware of the contexts of the OT passages they cite. Their OT usage is not always "atomistic," i.e., it does not always exploit scriptural passages opportunistically without respect for their context. Neither is it right to characterize the Jewish tradition of OT usage that the evangelists continue and develop as invariably atomistic.[7] Lars Hartman, for example, has shown in a close study of *1 Enoch* 46:1–8 that allusions to OT texts here draw their context with them, and Michael Fishbane points to the way in which, in the Wisdom of Solomon, "the exodus topos serves as the deep

---

[7]Against, e.g., Donald Juel (*Messianic Exegesis: Christological Interpretation of the Old Testament in Early Christianity* [Philadelphia: Fortress, 1988] 19–22), Jewish exegesis can be atomistic, but it is not always so. J. W. Doeve appropriately comments that a Jewish tradition "may mention a single [biblical] word in order to recall a whole context, and sometimes it may employ a single word it happens to need, while totally ignoring the context" (*Jewish Hermeneutics in the Synoptic Gospels and Acts* [Assen: Van Gorcum, 1953] 134; cf. Moo, *Old Testament*, 33, 56, 167).

structural matrix for a sermonic exposition."[8] While examples of atomistic exegesis can indeed be found in both the Jewish tradition and the NT (see, e.g., the analysis of Matt 27:57 in n. 17 below), instances where attention is paid to context are not rare. We will have occasion to point to some further examples of contextual awareness on the part of the evangelists as we proceed with this study.

Creation out of the Old Testament?

Both Matthew and Luke, then, embellish their passion narratives with features drawn from the OT lament psalms. It is unlikely that these embellishments reflect traditions available to Matthew and Luke but unknown to Mark; for the most part, the scenes we have been examining follow Mark, and the departures from Mark can easily be explained as reflecting the theological interests of Matthew and Luke respectively. This conclusion, however, raises a large question about the historicity of the passion narratives in general. If the Matthean and Lukan passion narratives sometimes embellish Mark on the basis of OT texts rather than historical memory, is it not likely that Mark's passion narrative has been created by similar concretion of OT texts, either by Mark himself or by the compiler of the pre-Markan passion narrative? And does this not imply that it is totally unhistorical?[9]

Perhaps Mark's passion narrative has been *partially* created out of OT texts. An example of a detail so created is the position of the women who witness Jesus' crucifixion, in the Synoptics, "from a distance" (ἀπὸ μακρόθεν, *apo makrothen*; Mark 15:40 par. Matt 27:55 par. Luke 23:49). In John, by way of contrast, they are standing by the cross, near enough to hold a conversation with the dying man (John 19:25–27). In this case, John may be more accurate historically than the Synoptics, since the Romans often allowed friends of crucified criminals to stand by them until they died, and the synoptic placement may well reflect a passage from one of the Psalms of the Righteous Sufferer, Ps 38:11: "My friends and companions stand aloof from my affliction, and my relatives stand afar off" (alt.) (LXX ἀπὸ μακρόθεν).[10] Perhaps this scripturally created detail goes back to Mark himself, since throughout his passion narrative

---

[8]Lars Hartman, *Prophecy Interpreted: The Formation of Some Jewish Apocalyptic Texts and of the Eschatological Discourse Mark 13 par.* (ConBNT 1; Lund: Gleerup, 1966) 118–26 (126); Michael Fishbane, *Biblical Interpretation in Ancient Israel* (Oxford: Clarendon, 1985) 432. Other examples of the same phenomenon could be multiplied; one might investigate, for example, the story of the struggle with Nicanor at the end of 2 Maccabees, where many features of the saga are drawn from the biblical narrative of David and Goliath.

[9]As suggested recently by Burton Mack, *A Myth of Innocence: Mark and Christian Origins* (Philadelphia: Fortress, 1988) 249–312.

[10]See Brown, *Death of the Messiah*, 2.1158.

he seems concerned to emphasize the forsakenness and aloneness of Jesus in the face of death.

It does seem, therefore, that OT texts have had an influence on the formation of the passion narrative, presumably from its earliest stages.[11] On the other hand, the extreme position that the narrative in its entirety has been created out of the OT is unwarranted. For example, the order of the allusions to Ps 22 in the four Gospels does not correspond to the psalm's own order.[12] It is difficult, moreover, to imagine that the church would have placed Ps 22:1 on the lips of the dying Jesus if the verse had not originally belonged there, since Jesus' use of this psalm verse created major difficulties. It has required considerable theological finesse for Christians down through the centuries to explain why Jesus, whom they have claimed to be the Son of God, complained in his dying moments that God had abandoned him. We have already seen that almost immediately after Mark another Gospel writer, Luke, found these words so distasteful that he changed them to something that was in his eyes more edifying. This impulse has continued down through the present day, as is witnessed by the commentators previously mentioned who suggest that Jesus really had the end of the psalm rather than its beginning in mind. The church probably would not have created such problems for itself; rather, the cry of dereliction was simply too securely rooted in the tradition about Jesus' death to be dislodged.[13] The other elements in the death narrative that echo Ps 22 (the division of the garments, the mockery) are at least plausible, though the particular terminology used to describe them reflects the psalm.

It is probably best, then, to adopt a nuanced position: the early Christians remembered certain details about Jesus' death because they believed them to have been prophesied in the Scriptures. Once having made the connection with the Scriptures, however, they discovered other, related OT passages that, in their view, *must* have been fulfilled in his death as well—and so they created narratives in which they *were* fulfilled.

The Suffering Servant of Isaiah

A similar process may have helped to produce the passion narratives' allusions to another, smaller body of OT texts, the passages in Isaiah that deal with the Lord's Suffering Servant (esp. Isa 50:4–9; 52:13–53:12). Here, however, the problems of historical reconstruction are more serious, since many scholars think it unlikely that Jesus

---

[11] See Dibelius, *From Tradition to Gospel*, 185.
[12] See Brown, *Death of the Messiah*, 2.1158.
[13] See Green, *Death of Jesus*, 305.

thought of himself as the Suffering Servant, a figure who dies a vicarious, violent death for the sins of others. The basic reason for this opinion is that to believe that Jesus saw himself as the Suffering Servant is to ascribe to him not only prescience about his own violent end but also an interpretation of it that dovetails suspiciously well with the church's emerging theology of atonement.

On the other hand, if Jesus thought of himself as the Righteous Sufferer of the Psalms, which is rendered likely by the cry of dereliction from the cross, he might have thought of himself as the Suffering Servant of Isaiah. The two figures were closely connected; the Suffering Servant figure is probably in its origin a prophetic adaptation of the Righteous Sufferer, and Jewish exegetes tended to amalgamate the two figures.[14] In similar fashion, the Gospel passion narratives interweave the two motifs, and it is sometimes difficult to tell whether a particular feature derives from the one or the other;[15] it is, in any case, doubtful that the readers of the Gospels would have thought of the Righteous Sufferer and the Suffering Servant as two separate figures.

We will return later to the problem of the origin of the Suffering Servant references in the Gospel passion narratives. First, however, the references need to be tabulated:

Gospels		*Isaiah*
Mark 14:10–11 par. Matt 26:15–16 par. Luke 22:4, 6; Mark 14:18 par. Matt 26:21; cf. John 13:21; Mark 14:21 par. Matt 26:24 par. Luke 22:22; Mark 14:41–42, 44 par. Matt 26:45–46, 48; Luke 22:48; Mark 15:1 par. Matt 27:2; Mark 15:10 par. Matt 27:18; Mark 15:15 par. Matt 27:26 par. Luke 23:25; cf. John 19:16	handed over (παραδιδόναι, *paradidonai*)	53:6, 12 LXX

---

[14]See Lothar Ruppert, *Jesus als der leidende Gerechte? Der Weg Jesu im Lichte eines alt- und zwischentestamentlichen Motivs* (SBS 59; Stuttgart: Katholisches, 1972) 19–20.

[15]See, e.g., the common usage of the verb παραδιδόναι (*paradidonai*, "to hand over") and the common motif of silence before accusers.

Mark 14:21 par. Matt 26:24	going [to death]; handed over	52:13–53:12
Mark 14:24 par. Matt 26:28 par. Luke 22:20	Mark: blood poured out for many; Matt: blood poured out for many for the forgiveness of sins; Luke: blood poured out for you	53:12 MT (poured out; LXX: delivered)
Luke 22:37	numbered among the transgressors	53:12 LXX
Mark 14:61 par. Matt 26:63; Mark 15:5 par. Matt 27:14; Luke 23:9	silence before accusers	53:7
Mark 14:65 par. Matt 26:27	spitting, slapping	50:6 LXX
Mark 15:5 par. Matt 27:14 (cf. Mark 15:39 par. Matt 27:5 par. Luke 23:47)	amazement of a Gentile ruler	52:15 LXX
Mark 15:6–15 par. Matt 27:15–26 par. Luke 23:17–25 par. John 18:39–40	criminal saved, innocent man delivered to murder	53:6, 12
John 19:1	scourging	50:6 LXX
Mark 15:19 par. Matt 27:30 par. John 19:3	spitting, slapping	50:6 LXX
Mark 15:27 par. Matt 27:38 par. Luke 23:33 par. John 19:18	associated with criminals in death	53:12
Luke 23:47	righteous, innocent (δίκαιος, *dikaios*)	53:11 LXX
Matt 27:57	buried by a rich man	53:9 LXX
[resurrection narratives]	[vindicated and exalted]	[52:13; 53:12]

Of these references, the most secure are Luke's unambiguous citation of Isa 53:12, the reference at the Last Supper to Jesus' blood poured out "for many," and the echoes of Isa 50:6 in the physical abuse meted out to Jesus after his two trials. While other allusions are more questionable[16] and the overall number is not as large as the number of references to the lament psalms, the allusions in the synoptic passion narratives to the Suffering Servant passages are nevertheless numerous enough and significantly enough placed to be important.

Indeed, the Suffering Servant passages may be important enough for the passion tradition that in some instances they are responsible for the narrative details in the passion stories, as we saw in the previous section that the Psalms of the Righteous Sufferer occasionally are. In Luke, for example, Jesus' explicit citation of Isa 53:12, "he was numbered with the transgressors" (Luke 22:37), looks like an early Christian creation, especially because the citation is unknown to the other evangelists and serves an apologetic purpose, as is indicated by the theme of fulfillment of Scripture.

Matthew, too, expands the passion tradition with features drawn from the Suffering Servant passages. For example, he adds to the Markan account of Jesus' "cup word" at the Last Supper the words "for the forgiveness of sins" (Matt 26:28)—apparently realizing the background of the saying in Isa 53:12 and filling it out with another allusion to that verse ("he bore the sin of many"; cf. Isa 53:6). He similarly adds to Mark's account of Jesus' burial the information that the donor of Jesus' tomb, Joseph of Arimathea, was a rich man (Matt 27:57). Although this description of Joseph is plausible, given that in Mark's narrative he is an esteemed member of the Jewish ruling council and therefore presumably well-off, the fact that Matthew feels called upon to mention Joseph's wealth explicitly may reflect Isa 53:9, "And they made his grave with the wicked and with a rich man in his death."[17]

---

[16]It is particularly troubling that the most pervasive putative "allusion" is the use of a single word, παραδιδόναι, "to be handed over." Here, however, the case is slightly stronger than at first appears. Earlier in the Synoptics, Jesus predicts his suffering, death, and resurrection three times (four times in Matthew), and two of these prophecies (three in Matthew) use παραδιδόναι (Mark 9:31 par. Matt 17:22–23 par. Luke 9:44; Mark 10:33 par. Matt 20:18–19 par. Luke 18:32; Matt 26:2). The second of these prophecies, Mark 10:33 par. Matt 20:18–19 par. Luke 18:32, combines παραδιδόναι (used twice in Mark and Matthew) with language recalling Isa 50:6 (spitting, scourging). Generalizing from this earlier passage, we may cautiously assert that the use of παραδιδόναι elsewhere in the Synoptics is probably intended to awaken echoes of the Suffering Servant passages.

[17]If so, however, Matthew is ignoring the context of the Isaianic passage, since Isaiah's parallelism implies that the rich man is wicked, whereas Matthew certainly does not think Joseph is. Brown (Death of the Messiah, 2.1224 n. 49) therefore doubts the allusion to Isaiah here, since "in instances of biblical

In an analogous way, in Mark itself the reference to the abuse meted out to Jesus at the end of the Sanhedrin trial (Mark 14:65 par. Matt 26:27) may have been supplied partly from the doublet in the trial before Pilate and partly from Isa 50:6. This is especially likely because there are many historical problems with the Sanhedrin trial, and it probably reflects a minimal amount of historical information, if indeed it took place at all.[18] Old Testament texts such as Isa 50:6, as well as the conflated allusion to Ps 110:1/Dan 7:13 in Mark 14:62 par. Matt 26:64,[19] may have rushed into this historical vacuum.

It is difficult to decide to what extent the remaining allusions to the Suffering Servant passages have been created by a similar process of concretion of OT texts or to what extent they are historical. This question is especially crucial for the "cup word" in Mark 14:24 par. Matt 26:28 par. Luke 22:20, since this is one of only two synoptic passages in which Jesus speaks of the saving purpose of his death—the other being Mark 10:45 par. Matt 20:28, also an allusion to Isa 53. On the one hand, against historicity is the observation made above that in this passage Matthew seems to have expanded Mark on the basis of Isa 53; it is not implausible, therefore, that the Markan account itself may have been heavily influenced by the same text. On the other hand, in favor of historicity is that a theology of vicarious expiation of sin partly based on Isa 53 seems to have been abroad in the Judaism of Jesus' time,[20] so it cannot be totally excluded that he would have expressed such ideas, especially with death staring him in the face. Jewish exegesis, however, tends to interpret the Suffering Servant as a collective rather than an

---

citation Matt[hew] likes every detail fulfilled." I do not think, however, that we should expect absolute consistency from Matthew, any more than from other Jewish exegetes; see n. 7 above. Moo (*Old Testament*, 144–45) attempts to evade the difficulty with the assertion that the structure of Isa 53:9 could be construed as an antithesis: "While the servant's grave was intended to be with the wicked, it turned out to be with the rich." But there is nothing in the original to suggest that the parallelism is other than straightforwardly synonymous; the only reason for questioning this analysis is the difficulty it poses for Matt 27:57, which of course is irrelevant for the original meaning.

[18] See Green, *Death of Jesus*, 281.

[19] Psalm 110:1 and Dan 7:13 are commonly used elsewhere in the NT to speak of Jesus' present exaltation and future return; see the references to these verses in the section "Loci Citati vel Allegati ex Vetere Testamento" in the Nestle-Aland edition of the Greek NT, and on Ps 110:1 see also David M. Hay, *Glory at the Right Hand: Psalm 110 in Early Christianity* (SBLMS 18; Nashville: Abingdon, 1973).

[20] See, e.g., 2 Macc 7:37–38; 4 Macc 6:28–29 (on these texts see Green, *Death of Jesus*, 168 n. 29 and the bibliography there); 1QS 8.3–7, 10; 1QSa 1.1–3 (on these texts see Marcus, *Way of the Lord*, 191–92). It should be noted, however, that in the Qumran texts the community, rather than the individual, makes expiation for the sins of the people and that the pre-Christian dating of 4 Maccabees is disputed (see n. 23).

individual figure,[21] so Jesus' putative application of it to himself would have been something of a novelty. But the individual interpretation has some rather secure warrants in the Isaianic text itself,[22] and if 4 Macc 6:28–29 is pre-Christian (which is disputed), then this view is attested in pre-Christian Judaism;[23] we cannot, moreover, exclude the possibility that Jesus' biblical exegesis was somewhat off the beaten track.

The argument goes back and forth, and is ultimately inconclusive. The only historically responsible judgment would seem to be an agnostic one: it is simply impossible to tell on historical grounds alone whether the "cup word" goes back to Jesus, and one's ultimate assessment of this question will partly depend on an a priori judgment about whether he could have foreseen an atoning death for himself.

In any case, regardless of whether or not Jesus thought of himself as the Suffering Servant, the Gospel writers did. This figure is important to the evangelists, especially Mark and Matthew, in part because of two elements that go beyond the picture of the Righteous Sufferer in the Psalms: the Isaianic Servant not only suffers but also dies, and his suffering and death are not only necessary but also redemptive. In the passion narratives, these elements are especially emphasized by means of the allusion in Mark 14:24 par. Matt 26:28, though they would perhaps be implied for some biblically literate readers of the Gospels by the other allusions to the Suffering Servant passages as well.

Zechariah 9–14

Besides the Psalms of the Righteous Sufferer and the deutero-Isaian Suffering Servant passages, the other major scriptural resource employed in the passion narratives is Zech 9–14. This distinct unit within Zechariah is cited and alluded to extensively in the NT generally, whereas Zech 1–8 is infrequently invoked.[24]

---

[21]See Marcus, *Way of the Lord*, 190–93.

[22]See Christopher Richard North (*The Suffering Servant in Deutero-Isaiah: An Historical and Critical Study* [London: Oxford University, 1948] 202–7), who cites the concreteness of detail, the innocence of the Servant's suffering, and the fact that he appears to have a mission to Israel.

[23]For a summary of the arguments about the dating of 4 Maccabees, see Hans-Josef Klauck, *4. Makkabäerbuch* (JSHRZ 3:6; Gütersloh: Gerd Mohn, 1989) 668–69. The inclusion of the work in the LXX and its quick acceptance among early Christians push Klauck back from the second-century C.E. dating advocated by Dupont-Sommer towards a first-century dating, though late in the century.

[24]See M. C. Black, "The Rejected and Slain Messiah Who Is Coming with the Angels: The Messianic Exegesis of Zechariah 9–14 in the Passion Narratives" (Ph.D. diss., Emory University, 1990) 35–48.

Within the passion narratives, the prophecy of the smiting of the shepherd and the scattering of the sheep (Zech 13:7) is introduced by a citation formula in Mark 14:27 par. Matt 26:31, and the prophecy of the inhabitants of Jerusalem "look[ing] on him whom they have pierced" (Zech 12:10) is similarly introduced in John 19:37. Indeed, according to Moo's count, four of the ten references to Zech 9–14 in the Gospels are explicit citations—an unusually high percentage, perhaps reflecting the relative lack of familiarity with these passages in the early church.[25]

The explicit citation of Zech 13:7 in Mark 14:27 par. Matt 26:31 is the center of a small cloud of embedded citations, which are shown in the following chart, along with three other allusions found elsewhere in the Matthean and Johannine passion narratives:[26]

Gospels		*Zechariah*
Mark 14:24 par. Matt 26:28	my blood of the covenant	9:11 LXX
Mark 14:25 par. Matt 26:29	that day, kingdom of God	14:4, 9 LXX
Mark 14:26 par. Matt 26:30	Mount of Olives	14:4 LXX
Mark 14:27 par. Matt 26:31; cf. John 16:32	strike the shepherd, and sheep will be scattered	13:7 MT (scattered; LXX: draw out)
Mark 14:28 par. Matt 26:32	restoration of scattered "sheep"	13:8–9
Mark 14:28 par. Matt 26:32	resurrection	14:4–5 (according to Jewish interpretations)
Matt 27:3–10	thirty pieces of silver	11:12–13 (but ascribed to Jeremiah)
Matt 27:51–53	splitting of earth, resurrection of holy ones	14:4–5
John 19:37	they shall look upon him whom they have pierced	12:10 MT (pierced; LXX: mocked)

---

[25] Moo, *Old Testament*, 221–24.
[26] On the Matthean allusions, see Allison, *End of the Ages*, 43–44.

While most of the Markan allusions are probably part of the pre-Markan passion narrative, one, the prophecy of resurrection and reconciliation in 14:28, seems to have been added by Mark himself.[27] What seems to have happened is this: Mark, realizing that "Strike the shepherd, and the sheep will be scattered" is a citation of Zech 13:7 but wanting to interject a more positive note into the dark prophecy of the disciples' desertion, adds an allusion to the hopeful continuation of the Zecharian passage by having Jesus predict a restoration of the disciples' fellowship with him after the resurrection. Mark, then, recognizes the scriptural background of his source, the pre-Markan passion narrative, and expands upon it—a technique we have observed to be characteristic of all three Synoptics throughout the passion narrative.

It is striking that the Markan allusions to Zech 9–14, unlike those to the Psalms of the Righteous Sufferer and the Suffering Servant passages, are not spread throughout the narrative but confined to the two consecutive pericopes of the Last Supper (Mark 14:22–26) and the prediction of desertion (Mark 14:27–31). This concentration suggests, perhaps, that the majority of the allusions actually go back to the events described rather than being an imposition of the early church. In the latter case, we might expect that allusions to Zech 9–14 would surface elsewhere in the passion narrative as well as here. Since they do not, it is easier to imagine that they go back to the historical Jesus, whose mind may have turned to this section of Zechariah as he prepared for, and then went to, his nocturnal vigil on the Mount of Olives—a location significantly mentioned only twice in the Scriptures, one of those instances being Zech 14:4.[28] Rootedness in the history of Jesus is further supported by the fact that apart from this reference to the Mount of Olives, all of the allusions to Zech 9–14 here are framed as words of Jesus instead of being more evenly divided between sayings and narrative.

Other Old Testament Texts

Aside from the Psalms of the Righteous Sufferer, the Isaianic Suffering Servant passages, and Zech 9–14, other sections of the OT have been alleged to have had a wide impact on the Gospel passion narratives, but such impact is often hard to prove. For example, the story in Gen 22 of Abraham's attempted sacrifice of Isaac was expanded in later Judaism in ways that emphasized the atoning merit of the actions of both Abraham and Isaac, and some scholars have seen such midrashic

---

[27] See Marcus (*Way of the Lord,* 154–55), citing the interruption of the logical connection between 14:27 and 14:29, the characteristic Markan preoccupation with Galilee, and the similarity to 16:7, which also disrupts its context and speaks of Galilee.

[28] The other instance is in 2 Sam 15:30, on which see the following section.

expansions as background for the Gospels' portrayal of Jesus' willing self-sacrifice. As Brown shows in an appendix devoted to this theory, however, the parallels between the midrashic expansions and individual Gospel passages are too subtle to be convincing.[29]

Brown himself is more positive about allusions to the narrative in 2 Sam 15, in which King David, betrayed by his trusted advisor Ahithophel, goes out of Jerusalem, crosses "the winter-flowing Kidron," ascends the Mount of Olives, weeps, and prays to God; Ahithophel subsequently hangs himself (2 Sam 17:23). In the Gospels, similarly, Jesus crosses "the winter-flowing Kidron" (John 18:1), goes out to the Mount of Olives (Mark 14:26 par. Matt 26:30 par. Luke 23:39 par. John 18:1), and prays in great sorrow; in Matthew, moreover, the betrayer Judas subsequently hangs himself (Matt 27:5).[30]

This is an intriguing set of parallels, but the only verbal correspondences are ἐξέρχεσθαι (*exerchesthai*, "to go out"), an extremely common verb; the Matthean ἀπήγξατο, *apēnxato*, the normal term for hanging oneself; and the Johannine "winter-flowing Kidron," which after all exactly describes the Kidron, a dry riverbed, or wadi, that contains water only in winter.[31] In the absence of closer verbal likenesses, it is difficult to be sure whether the allusions to 2 Sam 15 and 17 are actually intended, though they would make sense because the Messiah was expected to be a second David.[32]

CONTINUITY WITH JEWISH EXEGESIS

Eschatological Exegesis

Of the three main bodies of OT texts studied in the previous section, one, Zech 9–14, is a thoroughly eschatological section of the OT. It

---

[29] Brown, *Death of the Messiah*, 2.1435–44.

[30] See the summary in Brown, *Death of the Messiah*, 2.1448; also the index under "Ahithophel."

[31] Brown (*Death of the Messiah*, 1.257) mentions that Jesus' word for Judas in Matt 26:50, ἑταῖρος (*hetairos*, "friend"), is also used in 2 Sam 15:37 and 16:17, but there it is used not for Ahithophel but for David's loyal follower Hushai. Brown thinks that Matthew is using ἑταῖρος ironically to refer to the OT text, but this sounds like special pleading.

[32] I am slightly more favorable to seeing 2 Sam 15 behind the passion narratives of Matthew and John, because of the verbal correspondences, than I am to seeing it behind those of Mark and Luke. In the case of Matthew, moreover, the absence of reliable historical information about the mode of Judas's death (see Brown, *Death of the Messiah*, 2.1404–10) may have meant that Matthew had nothing to go on except OT typology in constructing a narrative about the just death of the traitor.

describes, somewhat obscurely, the expected events of the end (ἔσχατον, eschaton), in which God will refine and judge his people, the nations, and indeed the world and usher in a new era of paradisiacal peace. The employment of these eschatological prophecies from the OT in the Gospel passion narratives expresses the conviction of the early church that the events of Jesus' suffering, death, and resurrection were the beginning of this prophesied new age. For the early church, this new age would be brought to its full public manifestation in the imminently expected return of Jesus in glory, but for those with eyes to see, it was already present since Easter.

This conviction of eschatological breakthrough permeates the passion narratives and explains some otherwise puzzling biblical allusions. For example, in Mark 15:33 par. Matt 27:45 par. Luke 23:44–45 we read that when Jesus was crucified, there was darkness "over the whole earth" (NRSV margin) from the sixth hour (i.e., noon) on; this is probably an allusion to Amos 8:9, which prophesies that "on that day"—i.e., the day of judgment—God "will make the sun go down at noon, and darken the earth in broad daylight." As Jesus dies, then, the eschatological day of God's judgment prophesied in the OT has fallen like a terrible shadow over the earth.

Passages such as Amos 8:9 and Zech 9–14 were eschatological from their inception, so it is no surprise that they are used in passion narratives that interpret Jesus' death as the decisive end-time event.[33] Certain other OT passages, which were not properly eschatological in their original contexts, were nevertheless interpreted eschatologically in later Judaism. The LXX, for example, seems to interpret the Psalms of the Righteous Sufferer eschatologically,[34] and the Dead Sea Scrolls continue this pattern, offering eschatological interpretations, for example, of some of the same psalms that play an important role in the Gospel passion narratives.[35] Similarly, the Suffering Servant passages in Deutero-Isaiah, along with the other passages that speak of the Lord's Servant (Isa 42:1–4; 49:1–6; 50:4–9; 52:13–53:12), are interpreted eschatologically in the Dead Sea Scrolls, the Targums, and rabbinic traditions.[36] The early Christian understanding of the lament psalms and the Suffering Servant passages as prophecies of eschatological

---

[33]Two other eschatological texts, Dan 7:13 (conflated with Ps 110:1) and Hos 10:8, are used within the passion narrative to speak of the Second Coming (Mark 14:62 par. Matt 26:64; Luke 23:30).

[34]The enigmatic heading of most of them in the Hebrew Bible, למנצח (lmnṣḥ), is interpreted consistently as εἰς τὸ τέλος (eis to telos, "to or for the end"); cf. b. Pesaḥ. 117a.

[35]E.g., the allusions to Ps 22:15 in 1QH 5.31, to Ps 22:14–17 in 4QPsᶠ, to Ps 41:9 in 1QH 5.23–24, and to Ps 42:5 in 1QH 8.32.

[36]E.g., 1QS 8.3–7, 10; 1QSa 1.1–3. For the targumic and rabbinic passages, see Jeremias, "παῖς θεοῦ," TDNT 5.684–700; cf. Marcus, Way of the Lord, 191–92.

events now being fulfilled, therefore, was anticipated and probably prepared for by a Jewish tendency to interpret these texts in a similar contemporizing way.

Communal Interpretation

Nor is this the only way in which the use of the OT in the passion narratives follows lines laid down in postbiblical Judaism. For example, the lament psalms are often interpreted communally in Jewish traditions—a logical enough interpretation, given that the "I" who speaks them sometimes seems to include the group with whom the speaker identifies himself. Psalms 7 and 9, for example, are individual laments that contain the anomalous communal motif of the judgment and defeat of the nations, and Pss 10 and 22—which play a role in the Gospel passion narratives—end with the proclamation of God's kingship over the world. The Qumran *Hodayoth* are a similar mixture of individual and communal elements, based on the biblical lament psalms (see, e.g., 1QH 2.8–9, 20–30).

This communal dimension seems to have left its mark on the passion narratives' use of these texts as well. For example, we have previously spoken of the reference to Ps 35:19 par. 69:4 ("they hated me without a cause") in John 15:25. It is noteworthy that this Johannine allusion occurs in a context in which Jesus is stressing the profound connection between his own suffering and that of his disciples (John 15:18, 20). It is probably not just a coincidence that in the two psalms to which reference is here made, the "me" who is hated without a cause is linked with the suffering people of God generally.[37] The Johannine connection between Jesus' suffering and that of his followers was probably at least partly suggested by the connection between the individual and the collective in the psalms.

For the readers of the Gospels, this idea of the community's unity with Christ in his suffering would perhaps have been reinforced by their own familiarity with the Psalms of the Righteous Sufferer from the liturgy (see above). If readers were accustomed to praying these psalms as their own experience, then when they saw Jesus portrayed as praying and living through these same psalms, they would inevitably be drawn to make the linkage between their situation and his.

Similar remarks apply to the figure of the Lord's Suffering Servant from Isaiah. This figure has a strong collective dimension in the OT and in Jewish exegesis. Already in the Hebrew original of Isaiah the figure

---

[37] In Ps 35:20, the psalmist's enemies are those who conceive words of deceit against people who are quiet in the land. At the end of Ps 69, the psalmist's own vindication is linked with the salvation of Zion, the rebuilding of the cities of Judah, and the occupation of those cities by God's servants.

designated "the Lord's Servant" oscillates between a singular and a collective identity, and the LXX considerably extends the collective referent.[38] A collective interpretation of Isa 53 is found in the Diaspora in the Wisdom of Solomon (2:12–20; 5:1–7) and in Palestine in two Qumran texts that speak of the leaders of the community expiating iniquity, upholding the righteous cause, bearing anguish, and making propitiation for the land (1QS 8.3–10; 1QSa 1.1–3). Perhaps in contradiction to the Christian application of Isa 53 to Jesus, this collective interpretation later became dominant among Jews, as is attested by Origen's report that he disputed with Jews who interpreted the passage as a reference "to the people, understood as a single person, which has been dispersed and tormented" (*Against Celsus* 1.55)—a foreshadowing of medieval disputes between Jews and Christians about the interpretation of Isa 53.

Although in these later disputes Christians, for obvious reasons, defended the individual interpretation of Isa 53, in NT times they probably had not lost sight of the collective dimension of the Suffering Servant. Thus in Matt 24:9; Mark 13:9, 12 par. Matt 10:17, 21 par. Luke 21:12, 16, the verb παραδιδόναι (*paradidonai*, "to hand over"), which, as we have seen, has significant background in Isa 53, is applied to the future betrayal of the disciples,[39] and earlier in the Gospels the predictions of Jesus' passion, which prominently apply this verb to Jesus, are followed by instruction in discipleship (Mark 9:30–37 par. Matt 17:22–18:5 par. Luke 9:43–48; Mark 10:32–45 par. Matt 20:17–28). Thus Jesus' fate as Suffering Servant seems to involve that of his disciples as well.[40]

Other Jewish Exegetical Features

Besides the tendency of Jewish exegesis to interpret OT passages eschatologically and collectively, other Jewish exegetical techniques and traditions are visible in the scriptural usage of the passion narratives.

---

[38]According to Jeremias ("παῖς θεοῦ," 682–84), nine of the references to the Lord's Servant in Isa 41–53 are collective (41:8–9; 44:1, 2, 21 [twice]; 45:4; 48:20; 49:3). The LXX extends the collective references to 42:1, 19; 44:26; 48:20.

[39]In Matt 10:17 παραδώσουσιν (*paradōsousin*, "they will hand [you] over") is combined with μαστιγώσουσιν (*mastigōsousin*, "they will scourge [you]"); the latter word is cognate with μάστιγας (*mastigas*, "scourges"), which appears in Isa 50:6 LXX. In Matt 24:9, moreover, παραδώσουσιν is combined with θλῖψιν (*thlipsin*, "affliction"), creating a conceptual echo of Isa 53:11–12.

[40]Cf. Jane Schaberg, "Daniel 7–12 and the New Testament Passion-Resurrection Predictions," NTS 31 (1985) 215–17. Since, as will be shown below, the citation of Zech 13:7 in Mark 14:27 par. Matt 26:31 involves a sidelong glance at Isa 53, it is also relevant that this passage links the attack on the shepherd with the scattering of the sheep and thus implies a collective dimension to the shepherd. See also the parallel between the suffering of the pierced figure in Zech 12:10 and that of the flock doomed to slaughter in Zech 11:4–7, 15.

Sometimes particular Jewish interpretations are in view. For example, we have already mentioned the plethora of allusions to Zech 9–14 in Mark 14:26–28 par. Matt 26:30–32. One of the passages alluded to, Zech 14:4, is a prophecy that at the eschaton the Lord will stand on the Mount of Olives, the mountain will split in half, and the Lord will come with his holy ones. Later Jewish exegesis is fairly consistent in its interpretation that this split will open the earth so that the righteous dead (i.e., the holy ones) may rise, a belief that explains the presence of Jewish graveyards on the Mount of Olives from ancient times until our own day.[41] It is in line with these Jewish interpretations of Zech 14 that Jesus, in the Gospel passage under consideration, should speak of his resurrection as he stands on the Mount of Olives. A similar usage of this tradition of exegesis may undergird Matt 27:51–53, where we hear of an earthquake and a resurrection of the dead at a location just outside Jerusalem.[42]

More commonly, however, the passion narratives' debt to Jewish exegesis does not appear in particular interpretations but in the method of interpretation. For example, the merging or conflation of OT passages in order to create a more serviceable fused text is characteristic of Jewish exegesis,[43] and it is also found several times in the passion narratives. We have already referred, for example, to the conflation of Ps 110:1 and Dan 7:13 in Mark 14:62 par. Matt 26:64.[44] We have also mentioned that Mark 14:24 par. Matt 26:28 ("my blood of the covenant which is poured out for many") reflects the influence of Zech 9:11 and of Isa 53:12; this verse also alludes strongly to Exod 24:8 and thus can be considered a conflation of three OT texts.[45] Another probable example is John 19:36, "None of his bones shall be broken," which seems to invoke both the paschal lamb in the Pentateuch (Exod 12:10 [LXX], 46; Num 9:12) and the Righteous Sufferer in Ps 34:20.[46]

Already mentioned in other contexts, Mark 14:27 par. Matt 26:31 provides another interesting example. Here the text basically follows the LXX of Zech 13:7, in which God says to the sword in his hand, "Strike the shepherd, that the sheep may be scattered." God, then, is in effect calling upon himself to smite the shepherd, though this is not said in so many words. In the Gospels, however, this divine responsibility for the attack on the shepherd is made explicit; the LXX's second-person-plural imperative ("Strike!") is changed to the first-person-singular

---

[41] See, e.g., the Targum on Zech 14:4 and on Cant 8:5; these texts are consistent with the depictions on the north wall of the Dura Europa synagogue. Cf. Allison, *End of the Ages*, 43–44.

[42] Allison, *End of the Ages*, 43–44.

[43] See Kee, "Function," 181.

[44] Luke 22:69 omits one of the texts and thus avoids the conflation.

[45] Again, Luke drops the "my" and thus loses the reference to one of the conflated texts (Zech 9:11).

[46] See Brown, *Death of the Messiah*, 2.1184–87.

future ("I will strike"). This forthright acknowledgment of the divine role in the wounding of the shepherd may be plausibly ascribed to the influence of Isa 53:6, 10, which speaks of God bruising his chosen Servant for the benefit of his people. Thus the text from Zech 13 has been infiltrated by a feature of Isa 53, which speaks of the vicarious and redemptive wounding of the Servant for the sin of his people. For biblically literate readers, this infiltration would perhaps introduce a note of redemption into the citation of Zechariah's gloomy words about the assault on the shepherd.[47]

The techniques and traditions of usage of OT texts found in the Gospel passion narratives, then, are very much in continuity with those found among Jewish exegetes in the evangelists' environment. We shall see additional examples of this continuity in the next section.

THE OLD TESTAMENT IN THE PASSION NARRATIVES OF THE INDIVIDUAL GOSPELS

So far our study has generalized about the passion narratives' OT usage; it is now time to look at distinctive characteristics of the individual Gospels' usage.

Mark and Matthew

Most of what we have said so far relates to Mark, whose passion narrative is the basis for the narratives of Matthew and Luke. The usage of the Psalms of the Righteous Sufferer dominates Mark's passion narrative from beginning to end, but there are also several allusions to the Suffering Servant of Isaiah throughout the narrative and a concentrated burst of allusions to Zech 9–14 at one particular point. There are also allusions to isolated eschatological passages at various points; Dan 7:13 (conflated with Ps 110:1) is part of Jesus' reply to the high priest's question in Mark 14:62, and the cosmic darkness in 15:33 is probably an allusion to Amos 8:9.

Matthew generally follows Mark's passion narrative scriptural usage quite closely, only occasionally embellishing it. As we have seen, some of these embellishments reveal Matthew's awareness of the context of the OT passages to which Mark alludes.

Another example of the same awareness is Matt 27:34, where the crucified Jesus refuses an offer of wine mixed with gall. This refusal is

---

[47] It is impossible to say whether the echo of Isa 53 in Mark 14:27 par. Matt 26:31 was already present in the pre-Markan passion narrative or has been added by Mark. It is consonant, however, with the Markan addition of 14:28 in that both attenuate the severity of Zech 13:7.

interesting because it doubles the reference to Ps 69:21, the second half of which was already alluded to in the Markan passion narrative, where Jesus was given vinegar to drink (Mark 15:36). Matthew follows Mark here (27:48), but a few verses earlier in his narrative, he inserts an allusion to the first half of the psalm verse, so that both halves are covered, as is shown in the following chart:

Ps 69:21	*Matt 27:34*	*Matt 27:48*
they gave me gall for food	they offered him wine to drink, mingled with gall	
and for my thirst they gave me vinegar to drink		one of them . . . filled [a sponge] with vinegar . . . and gave it to him to drink

Contrary to the probable intention of the original OT text, where the offers of gall and of vinegar are meant to be synonymous, Matthew apparently understands the parallelism in Ps 69:21 to be fulfilled in two separate acts: first Jesus is given gall, then he is given vinegar. This overly literal fulfillment of a scriptural instance of synonymous parallelism is similar to that in Matt 21:1–7, where Matthew takes the reference in Zech 9:9 to the coming king mounted "on a donkey, and on a colt the foal of a donkey," as a reference to Jesus riding into Jerusalem on two animals.[48] Later in this study, we will see another instance of overexact fulfillment of Hebrew parallelism in John, and we will speculate about the ramifications of this exegetical technique for the questions of the audience and the purpose of the OT usage of Matthew and John.

The other Matthean passage, 27:9–10, is more puzzling and complicated. Here Matthew tells a story, absent from the other Gospels, in which Judas's blood money for the betrayal of Jesus is used by the chief priests to buy a potter's field. This incident, Matthew says, fulfills

> what had been spoken by the prophet Jeremiah, saying, "And they took the thirty pieces of silver, the price of him on whom a price had been set by some of the sons of Israel, and they gave them for the potter's field, as the Lord directed me." (RSV)

The trouble is that except for the reference to the purchase of a potter's field, which recalls two separate passages from Jeremiah (18:1–2, Jeremiah's

---

[48]Cf. Krister Stendahl, *The School of St. Matthew and Its Use of the Old Testament* (1954; reprint, Philadelphia: Fortress, 1968) 119; and Brown, *Death of the Messiah*, 2.942–43, 1059–60.

visit to a potter; and 32:6–9, his purchase of a field), what Matthew quotes is a loose adaptation of a text from Zech 11:12– 13, not from Jeremiah. The Zecharian text probably originally spoke of thirty shekels of silver, the price set on the shepherd of the flock, being thrown by him into the temple *treasury*, Hebrew אוֹצָר, *ʾwṣr*; the text in its present form, however, speaks of the money being thrown to the *potter*, Hebrew יוֹצֵר *ywṣr*—a difference of just one letter in the Hebrew.[49] Matthew, or the tradition upon which he draws, seems to know of both readings, since in 27:5 he has Judas throw down the blood money in the *temple* but continues the story with the purchase of the field of a *potter*.

The inaccurate attribution to Jeremiah has occasioned a great many explanations.[50] Some have suggested that Matthew is simply making a mistake, either because of a fault in his own memory or because he is drawing his biblical quotations from a testimony book, a collection of OT passages grouped around related themes. Ancient Jewish analogies to such misquotation exist.[51] It seems more likely, however, given Matthew's special interest in Jeremiah (cf. 2:17–18; 16:14), that he is deliberately invoking the image of the OT prophet, whose life was one of suffering witness to the word of God and rejection by religious authorities.[52]

Luke

While, aside from passages such as Matt 27:9–10 and 27:34, Matthew's OT usage follows Mark's rather closely, Luke's OT usage departs from Mark's more frequently, often lessening the connection between the passion description and the scriptural background.[53] Sometimes the reason for this diminution may be that Luke simply does not recognize the scriptural echo or because grammatical smoothness is more important to him, but on other occasions it reflects a more profound discomfort with the Markan text.

Thus, many of the less dignified aspects of the Righteous Sufferer of the Psalms or the Suffering Servant of Isaiah are eliminated. In Luke,

---

[49] On the text and its problems, see Carol L. and Eric M. Meyers, *Zechariah 9–14: A New Translation with Introduction and Commentary* (AB 25C; New York: Doubleday, 1993) 276–78.

[50] See Michael Knowles (*Jeremiah in Matthew's Gospel: The Rejected Prophet Motif in Matthean Redaction* [JSNTSup 68; Sheffield: JSOT, 1993] 60–77), who lists nine different possibilities.

[51] See Joseph A. Fitzmyer, "'4Q Testimonia' and the New Testament," in *Essays on the Semitic Background of the New Testament* (SBLSBS 5; Missoula, Mont.: Scholars, 1971) 59–89.

[52] See Knowles, *Jeremiah in Matthew's Gospel*, 77–81.

[53] See our three charts, in which it is often the case that a Lukan parallel is lacking for a Markan/Matthean parallel; we may also note the omission of the allusion to Dan 7:13 in Luke 22:69 par. Mark 14:62.

for example, Jesus no longer expresses his emotional distress in Geth-semane or his sense of abandonment on the cross, nor is he physically and verbally abused at his trials and his execution to the same extent that he is in Mark and Matthew. Similarly, while some of the references to Zech 9–14 may be omitted simply because Luke does not recognize or care about their echoes, the reason for the elimination of the allusion to Zech 13:7 in the parallel to Mark 14:26 is almost certainly that for Luke, the sheep/disciples are not scattered but remain with Jesus up to the very end (see Luke 23:49). The elimination of these undignified elements may have something to do with Luke's more cultured audi-ence, which might have taken offense at them.[54]

It is more difficult to tell why Luke has diminished the echo of Isa 53 in the "cup word" of Luke 22:20 by eliminating the word "many" (Mark 14:24); it may simply be that the referent of "many" is obscure. Some would say, however, that Luke has a problem with the idea of the Suffering Servant's redemptive death and point for support to Luke 22:27 par. Mark 10:45, where he leaves out the "ransom" saying.[55]

It may be, however, that Jesus' atoning death is an idea of such common currency in the early church that Luke can allude to it glanc-ingly without invoking it overtly. This view is supported by Acts 20:28, which does speak of Jesus' atoning death, and by the fact that in the Gospel itself, Luke introduces into the passion narrative its one explicit quotation of Isa 53 (Luke 22:37).[56] At the moment of Jesus' death, moreover, Luke creates another possible allusion to Isa 53 (Luke 23:47: δίκαιος [dikaios, "righteous" or "innocent"]; cf. Isa 53:11).[57] The omis-sion of Mark 10:45 is still troubling to this view, but a sound exegetical argument cannot be based only on what is not there in a single verse.

John

We have already alluded to the fact that John's passion narrative contains an example of overexact fulfillment of an OT text similar to the one we investigated in Matt 27:34. This passage is John 19:23–24, where

---

[54] See Hans Conzelmann ("Luke's Place in the Development of Early Chris-tianity," in *Studies in Luke–Acts*, ed. Leander E. Keck and J. Louis Martyn [1966; reprint, Philadelphia: Fortress, 1980] 298–316), who on p. 302 applies to Luke Martin Dibelius's somewhat anachronistic term "Christian bourgeoisie"; see also C. F. Evans (*Saint Luke* [TPINTC; London: SCM; Philadelphia: Trinity, 1990] 108–11) on Luke's apologetic purpose.

[55] See the summary of their opinions by Fitzmyer, who opposes them; even he, however, has to admit the difficulty of Luke 22:27, where Luke has omitted the Markan ransom saying "for some inscrutable reason" (*Luke*, 1.219–20).

[56] See Darrell L. Bock, *Proclamation from Prophecy and Pattern: Lucan Old Testament Christology* (JSNTSup 12; Sheffield: JSOT, 1987) 338 n. 204.

[57] Cf. Brown, *Death of the Messiah*, 2.1165.

John cites Ps 22:18, "They divide my garments among them, and for my clothing they cast lots" (alt.). The Synoptics already use this passage to refer to the distribution of Jesus' clothes (Mark 15:24 par. Matt 27:35 par. Luke 23:34), but John goes one step further, speaking, in two separate stages, of the division of the outer clothes into four portions ("they divide my garments among them") and of the raffling of the seamless undergarment ("for my clothing they cast lots"). Thus the synonymous parallelism of the OT text, which originally referred to a single action, is reinterpreted in a literalistic manner as a reference to two actions. The consonance between OT prophecy and NT fulfillment, therefore, is even more amazingly exact than it is in the Synoptics.[58]

A similar tendency to highlight the consonance between prophecy and fulfillment underlies a general characteristic of John's passion narrative: almost all the OT usage is found in explicit quotation of OT passages, introduced by citation formulas referring to the Scripture's "fulfillment" (19:24, 28, 36–37).[59] John has not been content, as the Synoptics usually have been, to leave the allusions to the OT in the passion narrative implicit and embedded in the story; rather, he actively calls the reader's attention to them every chance he gets. This is especially noticeable in the crucifixion scene, where four explicit OT citations explode in rapid-fire succession (19:24, 28, 36, 37).

Thus, both by splitting the parallelism of the OT original and by making his references to scriptural texts explicit, John manifests a concern to underline for his readers the exact fulfillment of Scripture. Matthew seems to share this concern; as we have seen, he too splits parallelisms, and his Gospel is famous for its "fulfillment citations" of the OT (1:22; 2:15, 17, 23, etc.)—though only one of these occurs in the passion narrative (27:9–10).

What is behind this concern with exact fulfillment? One possibility is simple ignorance—Matthew and John's ignorance of the true nature of Hebrew parallelism, and their communities' biblical illiteracy, so that scriptural fulfillment has to be pointed out to them in a heavy-handed way. This explanation would point to authors and audiences relatively unfamiliar with the Bible and therefore probably Gentile.[60]

Jewish analogies, however, suggest that this explanation is not the correct one. Forced exegesis is not necessarily a sign of ignorance; the

---

[58] See Brown, *Death of the Messiah*, 2.953–54.

[59] In spite of John's insistence on exact fulfillment, two of his scriptural citations in the passion narrative are difficult to identify (cf. also the mysterious "scripture" in 7:38). Scholars debate whether "I am thirsty" in 19:28 refers to Ps 22:15 or 69:21 and whether "none of his bones shall be broken" in 19:36 refers to Exod 12:10 LXX, 46; Num 9:12; or Ps 34:20 (see Brown, *Death of the Messiah*, 2.1072–74, 1184–87).

[60] See, e.g., John P. Meier, *The Vision of Matthew: Christ, Church, and Morality in the First Gospel* (New York: Paulist, 1978) 21–22.

famous rabbinic sage Rabbi Akiba, for example, practiced such exegesis, believing that because of its divine origin every word in the Bible must be loaded with meaning, even when an unprejudiced observer would say that it was not.[61] The sectaries from Qumran, whose hermeneutics was controlled by their eschatological convictions, used a similarly forced exegesis to find references to their own time in biblical prophecy. Their biblical commentaries, or *pesharim*, moreover, express their conviction of eschatological advent by explicit citation of Scripture and emphasis on its fulfillment in present events.[62]

The Qumran analogy suggests a different explanation for the splitting of parallelism and explicit citation of Scripture in the Matthean and Johannine passion narratives and elsewhere in the Gospels; these phenomena reflect not ignorance but a situation in which believers' faith is being challenged and they need to be reminded that God's guiding hand was behind every incident in Jesus' death, which is understood as an apocalyptic event. This apologetic explanation is supported by the fact that it is in the crucifixion scene that we find both examples of split parallelism and the greatest concentration of explicit OT citations. This observation coheres with our apologetic explanation, since, as we noted at the beginning of this study, the central problem that gave rise to the passion narratives was explaining how the Messiah came to be crucified.

The same point may be made in another way by looking at the specific formulas of citation employed in John's Gospel. Craig A. Evans has noted a consistent pattern in these formulas: from 12:38 on, with insignificant exceptions, they use the formula ἵνα πληρωθῇ (*hina plērōthē*, "in order that it might be fulfilled," 12:38–39; 13:18; 15:25; 19:24, 28, 36–37), whereas previous to that point in the Gospel this formula does not occur (1:23; 2:17; 6:31, 45; 7:42; 10:34).[63] Evans's

---

[61] See Stendahl (*School*, 119) on Matthew's literalistic interpretation of Zech 9:9 in Matt 21:5: "It is in no way a sign that he was unfamiliar with Jewish exegesis, but on the contrary gives evidence of his acquaintance with the hermeneutic methods of the rabbis." Cf. James L. Kugel (*The Idea of Biblical Poetry: Parallelism and Its History* [New Haven: Yale University, 1981] 96–134), who speaks of a rabbinic "forgetting" of the meaning of biblical parallelism, though his own analysis suggests that it is not so much a forgetting as an exaggeration of the "sharpening" already present in biblical parallelism. On Akiba's method, see also Rimon Kasher, "The Interpretation of Scripture in Rabbinic Literature," in *Mikra: Text, Translation, Reading, and Interpretation of the Hebrew Bible in Ancient Judaism and Early Christianity*, ed. Martin J. Mulder (CRINT 2:1; Minneapolis: Fortress, 1990) 568–71. Akiba's forced exegetical method is opposed to Rabbi Ishmael's more commonsense attitude that "the Torah speaks the language of human beings."

[62] See William H. Brownlee, "Biblical Interpretation among the Sectaries of the Dead Sea Scrolls," *BA* 14 (1951) 54–76.

[63] Craig A. Evans, "On the Quotation Formulas in the Fourth Gospel," *BZ* 26 (1982) 79–83. The exceptions are 12:39 and 19:37, in both of which cases

explanation for this pattern is plausible: for John, God's ultimate purpose is fulfilled in the death of Jesus, which is brought about by the divinely willed opposition to him, and it is to these twin realities that the Johannine "fulfillment citations" point. This analysis reinforces our thesis of apologetic purpose, since aside from Jesus' death on a cross, his own people's opposition to him was the most difficult feature of his story for Christians to explain.

Such an apologetic intention, however, at first seems somewhat surprising in a Gospel that often distances itself from Jews and things Jewish, even from the OT.[64] (Matthew, who uses techniques similar to John's, manifests a similar ambivalence about Judaism.)[65] John's profound ambivalence about these matters is well captured by 15:25: "It is to fulfill the word that is written in their law, 'They hated me without a cause'" (Ps 35:19 par. 69:4). Here there is both a linkage with the OT and with Jewish traditions (the idea of fulfillment of Scripture and the closeness to Jewish usages that refer to the non-Pentateuchal portions of Scripture as part of the Law)[66] and a distancing from "the Jews"[67] and their Scripture ("they hated me," "their law").

This ambivalence probably reflects the origin of John's Gospel in a Jewish-Christian community that has undergone a traumatic separation from its synagogue home—an origin shared by Matthew's community as well. But what function would the passion apologetic[68] have performed in such a setting? Probably not to convince hostile or wavering non-Christian Jews; no document that commonly uses the term "the Jews" as a technical term for Jesus' enemies is likely to have functioned as a missionary tract to convert the children of Israel. Rather, the OT usage in the Johannine passion narrative is probably designed to reinforce the belief of those within the community, to convince them anew that God's plan has reached its ultimate purpose in Jesus' death and that therefore they have been right to throw in their lot with the Christians. There is a close analogy in the *pesharim* from Qumran, which, as we have seen, often use forced exegesis to bolster the faith of

---

ἵνα πληρωθῇ has just been used in the preceding verse, and 19:28, where the synonymous ἵνα τελειωθῇ, *hina teleiōthē*, is used.

[64] See Martyn, *History and Theology*, esp. ch. 6.

[65] See Graham N. Stanton, *A Gospel for a New People: Studies in Matthew* (Edinburgh: T. & T. Clark, 1992).

[66] See, e.g., *t. Ḥul.* 2.24; *b. Sanh.* 91b; *b. Sukk.* 51b; cf. Str-B 2:542–43; 3:159, 462–63; and the similar usages in John 10:24, 34; Rom 3:19; 1 Cor 14:21.

[67] Although this term does not appear in the immediate context, it is the standard Johannine term for the opponents of Jesus; see Brown, *John*, 1.lxxi–lxxiii.

[68] The term comes from Barnabas Lindars, *New Testament Apologetic: The Doctrinal Significance of the Old Testament Quotations* (London: SCM, 1961) 75–137.

insiders that God is working out his eschatological purposes through their beleaguered community.

John's OT usage, therefore, is indeed apologetic or defensive in function, but its apologetic is indirect rather than direct.[69] It is designed to defend the faith of the community, but not directly to counter the attacks of outsiders; it is meant, rather, to put heart back into the Johannine Christians and to arm them with scriptural ammunition so that they become ready to return to their life of witness to, and suffering for, the gospel.

CONCLUSION

Indeed, it is probably accurate to say that most of the OT usage in the Gospels is intended to function as indirect apologetic and that this motive for scriptural usage was present from the beginning of the church. The apologetic purpose of primitive Christian OT usage can be glimpsed, for example, in the Scripture-laden speeches in Acts, which, though they are later products, probably mirror the missionary strategy of the early church.[70] It is even more directly observable in the passage from 1 Corinthians, cited early in this chapter, in which Paul reminds the Corinthians that the Messiah's death "in accordance with the Scriptures" was part of the gospel, the good news, that he originally proclaimed to them (1 Cor 15:1-3). The scriptural shape of Jesus' death, therefore, was part of Paul's missionary preaching.

This scriptural background was, and is, part of the good news because it helps to show that the news really is good—good because planned by the good and trustworthy God, who has always remained faithful to his promises and has shown through the Scriptures that he can turn the weakness, suffering, despair, and even death of human beings into triumph. The early Christians believed that this same gracious God, who had spoken of old through the prophets, had now spoken his final word through his Son (Heb 1:1-2). This new word gave a definitive proof of God's victory by pointing to the resurrection from the dead of a familiar biblical figure—the sold and wounded shepherd, the Righteous Sufferer, the innocent Servant cut off from the land of the living for the fault of others—and by pointing to the people with whom, in line with the biblical pattern, this righteous, suffering, risen shepherd and servant had mysteriously united himself.

---

[69] I owe this terminology to my Glasgow colleague John Barclay.

[70] See Ernst Haenchen, *The Acts of the Apostles: A Commentary* (Philadelphia: Westminster, 1971) 82.

 TWELVE

THE DEATH OF JESUS AND THE MEANING OF DISCIPLESHIP

Donald Senior, C.P.
President and Professor of New Testament Studies
Catholic Theological Union, Chicago

To consider the link between the death of Jesus and the meaning of Christian discipleship is to consider the most fundamental reality of Christian faith. Other essays in this volume have, in effect, viewed this link under many guises as they have examined various NT perspectives on the death of Jesus.

Rather than attempt an overly ambitious synthesis, this chapter will understand "discipleship" not in an abstract and comprehensive sense, as a cipher for the totality of Christian life, but in a more specific and concrete mode. The guiding question of this exploration will be, What are some of the explicit links that the passion narratives themselves make between the passion and death of Jesus and the disciples, particularly on the public character of Christian discipleship? Even though more limited and definable, such a review still catapults the reader into broad and powerful currents of NT theology.

A working assumption for this study is that the passion stories, like the Gospels as a whole, were designed in part to invite reflection on the meaning of discipleship. Certainly christological interests are also at work in the passion accounts: explaining how the crucifixion of Jesus was in accord with God's will. But such episodes as the tragic betrayal of Judas, the poignant question of the disciples—"Is it I?"—the public denial of Peter and his bitter tears, the disciples' sleep and their terrified flight, and the presence of the beloved disciple at the cross are all obvious invitations for the hearer of the Gospels to ponder these incidents and the questions they pose for Christian life. The dramatic force of the passion stories and the vivid, if limited, part played by the disciples in each of the narratives provide the evangelists with ready opportunities to proclaim the Christian message to their communities. This dimension of the passion stories has been apparent to Christian readers and listeners throughout the centuries. The role of the passion story in the church's liturgies, the retelling of the passion in church drama, art, and music—all of these play on the assumption that Christians are to insert themselves into the fateful events of the passion, particularly those scenes in which the disciples play a part.

THE DISCIPLES AND THE PASSION STORY

The disciples of Jesus have a significant, though restricted, role in the four Gospel passion accounts, with each evangelist portraying them in the distinctive manner that characterizes his Gospel as a whole.

Mark sets the basic pattern for the synoptic accounts, particularly for Matthew, who follows his source closely. The disciples are prominent in the opening scenes of Mark's passion narrative, which begins in 14:1 with the conspiracy against Jesus and continues through the episodes of the anointing, the preparation for the Passover meal, the meal itself, and the prayer in Gethsemane. But at the moment of the arrest, the disciples all flee (14:50–51), and with Peter's denial following (14:66–72), they are notably absent for the remainder of the story. None of the Gospels in fact will present the disciples generally as responding in heroic fashion to the passion and death of Jesus.

The overall portrayal of the disciples takes a different tone in Luke, but he too conceives of the passion as a time of crisis and testing for the disciples. The passion is the "opportune moment" for which Satan had been waiting since the beginning of Jesus' ministry (Luke 4:13), and with the approach of the fated Passover, the devil enters into Judas to trigger the events that lead to Jesus' death (22:3). But because the Twelve will form the nucleus of the Jerusalem community in Acts and provide the continuity between the life of Jesus and the birth of the church, Luke turns the spotlight away from the failure of the disciples. Thus Jesus acclaims their perseverance in the midst of trials and promises them thrones to judge the tribes of Israel in the kingdom of God (22:28–30). Nevertheless they are warned about the impending crisis and urged to be ready and vigilant (22:35–40). The entrance of the armed guards into the garden to arrest Jesus is described as the "hour of darkness" (22:53).

Although Luke does not record the disciples' flight at the time of the arrest, the reader cannot fail to note their absence. Even though Peter's denial may be softened by the fact that Jesus looks directly at him and prompts the apostle to weep tears of repentance (22:61–62), still the terrible threat of the passion is clear. Luke may wish to hint that the disciples return to witness the death of Jesus when he notes that some of those "who knew him" "stood at a distance" (23:49), but if so, the evangelist does it with a light hand.[1] As in the accounts of Mark and Matthew, the disciples are not present for the momentous events of the Roman trial and the crucifixion of Jesus. The comportment of the disciples in the Emmaus story, whose hearts are heavy with disillusionment (24:13–35), and the terrified fear of the other disciples at the moment of the resurrection appearance (24:37) indicate that Luke envisages the death of Jesus as a moment of crisis and a withering test for the community.

Predictably, the Johannine story takes a different route altogether. During the last discourse, Jesus does warn his disciples that the coming "hour" is a time when they will "scatter, each one to his home, and you will leave me alone" (16:32). Yet in the narrative the focus falls on Jesus' heroic encounter with his enemies, with the response of the disciples eclipsed by this brilliant spotlight. The disciples' departure comes because Jesus secures their release, not because they flee (18:8). It is true that Peter's denial remains in John's story, but the failure of Simon Peter is offset by the fidelity of the beloved disciple, who accompanies Peter into the courtyard of the high priest (18:15) and will be present at the cross, there to become a member of Jesus' new family (19:26–27).

Thus in John's passion story attention falls almost exclusively on Jesus, with only a minimal role for the disciples. The fidelity of the beloved disciple softens the impact of the passion as crisis or test for the community. The death of Jesus becomes instead the "hour" in which the Son of humanity (ὁ υἱὸς τοῦ ἀνθρώπου, ho huios tou anthrōpou) is glorified and the moment in which God's love for the world and the mission of the community are revealed.

It is not only in this array of scenes in the four passion stories that an explicit link to discipleship is made. Throughout the passion Jesus himself is obviously presented as an example for the disciples. His commitment to the will of the Father, his comportment at the moment of his arrest and trial, and his suffering on the cross portray Jesus as the obedient Son of God, as the faithful Just One of Israel, as the prophet-martyr dying with integrity.

Other characters, too, not necessarily identified as disciples yet demonstrating fidelity and responsiveness to Jesus, appear in the stories and become beacons to the reader. The woman who anoints Jesus, the repentant criminal, the centurion, the women at the cross and burial, and the figures of Joseph of Arimathea and, in John, Nicodemus also play exemplary roles in the drama.[2]

---

[1] See the discussion in ch. 4 above. Brown suggests that Luke may be referring not to the Eleven (since he would have been more explicit) but to "other disciples and/or friends of Jesus" (*Death of the Messiah*, 2.1171–73).

[2] See below, pp. 245–51.

While each of the Gospels has a distinctive theology of the death of Jesus, the passion remains inherently, in all four Gospels, a moment of crisis and threat, an opportunity for heroic fidelity and abject failure, an arena in which the forces of evil and death clash violently with God's anointed Messiah as Jesus makes his passage from death to life. Thus it is not surprising to detect within the passion narratives certain overarching themes of discipleship, each played out within the distinctive language and theological perspectives of the evangelists. I propose to focus on three such themes.

THE PASSION AND THE CALL TO VIGILANCE AND PRAYER

Particularly, but not exclusively, within the Synoptic Gospels, the death of Jesus is presented in quasi-apocalyptic tones as the crucial and definitive moment when the power of death assaults the power of God embodied in Jesus. As such, the passion of Jesus becomes a harbinger of the travails of the end time, when human history would be consummated. The Christian stance before this time of testing and struggle must be one of vigilance for the unexpected arrival of the day of the Lord and earnest prayer for deliverance from its overwhelming travails.

This perspective is clearly present in Mark but finds resonance in each of the Gospels.[3] Mark makes a strong link between the passion of Jesus and what could be called the "passion of the community" in ch. 13, immediately prior to the beginning of his passion narrative. There the disciples are warned that before the end time the community will experience a chaotic history, marked by division among nations (13:8); natural disasters (13:8); and divisions, strife, and the seductions of false messiahs and errant prophets within the community itself (13:5–7, 21–22). The sufferings that will be experienced in the course of the community's mission provide a tie into the passion of Jesus (see esp. 13:9–12). The disciples of Jesus will be handed over to councils, beaten, tried before governors, and betrayed to death by some of their own brethren—just as Jesus himself will suffer in the passion story.[4]

These events are antecedent to the end time. When the mission of the community is completed (13:10), then the Son of humanity will come in triumph to gather the elect from the "four winds, from the ends of the earth to the ends of heaven" (13:26–27). To prepare for these

---

[3]Without detouring into the issue of sources, I want to state that I share the view of those who believe that Mark was the primary source for the passion accounts of both Matthew and Luke. The relationship of John to Mark is more difficult to assess, but even there evidence exists that the Fourth Gospel had some contact with Mark.

[4]See ch. 2 above.

events, the community must be "awake" (γρηγορεῖν, *grēgorein*), alert and watching for the unexpected coming of the Son of humanity in history. The final words of Jesus in Mark's discourse drive home the point: "Therefore, keep awake—for you do not know when the master of the house will come, in the evening, or at midnight, or at cockcrow, or at dawn, or else he may find you asleep when he comes suddenly. And what I say to you I say to all: Keep awake" (13:35–37).

The anticipation of the passion story is evident. The watches of the night enumerated here become the framework for Mark's passion story: the passion events begin in the evening (14:17); the cockcrow punctuates Peter's denials (14:68, 72); and at dawn Jesus is brought to Pilate (15:1). The Markan passion story begins almost abruptly in 14:1, following immediately on the exhortation to "keep awake" in 13:37. The passage of Jesus through suffering and death, therefore, anticipates and illumines the sufferings the community will encounter as it carries out its mission in history. Elements of the passion correspond to what is predicted for the community: Jesus, too, is betrayed by one of his own, "one of the Twelve, one who is dipping bread into the bowl with me" (14:20), and the "sleep" of the disciples in Gethsemane will betray their failure to be ready for the moment of crisis (14:32–42). As he goes to prayer, Jesus exhorts Peter, James, and John to "keep awake" (14:34), and Simon is urged, "Keep awake and pray that you may not come into the time of trial" (14:38). Mark makes a point of emphasizing the failure of the disciples by having Jesus come three times to find them sleeping.[5]

The exhortations to vigilance and prayer in ch. 13 and in the passion story—as well as the disastrous failure of the disciples to heed them—serve as both warning and encouragement to the Markan community. The travails in their mission evoke the passion of Jesus, the Son of humanity, who suffered humiliation and death but was raised up by God; their sufferings also anticipate the end time, when through God's power they will endure and be gathered by the triumphant Son of humanity into God's kingdom.

Matthew's Gospel emphasizes the apocalyptic significance of Jesus' death, as his addition of the cosmic signs that follow in the wake of Jesus' death indicates (27:51–53).[6] Matthew also retains Mark's exhortations to vigilant prayer. The clear link between the apocalyptic discourse in chs. 24–25 and Matthew's passion narrative in chs. 26–27 is somewhat blunted by virtue of Matthew's redaction of this material.

---

[5]See Mark 14:37, 40, 41. While noting that the disciples sleep, Matthew shifts the focus to the repeated prayer of Jesus by enumerating the times he goes to pray (Matt 26:42, 44). In Luke, Jesus returns from prayer only once, to discover the disciples asleep "from grief" (Luke 22:45).

[6]See Donald Senior, "The Death of Jesus and the Resurrection of the Holy Ones (Mt 27:51–53)," *CBQ* 38 (1976) 312–29; and idem, *Passion of Jesus in Matthew*, 143–48.

Matthew, for example, omits the reference to the watches of the night found in Mark 13:35–37, and the series of judgment parables of ch. 25 stand between Jesus' exhortation to vigilance and the formal beginning of Matthew's passion story (see 24:36–42; 26:1).

Yet the theme of alert watchfulness in view of the unexpected coming of the end time remains a strong Matthean theme, one amplified in the parable of the bridesmaids (25:1–13; see esp. 25:13). In 26:18 Matthew underscores this motif by having Jesus refer to the impending passion as his καιρός, *kairos*, thus employing a term consistently used of the end time to describe the passion itself.[7] And in Gethsemane Matthew retains Mark's exhortation by Jesus that the disciples "stay awake and pray that you may not come into the time of trial" (26:41). In his version of the Gethsemane scene, Matthew, unlike Mark, focuses more on the repeated prayer of Jesus than on the threefold discovery of the disciples sleeping.[8] Jesus himself remains the paradigm of vigilant prayer as his καιρός approaches (26:44–46).

For Luke's account, too, one dimension of the passion is its lesson on the need for earnest and vigilant prayer in the face of deadly trials. Luke does not emphasize the failure of the disciples, so they are not presented as exemplars of morbid sleep in the face of the end time: they sleep because of "grief" (22:45). Yet the exhortation to vigilance in view of the aggressive force of evil and death remains strong in Luke's account. Luke follows Mark's lead in seeming to anticipate this theme of the passion in Jesus' temple discourse. The warnings about division, false prophets, and persecution in the cause of the mission are repeated (see 21:7–19). Typical Lukan concerns are also introduced: the disciples are urged to "persevere" (21:19; see 22:28), to "be alert at all times," and to pray that they might "have the strength to escape all these things that will take place" (21:36).

These themes return in the passion story in passages unique to Luke. At the Passover meal the disciples are praised as ones "who have stood by me in my trials" (22:28). Peter is warned that Satan has demanded to "sift all of you like wheat" (22:31). Simon and the rest of the disciples are spared only because Jesus has prayed for their deliverance. And Simon is told to "strengthen [his] brothers" once he has escaped the ordeal (22:32). At the conclusion of the meal—again in a passage unique to Luke—Jesus seems to alert the disciples once more to the ordeal of the passion. In contrast to previous missions, when they did not need to take purse, bag, or sandals, now they are urged to bring a purse and bag and to purchase a sword (22:35–38). The looming passion will be a πειρασμός, *peirasmos*, a struggle with the power of evil, against which one must be "armed."[9]

---

[7]See, for example, Matt 8:29 and 13:30 (and also 13:40, where the parable is explained as referring to the "end of the age").

[8]See n. 5 above.

[9]This motif in Luke has been discussed by Schuyler Brown in *Apostasy and*

And if Luke spares the disciples embarrassment at the moment of the arrest by not alluding to their flight, the theme of vigilance and earnest prayer for deliverance from the withering trial remains. When they reach the "Mount of Olives," Jesus instructs the disciples, "Pray that you may not come into the time of trial" (22:40; repeated in v. 46). His own prayer takes the form of a great struggle in which he prays for deliverance, receiving the comfort of an angel in the midst of his agony (22:41–44).

By introducing a more explicit role for Satan in the passion story, Luke seems to intensify the apocalyptic theme of prayer in the face of the "test."[10] The betrayal of Jesus is ultimately engineered by Satan, who takes possession of Judas at the opportune moment (22:3; see 4:13), and only the prayer of Jesus has protected Simon and the rest of the disciples from a similar fate (22:31–32). The arrest of Jesus is the hour when the "power of darkness" holds sway (22:53). Thus Luke's community is instructed to pray not simply for strength in the midst of trial but for the grace not to have to undergo the trial because of its ferocious power. The women of Jerusalem and the crowds that follow Jesus on his way of the cross are told to weep "for themselves and for their children" because they will not be spared the test (23:27–31). The disciples, however, are blessed because they have persevered with Jesus during his trials. The importance of persevering will become clear in Acts. The apostles will form the nucleus of the community after the resurrection, whereas Judas has gone astray in betraying Jesus (Acts 1:25). Only one of those who "have accompanied us during all the time that the Lord Jesus went in and out among us, beginning from the baptism of John until the day when he was taken up from us," can be a witness for Jesus and fill up the number of the Twelve (1:21–22).

Luke's pastoral theology becomes clear: to weather the storms of history, the disciple must remain with Jesus in vigilant prayer or else undergo deadly testing and even destruction under the power of evil.

John's Gospel treats this motif almost exclusively in the last discourse of chs. 13–17, the introductory section of his passion story, which roughly parallels the series of incidents that Mark and the other Synoptics treat in the multiple episodes prior to the arrest of Jesus. Missing from John are the disciples as exemplars either of torpid failure to be vigilant (Mark and Matthew) or of perseverance in the midst of trial (Luke). But John does portray Jesus as warning his community about the impending passion as an experience of persecution and trial. In 16:32–33 he predicts that in the coming "hour" the disciples will be "scattered." In the world the disciples will face persecution, but they are

---

Perseverance in the Theology of Luke (Rome: Biblical Institute, 1969); on this passage as a whole, see Senior, Passion of Jesus in Luke, 79–83.

[10]See Garrett, Demise of the Devil, 54–55; Soards, Passion according to Luke, 109–11; Neyrey, Passion according to Luke, 31–33.

to take courage because Jesus has "conquered the world" (16:33). A similar exhortation is found in 15:18–25. Jesus warns the disciples that the world will "hate" them, just as it hated Jesus. What they do to Jesus they will do to the disciples, so they should expect persecution "on account of my name" (15:20–21). The theme reemerges in the so-called priestly prayer of ch. 17. Jesus prays that the Father will protect the disciples from "the evil one" because the world will hate them, just as it hated Jesus (17:14–16).

These exhortations and prayers immediately precede the arrest in the garden, where the confrontation between Jesus and his enemies will take place in dramatic fashion. In John the focus falls almost exclusively on Jesus. The divine power that emanates from Jesus overwhelms his enemies, driving them to the ground even as they move to arrest him (18:6). Peter's feeble attempt at defending Jesus by cutting off the ear of Malchus, the high priest's slave, only serves to highlight Jesus' own freedom in submitting to his captors: "Am I not to drink the cup that the Father has given me?" (18:11). Thus John displays in one episode both the reality of Jesus' prediction about the world's hatred for Jesus and his power to overcome the world.

Each of the passion stories, therefore, exhibits in varying degree an understanding of the passion that links it to the experience of persecution and suffering in the history of the post-Easter community. These sufferings, it should be noted, are not so much depicted as individual or spiritual sufferings as they are linked to the community's mission in the world. On a fundamental level, the passion of Jesus is understood as a definitive encounter with the power of evil and death—as part of the struggles of the end time, as an assault of Satan, as the world's hatred. The disciples alone would not be able to withstand this test.

The various ways the Gospels portray Jesus in his passion exhibit the stance the Christian must take: immersed in prayer in Gethsemane, alert for the onslaught of evil at the moment of arrest, clinging to his trust in God as the fierce power of death threatens to overwhelm him on the cross. Therefore, the essential stance of the community of disciples in the world, too, is to "stay awake," ever watchful for the reality of evil and the presence of grace, remaining in communion with Jesus, and praying earnestly for deliverance.

THE PASSION AND THE WITNESS OF FAITH

The public character of the passion story and its inherent dramatic confrontation between the power of God and the forces of evil lead to another link between the death of Jesus and the meaning of discipleship, that of witness. While the passion stories may not employ all of the features of Jewish martyrdom accounts, there is little doubt that the call to fearless witness under the threat of persecution and death is an underlying motif in all four passion accounts.[11] Here, too, the role of the disciples in the passion narratives is not as heroic exemplars but primarily as foils to Jesus' own example of fearless witness.

Mark's story establishes a pattern that is repeated in the other accounts. When Jesus predicts that all of the disciples will be "scandalized" in him (14:27), Peter vigorously protests, "Even though all would be scandalized in you, I will not." Even Jesus' prediction of his threefold denial does not deter Peter's bravado: "Even though I must die with you, I will not deny you." The rest of the disciples "said the same" (14:31).

The commitment to follow Jesus to death clearly introduces the motif of heroic witness, a commitment to be carried out by Jesus and sadly abandoned by Peter and the other disciples. At the moment of the arrest, all of the disciples flee from the armed band. And in the case of Peter, Mark underscores the contrast between Jesus' heroic confession of his identity before the high priest (14:62) and Peter's public apostasy by sandwiching the interrogation before the high priest between segments of the denial story.[12]

While Matthew follows Mark's lead closely, treating the flight of the disciples and Peter's denial in virtually the same terms as Mark, Luke has a distinctive presentation.[13] Luke presents Jesus as the "prophet-martyr," one whose God-given mission to Israel meets rejection, persecution, and even death, just as the prophets experienced rejection.[14] Yet the prophet-martyr remains constant even in suffering and gives public witness of his fidelity to God. So Jesus the prophet, anointed with God's spirit of justice (4:16–30), the one who set his face toward Jerusalem (9:51) and predicted that he would suffer rejection just as the prophets before him (13:31–35), encounters the power of evil in the passion. His prayer on the Mount of Olives is a prayer for strength before the test. Luke alone presents Jesus' prayer in these terms, experiencing "agony,"

---

[11] For a discussion of ideas on martyrdom as a voluntary death in a noble cause, see David Seeley, *The Noble Death: Graeco-Roman Martyrology and Paul's Concept of Salvation* (JSNTSup 28; Sheffield: JSOT, 1990). The sobriety of the passion accounts about the physical suffering of Jesus contrasts, however, with many of the stories found in Maccabees.

[12] The nocturnal interrogation (14:55–65) is introduced with Peter warming himself at a fire in the courtyard (vv. 53–54) and concludes with his denial (vv. 66–72).

[13] Matthew does, however, intensify the account of Peter's denial by having the apostle deny Jesus "with an oath" (26:72) and having him weep "bitterly" (26:75).

[14] On this motif in Luke, see Richard J. Dillon, *From Eye-Witnesses to Ministers of the Word: Tradition and Composition in Luke 24* (AnBib 82; Rome: Biblical Institute, 1978).

sweating profusely as an athlete straining before the exertion and release of the contest, and having an angel to comfort and strengthen him for the ordeal ahead (22:39–46).[15] And as the passion unfolds, Jesus gives heroic witness: despite the violence, mockery, and unjust condemnation he must suffer, Jesus eschews violence and heals the severed ear of the high priest's slave (22:51), offers Peter a look of compassion at the very moment the disciple denies his master (22:61), forgives his executioners (23:34), offers salvation to a malefactor (23:43), and dies with a prayer of reverent obedience to God on his lips (23:46). As the centurion acclaims in Luke's version, "Truly this was a just man" (23:47)—whose noble and heroic death incites lament in the Jerusalem crowds (23:27) and brings a criminal (23:40–43) and those who witness his death (23:48) to repentance.

Luke follows through on this portrayal in Acts. The Jerusalem apostles, such as Peter and James, continue to witness to Jesus despite the threat of arrest and torture (e.g., Acts 4:1–31), and Stephen endures a martyr's death in a manner that recalls Jesus' own heroic passion (6:8–8:1).

Luke, therefore, uses the passion story as a moment to proclaim a fundamental quality of discipleship: the call to witness publicly, even heroically, to the gospel despite the threat of persecution and death. Jesus dies witnessing to the triumph of God's prophetic word, and the disciples of Jesus must aspire to the same calling. Within the passion story itself, the Lukan disciples can hardly be considered witnesses. At the supper they argue about who would be regarded as the greatest among them at the very moment Jesus presents the bread as his body "given for you" and the cup as the new covenant poured out in his blood "for you" (22:24–27). When Peter trumpets his readiness "to go with you to prison and death" (22:33), Jesus predicts his threefold denial. The warning on the impending struggle with evil in Jesus' instruction about the sword seems to be misunderstood (v. 38). And if the disciples are present at all at the moment of Jesus' death, it is only "at a distance" (23:49). Only after Jesus' death and under the impact of the risen Christ's presence and the power of the Spirit will the disciples be able to give heroic witness in the name of Jesus.

The testimony or witness motif is also an important feature of John's Gospel. Here, Jesus is the model of fearless witness. In ch. 8, a section of the Gospel with strong echoes in the passion story, Jesus confronts his enemies and presents his entire mission as a fearless witness of God's word to the world. Jesus' testimony is valid because he

---

[15]Neyrey contends that the term ἀγωνία, *agōnia*, has the connotation in Greco-Roman literature of exertion in preparation for an athletic contest or combat (*Passion according to Luke*, esp. 58–62; also Brown, *Death of the Messiah*, 1.189–90).

comes from God and speaks the truth, a truth his opponents cannot recognize and therefore reject. In their anger they will attempt to kill "a man who has told [you] the truth that I heard from God" (8:40). The strong polemical tone of this chapter and of its conclusion, where the Jews pick up stones to kill Jesus, evokes the passion account, particularly the exchange between Jesus and Annas.[16] Jesus proclaims to the high priest, "I have spoken openly to the world"—testimony that is once more rejected by the religious authorities (18:19–24).

The theme of testimony in John's Gospel reflects a fundamental mode of his Christology. Jesus is God's Word to the world; he is the revelation of God's love for the life of the world. Giving witness to God's word is the summation of Jesus' God-given mission, a mission that is to be taken up by the disciples themselves under the power of the Paraclete once Jesus has gone to the Father (17:18–19). The consummation of that mission comes with Jesus' sacrificial death—a death that will "gather into one all the dispersed children of God," as Caiphas unwittingly prophesied (11:47–53), a death that is the ultimate act of friendship love (15:13).

Within the passion story, John illustrates this fundamental understanding of Christian mission not only by presenting Jesus as the embodiment of God's word who proclaims God's enduring love for the world in his death and in his public testimony but also by drawing the contrast between Peter and the beloved disciple, a unique feature of John's passion narrative. As in the synoptic versions, Peter's commitment to follow Jesus even to death—"I will lay down my life for you" (13:37)—sets up a poignant example of failure in his public denial of his discipleship (18:25–27). John may prepare the reader for this by identifying Peter as the one who slashes the ear of the high priest's slave at the moment of the arrest (18:10–11), a fruitless exercise of violence that seems to overlook the power of Jesus. Chapter 21 of John attempts to remedy this abject example by having the risen Jesus exact a threefold testimony of love from Peter in Galilee and by predicting that he would die as a martyr (21:15–19).

Peter's failure to give testimony on behalf of Jesus contrasts with the comportment of the beloved disciple, the mysterious and representative follower of Jesus who first appears within the passion story of John.[17] In each instance, the beloved disciple outshines Peter: he reclines next to Jesus, and Peter must question Jesus through him (13:23–26); only because of this disciple is Peter able to enter the courtyard of the high priest (18:16); and while Peter denies his discipleship, the beloved

---

[16] See Brown, *Death of the Messiah*, 1.416; Senior, *Passion of Jesus in John*, 61–63.

[17] On this point, see Pheme Perkins, *Peter: Apostle for the Whole Church* (Columbia: University of South Carolina, 1994) 95–101.

disciple takes up vigil next to the cross with the mother of Jesus (19:26). There he will be inducted into the family of Jesus (19:26–27). John seems to imply that this is the disciple who gives testimony about the blood and water that flows from the open side of the crucified Jesus: "He who saw this has testified so that you also may believe. His testimony is true, and he knows that he tells the truth" (19:35). The words evoke Jesus' description of his own mission to the world and become an instance of faithful Johannine discipleship. This is ratified in ch. 21, where the disciple is described as one "whom Jesus loved," as "the one who had reclined next to Jesus at the supper" (21:20), and as "the disciple who is testifying to these things and has written them, and we know that his testimony is true" (21:24).[18]

For John's Gospel, the essence of discipleship consists in coming to understand the meaning of Jesus' death as God's word of love for the world and as a triumph over evil, and in giving living testimony to that "word" to the world.

Thus all four evangelists understand the passion and death of Jesus as an example of witness, as authentic martyrdom on behalf of the gospel. With the exception of the beloved disciple in John, the chosen disciples are presented as not yet ready or capable of such heroic witness; they therefore experience weakness and failure. No doubt this extraordinary example was meant as encouragement to communities who knew firsthand examples of both heroic witness and the scandal of apostasy and failure in the face of suffering and persecution.[19]

But the passion accounts also offer brief, cameo instances where individuals other than the designated disciples do respond generously and sometimes heroically. These counterexamples stand in contrast to the disciples and undoubtedly were meant as encouragement to the communities who received the Gospel accounts. The woman who anoints Jesus in Mark 14:3–9, for example, seems to understand that Jesus' destiny is death—a point consistently misunderstood by the Markan disciples. Recognizing Jesus' destiny, she acts generously, anointing Jesus on the head, an action that Jesus calls "beautiful" over the protests of the bystanders and interprets as his burial anointing (14:6–8). That this is meant as an example of generous discipleship is underscored by the extraordinary word of Jesus that concludes the scene: "Truly I tell you, wherever the good news is proclaimed in the whole world, what she has done will be told in remembrance of her" (14:9).

In Luke the brief vignette of Simon of Cyrene is transformed into an image of discipleship, as Simon "carries the cross after Jesus" (23:26)—language that recalls the discipleship saying of Jesus about

---

[18] See Brown, *Death of the Messiah*, 2.1182–84.
[19] See also Brown, *Death of the Messiah*, 1.621–26, for examples.

taking up the cross and following "after" him (see 9:23; 14:27). If the laments of the Jerusalem crowds who follow Jesus on the way of the cross (23:27) and the beating of breasts by the crowds who witness Jesus' death (23:48) are ambiguous signs of repentance, the response of the criminal who is crucified next to Jesus is clear. He rebukes the other malefactor taunting Jesus, confesses his sins, and asks that Jesus remember him as he enters his kingdom—all genuine signs of repentance approved by Luke's Gospel and earning the malefactor a promise of accompanying Jesus into paradise (23:39–43).

In each of the Synoptic Gospels, the Roman centurion who leads the execution detail becomes an unexpected and remarkable witness.[20] In Mark the centurion who acclaims Jesus as truly the "Son of God" after witnessing "how he died" (15:39) is the first and only human being in the Gospel to acclaim Jesus by this title.[21] In Matthew the centurion is joined by those who stand guard with him in confessing Jesus as Son of God after they witness the spectacular cosmic signs that erupt after his death (27:54; cf. 27:36). And in Luke the centurion "praised God" and acclaims Jesus as a "just" man, resonating with Luke's presentation of Jesus as God's suffering Just One (23:47).[22]

There are other, perhaps more ambiguous instances of heroism in the passion stories. In the Synoptics, when Joseph of Arimathea claims the body of Jesus from Pilate to give it a reverent burial, this is surely understood as an act of devotion, even if muted. In Mark he is described as a "respected member of the council, who was also himself looking for the kingdom of God" (15:43). He "takes courage" in deciding to go to Pilate; Mark may be suggesting that there was some risk on Joseph's part to identify himself in this manner with a man who was just condemned both by the Sanhedrin and by the Romans.[23] Luke portrays

---

[20] In John's account the "confession" of the centurion is in effect supplanted by the testimony of the beloved disciple (John 19:35).

[21] Until this point in Mark's narrative, only the demons recognize Jesus as "Son of God" (see Mark 5:7; in 3:24 the demoniac addresses Jesus as "the holy one of God"). The high priest asks if Jesus is "the Son of the Blessed One" but considers his affirmative answer blasphemy (Mark 14:62).

[22] See Robert J. Karris, "Luke 23:47 and the Lukan View of Jesus' Death," *JBL* 105 (1986) 65–74; also Matera, "Death of Jesus according to Luke," 483–84.

[23] Brown's contention that Joseph is simply a pious Jew who wants to have Jesus buried before sundown seems strained (*Death of the Messiah*, 2.1216). He believes that the "Achilles heel" of interpreting Joseph as a "disciple" is the fact that Mark does not show the women and Joseph cooperating in the burial. This is a weak argument from silence. And Mark does not have to portray Joseph as a "disciple" to make this action more than a response of Jewish piety. Joseph's search for the kingdom is being expressed in the fact that he is taking courage to perform an act of devotion for the crucified Jesus. Otherwise why would Mark have noted his search for the kingdom of God?—not unlike the encomium given to the scribe in Mark 12:34, a figure Mark surely presents in a positive light. It

Joseph in a similar manner, adding that he was a "good and just man who had not consented to their purpose and deed" (23:50–51). Matthew has another nuance, identifying Joseph not as a member of the Sanhedrin but as a "rich man" and a "disciple" who wraps the body of Jesus in a "clean" linen shroud and places the body in "his own new" tomb (27:57–60)—all details that suggest Matthew views Joseph's actions as the proper kind of devotion a rich disciple is able to provide. Does he also intend to imply some degree of risk for Joseph as a rich disciple exposing his allegiance to Jesus by such open devotion, as Mark's version does for one who is a member of the council? The point is subtle, if present.[24]

Even more ambiguous in the view of some interpreters is John's account. Here Joseph is identified as a "disciple" but "secretly, for fear of the Jews" (19:38). Earlier in the Gospel, John seems to judge harshly such fearful disciples as "loving human glory more than the glory that comes from God" (12:42–43). This same type of fear is exhibited by the people in 7:13, by the parents of the man born blind (9:22), and by the disciples themselves as they huddle behind locked doors after the death of Jesus (20:19). Joseph is joined by Nicodemus, who, the evangelist recalls, "had at first come by night" but now comes to the tomb bringing an extravagant amount of spices to anoint Jesus' body for burial (19:39).

Are these examples of inadequate discipleship? Or does John begin to show us the impact of Jesus' death, which is transforming secret and fearful disciples into ones who publicly give witness of their allegiance to the crucified Jesus? I believe the latter is what the evangelist had in mind. His account, in effect, amplifies and illustrates Mark's reference to "taking courage." Nicodemus, John notes, "at first" came to Jesus under the cover of night, but—the contrast is implicit—now under the impact of Jesus' death he steps out openly into the light.[25]

Another set of possibly ambiguous counterexamples of discipleship are the women at the cross. Once again Mark establishes a pattern that is taken up by the other two synoptic evangelists.[26] Mark indicates that along with the centurion, "there were also women looking on from a distance": Mary Magdalene, Mary the mother of James the younger and

---

seems to me that both Luke and Matthew—and perhaps John if we can assume dependence—read more into Mark's account than Brown is willing to concede.

[24] See the discussion of this text in Donald Senior, "Matthew's Account of the Burial of Jesus," in *The Four Gospels 1992: Festschrift Frans Neirynck*, ed. Frans Van Segbroeck et al. (3 vols.; BETL 100; Louvain: Leuven University, 1992) 2.1433–48, esp. 1444–45.

[25] See Robert J. Karris, *Jesus and the Marginalized in John's Gospel* (ZSNT; Collegeville, Minn.: Liturgical, 1990) 96–101.

[26] In John the role of witness at the cross is taken over by the beloved disciple, who, along with the mother of Jesus, becomes a privileged witness of Jesus' death.

of Joses, and Salome (15:40). Mark adds that "these used to follow him and provided for him when he was in Galilee; and there were many other women who had come up with him to Jerusalem" (15:41). Two of these women are mentioned in the burial scene: "Mary Magdalene and Mary the mother of Joses saw where the body was laid" (15:47).

An important role awaits them at the tomb on Sunday morning, an enigmatic scene that has captured the attention of modern interpreters of Mark. The three witnesses come to anoint Jesus, now that the Sabbath is over, and discover instead the empty tomb. A "young man" dressed in a white robe proclaims to them the message of resurrection and instructs them to announce it to "his disciples and Peter." They leave, trembling and in ecstasy, and "say nothing to anyone, for they were afraid" (16:8).

How does Mark understand the role of these women? For some interpreters, the women are destined to join the rest of the Markan disciples as examples of failure. Their presence at the cross is not heroic, since they stand "at a distance." At the burial they are a passive presence. And instead of proclaiming the resurrection message to the disciples, they lapse into fear and silence, failing, as the other disciples had before them, to grasp the gospel of God concerning Jesus.[27]

This line of interpretation depends in large measure on the meaning of 16:8. In my own view, which I have argued at some length elsewhere, the women's silence is not to be interpreted as another instance of discipleship failure.[28] The final verse should be understood not in isolation but in the context of the final scene as well as in the light of Jesus' own promises in the body of Mark's Gospel. From a literary standpoint, Mark presents Jesus as the most reliable witness: what he predicts comes true. Therefore, the disciples do hear the message because Jesus has already predicted both their failure and their redemption at the supper (see 14:27–28). They *will* see Jesus in Galilee—the message the women are to transmit—because Jesus has predicted they would. The women's "trembling," "ecstasy," "fear," and silence can be understood as reactions to the overwhelming theophany revealed to them by the young man at the tomb—Jesus the crucified one has been raised!

This interpretation explains the presence of the women at the death and burial; in both instances they "observe" the reality of Jesus' death and burial. They become the unlikely witnesses to the marvel of Jesus' resurrection, just as they were the witnesses of his death. Both are important in Mark's theology. While Mark does not explicitly identify the women as "disciples," he notes that they had "followed" Jesus (ἠκολούθουν αὐτῷ,

---

[27]See most recently Brown, *Death of the Messiah*, 2.1158–59, who also interprets this passage as a critique of the women.

[28]Senior, *Passion of Jesus in Mark*, 135–37.

ēkolouthoun autō), "served" him (διηκόνουν, *diē-konoun*), and come up with him (συναναβᾶσαι, *synanabasai*) to Jerusalem—all characterizations of discipleship in Mark's schema (see Mark 15:41). And in the wake of Mark's emphasis on the flight of the other disciples at the beginning of the passion story, the presence of these followers at the death of Jesus—even if hesitant—is noteworthy.[29]

The women, in fact, follow on a string of unlikely respondents in the Gospel, such as Levi (2:13–17), the Gadarene demoniac (5:1–20), the woman with the hemorrhage (5:25–34), the Syrophoenician woman (7:24–30), Bartimaeus (10:46–52), the scribe (12:28–34), the widow (12:41–44), and the woman who anoints Jesus (14:3–9). In a way similar to these examples, the women exhibit faith in Jesus whereas the disciples fail, and—in this instance at least—these unlikely witnesses will become the means by which the disciples hear the Easter message.

This reading of Mark may be confirmed by Matthew's rendition. He too places women at the cross: Mary Magdalene and Mary the mother of James and Joseph and "the mother of the sons of Zebedee" (27:56). He gives a slight emphasis to their presence along with the centurion and the other witnesses by adding the emphatic ἐκεῖ, *ekei* (27:55). Two of these women, Mary Magdalene and the "other Mary," are at the tomb, where they seem to take up a vigil, "sitting opposite the tomb," almost as if in contrast to the guard that would be set up at the request of the Jewish leaders (27:62–66). In 28:1 the two women come "to see the tomb" and are greeted by an earthquake and an "angel of the Lord" who rolls back the stone to reveal an empty tomb. They are also entrusted with the Easter message, but there is no ambiguity in Matthew's description: "So they left the tomb quickly with fear and great joy, and

---

[29]Brown's hesitation on this score is curious (see *Death of the Messiah*, 2.1157–59). He suggests that a negative contrast between the fact that the women stand "at a distance" and the centurion's proximity to, and confession of, Jesus is Mark's point, rather than a contrast between the presence of the women and the absence of the other disciples. While one can share his hesitation to present anachronistically a feminist perspective in which the women in this scene are contrasted with male failure by the other disciples, this caution can be carried too far. Brown's protest that Mark could not have meant a comparison with an incident that occurred "66 verses earlier" seems odd for any interpreter who believes Mark has prepared for the passion story as early as ch. 1 of the Gospel. Is it likely that the reader of Mark would already have forgotten such incidents as the headlong flight in the garden or Peter's denial? If in fact one dramatized the Gospel, the presence of these women as the only followers of Jesus at the cross would certainly remind the audience of the absence of the other disciples. Brown, in fact, is willing to allow such a contrast in the case of Joseph of Arimathea in Matthew's account; here Brown notes that Matthew "presents one male *disciple* [italics original] who has remained with Jesus to the death" "over against the most famous male *disciples* of Jesus (the Twelve) who had fled" (2.1224).

ran to tell his disciples" (28:8). Their fear and joy are consummated when they encounter the risen Christ himself and worship him (28:9). Thus for Matthew the women are clearly the first witnesses of Easter, bringing to the scattered Eleven the message of the empty tomb and their first encounter with the risen Christ.

Luke moves in a similar fashion. The "women who had followed him from Galilee [συνακολουθοῦσαι αὐτῷ, synakolouthousai autō]," along with "those who knew him," stand at a distance "watching these things [ὁρῶσαι ταῦτα, horōsai tauta]" (23:49). They are noted again at the burial with a similar description: "The women followed after [Joseph] who had come up with him [συνεληλυθυῖαι, synelēlythuiai] from Galilee, and they saw the tomb and how his body was laid" (23:55). This provides a link to the empty tomb story because Luke notes: "Then they returned, and prepared spices and ointments. On the Sabbath they rested according to the commandment. But on the first day of the week, at early dawn, they came to the tomb, taking the spices that they had prepared" (23:56–24:1).

Upon arriving at the tomb, the women find two men in dazzling clothes and, as in Mark and Matthew, receive the Easter proclamation. In contrast to Mark and Matthew, Luke narrates the actual report of the women to the "Eleven" (24:8–10): remembering Jesus' words, "they told all this to the Eleven and to all the rest. Now it was Mary Magdalene, Joanna, Mary the mother of James, and the other women with them who told this to the apostles."

The fact that Luke intends this reporting to be an example of witness on behalf of Jesus—and one that contrasts with the other disciples—is driven home by the reaction of the Eleven: "But these words seemed to them an idle tale, and they did not believe them" (24:11). Only after Peter's own visit to the tomb (24:12), the appearances to the disciples on the road to Emmaus (24:13–35), and Jesus' own appearance to the whole assembly (24:36–43) is the Easter message accepted. Then the risen Christ opens the disciples' minds to understand the Scriptures and commands them to be "witnesses of these things" (24:44–48).[30]

Thus, along with the more explicit emphasis on the witness motif illustrated in the comportment of Jesus and his disciples in the passion stories, there are other examples where cameo characters respond to Jesus' passion and death in a manner that exemplifies dimensions of authentic discipleship. All of these examples, even those that are ambiguous, draw their cogency from the fact that Jesus' death was a crucifixion, a public execution at the hands of the Roman authorities

---

[30]On the role of the women as witnesses at the tomb, see the interesting discussion of Carolyn Osiek, "The Women at the Tomb: What Are They Doing There?" *Ex Auditu* 9 (1993) 97–107.

and with the approval of the religious leaders. I am speaking here not so much on a historical level—although the crucifixion of Jesus is a sure historical fact—but within the dramatic context of the Gospel stories. Because Jesus is publicly condemned by the authorities to a shameful death by capital punishment, his own courage and the response of his followers and those attracted to him have a new level of meaning. Through the witness motif the evangelists reminded their communities that allegiance to Jesus could not be hidden. In an atmosphere of hostility and misunderstanding, authentic disciples of Jesus would not hesitate to give public witness to their faith, even if that might result in persecution or death.

THE PASSION AND THE CRITIQUE OF ABUSIVE POWER

Another link between the death of Jesus and discipleship is found in the pervasive critique of abusive power that emerges in all four accounts. Once again taking Mark as our lead, we can find an entry point in the arrest story (14:43–52). Here in dramatic fashion Jesus' opponents, brandishing swords and clubs, publicly confront him. The underlying tension of the Gospel stands out clearly: on one side is a crowd intent on violence, with Judas the betrayer of Jesus leading them; on the other stand Jesus and his disciples. In the mayhem surrounding the arrest, a "bystander" draws his sword, striking the slave of the high priest and cutting off his ear (14:47). Mark does not identify the sword-bearer as a disciple, and there is no compelling reason to do so; the evangelist may think of him as one of the crowd who accidentally strikes the servant in the chaos of the arrest, or perhaps this is a deliberate blow by a third party who happened to be standing by.[31] In any case, this incident is part of the atmosphere of violence to which Jesus directs his rebuke: "Then Jesus said to them, 'Have you come out with swords and clubs to arrest me as though I were a bandit?'" (14:48). After that confrontation the disciples all flee, leaving Jesus to the mercy of his captors (14:50–51). Jesus' words are an unmistakable rebuke to the treachery and violence ("with swords and clubs") of his captors.[32]

The other evangelists use this same moment to introduce more explicit teaching on discipleship. Matthew, for example, makes the

---

[31] See the discussion of this text in Brown, *Death of the Messiah*, 1.266–68; Senior, *Passion of Jesus in Mark*, 82–83.

[32] On the meaning of this text in relation to Markan theology and the background of his community, see Donald Senior, " 'With Swords and Clubs . . . ': The Setting of Mark's Community and His Critique of Abusive Power," *BTB* 17 (1987) 10–20.

sword-bearer a disciple—"one of those with Jesus" (26:51) who in the excitement of the moment draws his sword to defend Jesus from arrest. Jesus, in turn, rejects this use of violence:

> Put your sword back into its place; for all who take the sword will perish by the sword. Do you think that I cannot appeal to my Father, and he will at once send me more than twelve legions of angels? But how then would the Scriptures be fulfilled, which say it must happen in this way? (26:52–54)

Both the style and content of these words resonate with Jesus' teaching elsewhere in Matthew's Gospel, particularly in the Sermon on the Mount, where Jesus condemned violent retaliation and taught love of enemies (see 5:39, 43–45). The arrest scene, with the threat of violence against Jesus and the seduction of the disciples to retaliate in kind, offers Matthew a perfect opportunity to drive home this teaching of Jesus.

Luke, too, follows this pattern, explicitly posing the question that this scene raises for discipleship: "And when those who were about him saw what would follow, they said, 'Lord, shall we strike with the sword?'" (22:49). Without waiting for the answer, "one of them" strikes the high priest's servant and cuts off his right ear. Jesus' rejection of such violence is eloquent: "No more of this," he commands and then heals the ear of the slave (22:51). The finale to the arrest scene gives a new dimension to this violence. Luke has Jesus directly address the "chief priests and captains of the temple and elders who had come out against him" (compare the "crowds" [Mark] and "them" [Matthew]), and to Jesus' saying about coming with swords and clubs Luke adds, "But this is your hour and the power of darkness" (22:53). Behind the violent arrest stands the power of the demonic that possessed Judas to betray Jesus and to lead this violent crowd against Jesus.

John, too, retains this element of the arrest scene. Now the sword-bearer is identified as "Simon Peter" (18:10), another instance in John where Peter's discipleship will be less than ideal. Jesus commands him, "Put your sword into its sheath; shall I not drink the cup which the Father has given me?" (18:11). Another saying of Jesus later in John's passion story illumines this incident. During the Roman trial, Jesus contrasts his power with that of a kingdom "from this world": "My kingship is not of this world; if my kingship were of this world, my servants would fight, that I might not be handed over to the Jews; but my kingship is not from this world" (18:36). In Johannine terms, taking up the sword to prevent Jesus' arrest is a succumbing to the manner of this world's kingdoms. Jesus' power is radically different.

These examples of direct instruction about not wielding the sword, coming at a violent moment, point to an underlying and sometimes overlooked aspect of the passion stories: the contrast drawn between

Jesus' exercise of power and the violent and abusive power displayed by Jesus' opponents. In Mark's theology, for example, the passion provides a vivid and definitive contrast between the Son of humanity, who has come "not to be served but to serve, to give his life in ransom for the many" (10:45), and secular rulers whose power is oppressive and brutal. This text, with its reference to the death of Jesus, climaxes a pericope in which Jesus draws an explicit contrast between the way power is exercised among the "Gentiles" in "lording it over" others and "making their power felt" and the manner of authority in the Christian community, which is to be expressed in self-transcending service (see 10:42–44).[33] And in the apocalyptic discourse immediately prior to the passion story, the disciples were warned by Jesus to expect arrest, beatings, and trials from both religious and imperial authorities in the course of their mission (13:9–11).

Virtually the entire Markan passion story can be read in this light. Jesus is arrested at night by an armed band led by his betrayer; he is brought before the Sanhedrin for interrogation and tortured by the guards (14:65). He is then brought for trial before Pilate and, with the verdict of death, is mocked and beaten by the soldiers (15:16–20). The mockery is directed at Jesus' supposed pretensions to royal power, thus setting up a parody of kingship: a purple cloak, a crown of thorns, mock homage that turns violent. This introduces a strong note of irony into the passion story, one that carries through the entire Roman trial and the crucifixion. Jesus is mocked and ultimately rejected because he pretends to be a "king." The religious leaders and other bystanders continue to hurl this mockery at Jesus even as he hangs on the cross: "Let the Messiah, the King of Israel, come down from the cross now, so that we can see and believe" (14:32). Mark's reader knows that Jesus *is* a king but not in the manner of Roman imperial authority or the manner of authority exercised by the Sanhedrin. Thus the symbols of power used against Jesus turn back on themselves: the crown, the cloak, and those who wear them are, in effect, bankrupt symbols of power.[34] In Mark's perspective, not unlike Pauline theology, God's power will ultimately be revealed in weakness; at the very moment Jesus dies in seemingly abject fashion, God's power will raise him from the dead. This theology is an implicit critique of abusive power, one that might not be lost on an early Christian community that had experienced the brutality of arbitrary imperial authority.[35]

---

[33] See Senior, "With Swords and Clubs," 14–20.

[34] On the symbol of kingship in Mark's theology of the passion, see esp. Matera, *Kingship of Jesus.*

[35] This would be particularly acute if the community addressed by Mark's Gospel is located at Rome in the wake of the Neronic persecution. There is much to recommend this traditional setting for Mark's Gospel; on this point,

And surely this theme is not absent in John's Gospel, where the dialogue between Jesus and Pilate and the symbol of kingship dominate the passion story. Through his life-giving death, a death that exemplifies friendship love (15:13), Jesus demonstrates his conquest of the world's power. For John, as in the other Gospels, the immediate concern is theological, not political. Yet the proclamation of Jesus' authority in the very act of dying through crucifixion—even with Pilate presented as a sympathetic if weak player in the drama—unavoidably relativizes imperial power and implicitly critiques it.[36]

Each of the motifs we have considered illustrates that the evangelists and their communities saw deep and abiding connections between the death of Jesus and the meaning of Christian discipleship. What is also striking is that the passion accounts enable the community to reflect on the public character of Christian faith. This is immediately apparent in the motifs of witness under persecution and the critique of abusive power. But it is also implicit in the exhortation to vigilance and prayer; the threats of suffering and calamity that call forth vigilant prayer are experienced precisely as the community carries out its mission to the world.

As I have suggested above, the very nature of the passion story lends itself to reflection on the public character of discipleship. The passion of Jesus is a "public" event, culminating in official condemnation and crucifixion at a crossroads. Jesus does not suffer and die alone but surrounded by his opponents: the Sanhedrin, the palace guards, Pilate, the crowds, and the Roman soldiers. The fundamental passion story opens an opportunity for the evangelists to reflect on how discipleship must be lived not only in public but in a threatening environment. The terrible reality of Jesus' crucifixion brings into focus the raw power of death and evil, a power the community itself would have to face in history. There, in a world that would often be hostile and threatening, the disciples of Jesus would be called to a life of fidelity, indeed to a life of public and prophetic witness on behalf of the gospel. Only by vigilance and by earnest prayer for strength and deliverance could the community hope to remain faithful until the end.

One is reminded of Dietrich Bonhoeffer's meditation on the meaning of community:

> Jesus Christ lived in the midst of his enemies. At the end all his disciples deserted him. On the Cross he was utterly alone, surrounded by evildoers and mockers. For this cause he had come, to bring peace

see Senior, "With Swords and Clubs," 11–14; and Hengel, *Studies in the Gospel of Mark.*

[36]This feature of Johannine theology is relatively neglected; but see David Rensberger, *Johannine Faith and Liberating Community* (Philadelphia: Westminster, 1988); and Cassidy, *John's Gospel.*

to the enemies of God. So the Christian, too, belongs not in the seclusion of a cloistered life but in the thick of foes. There is his commission, his work.[37]

For some Christians who believe they can lead a life of discipleship without rancor such reflections may seem melodramatic. But for many contemporary Christians around the globe, the cost of discipleship proclaimed in the passion stories is a daily reality.

---

[37] Dietrich Bonhoeffer, *Life Together* (San Francisco: Harper & Row, 1954) 17.

✛ THIRTEEN

THE DEATH OF JESUS AND THE MEANING OF THE ATONEMENT

INTRODUCTION

At the beginning of his classic study, *The Death of Christ*, issued almost a century ago, James Denney justifies the publication of his treatise by noting that "the death of Christ has not the place assigned to it, either in preaching or theology, which it has in the New Testament."[1] Denney's own work significantly addressed this deficiency at the turn of the twentieth century, and it was joined by another important work at midcentury, Vincent Taylor's *Atonement in New Testament Teaching*.[2] In spite of these and more recent examinations,[3] Denney's allegation is perhaps no less true today than when he first wrote it—even if the reasons for this failing may have shifted with the passing decades.

Today NT teaching on the atonement is not so much neglected in some circles as purposely set aside. For an increasing number of persons and faith communities, atonement theology is irrelevant. What is more, a faith rooted in the divine drama of the crucifixion has been relegated for many to barbaric status. The reason is not, as Herman-Emiel Mertens has suggested, that traditional models of redemption—e.g., those of Luther and Anselm and Irenaeus—have become obsolete. For him, "the one who accepts these traditional models without reserve and

---

[1] Denney, *Death of Christ*, v.

[2] Taylor, *Atonement in New Testament Teaching*. Cf. also his *Jesus and His Sacrifice: A Study of the Passion Sayings in the Gospels* (London: Macmillan, 1937); and *Forgiveness and Reconciliation: A Study in New Testament Theology* (London: Macmillan, 1941).

[3] See the helpful introductory book by Paul S. Fiddes, *Past Event and Present Salvation: The Christian Idea of Atonement* (Louisville: Westminster/John Knox, 1989).

passes them on untranslated, does not at all serve the religious community well."[4] For others, criticism of atonement teaching is much more radical. Especially for many feminist theologians, but not only for them, the message of the cross does not simply stand in need of reinterpretation; the cross itself and the divine drama it represents—therein lies the problem. Unlike some liberation theologies, where those NT materials struggling to make sense of the death of Jesus are important precisely for the seriousness with which they grapple with suffering,[5] feminist theologies generally find atonement imagery offensive. Does not biblical imagery perpetuate patriarchal patterns of power and encourage victims of abuse to submit to unjust suffering? Can the NT understanding of the atonement have relevance at the turn of the twenty-first century?

In order to address more fully these concerns with the status of atonement theology in contemporary theology and proclamation, it will be helpful, first, briefly to rehearse what is often meant today by "atonement theology." This will provide some background for understanding the objections raised against this classical doctrine in its contemporary dress. A survey of these objections naturally leads to a reexamination of the NT materials both to inquire whether they have been appropriated faithfully in the current discussion and to ask in what interpretive direction they might point for constructive theological engagement today.

THE SALVIFIC DEATH OF JESUS: CLASSICAL THEORIES AND MODERN OBJECTIONS

According to the earliest tradition, Jesus' death was "for us."[6] That is, the followers of Jesus have never been content with the "brute" fact that Jesus died but have always been concerned with the interpretation of this fact. "Christianity proclaims not merely that Christ died, but that his death had significance for the otherwise apparently absurd course of human history."[7] The salvific significance of the death of Jesus is the subject of the atonement.

---

[4]Herman-Emiel Mertens, *Not the Cross, but the Crucified: An Essay in Soteriology* (LTPM 11; Louvain: Peeters; Grand Rapids: Eerdmans, 1992) 85.

[5]Cf., e.g., Leonardo Boff, who writes in the introduction to his study of Jesus' passion, "I hope that my experiment will be a help to those who, in their pain, seek to confer a meaning on the painful passion of the world" (*Passion of Christ*, xiii).

[6]Cf. Lohse, *Märtyrer und Gottesknecht*.

[7]Thomas C. Oden, *Systematic Theology*, vol. 2, *The Word of Life* (San Francisco: Harper & Row, 1989) 345.

Historical Views of the Atonement

Throughout the history of the Christian church, beginning with the apostolic era itself, theologians have formulated theories to explain how Jesus' death is effective for our salvation. What is the nexus between liberation and violent, unjust death?

> There are no pat answers. There are only theories which try to assimilate a wide array of biblical images, theories which try to explain a mystery, theories which fit some cultural milieus better than others, theories which all have their flaws and glitches.[8]

Numerous models have been proposed—e.g., incarnational, satisfaction, moral influence, dramatic, governmental, mimetic, ransom, penal substitution, and so on. Three of these have achieved ascendancy.[9]

The first is the soteriological model of *satisfaction*, formulated by Anselm of Canterbury (1033–1109). Arguing against an earlier "ransom theory"—i.e., that the death of Jesus was a ransom paid to the devil in order that sinful humanity might be released from the devil's grip—Anselm saw that the problem with redemption is not concerned fundamentally with any "devil's right" but with the wrong done to God. Called to faithfulness and service, humans have instead chosen sin. The justice of God, then, requires satisfaction, a settlement, before humanity can be forgiven. The dilemma is this: reparations must be made from the human side, since humans have sinned against God, but sin is so far-reaching, so heinous, that only God is capable of making amends. Why did God become human?[10] Anselm answers that without the incarnation, redemption is impossible, since only Christ, divine and human, could live the faithful life required of all humans and offer his life in death to satisfy the justice of God.

A second view, roughly contemporaneous with that of Anselm, was championed by the Parisian Peter Abelard (1079–1142). For him the notions of a ransom paid to the devil or reparations surrendered to God are unthinkable. Instead he characterizes the atonement as the ultimate revelation of the love of God, which in turn elicits a reciprocal response of love from humanity.

Third, drawing on the earlier views of Irenaeus and Luther, Gustaf Aulén sees the cross of Christ as a great struggle against, and victory over, the devil. Jesus' death is the decisive moment in a great cosmic

---

[8]Margo G. Houts, "Classical Atonement Imagery: Feminist and Evangelical Challenges," *Catalyst* 19, no. 3 (1993) 1, 5–6 (1).

[9]Cf. Gustaf Aulén, *Christus Victor: An Historical Study of the Three Main Types of the Idea of the Atonement* (London: S.P.C.K., 1950); also Mertens, *Not the Cross, but the Crucified*, 63–132.

[10]Anselm, *Cur Deus Homo*.

drama pitting good and evil against each other. At the cross of Christ, the devil experiences defeat and loses his power over sinful humanity. In this decisive moment, God is revealed as the chief actor in the salvation-historical story; indeed, God is both subject and object of this dramatic salvation-historical act. The consequence is reconciliation between God and the world.

Feminist Criticism of Popular Atonement Theology

Although the myriad theories of atonement postulated throughout the history of the church are often subsumed under these three headings, one has come to dominate the landscape of Christian faith in America, especially in its more popular expressions. This is the model of penal substitution, often attributed to Anselm or at least understood as having its derivation in his theory of satisfaction. According to this theory, humanity has, in its sin, turned away from God and so merits divine punishment. Jesus, in his death on the cross, died in place of (as a substitution for) sinful humanity at God's behest, and in doing so he took upon himself the punishment humanity ought to have suffered.

The most adamant objections to atonement theology, understood popularly as penal substitution, have come from feminist theologians. This is not to say that feminist theologians are the first to raise questions against this atonement imagery or that feminist theologians are univocal in their assessment of atonement theology. Nevertheless, feminist theologians have raised two broad concerns that help to focus our thinking here.[11]

First, for many feminist theologians, atonement imagery raises important questions about the nature of God. Second, and intimately related, the troublesome metaphors reflecting the character of God that are accorded privilege in atonement theology lead easily and naturally to the incarnation of these characteristics in human relationships—i.e., among those whose vocation is to reflect the divine image.

What, according to feminist theological analysis, does atonement theology teach about God's character? According to the predominant model, God is envisaged as the powerful patriarch in the greater household of the human family. This God demands absolute allegiance and punishes any act of disobedience. The cross of Christ, according to this model, becomes a manifestation of God's wrath and a paradigm of parental punishment: God is the patriarch who punishes his son in order to satisfy God's own parental honor and sense of justice. Atonement theology may urge images of the grace of God, but according to

---

[11] See Houts, "Classical Atonement Imagery."

Rita Nakashima Brock, it can do so only at the expense of "the abuse of the one perfect child."

> The experience of grace is lodged here, I believe, in a sense of relief at being relieved of punishment for one's inevitable failings and not in a clear sense of personal worth gained from an awareness of the unconditional nature of love. *The shadow of the punitive father must always lurk behind the atonement. He haunts images of forgiving grace.*[12]

Pushing further, Beverly W. Harrison and Carter Heyward have insisted, "As the classical portrait of the punitive character of this divine-human transaction, Anselm of Canterbury's doctrine of atonement . . . probably represents the sadomasochism of Christian teaching at its most transparent."[13] God plays the role of the sadist who willfully inflicts punishment, and Jesus embraces the character of the masochist who willingly suffers it.[14]

Where might this imagery lead? Feminist theologians have been quick to observe that atonement theology construed along these lines legitimates and perpetuates abuse in human relationships, not least in the home. What is more, locating Jesus, characterized as the willing victim of unjust suffering, at the heart of Christian faith is for some tantamount to idealizing the values of the victim and advising the abused to participate in their own victimization.[15]

Some Critical Responses

What are we to make of these criticisms? First, it must be acknowledged that legitimate concerns lie behind these objections. However we might want to urge (as we want to do momentarily) that atonement theology, either biblically or classically understood, is misappropriated and misrepresented when coerced into the popular mold of the model of penal substitution, the fact remains that study groups, songs, and other manifestations of popular church life in America often represent this model as nothing less than the historical teaching of the Christian

---

[12] Rita Nakashima Brock, "And a Little Child Will Lead Us: Christology and Child Abuse," in *Christianity, Patriarchy, and Abuse: A Feminist Critique*, ed. Joanne Carlson Brown and Carole R. Bohn (New York: Pilgrim, 1989) 42–61 (52–53); emphasis added.

[13] Beverly W. Harrison and Carter Heyward, "Pain and Pleasure: Avoiding the Confusions of Christian Tradition in Feminist Theory," in Brown and Bohn, *Christianity, Patriarchy, and Abuse*, 148–73 (153).

[14] See also Rita Nakashima Brock, *Journeys by Heart: A Christology of Erotic Power* (New York: Crossroad, 1988); Dorothee Sölle, *Thinking about God: An Introduction to Theology* (London: SCM; Philadelphia: Trinity, 1990).

[15] Cf. Joanne Carlson Brown and Rebecca Parker, "For God So Loved the World?" in Brown and Bohn, *Christianity, Patriarchy, and Abuse*, 1–30.

church. When criticisms of this view are raised, it must be admitted straightforwardly that on biblical and traditional grounds, this contemporary manifestation of atonement theology is both deficient and disturbing. That atonement theology might be placed in the service of abusive behavior, and indeed serve to provide the divine imprimatur for that behavior, is a scandal that calls for repentance and repudiation. (But is the culprit atonement theology per se?)

Second, though, it is important to remember that the classical view of the atonement put forward by Anselm is not the penal-substitutionary theory popularized in our day. As Richard Swinburne has observed: "Punishment is something imposed by the wronged party (in this case, God); atonement is offered voluntarily. Anselm writes of 'satisfaction, that is . . . voluntary payment of the debt' which overrides the need for 'punishment.' "[16] Indeed, what matters to Anselm is not God's embarrassment at having been wronged by humanity. The crucifixion of Jesus is not an attempt to appease a vindictive God; rather, the focus for Anselm falls on the consequences of sin for humanity and the cosmos.

On the other hand, it is equally critical to situate Anselm in his own social history. According to the patronal ethics of Anselm's feudal world, a lord and his vassals lived in peace at the intersection of reciprocal obligations. The lord provided capital and protection, the vassal loyalty and tribute. In this microworld, social order depended on honoring and serving the landowner. Within this cultural environment, God is presented by Anselm as a feudal lord, and this within a larger criminal-justice framework that may seem alien to us. The legal system in the United States is oriented around punishment of the guilty; in Anselm's day, however, the working of justice depended first on satisfaction, paying what was due.

This suggests already that any interpretation of the salvific significance of the cross takes shape within a certain culture. It also suggests how, even stripped of its caricature as a model of penal substitution, Anselm's view of the atonement is limited in its cultural specificity. Indeed, taken on its own terms (and not as filtered through subsequent reconceptualizations that accord greater privilege to notions of God's supposed vindictive nature), Anselm's theory leaves itself open immediately to attack from the perspective of those on whose backs the feudal system was made to work. Anselm's thought reflected a culture of patronage in a way that tended to provide a divine sanction for the feudal system; his understanding of Jesus' death might well have been developed along contrary lines so as to call that system into question.[17]

---

[16] Richard Swinburne, *Responsibility and Atonement* (Oxford: Clarendon, 1989) 155. See further Mertens, *Not the Cross, but the Crucified*, 71–74.

[17] See ch. 9 above.

Third, thoroughgoing criticism of atonement theology by some feminist theologians reflects our common problem of dependence on metaphorical language to communicate what is beyond language.[18] Especially from feminist quarters, we have been cautioned about the limits of our religious language. Hence, it is ironic that some of those same feminist theologians are themselves guilty of treating as literal the metaphorical language of atonement theology.[19] Alternatively, it might better be said that metaphorical language related to the atonement has been literalized in popular expressions of American Christianity, but in this case, instead of addressing the problem of metaphor in communicating the atonement, some feminists have demonized the doctrine of atonement itself. Perhaps people on all sides are implicated in a common refusal to recognize the limits of language or, more particularly, the reach of metaphor.[20]

Metaphors are two-edged: they reveal and conceal, highlight and hide. This means, first, that no one metaphor will capture the reality of the atonement. Metaphors from Israel's sacrificial system communicate something important about the death of Jesus, but they cannot contain the profundity of the cross of Christ.

The nature of metaphor suggests another interpretive imperative: Not all properties are necessarily embraced or legitimated in a given use of a metaphor.[21] Mark 10:45 ("For the Son of humanity [ὁ υἱὸς τοῦ ἀνθρώπου, ho huios tou anthrōpou] came not to be served but to serve and to give his life a ransom for many") employs the ransom metaphor, but this usage need not encourage speculation on the nature of this business transaction. Who pays the ransom? To whom is it paid? These questions are not addressed by the text, either by this verse or by the larger cotext in Mark's Gospel.

Umberto Eco provides an interesting example of this problem from a medieval encyclopedia, where everything that exists is nothing other than "an emanative outpouring" of God. In this shared understanding

---

[18]Cf. Colin E. Gunton, *The Actuality of the Atonement: A Study of Metaphor, Rationality, and the Christian Tradition* (Edinburgh: T. & T. Clark; Grand Rapids: Eerdmans, 1989) esp. ch. 2.

[19]Of course, in some cases the problem to which feminist and other critics address themselves is that the metaphors chosen are already implicated in problematic understandings of the world. In at least some cases, however, the prior question may revolve around our need to respect the limits of metaphorical language. As we will argue below, we need new metaphors for communicating the mystery of the atonement in our world, but even these new metaphors will conceal as they reveal.

[20]Cf. George Lakoff and Mark Johnson, *Metaphors We Live By* (Chicago/London: University of Chicago, 1980).

[21]Cf. Umberto Eco, *Semiotics and the Philosophy of Language* (AS; Bloomington: Indiana University, 1984) ch. 3.

of the world, "every being functions as a synecdoche or metonymy of the One." The code, however, is ambiguous. Is the lion a figure of Christ? Or of antichrist? On the one hand, "the lion erases his tracks with his tail . . . and is thus a figure of Christ canceling the traces of sin." On the other, according to a medieval exegesis of Ps 21, the "terrible maw of the beast . . . becomes a metaphor of Hell" and thus of the antichrist. How might one disambiguate any particular usage of the lion metaphor? "In order to decide whether the lion must be seen as a *figura Christi* or as a figure of the Antichrist, a *co-text* is necessary."[22] That is, one must refer to the sentences and larger textual units surrounding the metaphorical reference and relating to it so as to constrain its interpretation.

Of course, Eco's example raises another issue. Apart from avid readers of the Book of Revelation or of C. S. Lewis's *Chronicles of Narnia*, not many of our contemporaries would struggle with the aforementioned ambiguity at all. We do not as a matter of course employ the lion metaphor in order to refer to Christ. Hence, the success of a metaphor is a function not only of interpretive attention being paid to cotext but also of shared sociohistorical presuppositions. Anselm's model of the atonement arose out of and reflects a particular sociohistorical moment relatively foreign to us. One important way of analyzing his model would therefore be to inquire into its ability to communicate within and/or against the world in which Anselm worked.

Anselm, of course, never argued that his model was rooted in Scripture, and herein lies a fourth difficulty with modern criticism of atonement theology. Atonement theology has often been equated with the theory of penal substitution, the theory of penal substitution has often been attributed to Anselm, and Anselm's thought has often been assumed to derive from the Apostle Paul. We have seen that this is a troublesome caricature of Anselm and that in this whole discussion, metaphorical language has been pressed into service in ways it is not capable of handling. To these responses we may add a further one— namely, the significant degree to which criticisms of this sort fail to take the biblical witness on its own terms. In fact, Paul uses an almost inexhaustible series of metaphors to represent the significance of Jesus' death, and penal substitution (at least as popularly defined) is not one of them.[23] We can go further, highlighting key points developed more fully in ch. 6 above.

---

[22] Eco, *Semiotics and the Philosophy of Language*, 103–4.

[23] Fiddes notes that Paul has a "penal view" of Christ's suffering and that he conceives of Christ as a substitute and representative of humankind, but he denies that these two concepts can be joined in Paul into a theory of "penal substitution," in which atonement is achieved via a transfer of penalty (*Past Event and Present Salvation*, 98).

(1) It is not only that Paul commissions a wide array of metaphors for communicating the significance of Jesus' death to his diverse audiences.

(2) It is also that Paul never operates with the picture of God or the God-Jesus relationship attributed to Paul by recent critics. For Paul, notions of punishment and retribution are peripheral at best. As Stephen Travis has argued, "He understands both salvation and condemnation primarily in relational terms: people's destinies will be a confirmation and intensification of the relationship with God or alienation from him which has been their experience in this life."[24] The "wrath of God" is, for Paul, not an affective response on the part of God, not the striking out of a vengeful God. As we have indicated, Paul's concern is not with retributive punishment.

(3) Moreover, Paul's conception of sin is not one that accords particular emphasis to individual sinful acts, each of which, it might be thought, attracts divine punishment. Sin, rather, is a general disposition of hostility toward God and God's purpose, a refusal to honor God as God. Sin is a relational problem. Hence, although Paul's notion of atonement takes sin with utmost seriousness, it is concerned above all with the restoration of the divine-human relationship, not with the mollification of a God angered by masses of misdeeds.

(4) Nor does Paul treat God as the subject and Jesus as the object of the cross. S. W. Sykes has suggested that the NT juxtaposes two principal narrative sequences in its representation of Jesus' death as a sacrifice. Each of these story lines has its own primary actors—for the one, God; for the other, Jesus. Although these two are not independent of each other, inasmuch as they both focus on the cross of Christ, neither is the one assimilated into the other.

> The one story has to do with God's appointment of Jesus as his "means of dealing with sin." The other story has to do with Jesus' own voluntary self-offering. Told as a single trinitarian drama, this becomes all too easily a monstrous saga in which the Father plans the immolation of his own Son in appeasement of his wrathful rejection of the human race. *But it is highly significant that at no stage is this inference explicitly drawn in the New Testament, where the two narrative sequences tend to occur in somewhat different contexts.*[25]

Jesus, then, is not a victim only but is himself the priest.

---

[24]Travis, "Christ as Bearer of Divine Judgment," 332; cf., idem, *Christ and the Judgment of God* (Basingstoke: Marshall, Morgan & Scott, 1986); and idem, "Wrath of God (NT)," *ABD*, 6.996–98. Contra (among recent interpreters), Morris, *The Cross in the New Testament*, 382–88.

[25]S. W. Sykes, "Outline of a Theology of Sacrifice," in *Sacrifice and Redemption*, 282–98 (294–95); emphasis added. See also his earlier essay, "Sacrifice in the New Testament and Christian Theology," in *Sacrifice*, ed. M. F. C. Bourdillon and Meyer Fortes (London: Academic, 1980) 61–83.

(5) What is more, Jesus' self-offering was not the courageous exploit of one who sought his own death, in the same way that the suffering experienced by Paul was not suffering for its own sake. As we have indicated above,[26] Jesus and Paul were not committed to agony and pain and did not idolize unjust suffering. In Jesus' commitment to the divine redemptive purpose, in his solidarity with God's project and with those suffering in a world hostile to God's purpose, Jesus encountered pain in the form of a Roman cross.

Taken on its own terms, then, Paul's theology of the atonement, and that of the NT as a whole, is not as susceptible to the charge of glorifying abuse as some have thought. Having raised the issue of faithful engagement with the biblical materials, we are now in a position to turn our attention more directly to the atonement in NT teaching.

THE ATONEMENT IN THE NEW TESTAMENT

Within the pages of the NT, the salvific effect of the death of Jesus is represented chiefly (though not exclusively) via five constellations of images. These are borrowed from significant spheres of public life in ancient Palestine and the larger Greco-Roman world: the court of law (e.g., justification), commercial dealings (e.g., redemption), personal relationships (whether among individuals or groups—e.g., reconciliation), worship (e.g., sacrifice), and the battleground (e.g., triumph over evil). Each of these examples provides a window into a cluster of terms and concepts that relate to that particular sphere of public life.

For example, without using the actual term "sacrifice" (which, in any case, might be used to refer to a variety of cult-related practices, each with its own aim), Paul and John can refer to Jesus as the "Passover Lamb" (1 Cor 5:7) and "the Lamb of God who takes away the sin of the world" (John 1:29; cf. John 1:36; Rev 5:6); Peter can relate how Jesus "bore our sins in his body on the tree" (1 Pet 2:24; cf. 1:19); Jesus' death can be characterized by NT writers as "first fruits" (1 Cor 15:20, 23; cf. Lev 23; Deut 16) and the "blood of the covenant" (Mark 14:23; cf. Exod 24:8); and the handing over of Jesus can recall the binding of Isaac (Rom 8:32; cf. Gen 22). The writer of Hebrews qualifies the salvific significance of Jesus' death specifically in terms borrowed from Israel's sacrificial cult (cf., e.g., 9:11–14). Similarly, "reconciliation" can be represented by the καταλλασσ- (*katallass-*, "reconciliation," "to reconcile") word group (Rom 5:10, 11; 11:15; 1 Cor 7:11; 2 Cor 5:18, 19, 20; Eph 2:16; Col 1:20, 22; cf. also Matt 5:24: διαλλάσσομαι, *diallassomai*, "to reconcile oneself") but also by the terminology of peace (Eph 2:14–18) and the

---

[26]See chs. 6 and 9 above.

multitudinous acts (e.g., Rom 16:16), pleas (e.g., Philemon), and testimonies (e.g., Acts 15:8–9; Gal 3:26–29) of reconciliation that dot the landscape of the NT.

Why are so many images enlisted in the atonement theology of the NT? Our earlier reflections point immediately to one reason for this plurality. Language for the atonement is metaphorical (cf., though, the concreteness of the concept of reconciliation as a description of the new relationship between God and humanity that follows from the cross of Christ);[27] given the nature of metaphor, it is unthinkable that one soteriological model could express all of the truth. Hence, even if Christians have always spoken with one voice in their affirmation of Jesus as our Savior, already in the NT, and certainly since, this affirmation has been understood in a variety of ways.[28]

A second reason for this plurality is pastoral. The language in which one construes the efficacy of Jesus' death is dependent in part on the needs one hopes to address. "Very different models and categories are used to describe the 'lost' condition of the human race prior to Christ. . . . Different descriptions of the human situation inevitably lead to different explanations of how this has been altered by the work of Christ."[29] If people are lost, they need to be found. If they are oppressed by hostile powers, they need to be delivered. If they exist in a state of enmity, they need to be reconciled. And so on.

More particularly, images of atonement are often used in the NT because of the specific needs of a local congregation.[30] The image of reconciliation, for example, which comes very much to the fore in 2 Cor 5:14–6:13, helps Paul to lay bare the nexus between the Corinthians' relationship toward him and their status before God. In this context, reconciliation with God would work itself out also as reconciliation with Paul. This lies behind Paul's dual request: "Be reconciled to God!" and "Open wide your hearts [to us]!"

Third, because of wider cultural considerations, a plurality of metaphors is used to draw out the salvific significance of Jesus' death. If the message of salvation is universal—and this is one of the constants in NT atonement theology—and if that message is to be grasped in ever-expanding cultural circles, then the message must be articulated in culture-specific ways. As Mertens observes: "Images of Christ and conceptions of salvation bear the mark of the prevailing cultural consciousness and are only temporarily relevant. They do not remain

---

[27]I. Howard Marshall, "The Meaning of 'Reconciliation,' " in *Jesus the Saviour: Studies in New Testament Theology* (London: S.P.C.K.; Downers Grove, Ill.: InterVarsity, 1990) 258–74.

[28]Mertens, *Not the Cross, but the Crucified*, 95.

[29]Christopher M. Tuckett, "Atonement in the NT," *ABD* 1.518–22 (518).

[30]Cf. Driver, *Understanding the Atonement*; Boff, *Passion of Christ*, 78–84.

always and everywhere equally useful. Some 'age' quicker than others."[31] For the atonement, images in the NT are drawn from a range of possibilities in the wider public discourse. Even if they are, to varying degrees, transformed by their association with the crucifixion of Jesus of Nazareth, they nevertheless take their interpretive point of departure from prominent, shared, social intercourse.

To root ourselves more fully in the atonement theology of the NT, we will examine selected images employed by various NT writers. Following this, we will turn to some implications of this discussion for atonement thought today.

Redemption

Louw and Nida identify the key terms for "redemption"[32]—λυτρόομαι (*lytroomai*, "to release or set free"), λύτρωσις (*lytrōsis*, "redemption"), ἀπολύτρωσις (*apolytrōsis*, "redemption"), λυτρωτής (*lytrōtēs*, "redeemer"), λύτρον (*lytron*, "means of release," "ransom"), and ἀντίλυτρον (*antilytron*, "ransom")—in the semantic subdomain of "Release, Set Free," together with a number of other terms in the NT that sometimes refer to salvation: λύω, ἀπολύω, ἀπαλλάσσω (*lyō, apolyō, apallassō*, "to release, to set free"); ἀγοράζω, ἐξαγοράζω (*agorazō, exagorazō*, "to purchase, to redeem"); ἄφεσις (*aphesis*, "the process of setting free or liberating"); ἐλευθερία, ἐλεύθερος, ἐλευθερόω (*eleutheria, eleutheros, eleutheroō*, "to be free," "to set free").[33] We list these terms to illustrate again the linguistic variety available to early Christians as they sought to articulate the significance of Jesus' death—in this case even within the general framework of "redemption."

Luke–Acts collects a number of these terms (cf. Luke 1:68, 77; 2:38 [cf. 2:25]; 21:28; 24:21; Acts 7:35) to link the concept of redemption with the prototypical act of deliverance in the OT: the liberation of God's people from Egypt. This is accomplished in a way that underscores the agency of Jesus (like Moses) as deliverer and that identifies God's action in Jesus as deliverance from sociopolitical oppression and as the forgiveness of sins. But rather than draw a bridge from Jesus' death to this full-bodied notion of redemption, characters within Luke's story understand the crucifixion as a denial of their hope that Jesus would be the one to redeem Israel (Luke

---

[31] Mertens, *Not the Cross, but the Crucified*, 63–64.

[32] See I. Howard Marshall, "The Development of the Concept of Redemption in the New Testament," in *Jesus the Saviour*, 239–57.

[33] Johannes P. Louw and Eugene A. Nida, eds., *Greek-English Lexicon of the New Testament Based on Semantic Domains* (2 vols.; New York: United Bible Societies, 1988) 1.§§37,127–38. They also mention δικαιόω (*dikaioō*, usually "to justify" but in Rom 6:7 "to release [from the power of sin]").

24:19–21). Even though the narrator labels this view a profound misunderstanding, he goes on to show only that the cross was not a contradiction of such longings, not that the cross was directly instrumental in instigating God's redemption.[34] For Luke the totality of Jesus' ministry—his coming, his public mission, his death, his exaltation, and his present activity via the Spirit—plays this role.

More to the point for discerning the role of the concept of redemption in the larger drama of the atonement in the NT are data from other NT writers. The authenticity of the "ransom-saying" ("For the Son of humanity came not to be served but to serve and to give his life a ransom [λύτρον, lytron] for many"—Matt 20:28; Mark 10:45; cf. 1 Tim 2:6; Tit 2:14) has been the focus of ongoing debate.[35] Nonetheless, in the first two Gospels, this logion plays a central role, since it identifies the cardinal purpose of Jesus' mission as service toward others, then identifies the death of Jesus as the ultimate expression of a life lived on behalf of others. The author of 1 Timothy makes a similar point, identifying Jesus' death as the means of deliverance and clarifying, with the use of "all," that in his death Jesus was the mediator between God and the whole of humanity.

Paul uses the language of redemption (ἀπολύτρωσις, apolytrōsis) in Rom 3:21–26 (esp. vv. 24–25), where the primary emphasis is on God's own integrity but where God's integrity is certified by the assertion that redemption is in Christ, through his death now understood as an atoning act. In Rom 8:23 the term is used in a different, eschatological sense for the divine consummation of God's deliverance on a cosmological scale. According to Col 1:13–14, redemption is set in interpretive apposition to the forgiveness of sins but is also developed in the context of talk about competing kingdoms. Redemption entails freedom from the "power of darkness" for new life and loyalty to God's Son. In other cases, Paul employs the language of purchase leading to the release of slaves to represent the salvific effect of the cross. "You have been bought with a price," he writes to the Corinthians, reminding them that through Christ's death they have been set free from bondage to sin but now belong to the Lord (1 Cor 6:20; 7:23). In this context Paul insists that Christians have been freed through the cross for service to Christ.

---

[34]Cf., however, Acts 20:28; Green, "Death of Jesus, God's Servant," 3–7.

[35]Mertens speaks for many when he asserts, "Jesus can not possibly have said this" (Not the Cross, but the Crucified, 50); such an assertion, however, does not take with adequate seriousness such arguments as those posed by, e.g., Stuhlmacher, "Vicariously Giving His Life for Many, Mark 10:45 (Matt. 20:28)," in Reconciliation, Law, and Righteousness, 16–29; Sydney H. T. Page, "The Authenticity of the Ransom Logion (Mark 10:45b)," in Studies of History and Tradition in the Four Gospels, ed. R. T. France and David Wenham (GP 1; Sheffield: JSOT, 1980) 137–61; Robert H. Gundry, Mark: A Commentary on His Apology for the Cross (Grand Rapids: Eerdmans, 1993) 587–93.

Elsewhere he writes, "Christ has redeemed you from the curse of the law" (Gal 3:13). Among the Galatians, then, Paul portrays the law as a powerful force holding the Jewish people captive; in his death, the apostle argues, Christ has set them free by putting into effect the universal blessing of the divine covenant (to both Jew *and* Gentile). The law has not been destroyed, as though the freedom won in Christ might lead to gratification of "fleshly desires": "Do not use your freedom as an opportunity for self-indulgence, but through love become slaves to one another" (Gal 5:15). (For "redemption" in the wider Pauline circle, see also Eph 1:7–8, 14; 4:30.)

Likewise, the Book of Revelation communicates the idea of the "purchase" of believers through the death of Jesus (e.g., 5:9); ransomed, they are made into a new people serving God. Given the content of Revelation as a whole, redemption must be understood as deliverance from evil powers, together with unyielding allegiance to the Lamb. First Peter 1:18–19 affirms that believers were "ransomed" from the futile ways of their ancestors "with the precious blood of Christ" (cf. Eph 1:7; 2 Pet 2:1). In these and related passages, NT writers are drawing on a wealth of what would have been shared experience in the larger Greco-Roman world. Those familiar with the history of Israel, of course, would have heard reverberations of the story of the exodus in the background of such references (e.g., Exod 6:6; cf. Isa 51:11). Others, however, might have been led to conjure up images of the "redemption" of slaves or of prisoners of war.

This raises a question: If Jesus' death "purchased" believers, to whom was the purchase price paid? The devil? The demonic world? It is here, at this juncture, that we encounter the limits of the metaphor of redemption. Israel might think of God's redeeming them from Egypt without assuming thereby that God actually paid Pharaoh a price for his former slaves. In the same way, a number of NT texts present Jesus' death as a ransom without identifying or even conveying the notion of a recipient of that "price." Underscored instead are the result of being purchased—namely, service to Christ—and the high cost of the deliverance that Christ's death wins.

Sacrifice

As Howard Marshall has indicated, from the concept of redemption it is not far to a further constellation of images, that related to sacrifice. The reason is that in developing the concept of redemption, NT writers were already drawing on the world of the sacrificial cult; for many of the pertinent texts, "redemption is accomplished by the offering of a sacrifice."[36]

---

[36]Marshall, "Concept of Redemption," 243.

The importance of this category for explicating the death of Jesus in the NT is intimated simply by its prevalence and the variety of ways it appears. The formulaic expression "Christ died for all," with its many variants (cf., e.g., Mark 10:45; 14:24; Rom 5:6, 8; 1 Cor 8:11; 15:3; Gal 2:21; 1 Thess 5:10; 1 Pet 3:18), points to an understanding of Jesus' death as sacrificial in some sense, just as do references to the salvific implications of his blood (e.g., Acts 20:28; Rom 5:9; Col 1:20). Jesus' death is interpreted as a covenant sacrifice (e.g., Mark 14:24; 1 Cor 11:25; Heb 7:22; 8:6; 9:15), a Passover sacrifice (e.g., John 19:14; 1 Cor 5:7–8), the sin offering (Rom 8:3; 2 Cor 5:21), the offering of first fruits (1 Cor 15:20, 23), the sacrifice offered on the Day of Atonement (Hebrews 9–10), and an offering like that of Isaac by Abraham (e.g., Rom 8:32).[37] As the writer of Ephesians affirms, "Christ loved us and gave himself up for us as a fragrant offering and sacrifice to God" (5:2).

Of course, "sacrifice" has no monolithic meaning in ancient Israel. One must not only think of the various types of regular and special sacrifices (e.g., the burnt offering, the cereal offering, the guilt offering, the Passover sacrifice). One must also keep in mind the development of the "sacrifice of obedience"—i.e., the preference in some prophetic literature for obedience over sacrifice (e.g., Isa 1:10–17; Amos 5:21–25; Mic 6:6–8). The latter development is explicitly highlighted by the author of Hebrews (10:5–10), though not to the exclusion of the use of sacrificial imagery in a more material way, and is not far from the background of an overall NT witness to the faithfulness/obedience of Jesus Christ.[38] Complicating this picture further, sacrifice was a category known to people in the larger Greco-Roman world quite apart from the sacrificial cult of Israel.[39] Indeed, the idea of *human* sacrifice, the more specific way in which Jesus' death is understood in various NT writings, is known best outside narrowly defined Jewish circles. This does not mean that one must step outside the trajectories of Israel's religion to come to terms with Jesus' death as a sacrifice. After all,

---

[37] Jon D. Levenson proposes further that Jesus' crucifixion would have been understood within the framework of the longstanding idea in Israel of sacrificing the firstborn son; this thesis is worth exploring, irrespective of how his theory on the actual practice of child sacrifice in ancient Israel is evaluated (*The Death and Resurrection of the Beloved Son: The Transformation of Child Sacrifice in Judaism and Christianity* [New Haven/London: Yale University, 1993]).

[38] On which see Richard N. Longenecker, "The Foundational Conviction of New Testament Christology: The Obedience/Faithfulness/Sonship of Christ," in Green and Turner, *Jesus of Nazareth*, 473–88.

[39] See Hengel, *Atonement*, 1–32; Sam K. Williams, *Jesus' Death as Saving Event: The Background and Origin of a Concept* (HDR 2; Missoula, Mont.: Scholars, 1975). David Seeley, in fact, turns away from the temple cultus and other more non-Greek Jewish categories to Greco-Roman martyrology (and more specifically to the category of the "noble death") to make sense of Paul's soteriology (*Noble Death*).

within Hellenistic Judaism one finds precursors to the sacrificial interpretation of Jesus' death, above all in the effective deaths of martyrs as
narrated in 1 Macc 2:7–38; 2 Macc 6:18–7:42; 4 Macc 6:24–30. In these
texts the execution of the faithful is given special meaning in God's
purpose—e.g., as a means of resisting evil or of bringing forward God's
vindication of his people, and even as an act atoning for one's own sins
or sins of the nation.

Moreover, the interpretations of the deaths of the martyrs as atoning
in 2 and 4 Maccabees themselves build on OT images of sacrifice and
the Isaianic portrayal of the Servant of Yahweh, whose suffering would
be for the benefit of God's people. This connection is usually not taken
with sufficient gravity by those who attempt to locate the immediate
background to Paul's atonement theology in 4 Maccabees.[40] Would not
Jesus and his followers be capable of participating in a similar, parallel
creative appropriation of those sacrificial metaphors and Servant
passages?

In what way(s) is Jesus' death presented as a sacrifice in the NT? We
have already collected a number of pertinent references, but it will be
helpful to examine in brief detail the sacrificial imagery of a few NT
writers. In Rom 3:25, Paul can hardly have anything in mind other than
Jesus' death as a sacrifice, referring as he does to the lid of the ark, the
ἱλαστήριον, *hilastērion*, "the place at which atonement was made for
the entire community of Israel on the great Day of Atonement in
accordance with God's ordinance."[41] In its cotext in Romans, Paul's
usage of this term probably refers not so much to the "place" of
atonement as to its "means."[42] Here, as in Rom 8:3 and 2 Cor 5:21,
where Jesus' death is likened to the sin offering, Paul underscores the
magnitude of sin's reach and power. God's condemnation of sin is
effected via the death of Jesus, and the death of Jesus marks the end of
sin's power.

The Fourth Gospel identifies Jesus' death as sacrificial in three
related passages. First, in greeting Jesus, John the Baptist identifies him
as "the Lamb of God who takes away the sin of the whole world" (John
1:29, 36). A clue to the appropriate interpretation of this identification
appears much later, in John 19:14 (cf. 18:28; 19:31), where the fourth
evangelist emphasizes that Jesus' execution took place at the time of the
slaughter of the Passover sacrifice. Hence, even though other interpretations might be suggested by the currency of the phrase "lamb of God"
in contemporary literature (e.g., the lamb sacrificed in the burnt offering, the messianic lamb/ram of apocalyptic literature, the lamb/Servant

---

[40] E.g., Williams, *Jesus' Death as Saving Event*; Seeley, *Noble Death*.

[41] Jürgen Roloff, "ἱλαστήριον," *EDNT*, 2.185–86.

[42] See the discussion in James D. G. Dunn, *Romans* (2 vols.; WBC 38a–38b;
Dallas, Tex.: Word, 1988) 1.170–72.

of Yahweh silent before the shearers), this interpretation can hardly be ruled out.[43]

In ch. 5 of the Book of Revelation, John records a crisis caused by the quandary about who might be able to open the scroll containing the hidden purpose of God. The initial identification of the one determined to be worthy to open the scroll, "the Lion of the Tribe of Judah" and "the Root of David," suggests powerful images of the Davidic Messiah, the conquering one. This is all immediately and radically reinterpreted, however, as this messianic figure is further identified as the Lamb whose sacrificial death has redeemed people from all nations (5:5–10). The victory of the Messiah—and, indeed, of the people of God—is won through a sacrificial death. Following this, the Lamb serves as a chief christological image for the book as a whole; from this text onward, however, we understand that the defeat, portrayed throughout Revelation, of all that opposes the rule of God has been accomplished by his sacrificial death.[44]

Finally, it is imperative to recognize that the sacrificial interpretation of Jesus' death pervades the letter to the Hebrews. The author of Hebrews observes that "without the shedding of blood there can be no forgiveness of sins" (9:22) and builds a case that in his role as both priest and sacrificial victim, Jesus has "appeared once for all at the end of the age to remove sin by his own sacrifice" (9:26). This author, however, has not set for himself the task of defending or explicating the sacrificial system of Israel. Quite the contrary, he uses Israel's categories to show how Israel's past has been superseded by the work of Christ. Jesus' death has instituted a new covenant—one in continuity with, but superior to, the former covenant.

Revelation

The concept of atonement is not often developed in terms of the revelatory character of Jesus' death, but in significant strands of NT thought the cross has this function. The human predicament is imagined in terms of "blindness" or "lack of perception." It is striking, e.g., that human beings in the Gospel of Mark struggle, from the beginning of the narrative, with the question of Jesus' identity; finally, having seen the manner of Jesus' death, the centurion recognizes what the narrator and God have been saying all along—that Jesus is the Son of God (Mark 1:1, 9–11; 9:2–8; 15:39). Not only in his powerful and authoritative

---

[43]Cf. the helpful discussion in Schnackenburg, *John*, 1.297–301; I. Howard Marshall, "Lamb of God," *DJG*, 432–34.

[44]Cf. Richard Bauckham, *The Theology of the Book of Revelation* (NTT; Cambridge: Cambridge University, 1993) 73–76.

teaching but also in light of his death must Jesus and his mission be understood.[45]

The third evangelist has his own way of presenting the revelatory character of Jesus' mission. By bringing repeatedly into the foreground the question of the quality of life within the community of believers, Luke draws particular attention to Jesus' life of service toward others. In affirmations of Jesus' present orientation toward service (22:24–27) and his future, eschatological diaconal comportment (12:35–38), we gain a glimpse of the character of God—known not for "lording it over" others or otherwise taking advantage of humans through abusive expressions of power but for mercy and grace. As we have intimated, though, this emphasis on revelation is not focused, for Luke, narrowly on the death of Jesus but is manifest in the character of his whole life and ongoing mission.

The Fourth Gospel, on the other hand, points in a more emphatic way to the revelatory character of the cross. John's overarching concern with the theme of revelation is transparent in his ample use of the language of ignorance and knowing, blindness and seeing, and so on. Of Jesus John writes, "The true light, which enlightens everyone, was coming into the world" (1:9). The drama of the Fourth Gospel develops more pointedly around the theme of the coming of the "hour," however, and this is the "hour" of Jesus' being "lifted up," his glorification, his return to the Father. And these images reach their acme for John in the crucifixion of God's Son. What about God is revealed in the cross? In a passage with interesting parallels to the hymn to Christ in Phil 2:6–11, John interprets the purpose of the incarnation in terms of Jesus' self-giving (13:1–17). This self-giving is expressed both in the disgraceful act of a Teacher and Lord washing the feet of his followers and in his life-giving death. If, then, the cross is the moment in which the full glory of God is revealed (17:1), this glory is framed in the majesty of other-centered love.

Reconciliation

Our final example may seem best suited to our present age, given our heightened concerns with social psychology and experience of community, on the one hand, and our increased awareness of our connectedness to the whole cosmos, on the other. Reconciliation as a term is not prominent in the NT, but as a conceptual umbrella it has wide currency among the NT writings. As an image, reconciliation assumes a state of hostility, and in the NT this hostility is understood to be present in a variety of relationships—i.e., between God and humanity;

---

[45] See ch. 2 above.

between humanity and the rest of creation, including the earth but also supernatural powers and principalities; and between humans (master and slave, male and female, Jew and Gentile, the sick and the well, Paul and his churches, rich and poor, and so on). The work of Jesus is effective in bringing peace in all of these arenas.

In Paul and the wider Pauline circle, the language of reconciliation proves to be remarkably elastic.[46] In Paul's hands, reconciliation underscores the primacy of God's initiative in providing for salvation and promoting human recovery. Centered on the crucifixion of Jesus in human history, the act of reconciliation nevertheless has eschatological and cosmic ramifications. Just as cosmic forces were created through the agency of Christ, so in his death are they reconciled to God, restored to their authentic vocation in God's divine purpose. Reconciliation is a past event, since it is rooted in the cross, but the work of reconciliation continues until the eschaton; Paul urges the family of God, then, to ongoing reconciliation both with God and with others. Paul himself writes his job description in such terms: his is a "ministry of reconciliation" (2 Cor 5:18). The apostle lays the conceptual groundwork, but the writer of Ephesians makes explicit the connection between the vocabulary of reconciliation and the destruction of the barriers that separate Jewish from Gentile people. Salvation as portrayed in the Pauline concept of reconciliation, then, has personal and social, human and cosmic, spiritual and material, religious and ethnic meaning.

As we have outlined, many other images for explicating the significance of Jesus' death are noted in the NT and might have been explored here. Enough of these have been probed to indicate our great loss when the atonement theology of the NT writings is collapsed into one model or metaphor. And enough has been said to lay the groundwork for our final remarks on the constructive theological task.

THE NEW TESTAMENT AND ATONEMENT THEOLOGY TODAY: COMPASS POINTS

In this concluding section we do not need to present an apologia for discerning models—some new, others old—to communicate the salvific death of Jesus. The preceding discussion has indicated already the degree to which a plurality of metaphors has been used in Christian communities since the beginning of the Christian movement. Our dilemma lies

---

[46]Cf. Rom 5:10, 11; 11:15; 1 Cor 7:11; 2 Cor 5:18, 19, 20; Eph 2:16; Col 1:20, 22; Ralph P. Martin, *Reconciliation: A Study of Paul's Theology* (rev. ed.; Grand Rapids: Zondervan, 1990); Victor Paul Furnish, "The Ministry of Reconciliation," *CurTM* 14 (1977) 204–18; Marshall, "Meaning of 'Reconciliation.' "

elsewhere. First, today we must grapple with appropriating language suitable to communicating the profundity of Jesus' salvific work to people outside the Christian faith as well as those inside the church. Second, we must do so in a way that does justice to the biblical presentation of the work of Jesus. This means, first and foremost, that the cross can never be neglected or marginalized in Christian proclamation, given the centrality of the cross to the writings of the NT. If, according to the Gospel of Mark, Jesus cannot be understood as Son of God apart from the cross; if, according to Paul, the messiahship of Jesus is radically nuanced by the modifier "crucified"; if, according to the Book of Revelation, the Lion of Judah not only appears but triumphs over evil in all of its guises as the slain Lamb, then we today can scarcely attempt to think and act Christianly in a way that is not informed by the cross. In fact, it is precisely the theology of the cross—that mystery of God at work against all human expectations, the foolishness that reveals the wisdom of God—that works continuously to unseat our own pretensions and efforts to accord privilege to our own agenda and ethnocentrisms over against the way of God's mercy.

Reminding ourselves of the centrality of the cross for Christian faith and life does not mean that we should glorify suffering or justify abuse and victimization, however. For this reason, it may be helpful to modify our terminology, as Mertens has suggested:

> "Not the cross, but the Crucified" is our hope. This distinction is extremely important. We must not hope to find our own calvary, nor long for another Golgotha. . . . Well-understood, "cross-faith" does not at all affect the lust for life. But it surely illuminates the evangelical paradox that "whoever loses his [sic] life . . . will save it" (Mark 8:35).[47]

Beyond this, how might we engage in a reflective, critical appropriation of NT atonement theology?[48] First, this means respecting the integrity of the various NT writings, accepting their invitations to enter into their worlds and to adopt a perspective from within these writings. We appreciate how the writers sought to communicate in language appropriate to their life situations, while at the same time we leave ourselves open to being challenged by their visions of reality and the purpose of God. This requires that we decenter our own self-interests so as to be addressed by the text as "other," to allow it to engage us in creative discourse, and to take the risk of being shaped, indeed transformed, in the encounter.[49]

---

[47] Mertens, *Not the Cross, but the Crucified*, 171.

[48] On what follows, see the critical observations in Green, *Theology of Luke*, ch. 6.

[49] Cf. Anthony C. Thiselton, *New Horizons in Hermeneutics: The Theory and Practice of Transforming Biblical Reading* (London: Collins; Grand Rapids: Zondervan, 1992) 16–29.

On the other hand, this does not mean that we lose ourselves in the various NT documents. These are first-century documents from the Mediterranean world; we are twentieth-century people, many of us from quite different worlds. Understanding how the message of these ancient writers articulates with and challenges their world may shed light on our own experience of the world and of God. Still, we come to these texts as late-twentieth-century people with our own needs and questions, not assuming that their questions are ours but inquiring into the strategies, sources of authority, and contours of those presentations that might inform our own communities of faithful discourse.

We engage in a reflective appropriation of the NT message of atonement not simply (and sometimes not at all) by reading its content directly into our world but also (and sometimes only) by inquiring into how those writers have engaged in the task of theology and ethics. This is true because Paul, Luke, John, and the others were concerned to shape a community that served God's aims more than they were interested in outlining the precise beliefs and habits of that community.

In *Communities of Discourse*, Robert Wuthnow has drawn attention to a helpful approach to questions of this sort. Although he is concerned with the Protestant Reformation, the Enlightenment, and the rise of European socialism, his methodological considerations are equally apropos to a reading of atonement theology in the NT.[50] He characterizes his investigation as a study of the problem of articulation—i.e., how ideas can both be shaped by their social situations and yet manage to disengage from and often challenge those very situations. In the case of atonement theology, we might ask, how can a given NT writer be situated in and reflect a particular sociohistorical environment and at the same time work to shape and perhaps undermine that environment? What strategies does he adopt? How has he engaged in theological and ethical reflection? How has he invited his audience into the reflective and constructive task of discourse on the meaning of Jesus' death and its implications for discipleship?

To think along these lines is immediately to realize, first, that the models championed in the NT for expounding the meaning of Jesus' suffering may not all be suited to our day. We realize, second, that we must inquire into how those models were used in, say, Paul's world and in his discourse, in order to perceive how Paul has adopted *and adapted* that language, those metaphors. Placing them within the divine drama, interpreting them in his letters, he is able to draw on shared experience and vocabulary without being ruled by their currency in the world at large. Having borrowed the language of purchasing slaves or prisoners

---

[50]Robert Wuthnow, *Communities of Discourse: Ideology and Social Structure in the Reformation, the Enlightenment, and European Socialism* (Cambridge/London: Harvard University, 1989).

of war, how does he mold that language to his own ends? As Marshall observes, "A preacher would surely have delighted to point out the differences between sacral manumission and Christian redemption, and especially to contrast the price paid by the slave in the secular world with the free gift of God in Christ."[51]

This, we may recall, is one reason Anselm's model for explaining the atonement was so limited. Not only was it rooted so deeply in the sociohistorical moment of his feudal society; it also failed to enter into critical engagement with that society. What is more, it failed to gain its determinative coordinates from the portrayal of Jesus' death in the NT. Had it done so, it might have reflected better Jesus' own penetrating critique of such relationships of debt and obligation, which provided the raw material for Anselm's own thinking.

In our attempt to engage the NT faithfully within the integrity of its own discourse and world as well as grapple with the needs, vocabulary, and values of our own communities, we can be guided by additional themes that are central to atonement thought in the NT. The first of these turns the spotlight on the human predicament. "Lostness" may be articulated in a variety of ways—blindness, deafness, hard-heartedness, slavery to an evil power, enmity, and so on—but one of the constants in the equation of NT thinking about the atonement is the acute need of the human community. Humanity does not have the wherewithal to save itself but needs help (salvation, redemption, deliverance, and so on) from the outside, from God.

A second coordinate is the necessity of human response that flows out of the gracious act of God. The salvific work of God has not yet run its full course, but the lives of God's people must already begin to reflect the new reality (new creation) to which God is moving history. We are saved *from*, it is true, but we are also saved *for*. Atonement theology in the NT does not simply hold tightly to the work of Christ but opens wide its arms to embrace and guide the lives of Christians. Believers—having been redeemed, reconciled, delivered, bought, justified, and so on—are now released and empowered to reflect in their lives the quality of life exemplified by their Savior. This life is cruciform in shape, diaconal in character. Atonement theology cannot be separated from ethics.

Between the human predicament and the imperative of human response is the divine drama, the ultimate manifestation of the love of God. This is the third coordinate: God, acting on the basis of his covenant love, on his own initiative, was at work in the cross of Christ for human salvation. The NT portrays Golgotha along two story lines—one with God as subject, the other with Jesus as subject. It will not do, therefore, to characterize the atonement as God's punishment

---

[51] Marshall, "Concept of Redemption," 242.

falling on Christ (i.e., God as subject, Christ as object) or as Christ's appeasement or persuasion of God (Christ as subject, God as object). At the same time, however paradoxical it may seem, what happened on the cross for our atonement was, according to the NT, a consequence of God's initiative, a demonstration of divine love. As Paul summarizes, employing one model among many possibilities, "God was in Christ reconciling the world to himself" (2 Cor 5:19). Again, "God displays his love for us in that while we were still sinners Christ died for us" (Rom 5:8).

Fourth, and as a corollary to the three previous themes, NT atonement theology accords privilege to no one group over another. What happened on the cross was of universal significance—in the language of the day, for Jew and Gentile, for slave and free, for male and female. The cross was the expression of God's grace for all, for all persons as well as for all creation. Atonement theology thus repudiates ancient and modern attempts at segregating people away from the gracious invitation of God or otherwise possessing as one's own the gift of God available to all humanity, for the whole world.

CONCLUSION

In his introduction to the contemporary theological scene, Clark Pinnock inquires, "What would happen if theology [took] the Christian mission seriously?" Such a theology, he contends, would require a renovation in theological language, focus, and thought structures and would be more concerned about being understood by outsiders.[52] We have maintained that the theology of atonement as set forth by the various NT writings is the product of just such a concern. The significance of Jesus' death "for us" could never be exhausted or captured, so early theologians searched the conceptual encyclopedias of their day in order to communicate in ever-widening circles the nature of God's good news in Christ. Such a range of metaphors, however, not only was useful in proclaiming the meaning of the cross to potential Christians but also was serviceable in the resulting archipelago of local Christian communities.

---

[52]Clark H. Pinnock, *Tracking the Maze: Finding Our Way through Modern Theology from an Evangelical Perspective* (San Francisco: Harper & Row, 1990) 5–7. This is not to suggest that theologians as a whole have not been concerned with such issues; one thinks immediately, e.g., of Wolfhart Pannenberg's wide-ranging attempts to explicate the locus of theological investigation in the university, or of Hans Küng's concern to render the Christian message intelligible in the context of the challenges of modern humanisms and world religions.

Working in a Japanese mission setting, Norman Kraus has sought to follow in the wake of those NT theologians who worked to portray the meaning of the atonement in culturally relevant ways.[53] In his missionary context, Kraus believes, an emphasis on shame and vicarious identification is more to the point than some of the other images employed in recent years in the West. Not coincidentally, his proposal has significant moorings in the NT, whose writings themselves arose from within a culture where the values of honor and shame were pivotal.

Kraus presents one illustration of what must surely be the ongoing work of Christian communities everywhere, if they in fact seek to be oriented biblically. We must continuously seek out metaphors, new and old, that speak effectively and specifically to our various worlds. If we would follow in the path of the NT writers, the metaphors we deploy would be at home, but never too comfortable, in our settings; those writers sought, and we seek, not only to be understood by but also to shape people and social systems around us. Moreover, we would not eschew earlier models or the reality to which they point but would carry on our constructive work fully in conversation with, and under the guidance of, the Scriptures of Israel and the church and apostolic testimony. Our hermeneutical work, like that of Paul, would be sensitive to the interplay of scriptural coordinates and the contemporary images that convey redemptive meaning.

---

[53] C. Norman Kraus, *Jesus Christ Our Lord: Christology from a Disciple's Perspective* (Scottdale, Pa.: Herald, 1987).

SELECT BIBLIOGRAPHY

Achtemeier, Paul J. "Suffering Servant and Suffering Christ in 1 Peter." In *The Future of Christology: Essays in Honor of Leander E. Keck*. Edited by Abraham J. Malherbe and Wayne A. Meeks. Pages 176–88. Minneapolis: Fortress, 1993.

Allison, Jr., Dale C. *The End of the Ages Has Come: An Early Interpretation of the Passion and Resurrection of Jesus*. Philadelphia: Fortress, 1985.

Attridge, Harold. *Hebrews*. Hermeneia. Philadelphia: Fortress, 1989.

Aulén, Gustaf. *Christus Victor: An Historical Study of the Three Main Types of the Idea of the Atonement*. London: S.P.C.K., 1950.

Balch, David. "Hellenization/Acculturation in 1 Peter." In *Perspectives on First Peter*. Edited by Charles H. Talbert. Pages 79–101. SSS 9. Macon, Ga.: Mercer University, 1986.

Bammel, Ernst, and C. F. D. Moule, eds. *Jesus and the Politics of His Day*. Cambridge: Cambridge University, 1984.

Barrett, C. K. *The Gospel according to St. John*. 2d ed. Philadelphia: Westminster, 1978.

Bassler, Jouette M. "Mixed Signals: Nicodemus in the Fourth Gospel." *JBL* 108 (1989) 635–46.

_____, ed. *Pauline Theology*. Vol. 1: *Thessalonians, Philippians, Galatians, Philemon*. Minneapolis: Fortress, 1991.

Batstone, David. *From Conquest to Struggle: Jesus of Nazareth in Latin America*. Albany: State University of New York, 1991.

Bauckham, Richard. *The Theology of the Book of Revelation*. NTT. Cambridge: Cambridge University, 1993.

Bauer, David R. "The Major Characters of Matthew's Story: Their Function and Significance." *Int* 46 (1992) 357–67.

Beck, Brian E. " 'Imitatio Christi' and the Lucan Passion Narrative." In *Suffering and Martyrdom in the New Testament: Studies Presented to G. M. Styler by the Cambridge New Testament Seminar*. Edited by William Horbury and Brian McNeil. Pages 28–47. Cambridge: Cambridge University, 1981.

Beker, J. Christiaan. *Paul the Apostle: The Triumph of God in Life and Thought*. Edinburgh: T. & T. Clark, 1980.

Berger, Peter L., and Thomas Luckmann. *The Social Construction of Reality: A Treatise in the Sociology of Knowledge*. New York: Doubleday, 1966.

Best, Ernest. *Mark: The Gospel as Story*. SNTW. Edinburgh: T. & T. Clark, 1983.

Betz, Hans Dieter. *Galatians: A Commentary on Paul's Letter to the Churches in Galatia*. Hermeneia. Philadelphia: Fortress, 1979.

Betz, Otto. *What Do We Know about Jesus?* London: SCM, 1968.

Black, C. Clifton. *The Disciples according to Mark: Markan Redaction in Current Debate*. JSNTSup 27. Sheffield: JSOT, 1989.

Black, M. C. "The Rejected and Slain Messiah Who Is Coming with the Angels: The Messianic Exegesis of Zechariah 9–14 in the Passion Narratives." Ph.D. diss., Emory University, 1990.

Blank, Josef. *Krisis: Untersuchungen zur johanneischen Christologie und Eschatologie*. Freiburg: Lambertus, 1964.

_____. "Die Verhandlung vor Pilatus Joh 18,28–19,16 im Lichte johanneischer Theologie." *BZ* 3 (1958–59) 60–81.

Blinzler, Josef. "The Trial of Jesus in the Light of History." *Judaism* 20 (1971) 49–55.

Bock, Darrell L. *Proclamation from Prophecy and Pattern: Lucan Old Testament Christology*. JSNTSup 12. Sheffield: JSOT, 1987.

_____. "The Son of Man Seated at God's Right Hand and the Debate over Jesus' 'Blasphemy.' " In *Jesus of Nazareth: Lord and Christ. Essays on the Historical Jesus and New Testament Christology*. Edited by Joel B. Green and Max Turner. Pages 181–91. Grand Rapids: Eerdmans; Carlisle: Paternoster, 1994.

Boff, Leonardo. *Passion of Christ, Passion of the World: The Facts, Their Interpretation, and Their Meaning Yesterday and Today*. Maryknoll, N.Y.: Orbis, 1987.

Bonhoeffer, Dietrich. *Life Together*. San Francisco: Harper & Row, 1954.

Boring, M. Eugene. *Revelation*. IBC. Louisville: John Knox, 1989.

Böttger, Paul Christoph. *Der König der Juden—das Heil für die Völker: Die Geschichte Jesu Christi im Zeugnis des Markusevangeliums*. Neukirchen-Vluyn: Neukirchener, 1981.

Bourdillon, M. F. C., and Meyer Fortes, eds. *Sacrifice*. London: Academic, 1980.

Brandon, S. G. F. "The Trial of Jesus." *Judaism* 20 (1971) 43–48.

Braund, David C. *Augustus to Nero: A Sourcebook on Roman History, 31 BC–AD 68*. London: Crook Helm, 1985.

Brawley, Robert L. *Luke–Acts and the Jews: Conflict, Apology, and Conciliation*. SBLMS 33. Atlanta: Scholars, 1987.

Broadhead, Edwin K. *Teaching with Authority: Miracles and Christology in the Gospel of Mark*. JSNTSup 74. Sheffield: JSOT, 1992.

Brock, Rita Nakashima. "And a Little Child Will Lead Us: Christology and Child Abuse." In *Christianity, Patriarchy, and Abuse: A Feminist Critique*. Edited by Joanne Carlson Brown and Carole R. Bohn. Pages 42–61. New York: Pilgrim, 1989.

_____. *Journeys by Heart: A Christology of Erotic Power*. New York: Crossroad, 1988.

Brown, Joanne Carlson, and Carole R. Bohn, eds. *Christianity, Patriarchy, and Abuse: A Feminist Critique*. New York: Pilgrim, 1989.

Brown, Joanne Carlson, and Rebecca Parker. "For God So Loved the World?" In *Christianity, Patriarchy, and Abuse: A Feminist Critique*. Edited by Joanne Carlson Brown and Carole R. Bohn. Pages 1–30. New York: Pilgrim, 1989.

Brown, Raymond E. *The Death of the Messiah—from Gethsemane to the Grave: A Commentary on the Passion Narratives.* 2 vols. ABRL. New York: Doubleday, 1994.

_____. *The Gospel according to John.* 2 vols. AB 29–29A. Garden City, N.Y.: Doubleday, 1966–70.

_____. "The Gospel of Peter and Canonical Gospel Priority." *NTS* 33 (1987) 321–43.

_____. "Incidents That Are Units in the Synoptic Gospels but Dispersed in John." *CBQ* 23 (1961) 143–60.

_____. "Not Jewish Christianity and Gentile Christianity but Types of Jewish/Gentile Christianity." *CBQ* 45 (1983) 74–79.

Brown, Schuyler. *Apostasy and Perseverance in the Theology of Luke.* Rome: Biblical Institute, 1969.

Brownson, James V. "Neutralizing the Intimate Enemy: The Portrayal of Judas in the Fourth Gospel." In *Society of Biblical Literature 1992 Seminar Papers.* Edited by Eugene H. Lovering, Jr. Pages 49–60. Atlanta: Scholars, 1992.

Bryan, Christopher. *A Preface to Mark: Notes on the Gospel in Its Literary and Cultural Settings.* New York/Oxford: Oxford University, 1993.

Büchele, Anton. *Der Tod Jesu im Lukasevangelium: Eine redaktionsgeschichtliche Untersuchung zu Lk 23.* FTS 26. Frankfurt: Knecht, 1978.

Bultmann, Rudolf. *The Gospel of John: A Commentary.* Philadelphia: Westminster, 1971.

_____. *The History of the Synoptic Tradition.* 1963. Reprint. Peabody, Mass.: Hendrickson, 1994.

Burkill, T. A. *Mysterious Revelation: An Examination of the Philosophy of St. Mark's Gospel.* Ithaca, N.Y.: Cornell University, 1963.

Caird, George B. *The Revelation of St. John the Divine.* BNTC 19. Peabody, Mass.: Hendrickson, 1966.

Cargal, Timothy B. " 'His Blood Be upon Us and upon Our Children': A Matthean Double Entendre?" *NTS* 37 (1991) 101–12.

Carroll, John T. "Jesus as Healer in Luke–Acts." In *Society of Biblical Literature 1994 Seminar Papers.* Edited by Eugene H. Lovering, Jr. Pages 269–85. Atlanta: Scholars, 1994.

_____. "Luke's Apology for Paul." In *Society of Biblical Literature 1988 Seminar Papers.* Edited by David J. Lull. Pages 106–18. Atlanta: Scholars, 1988.

_____. "Luke's Crucifixion Scene." In *Reimaging the Death of the Lukan Jesus.* Edited by Dennis D. Sylva. Pages 108–24, 194–203. AMT:BBB 73. Frankfurt am Main: Anton Hain, 1990.

_____. "Luke's Portrayal of the Pharisees." *CBQ* 50 (1988) 604–21.

_____. *Response to the End of History: Eschatology and Situation in Luke–Acts.* SBLDS 92. Atlanta: Scholars, 1988.

_____. "The Uses of Scripture in Acts." In *Society of Biblical Literature 1990 Seminar Papers.* Edited by David J. Lull. Pages 512–28. Atlanta: Scholars, 1990.

Cassidy, Richard J. *Jesus, Politics, and Society: A Study of Luke's Gospel.* Maryknoll, N.Y.: Orbis, 1978.

_____. *John's Gospel in New Perspective: Christology and the Realities of Roman Power.* Maryknoll, N.Y.: Orbis, 1992.

_____. *Society and Politics in the Acts of the Apostles.* Maryknoll, N.Y.: Orbis, 1987.

Catchpole, David R. *The Trial of Jesus: A Study in the Gospels and Jewish Historiography from 1770 to the Present Day*. SPB 18. Leiden: E. J. Brill, 1971.

Chance, J. Bradley. "The Jewish People and the Death of Jesus in Luke–Acts: Some Implications of an Inconsistent Narrative Role." In *Society of Biblical Literature 1991 Seminar Papers*. Edited by Eugene H. Lovering, Jr. Pages 50–81. Atlanta: Scholars, 1991.

Charlesworth, James H., ed. *Jews and Christians*. New York: Crossroad, 1990.

_____, ed. *The Messiah: Developments in Earliest Judaism and Christianity*. Minneapolis: Fortress, 1992.

Chatman, Seymour. *Story and Discourse: Narrative Structure in Fiction and Film*. Ithaca, N.Y./London: Cornell University, 1978.

Cohn, Haim. "Reflections on the Trial of Jesus." *Judaism* 20 (1971) 10–23.

_____. *The Trial and Death of Jesus*. New York: Harper & Row, 1971.

Collins, Adela Yarbro. *The Beginning of the Gospel: Probings of Mark in Context*. Minneapolis: Fortress, 1992.

_____. *Crisis and Catharsis: The Power of the Apocalypse*. Philadelphia: Westminster, 1984.

Conzelmann, Hans. "Luke's Place in the Development of Early Christianity." In *Studies in Luke–Acts*. Edited by Leander E. Keck and J. Louis Martyn. Pages 298–316. Philadelphia: Fortress, 1966.

_____. *The Theology of St. Luke*. New York: Harper & Row; London: Faber & Faber, 1960. Reprint. London: SCM, 1982.

Cousar, Charles B. *A Theology of the Cross: The Death of Jesus in the Pauline Letters*. OBT. Minneapolis: Fortress, 1990.

Crossan, Dominic M. "Anti-Semitism and the Gospel." *TS* 26 (1965) 189–214.

Crossan, John Dominic. *The Cross That Spoke: The Origins of the Passion Narrative*. San Francisco: Harper & Row, 1988.

Culpepper, R. Alan. *Anatomy of the Fourth Gospel*. FF. Philadelphia: Fortress, 1983.

Dahl, Nils A. "Messianic Ideas and the Crucifixion of Jesus." Revised by Donald H. Juel. In *The Messiah: Developments in Earliest Judaism and Christianity*. Edited by James H. Charlesworth. Pages 382–403. Minneapolis: Fortress, 1992.

_____. "The Passion Narrative in Matthew." In *Jesus in the Memory of the Early Church*. Pages 37–51. Minneapolis: Augsburg, 1976.

Darr, John A. *On Character Building: The Reader and the Rhetoric of Characterization in Luke–Acts*. LCBI. Louisville: Westminster/John Knox, 1992.

Dauer, Anton. *Die Passionsgeschichte im Johannesevangelium: Eine traditionsgeschichtliche und theologische Untersuchung zu John 18,1–19,30*. SANT 30. Munich: Kösel, 1972.

de Jonge, Marinus. *Jesus: Stranger from Heaven and Son of God*. SBLSBS 11. Missoula, Mont.: Scholars, 1977.

de la Potterie, Ignace. *The Hour of Jesus: The Passion and the Resurrection of Jesus according to John*. New York: Alba, 1989.

_____. "Jesus, King and Judge according to John 19:13." *Scripture* 13 (1961) 97–111.

Delling, Gerhard. *Der Kreuzestod in der urchristlichen Verkündigung*. Göttingen: Vandenhoeck & Ruprecht, 1972.

Denney, James. *The Death of Christ: Its Place and Intepretation in the New Testament*. 3d ed. New York: A. C. Armstrong & Sons, 1903.

Derrett, J. Duncan M. *The Victim: The Johannine Passion Narrative Reexamined*. Shipston-on-Stour, England: Drinkwater, 1993.

Descamps, A. "Rédaction et christologie dans la récit matthéen de la Passion." In *L'Évangile selon Matthieu*. Edited by M. Didier. Pages 359–415. BETL 29. Gembloux: Duculot, 1972.

Dibelius, Martin. *From Tradition to Gospel*. 1933. Reprint. Cambridge: James Clarke, 1971.

Dillon, Richard J. *From Eye-Witnesses to Ministers of the Word: Tradition and Composition in Luke 24*. AnBib 82. Rome: Biblical Institute, 1978.

_____. "The Psalms of the Suffering Just in the Accounts of Jesus' Passion." *Worship* 61 (1987) 430–40.

Doeve, J. W. *Jewish Hermeneutics in the Synoptic Gospels and Acts*. Assen: Van Gorcum, 1953.

Donahue, John R. "From Passion Traditions to Passion Narrative." In *The Passion in Mark: Studies on Mark 14–16*. Edited by Werner H. Kelber. Pages 1–20. Philadelphia: Fortress, 1976.

Donfried, Karl P. "Paul and Judaism: 1 Thessalonians 2:13–16 as a Test Case." *Int* 38 (1984) 242–53.

Dormeyer, Detlev. *Die Passion Jesu als Verhaltensmodell: Literarische und theologische Analyse der Traditions- und Redaktionsgeschichte der Markuspassion*. NTAbh n.s. 11. Münster: Aschendorff, 1974.

_____. *Der Sinn des Leidens Jesu: Historisch-kritische und textpragmatische Analysen zur Markuspassion*. SBS 96. Stuttgart: Katho-lisches, 1979.

Douglas, Mary. *How Institutions Think*. The Frank W. Abrams Lectures. Syracuse, N.Y.: Syracuse University, 1986.

Driver, John. *Understanding the Atonement for the Mission of the Church*. Scottdale, Pa.: Herald, 1986.

Duke, Paul D. *Irony in the Fourth Gospel*. Atlanta: John Knox, 1985.

Dunn, James D. G. *Jesus, Paul, and the Law: Studies in Mark and Galatians*. Louisville: Westminster/John Knox, 1990.

_____. "Messianic Ideas and Their Influence on the Jesus of History." In *The Messiah: Developments in Earliest Judaism and Christianity*. Edited by James H. Charlesworth. Pages 365–81. Minneapolis: Fortress, 1992.

_____. "Paul's Understanding of the Death of Jesus as Sacrifice." In *Sacrifice and Redemption: Durham Essays in Theology*. Edited by S. W. Sykes. Pages 35–56. Cambridge: Cambridge University, 1991.

_____. "Prolegomena to a Theology of Paul." *NTS* 40 (1994) 407–32.

_____. *Romans*. 2 vols. WBC 38a–38b. Dallas, Tex.: Word, 1988.

_____. *The Theology of Paul's Letter to the Galatians*. NTT. Cambridge: Cambridge University, 1993.

Dunnill, John. *Covenant and Sacrifice in the Letter to the Hebrews*. SNTSMS 75. Cambridge: Cambridge University, 1992.

Eco, Umberto. *Semiotics and the Philosophy of Language*. AS. Bloomington: Indiana University, 1984.

Ehrman, Bart D. "The Cup, the Bread, and the Salvific Effect of Jesus' Death in Luke–Acts." In *Society of Biblical Literature 1991 Seminar Papers*. Edited by Eugene H. Lovering, Jr. Pages 576–91. Atlanta: Scholars, 1991.

_____. "Jesus' Trial before Pilate: John 18:28–19:16." *BTB* 13 (1983) 124–31.

Elliott, John H. "1 Peter, Its Situation and Strategy: A Discussion with David Balch." In *Perspectives on First Peter*. Edited by Charles H. Talbert. Pages 61–78. SSS 9. Macon, Ga.: Mercer University, 1986.

_____. *A Home for the Homeless: A Sociological Exegesis of 1 Peter, Its Situation and Strategy*. Philadelphia: Fortress, 1981.

Ellis, E. Earle, and Erich Grässer, eds. *Jesus und Paulus: Festschrift für Werner Georg Kümmel zum 70. Geburtstag*. Göttingen: Vandenhoeck & Ruprecht, 1975.

Enslin, Morton S. "The Temple and the Cross." *Judaism* 20 (1971) 24–31.

Esler, Philip Francis. *Community and Gospel in Luke–Acts: The Social and Political Motivations of Lucan Theology*. SNTSMS 57. Cambridge: Cambridge University, 1987.

Eusebius. *The Ecclesiastical History*. 2 vols. Translated by John Ernest Leonard Oulton. Loeb Classical Library. Cambridge: Harvard University, 1932.

Evans, C. F. *Saint Luke*. TPINTC. London: SCM; Philadelphia: Trinity, 1990.

Evans, Craig A. "Jesus in Non-Christian Sources." In *Dictionary of Jesus and the Gospels*. Edited by Joel B. Green and Scot McKnight. Pages 364–68. Downers Grove, Ill.: InterVarsity; Leicester: InterVarsity, 1992.

_____. "On the Quotation Formulas in the Fourth Gospel." *BZ* 26 (1982) 79–83.

Farmer, William R., ed. *New Synoptic Studies: The Cambridge Gospel Conference and Beyond*. Macon, Ga.: Mercer University, 1983.

Farrer, Austin M. *A Rebirth of Images*. Westminster: Dacre, 1949.

Feldmeier, Reinhard. *Die Krisis des Gottessohnes: Die Gethsemaneerzählung als Schlüssel der Markuspassion*. WUNT 2:21. Tübingen: J. C. B. Mohr (Paul Siebeck), 1987.

Ferguson, Everett. "Psalms." In *Encyclopedia of Early Christianity*. Edited by Everett Ferguson et al. Garland Reference Library of the Humanities 846. New York/London: Garland, 1990.

Ferguson, Everett, et al., eds. *Encylopedia of Early Christianity*. Garland Reference Library of the Humanities 846. New York/London: Garland, 1990.

Fiddes, Paul S. *Past Event and Present Salvation: The Christian Idea of Atonement*. Louisville: Westminster/John Knox, 1989.

Fiorenza, Elisabeth Schüssler. *The Book of Revelation: Justice and Judgment*. Philadelphia: Fortress, 1985.

Fishbane, Michael. *Biblical Interpretation in Ancient Israel*. Oxford: Clarendon, 1985.

Fitzgerald, John T. *Cracks in an Earthen Vessel: An Examination of the Catalogues of Hardships in the Corinthian Correspondence*. SBLDS 99. Atlanta: Scholars, 1988.

Fitzmyer, Joseph A. "Crucifixion in Ancient Palestine, Qumran Literature, and the New Testament." In *To Advance the Gospel*. Pages 125–46. New York: Crossroad, 1981.

_____. *Essays on the Semitic Background of the New Testament*. SBLSBS 5. Missoula, Mont.: Scholars, 1971.

_____. " '4Q Testimonia' and the New Testament." In *Essays on the Semitic Background of the New Testament*. Pages 59–89. SBLSBS 5. Missoula, Mont.: Scholars, 1971.

_____. *The Gospel according to Luke: Introduction, Translation, and Notes.* 2 vols. AB 28–28A. Garden City, N.Y.: Doubleday, 1981–85.

_____. *Luke the Theologian: Aspects of His Teaching.* New York/Mahwah N.J.: Paulist, 1989.

_____. *To Advance the Gospel.* New York: Crossroad, 1981.

Flusser, David. "A Literary Approach to the Trial of Jesus." *Judaism* 20 (1971) 32–36.

Forestell, J. Terence. *The Word of the Cross: Salvation as Revelation in the Fourth Gospel.* AnBib 57. Rome: Biblical Institute, 1974.

France, R. T., and David Wenham, eds. *Studies in Midrash and Historiography.* GP 3. Sheffield: JSOT, 1983.

_____, eds. *Studies of History and Tradition in the Four Gospels.* GP 1. Sheffield: JSOT, 1980.

Friedrich, Gerhard. *Die Verkündigung des Todes Jesu im Neuen Testament.* BTS 6. Neukirchen-Vluyn: Neukirchener, 1982.

Fuchs, Albert. *Das Petrusevangelium.* SNTU 2. Linz, Austria; Freistadt: Plöchl, 1978.

Fuller, Reginald H. "The 'Jews' in the Fourth Gospel." *Dialog* 16 (1977) 31–37.

Furnish, Victor Paul. "The Ministry of Reconciliation." *CurTM* 14 (1977) 204–18.

Garland, David E. *One Hundred Years of Study on the Passion Narratives.* NABPRBS 3. Macon, Ga.: Mercer University, 1989.

Garrett, Susan R. *The Demise of the Devil: Magic and the Demonic in Luke's Writings.* Minneapolis: Fortress, 1989.

_____. "Exodus from Bondage: Luke 9:31 and Acts 12:1–24." *CBQ* 52 (1990) 656–80.

_____. "The Meaning of Jesus' Death in Luke." *WW* 12 (1992) 11–16.

George, Augustin. "Le Sens de la mort de Jésus pour Luc." *RB* 80 (1973) 186–217.

Gnilka, Joachim. "Wie urteilte Jesus über seine Tod?" In *Der Tod Jesu: Deutungen im Neuen Testament.* Edited by Karl Kertelge. Pages 13–50. QD 74. Freiburg/Basel/Vienna: Herder, 1976.

Gnuse, Robert. "Dream Genre in the Matthean Infancy Narratives." *NovT* 32 (1990) 97–120.

Goppelt, Leonhard. *A Commentary on 1 Peter.* Edited by Ferdinand Hahn. Translated by John E. Alsup. Grand Rapids: Eerdmans, 1993.

Gowler, David B. *Host, Guest, Enemy, and Friend: Portraits of the Pharisees in Luke and Acts.* New York: Peter Lang, 1991.

Grant, Robert M. "The Trial of Jesus in the Light of History." *Judaism* 20 (1971) 37–42.

Grassi, Joseph A. *Rediscovering the Impact of Jesus' Death: Clues from the Gospel Accounts.* Kansas City, Mo.: Sheed & Ward, 1987.

Green, Joel B. "Burial of Jesus." In *Dictionary of Jesus and the Gospels.* Edited by Joel B. Green and Scot McKnight. Pages 88–92. Downers Grove, Ill.: InterVarsity; Leicester: InterVarsity, 1992.

_____. "Crucifixion." In *Dictionary of Paul and His Letters.* Edited by Gerald F. Hawthorne and Ralph P. Martin. Pages 197–99. Downers Grove, Ill.: InterVarsity, 1993.

288 THE DEATH OF JESUS IN EARLY CHRISTIANITY

———. "Death of Christ." In *Dictionary of Paul and His Letters*. Edited by Gerald F. Hawthorne and Ralph P. Martin. Pages 201–9. Downers Grove, Ill.: InterVarsity, 1993.

———. "Death of Jesus." In *Dictionary of Jesus and the Gospels*. Edited by Joel B. Green and Scot McKnight. Pages 146–63. Downers Grove, Ill.: InterVarsity; Leicester: InterVarsity, 1992.

———. "The Death of Jesus, God's Servant." In *Reimaging the Death of the Lukan Jesus*. Edited by Dennis D. Sylva. Pages 1–28, 170–73. AMT:BBB 73. Frankfurt am Main: Anton Hain, 1990.

———. *The Death of Jesus: Tradition and Interpretation in the Passion Narrative*. WUNT 2:33. Tübingen: J. C. B. Mohr (Paul Siebeck), 1988.

———. "The Demise of the Temple as 'Culture Center' in Luke–Acts: An Exploration of the Rending of the Temple Veil (Luke 23:44–49)," *RB* 101 (1994) 495–515.

———. "The *Gospel of Peter*: Source for a Pre-canonical Passion Narrative?" *ZNW* 78 (1987) 293–301.

———. " 'The Message of Salvation' in Luke–Acts." *Ex Auditu* 5 (1989) 21–34.

———. " 'Salvation to the End of the Earth' (Acts 13:47): God as Savior in the Acts of the Apostles." In *The Book of Acts and Its Theology*. Edited by I. Howard Marshall and David Peterson. Grand Rapids: Eerdmans, 1995.

———. *The Theology of the Gospel of Luke*. NTT 3. Cambridge: Cambridge University, 1995.

———. *The Way of the Cross: Following Jesus in the Gospel of Mark*. Nashville: Discipleship Resources, 1991.

———, ed. *Hearing the New Testament: Strategies for Interpretation*. Grand Rapids: Eerdmans, 1995.

Green, Joel B., and Scot McKnight, eds., *Dictionary of Jesus and the Gospels*. Downers Grove, Ill.: InterVarsity; Leicester: InterVarsity, 1992.

Green, Joel B., and Max Turner, eds. *Jesus of Nazareth: Lord and Christ. Essays on the Historical Jesus and New Testament Christology*. Grand Rapids: Eerdmans; Carlisle: Paternoster, 1994.

Gundry, Robert H. *Mark: A Commentary on His Apology for the Cross*. Grand Rapids: Eerdmans, 1993.

Gunton, Colin E. *The Actuality of the Atonement: A Study of Metaphor, Rationality, and the Christian Tradition*. Edinburgh: T. & T. Clark; Grand Rapids: Eerdmans, 1989.

Haenchen, Ernst. *The Acts of the Apostles: A Commentary*. Philadelphia: Westminster, 1971.

Hafemann, Scott J. "Suffering." In *Dictionary of Paul and His Letters*. Edited by Gerald F. Hawthorne and Ralph P. Martin. Pages 919–21. Downers Grove, Ill.: InterVarsity, 1993.

Hanson, Anthony Tyrrell. *The Paradox of the Cross in the Thought of St. Paul*. JSNTSup 17. Sheffield: JSOT, 1987.

Harrison, Beverly W., and Carter Heyward. "Pain and Pleasure: Avoiding the Confusions of Christian Tradition in Feminist Theory." In *Christianity, Patriarchy, and Abuse: A Feminist Critique*. Edited by Joanne Carlson Brown and Carole R. Bohn. Pages 148–73. New York: Pilgrim, 1989.

Hart, Ray L. "Religious and Theological Studies in American Higher Education: A Pilot Study." *JAAR* 59 (1991) 715–827.

Hartman, Lars. *Prophecy Interpreted: The Formation of Some Jewish Apocalyptic Texts and of the Eschatological Discourse Mark 13 par.* ConBNT 1. Lund: Gleerup, 1966.

Harvey, A. E. *Jesus and the Constraints of History.* Philadelphia: Westminster, 1982.

_____. *Jesus on Trial: A Study in the Fourth Gospel.* London: S.P.C.K., 1976.

Hawthorne, Gerald F., and Ralph P. Martin, eds. *Dictionary of Paul and His Letters.* Downers Grove, Ill.: InterVarsity, 1993.

Hay, David M. *Glory at the Right Hand: Psalm 110 in Early Christianity.* SBLMS 18. Nashville: Abingdon, 1973.

_____, ed. *Pauline Theology.* Vol. 2: *1 and 2 Corinthians.* Minneapolis: Fortress, 1993.

Hays, Richard B. "Crucified with Christ: A Synthesis of the Theology of 1 and 2 Thessalonians, Philemon, Philippians, and Galatians." In *Pauline Theology.* Vol. 1: *Thessalonians, Philippians, Galatians, Philemon.* Edited by Jouette M. Bassler. Pages 227–46. Minneapolis: Fortress, 1991.

_____. *The Faith of Jesus Christ: An Investigation of the Narrative Substructure of Galatians 3:1–4:11.* SBLDS 56. Chico, Calif.: Scholars, 1983.

Heil, John Paul. *The Death and Resurrection of Jesus: A Narrative-Critical Reading of Matthew 26–28.* Minneapolis: Fortress, 1991.

Hengel, Martin. *The Atonement: The Origins of the Doctrine in the New Testament.* Philadelphia: Fortress, 1981.

_____. *Crucifixion in the Ancient World and the Folly of the Message of the Cross.* Philadelphia: Fortress, 1977.

_____. "The Gospel of Mark: Time of Origin and Situation." In *Studies in the Gospel of Mark.* Pages 1–30. London: SCM, 1985.

_____. *Studies in the Gospel of Mark.* London: SCM, 1985.

Hennecke, Edgar, Wilhelm Schneemelcher, and R. McL. Wilson, eds. *New Testament Apocrypha.* 2 vols. Philadelphia: Westminster, 1963–65. 2d ed., Louisville: Westminster/John Knox; Cambridge: James Clarke, 1991–92.

Herford, R. Travers. *Christianity in Talmud and Midrash.* London: Williams & Norgate, 1903.

Hock, Ronald F. *The Social Context of Paul's Ministry: Tentmaking and Apostleship.* Philadelphia: Fortress, 1980.

Hooker, Morna D. "Interchange and Atonement." *BJRL* 60 (1978) 462–81.

_____. "Interchange in Christ." *JTS* 22 (1974) 349–61.

Horbury, William, and Brian McNeil, eds. *Suffering and Martyrdom in the New Testament: Studies Presented to G. M. Styler by the Cambridge New Testament Seminar.* Cambridge: Cambridge University, 1981.

Houts, Margo G. "Classical Atonement Imagery: Feminist and Evangelical Challenges." *Catalyst* 19 no. 3 (1993) 1, 5–6.

Isaacs, Marie E. *Sacred Space: An Approach to the Theology of the Epistle to the Hebrews.* JSNTSup 73. Sheffield: JSOT, 1992.

Jeremias, Joachim. "Παῖς θεοῦ." *TDNT.* 5.654–717.

Jervell, Jacob, and Wayne A. Meeks, eds. *God's Christ and His People.* Nils A. Dahl Festschrift. Oslo: Universitetsforlaget, 1977.

Johnson, Luke Timothy. *The Gospel of Luke.* SP 3. Collegeville, Minn.: Liturgical, 1991.

_____. "The Social Dimensions of *Sōtēria* in Luke–Acts and Paul." In *Society of Biblical Literature 1993 Seminar Papers*. Edited by Eugene H. Lovering, Jr. Pages 520–36. Atlanta: Scholars, 1993.

Jones, F. Stanley. "The Pseudo-Clementines: A History of Research." *SecCent* 2 (1982) 1–33, 63–96.

Juel, Donald. *Messiah and Temple: The Trial of Jesus in the Gospel of Mark*. SBLDS 31. Missoula, Mont.: Scholars, 1973.

_____. *Messianic Exegesis: Christological Interpretation of the Old Testament in Early Christianity*. Philadelphia: Fortress, 1988.

Kähler, Martin. *The So-Called Historical Jesus and the Historic Biblical Christ*. Philadelphia: Fortress, 1964.

Kany, Roland. "Der lukanische Bericht von Tod und Auferstehung Jesu aus der Sicht eines hellenistischen Romanlesers." *NovT* 28 (1986) 75–90.

Karris, Robert J. *Jesus and the Marginalized in John's Gospel*. ZSNT. Collegeville, Minn.: Liturgical, 1990.

_____. *Luke: Artist and Theologian. Luke's Passion Account as Literature*. TI. New York/Mahwah, N.J./Toronto: Paulist, 1985.

_____. "Luke 23:47 and the Lukan View of Jesus' Death." *JBL* 105 (1986) 65–74.

Käsemann, Ernst. *The Testament of Jesus*. Philadelphia: Fortress, 1968.

Kasher, Rimon. "The Interpretation of Scripture in Rabbinic Literature." In *Mikra: Text, Translation, Reading, and Interpretation of the Hebrew Bible in Ancient Judaism and Early Christianity*. Edited by Martin J. Mulder. CRINT 2:1. Minneapolis: Fortress, 1990.

Keck, Leander E., and J. Louis Martyn, eds. *Studies in Luke–Acts*. Philadelphia: Fortress, 1966.

Kee, Howard Clark. "The Function of Scriptural Quotations and Allusions in Mark 11–16." In *Jesus und Paulus: Festschrift für Werner Georg Kümmel zum 70. Geburtstag*. Edited by E. Earle Ellis and Erich Grässer. Pages 165–88. Göttingen: Vandenhoeck & Ruprecht, 1975.

Kelber, Werner H. "Conclusion: From Passion Narrative to Gospel." In *The Passion in Mark: Studies on Mark 14–16*. Edited by Werner H. Kelber. Pages 153–80. Philadelphia: Fortress, 1976.

_____. *The Oral and the Written Gospel: The Hermeneutics of Speaking and Writing in the Synoptic Tradition, Mark, Paul, and Q*. Philadelphia: Fortress, 1983.

_____, ed. *The Passion in Mark: Studies on Mark 14–16*. Philadelphia: Fortress, 1976.

Kertelge, Karl. "Das Verständnis des Todes Jesu bei Paulus." In *Der Tod Jesu: Deutungen im Neuen Testament*. Edited by Karl Kertelge. Pages 114–36. QD 74. Freiburg/Basel/Vienna: Herder, 1976.

_____, ed. *Der Tod Jesu: Deutungen im Neuen Testament*. QD 74. Freiburg/Basel/Vienna: Herder, 1976.

Kingsbury, Jack Dean. *Conflict in Luke: Jesus, Authorities, Disciples*. Minneapolis: Fortress, 1991.

_____. *Matthew as Story*. 2d ed. Philadelphia: Fortress, 1988.

Klauck, Hans-Josef. *4. Makkabäerbuch*. JSHRZ 3:6. Gütersloh: Gerd Mohn, 1989.

Klijn, A. Frederik J. *Jewish-Christian Gospel Tradition*. Supplements to *Vigiliae Christianae* 17. Leiden: E. J. Brill, 1992.

_____. "The Study of Jewish Christianity." *NTS* 20 (1974) 419–31.

Knowles, Michael. *Jeremiah in Matthew's Gospel: The Rejected Prophet Motif in Matthean Redaction.* JSNTSup 68. Sheffield: JSOT, 1993.

Koester, Helmut. *Ancient Christian Gospels: Their History and Development.* Philadelphia: Trinity, 1990.

_____. "Apocryphal and Canonical Gospels." *HTR* 73 (1980) 105–30.

Kraus, C. Norman. *Jesus Christ Our Lord: Christology from a Disciple's Perspective.* Scottdale, Pa.: Herald, 1987.

Kugel, James L. *The Idea of Biblical Poetry: Parallelism and Its History.* New Haven: Yale University, 1981.

Kurz, William S. "Luke 22:14–38 and Greco-Roman and Biblical Farewell Addresses." *JBL* 104 (1985) 251–68.

_____. *Reading Luke–Acts: Dynamics of Biblical Narrative.* Louisville: Westminster/John Knox, 1993.

Kysar, Robert. *John, the Maverick Gospel.* Atlanta: John Knox, 1976.

Lakoff, George, and Mark Johnson. *Metaphors We Live By.* Chicago/London: University of Chicago, 1980.

Lauterbach, Jacob Zallel. *Rabbinic Essays.* Cincinnati: Hebrew Union College, 1951.

Laws, Sophie. *In the Light of the Lamb: Imagery, Parody, and Theology in the Apocalypse of John.* Wilmington, Del.: Michael Glazier, 1988.

Layton, Bentley, ed. *The Rediscovery of Gnosticism.* Vol. 1. Leiden: E. J. Brill, 1980.

Levenson, Jon D. *The Death and Resurrection of the Beloved Son: The Transformation of Child Sacrifice in Judaism and Christianity.* New Haven/London: Yale University, 1993.

Lindars, Barnabas. *New Testament Apologetic: The Doctrinal Significance of the Old Testament Quotations.* London: SCM, 1961.

_____. "The Passion in the Fourth Gospel." In *God's Christ and His People.* Edited by Jacob Jervell and Wayne A. Meeks. Nils A. Dahl Festschrift. Pages 71–86. Oslo: Universitetsforlaget, 1977.

_____. *The Theology of the Letter to the Hebrews.* NTT. Cambridge: Cambridge University, 1991.

Linnemann, Eta. *Studien zur Passionsgeschichte.* FRLANT 102. Göttingen: Vandenhoeck & Ruprecht, 1970.

Lohse, Eduard. *Märtyrer und Gottesknecht: Untersuchungen zur urchristlichen Verkündigung vom Sühntod Jesu Christi.* 2d ed. FRLANT n.s. 46. Göttingen: Vandenhoeck & Ruprecht, 1963.

Longenecker, Richard N. "The Foundational Conviction of New Testament Christology: The Obedience/Faithfulness/Sonship of Christ." In *Jesus of Nazareth: Lord and Christ. Essays on the Historical Jesus and New Testament Christology.* Edited by Joel B. Green and Max Turner. Pages 473–88. Grand Rapids: Eerdmans; Carlisle: Paternoster, 1994.

Louw, Johannes P., and Eugene A. Nida, eds. *Greek-English Lexicon of the New Testament Based on Semantic Domains.* 2 vols. New York: United Bible Societies, 1988.

Lovering, Eugene H., Jr., ed. *Society of Biblical Literature 1991 Seminar Papers.* Atlanta: Scholars, 1991.

_____, ed. *Society of Biblical Literature 1992 Seminar Papers*. Atlanta: Scholars, 1992.

_____, ed. *Society of Biblical Literature 1994 Seminar Papers*. Atlanta: Scholars, 1994.

Lüdemann, Gerd. *Paulus, der Heidenapostel*. Vol. 2. FRLANT 130. Göttingen: Vandenhoeck & Ruprecht, 1983.

Lull, David J., ed. *Society of Biblical Literature 1988 Seminar Papers*. Atlanta: Scholars, 1988.

_____, ed. *Society of Biblical Literature 1990 Seminar Papers*. Atlanta: Scholars, 1990.

Mack, Burton. *A Myth of Innocence: Mark and Christian Origins*. Philadelphia: Fortress, 1988.

MacLennan, Robert S. *Early Christian Texts on Jews and Judaism*. BJS 194. Atlanta: Scholars, 1990.

Maier, Johann. *Jesus von Nazareth in der talmudischen Überlieferung*. Darmstadt: Wissenschaftliche Buchgesellschaft, 1978.

Malherbe, Abraham J., and Wayne A. Meeks, eds. *The Future of Christology: Essays in Honor of Leander E. Keck*. Minneapolis: Fortress, 1993.

Malina, Bruce J. *The New Testament World: Insights from Cultural Anthropology*. Atlanta: John Knox, 1981.

Marcus, Joel. *The Way of the Lord: Christological Exegesis of the Old Testament in the Gospel of Mark*. Louisville: Westminster/John Knox, 1992.

Marshall, I. Howard. *Commentary on Luke*. NIGTC 3. Grand Rapids: Eerdmans, 1978.

_____. "The Development of the Concept of Redemption in the New Testament." In *Jesus the Saviour: Studies in New Testament Theology*. Pages 239–57. London: S.P.C.K.; Downers Grove, Ill.: InterVarsity, 1990.

_____. *Jesus the Saviour: Studies in New Testament Theology*. London: S.P.C.K.; Downers Grove, Ill.: InterVarsity, 1990.

_____. "Lamb of God." In *Dictionary of Jesus and the Gospels*. Edited by Joel B. Green and Scot McKnight. Pages 432–34. Downers Grove, Ill.: InterVarsity; Leicester: InterVarsity, 1992.

_____. "The Meaning of 'Reconciliation.' " In *Jesus the Saviour: Studies in New Testament Theology*. Pages 258–74. London: S.P.C.K.; Downers Grove, Ill.: InterVarsity, 1990.

Martin, Ralph P. *Mark: Evangelist and Theologian*. CEP. Grand Rapids: Zondervan, 1972.

_____. *Reconciliation: A Study of Paul's Theology*. Rev. ed. Grand Rapids: Zondervan, 1990.

Martyn, J. Louis. *History and Theology in the Fourth Gospel*. 2d ed. Nashville: Abingdon, 1979.

Marxsen, Willi. *Mark the Evangelist*. Nashville: Abingdon, 1969.

Matera, Frank J. "The Death of Jesus according to Luke: A Question of Sources." *CBQ* 47 (1985) 469–85.

_____. "Jesus before Annas: John 18,13–14.19–24." *ETL* 66 (1990) 38–55.

_____. "Jesus' Journey to Jerusalem (Luke 9.51–19.46): A Conflict with Israel." *JSNT* 51 (1993) 57–77.

_____. *The Kingship of Jesus: Composition and Theology in Mark 15*. SBLDS 66. Chico, Calif.: Scholars, 1982.

_____. *Passion Narratives and Gospel Theologies: Interpreting the Synoptics through Their Passion Stories*. TI. New York/Mahwah, N.J.: Paulist, 1986.

_____. "The Trial of Jesus: Problems and Proposals." *Int* 45 (1991) 5–16.

Meeks, Wayne A. *The Prophet-King: Moses Traditions and the Johannine Christology*. NovTSup 14. Leiden: E. J. Brill, 1967.

Meeks, Wayne A., and Robert L. Wilken. *Jews and Christians in Antioch in the First Four Centuries of the Common Era*. SBLSBS 13. Missoula, Mont.: Scholars, 1978.

Meier, John P. *A Marginal Jew: Rethinking the Historical Jesus*. Vol. 1: *The Roots of the Problem and the Person*. ABRL. New York: Doubleday, 1991.

_____. *The Vision of Matthew: Christ, Church, and Morality in the First Gospel*. New York: Paulist, 1978.

Mertens, Herman-Emiel. *Not the Cross, but the Crucified: An Essay in Soteriology*. LTPM 11. Louvain: Peeters; Grand Rapids: Eerdmans, 1992.

Metzger, Bruce M. *A Textual Commentary on the Greek New Testament*. New York: United Bible Societies, 1971.

Meyers, Carol L., and Eric M. Meyers. *Zechariah 9–14: A New Translation with Introduction and Commentary*. AB 25C. New York: Doubleday, 1993.

Miller, Robert J. "The Gospels That Didn't Make the Cut." *BibRev* 9, no. 4 (1993) 14–25, 56.

Mitchell, Stephen. *The Gospel according to Jesus: A New Translation and Guide to His Essential Teachings for Believers and Unbelievers*. New York: HarperCollins, 1991.

Moessner, David P. " 'The Christ Must Suffer': New Light on the Jesus, Stephen, Paul Parallels in Luke–Acts." *NovT* 28 (1986) 220–56.

_____. " 'The Christ Must Suffer,' the Church Must Suffer: Rethinking the Theology of the Cross in Luke–Acts." In *Society of Biblical Literature 1990 Seminar Papers*. Edited by David J. Lull. Pages 165–95. Atlanta: Scholars, 1990.

_____. *Lord of the Banquet: The Literary and Theological Significance of the Lukan Travel Narrative*. Minneapolis: Fortress, 1989.

Mohr, Till Arend. *Markus- und Johannespassion: Redaktions- und traditionsgeschichtliche Untersuchungen der Markinischen und Johanneischen Passionstradition*. ATANT 70. Zurich: Theologischer, 1982.

Moo, Douglas J. *The Old Testament in the Gospel Passion Narratives*. Sheffield: Almond, 1983.

Morris, Leon. *The Apostolic Preaching of the Cross*. 3d ed. Leicester: Inter-Varsity, 1965.

_____. *The Cross in the New Testament*. Grand Rapids: Eerdmans, 1965.

Mowery, Robert L. "God, Lord and Father: The Theology of the Gospel of Matthew." *BibRes* 33 (1989) 24–36.

Mulder, Martin J., ed. *Mikra: Text, Translation, Reading, and Interpretation of the Hebrew Bible in Ancient Judaism and Early Christianity*. CRINT 2:1. Minneapolis: Fortress, 1990.

Müller, Paul-Gerd. "βλέπω." *EDNT*. 1.221–22.

Müller, Ulrich B. "Die Bedeutung des Kreuzestodes Jesu im Johannesevangelium." *Kerygma und Dogma* 21 (1975) 49–71.

Myllykoski, Matti. *Die letzten Tage Jesu: Markus und Johannes, ihre Traditionen und die historische Frage*. 2 vols. Suomalaisen Tiedeakatemian

Toimituksia. Annales Academiae Scientiarum Fennicae B/256 and B/272. Helsinki: Suomalainen Tiedeakatemia, 1991–1994.

Neirynck, Frans. "The Apocryphal Gospels and the Gospel of Mark." In *The New Testament in Early Christianity*. Edited by Jean-Marie Sevrin. Pages 123–75. BETL 86. Louvain: Leuven University, 1989.

Neyrey, Jerome. *The Passion according to Luke: A Redaction Study of Luke's Soteriology*. TI. New York/Mahwah, N.J.: Paulist, 1985.

Nicholson, Godfrey C. *Death as Departure: The Johannine Descent- Ascent Schema*. SBLDS 63. Chico, Calif.: Scholars, 1983.

North, Christopher Richard. *The Suffering Servant in Deutero-Isaiah: An Historical and Critical Study*. London: Oxford University, 1948.

Oden, Thomas C. *Systematic Theology*. Vol. 2: *The Word of Life*. San Francisco: Harper & Row, 1989.

Osiek, Carolyn. "The Women at the Tomb: What Are They Doing There?" *Ex Auditu* 9 (1993) 97–107.

O'Toole, Robert F. *The Unity of Luke's Theology: An Analysis of Luke–Acts*. GNS 9. Wilmington, Del.: Michael Glazier, 1984.

Overman, J. Andrew. *Matthew's Gospel and Formative Judaism: The Social World of the Matthean Community*. Minneapolis: Fortress, 1990.

Page, Sydney H. T. "The Authenticity of the Ransom Logion (Mark 10:45b)." In *Studies of History and Tradition in the Four Gospels*. Edited by R. T. France and David Wenham. Pages 137–61. GP 1. Sheffield: JSOT, 1980.

Pagels, Elaine H. "Gnostic and Orthodox Views of Christ's Passion: Paradigms for the Christian's Response to Persecution?" In *The Rediscovery of Gnosticism*. Vol. 1. Edited by Bentley Layton. Pages 262–83. Leiden: E. J. Brill, 1980.

_____. *The Gnostic Gospels*. New York: Vintage, 1979.

_____. *The Gnostic Paul*. Philadelphia: Fortress, 1975.

Pannenberg, Wolfhart. *Jesus—God and Man*. London: SCM, 1968.

Perkins, Pheme. *Peter: Apostle for the Whole Church*. Columbia: University of South Carolina, 1994.

Pesch, Rudolph. *Das Abendmahl und Jesu Todesverständnis*. QD 80. Freiburg/Basel/Vienna: Herder, 1978.

Petersen, Norman R. *Literary Criticism for New Testament Critics*. GBS. Philadelphia: Fortress, 1978.

_____. *Rediscovering Paul: Philemon and the Sociology of Paul's Narrative World*. Philadelphia: Fortress, 1985.

Peterson, David. *Hebrews and Perfection: An Examination of the Concept of Perfection in the "Epistle to the Hebrews."* SNTSMS 47. Cambridge: Cambridge University, 1982.

Pinnock, Clark H. *Tracking the Maze: Finding Our Way through Modern Theology from an Evangelical Perspective*. San Francisco: Harper & Row, 1990.

Plank, Karl A. *Paul and the Irony of Affliction*. SBLSS. Atlanta: Scholars, 1987.

Pobee, John S. *Persecution and Martyrdom in the Theology of Paul*. JSNTSup 6. Sheffield: JSOT, 1985.

Powell, Mark Allan. "The Plot to Kill Jesus from Three Different Perspectives: Point of View in Matthew." In *Society of Biblical Literature 1990 Seminar Papers*. Edited by David J. Lull. Pages 603–13. Atlanta: Scholars, 1990.

Reif, Stefan C. *Judaism and Hebrew Prayer: New Perspectives on Jewish Liturgical History*. Cambridge: Cambridge University, 1993.

Reinbold, Wolfgang. *Der älteste Bericht über den Tod Jesu: Literarische Analyse und historische Kritik der Passionsdarstellungen der Evangelien*. BZNW 69. Berlin/New York: Walter de Gruyter, 1994.

Rensberger, David. *Johannine Faith and Liberating Community*. Philadelphia: Westminster, 1988.

Rese, Martin. *Die "Stunde" Jesu in Jerusalem (Lukas 22,1–53): Eine Untersuchung zur literarischen und theologischen Eigenart des lukanischen Passionsberichts*. Münster: Münster University, 1970–71.

Rhoads, David, and Donald Michie. *Mark as Story: An Introduction to the Narrative of a Gospel*. Philadelphia: Fortress, 1982.

Richard, Earl. "The Functional Christology of 1 Peter." In *Perspectives on First Peter*. Edited by Charles H. Talbert. Pages 121–39. SSS 9. Macon, Ga.: Mercer University, 1986.

Richardson, Cyril, ed. *Early Christian Fathers*. Philadelphia: Westminster, 1953.

Richter, Georg. "Die Deutung des Kreuzestodes Jesu in der Leidensgeschichte des Johannesevangeliums (Jo 13–19)." *BibLeb* 9 (1968) 21–36.

Ringe, Sharon H. *Jesus, Liberation, and the Biblical Jubilee: Images for Ethics and Christology*. OBT 19. Philadelphia: Fortress, 1985.

Rivkin, Ellis. *What Crucified Jesus? The Political Execution of a Charismatic*. Nashville: Abingdon; London: SCM, 1984.

Robinson, James M., ed. *The Nag Hammadi Library in English*. New York: Harper & Row, 1977.

Roloff, Jürgen. "ἱλαστήριον." *EDNT*. 2.185–86.

_____. *The Revelation of John: A Continental Commentary*. Minneapolis: Fortress, 1993.

Rossé, Gerard. *The Cry of Jesus on the Cross: A Biblical and Theological Study*. Mahwah, N.J.: Paulist, 1987.

Rudolph, Kurt. *Gnosis: The Nature and History of an Ancient Religion*. Edinburgh: T. & T. Clark, 1983.

Ruppert, Lothar. *Jesus als der leidende Gerechte? Der Weg Jesu im Lichte eines alt- und zwischentestamentlichen Motivs*. SBS 59. Stuttgart: Katholisches, 1972.

Sampley, J. Paul. *Walking between the Times: Paul's Moral Reasoning*. Minneapolis: Fortress, 1991.

Sanders, E. P. *Jesus and Judaism*. London: SCM, 1985.

Sanders, Jack T. *The Jews in Luke–Acts*. Philadelphia: Fortress, 1987.

Sandmel, Samuel. "The Trial of Jesus: Reservations." *Judaism* 20 (1971) 69–74.

Schaberg, Jane. "Daniel 7–12 and the New Testament Passion-Resurrection Predictions." *NTS* 31 (1985) 208–22.

Schaeffer, Susan E. "The 'Gospel of Peter,' the Canonical Gospels, and Oral Tradition." Ph.D. diss., Union Theological Seminary, 1990.

Schenke, Ludger. *Der gekreuzigte Christus: Versuch einer literarkritischen und traditionsgeschichtlichen Bestimmung der vormarki-nischen Passionsgeschichte*. SBS 69. Stuttgart: Katholisches, 1974.

_____. *Studien zur Passionsgeschichte des Markus: Tradition und Redaktion in Markus 14,1–42*. FB 4. Würzburg: Echter, 1971.

Schmidt, Daryl. "1 Thess 2:13–16: Linguistic Evidence for an Interpolation." *JBL* 102 (1983) 269–79.

Schnackenburg, Rudolf. *The Gospel according to St. John.* 3 vols. Vol. 1. New York: Herder & Herder, 1968. Reprint. New York: Crossroad, 1980. Vols. 2 and 3. New York: Crossroad, 1980–1982.

Schneider, Gerhard. *Verleugnung, Verspottung, und Verhör Jesu nach Lukas 22,54–71.* Munich: Kösel, 1969.

Schneider, Johannes. "ξύλον," *TDNT.* 5.37–41.

Schoeps, Hans-Joachim. *Theologie und Geschichte des Judenchristentums.* Tübingen: J. C. B. Mohr (Paul Siebeck), 1949.

Schreiber, Johannes. *Theologie des Vertrauens: Eine redaktionsgeschichtliche Untersuchung des Markusevangeliums.* Hamburg: Furche, 1967.

Schütz, Frieder. *Der leidende Christus: Die angefochtene Gemeinde und das Christuskerygma der lukanischen Schriften.* BWANT 89. Stuttgart: Kohlhammer, 1969.

Seeley, David. *The Noble Death: Graeco-Roman Martyrology and Paul's Concept of Salvation.* JSNTSup 28. Sheffield: JSOT, 1990.

Senior, Donald. "The Death of Jesus and the Resurrection of the Holy Ones (Mt 27:51–53)." *CBQ* 38 (1976) 312–29.

_____. "Matthew's Account of the Burial of Jesus." In *The Four Gospels 1992: Festschrift Frans Neirynck.* Edited by Frans Van Segbroeck et al. Vol. 2. Pages 1433–48. BETL 100. Louvain: Leuven University, 1992.

_____. *The Passion Narrative according to Matthew: A Redactional Study.* BETL 39. Louvain: Leuven University, 1975.

_____. *The Passion of Jesus in the Gospel of John.* PS 4. Collegeville, Minn.: Liturgical, 1991.

_____. *The Passion of Jesus in the Gospel of Luke.* PS 3. Wilmington, Del.: Michael Glazier, 1989.

_____. *The Passion of Jesus in the Gospel of Mark.* PS 2. Wilmington, Del.: Michael Glazier, 1984.

_____. *The Passion of Jesus in the Gospel of Matthew.* PS 1. Wilmington, Del.: Michael Glazier, 1985.

_____. " 'With Swords and Clubs . . .': The Setting of Mark's Community and His Critique of Abusive Power." *BTB* 17 (1987) 10–20.

Setzer, Claudia J. *Jewish Responses to Early Christians: History and Polemics, 30–150 C.E.* Minneapolis: Fortress, 1994.

Sevrin, Jean-Marie, ed. *The New Testament in Early Christianity.* BETL 86. Louvain: Leuven University, 1989.

Siker, Jeffrey S. *Disinheriting the Jews: Abraham in Early Christian Controversy.* Louisville: Westminster/John Knox, 1991.

Sloyan, Gerard S. *Jesus on Trial.* Philadelphia: Fortress, 1973.

_____. "The Last Days of Jesus." *Judaism* 20 (1971) 56–68.

Smith, D. Moody. *John among the Gospels: The Relationship in Twentieth-Century Research.* Minneapolis: Fortress, 1992.

_____. "Judaism and the Gospel of John." In *Jews and Christians.* Edited by James H. Charlesworth. Pages 76–99. New York: Crossroad, 1990.

Smith, Dennis E. "Table Fellowship as a Literary Motif in the Gospel of Luke." *JBL* 106 (1987) 613–38.

Soards, Marion L. *The Passion according to Luke: The Special Material of Luke 22.* JSNTSup 14. Sheffield: JSOT, 1987.

Sölle, Dorothee. *Thinking about God: An Introduction to Theology.* London: SCM; Philadelphia: Trinity, 1990.

Sommer, Urs. *Die Passionsgeschichte des Markusevangeliums: Überlegungen zur Bedeutung der Geschichte für den Glauben.* WUNT 2:58. Tübingen: J. C. B. Mohr (Paul Siebeck), 1993.

Stanton, Graham N. *A Gospel for a New People: Studies in Matthew.* Edinburgh: T. & T. Clark, 1992.

_____. "Jesus of Nazareth: A Magician and False Prophet Who Deceived God's People?" In *Jesus of Nazareth: Lord and Christ. Essays on the Historical Jesus and New Testament Christology.* Edited by Joel B. Green and Max Turner. Pages 164–80. Grand Rapids: Eerdmans; Carlisle: Paternoster, 1994.

Stendahl, Krister. *The School of St. Matthew and Its Use of the Old Testament.* Philadelphia: Fortress, 1954.

Stuhlmacher, Peter. "Eighteen Theses on Paul's Theology of the Cross." In *Reconciliation, Law, and Righteousness: Essays in Biblical Theology.* Pages 155–68. Philadelphia: Fortress, 1986.

_____. *Jesus of Nazareth—Christ of Faith.* Peabody, Mass.: Hendrickson, 1993.

_____. *Reconciliation, Law, and Righteousness: Essays in Biblical Theology.* Philadelphia: Fortress, 1986.

_____. "Vicariously Giving His Life for Many, Mark 10:45 (Matt. 20:28)." In *Reconciliation, Law, and Righteousness: Essays in Biblical Theology.* Pages 16–29. Philadelphia: Fortress, 1986.

Swinburne, Richard. *Responsibility and Atonement.* Oxford: Clarendon, 1989.

Sykes, S. W. "Outline of a Theology of Sacrifice." In *Sacrifice and Redemption: Durham Essays in Theology.* Edited by S. W. Sykes. Pages 282–98. Cambridge: Cambridge University, 1991.

_____. "Sacrifice in the New Testament and Christian Theology." In *Sacrifice.* Edited by M. F. C. Bourdillon and Meyer Fortes. Pages 61–83. London: Academic, 1980.

_____, ed. *Sacrifice and Redemption: Durham Essays in Theology.* Cambridge: Cambridge University, 1991.

Sylva, Dennis D. *Reimaging the Death of the Lukan Jesus.* AMT:BBB 73. Frankfurt am Main: Anton Hain, 1990.

Tabor, James D. "'A Pierced or Piercing Messiah? The Verdict Is Still Out." *BAR* 18, no. 6 (1992) 58–59.

Talbert, Charles H. *Learning through Suffering: The Educational Value of Suffering in the New Testament and in Its Milieu.* ZSNT. Collegeville, Minn.: Liturgical, 1991.

_____, ed. *Perspectives on First Peter.* SSS 9. Macon, Ga.: Mercer University, 1986.

Tambasco, Anthony J. *A Theology of Atonement and Paul's Vision of Christianity.* ZSNT. Collegeville, Minn.: Liturgical, 1991.

Tannehill, Robert C. "Israel in Luke–Acts: A Tragic Story." *JBL* 104 (1985) 69–85.

_____. *The Narrative Unity of Luke–Acts.* 2 vols. FF. Philadelphia/Minneapolis: Fortress, 1986–90.

Taylor, Vincent. *The Atonement in New Testament Teaching.* 2d ed. London: Epworth, 1945.

_____. *Forgiveness and Reconciliation: A Study in New Testament Theology.* London: Macmillan, 1941.

_____. *The Formation of the Gospel Tradition.* London: Macmillan, 1949.

_____. *Jesus and His Sacrifice: A Study of the Passion Sayings in the Gospels.* London: Macmillan, 1937.

_____. *The Passion Narrative of St. Luke: A Critical and Historical Investigation.* Edited by Owen E. Evans. SNTSMS 19. Cambridge: Cambridge University, 1972.

Thiselton, Anthony C. *New Horizons in Hermeneutics: The Theory and Practice of Transforming Biblical Reading.* London: Collins; Grand Rapids: Zondervan, 1992.

_____. "New Testament Interpretation in Historical Perspective." In *Hearing the New Testament: Strategies of Interpretation.* Edited by Joel B. Green. Grand Rapids: Eerdmans, 1995.

Thompson, Leonard. *The Book of Revelation: Apocalypse and Empire.* Oxford: Oxford University, 1990.

Toolan, Michael J. *Narrative: A Critical Linguistic Introduction.* Interface. London/New York: Routledge, 1988.

Toynbee, J. M. C. *Death and Burial in the Roman World.* London: Thames & Hudson, 1971.

Travis, Stephen H. *Christ and the Judgment of God.* Basingstoke: Marshall, Morgan & Scott, 1986.

_____. "Christ as Bearer of Divine Judgment in Paul's Thought about the Atonement." In *Jesus of Nazareth: Lord and Christ. Essays on the Historical Jesus and New Testament Christology.* Edited by Joel B. Green and Max Turner. Pages 332–45. Grand Rapids: Eerdmans; Carlisle: Paternoster, 1994.

_____. "Wrath of God (NT)." *ABD.* 6.996–98.

Trocmé, Etienne. *The Formation of the Gospel according to Mark.* London: S.P.C.K., 1975.

_____. *The Passion as Liturgy: A Study in the Origin of the Passion Narratives in the Four Gospels.* London: SCM, 1983.

Tröger, Karl-Wolfgang. "Die Passion Jesu Christi in der Gnosis nach den Schriften von Nag Hammadi." Diss., University of Berlin, 1978.

Tuckett, Christopher M. "Atonement in the NT." *ABD.* 1.518–22.

_____, ed. *The Messianic Secret.* IRT 1. Philadelphia: Fortress, 1983.

Tyson, Joseph B. "Conflict as a Literary Theme in the Gospel of Luke." In *New Synoptic Studies: The Cambridge Gospel Conference and Beyond.* Edited by William R. Farmer. Pages 303–27. Macon, Ga.: Mercer University, 1983.

_____. *The Death of Jesus in Luke–Acts.* Columbia: University of South Carolina, 1986.

_____. *Images of Judaism in Luke–Acts.* Columbia: University of South Carolina, 1992.

_____, ed. *Luke–Acts and the Jewish People: Eight Critical Perspectives.* Minneapolis: Augsburg, 1988.

Untergassmair, Franz Georg. *Kreuzweg und Kreuzigung Jesu: Ein Beitrag zur lukanischen Redaktionsgeschichte und zur Frage nach der lukanischen "Kreuzestheologie."* Paderborn: Schöningh, 1980.

Van Segbroeck, Frans, et al., eds. *The Four Gospels 1992: Festschrift Frans Neirynck.* 3 vols. BETL 100. Louvain: Leuven University, 1992.

Van Voorst, Robert E. *The Ascents of James.* SBLDS 112. Atlanta: Scholars, 1989.

Vermes, Geza. *Jesus and the World of Judaism.* London: SCM, 1983.

_____. *Jesus the Jew: A Historian's Reading of the Gospels.* Philadelphia: Fortress, 1973.

Vielhauer, Philipp. "On the Paulinism of Luke–Acts." In *Studies in Luke–Acts.* Edited by Leander E. Keck and J. Louis Martyn. Pages 33–51. Philadelphia: Fortress, 1966.

von Walde, U. C. "The Johannine Jews: A Critical Survey." *NTS* 28 (1982) 33–60.

Walaskay, Paul W. "The Trial and Death of Jesus in the Gospel of Luke." *JBL* 94 (1975) 81–93.

Watson, Francis. "Why Was Jesus Crucified?" *Theology* 88 (1985) 105–12.

Weber, Hans-Ruedi. *The Cross: Tradition and Interpretation.* London: S.P.C.K., 1979.

Wenham, David, ed. *The Jesus Tradition outside the Gospels.* GP 5. Sheffield: JSOT, 1985.

White, Hayden. "The Narratization of Real Events." *CI* 7 (1980–81) 793–98.

_____. "The Question of Narrative in Contemporary Historical Theory." *HT* 23 (1984) 1–33.

_____. "The Value of Narrativity in the Representation of Reality." *CI* 7 (1980–81) 5–27.

Wilcox, Max. " 'Upon the Tree'—Deuteronomy 21:22–23 in the New Testament." *JBL* 96 (1977) 85–99.

Wilde, Robert. *The Treatment of the Jews in the Greek Christian Writers of the First Three Centuries.* Washington: Catholic University of America, 1949.

Wilken, Robert. *John Chrysostom and the Jews.* Berkeley: University of California, 1983.

_____. *Judaism and the Early Christian Mind: A Study of Cyril of Alexandria's Exegesis and Theology.* New Haven: Yale University, 1971.

Williams, Sam K. *Jesus' Death as Saving Event: The Background and Origin of a Concept.* HDR 2. Missoula, Mont.: Scholars, 1975.

Winter, Paul. *On the Trial of Jesus.* 2d ed. SJ 1. Berlin: Walter de Gruyter, 1974.

Witherup, Ronald D. "The Cross of Jesus: A Literary-Critical Study of Matthew 27." Ph.D. diss., Union Theological Seminary in Virginia, 1985.

Wright, N. T. *The Climax of the Covenant: Christ and the Law in Pauline Theology.* Minneapolis: Fortress, 1991.

Wuthnow, Robert. *Communities of Discourse: Ideology and Social Structure in the Reformation, the Enlightenment, and European Socialism.* Cambridge/London: Harvard University, 1989.

Zehnle, Richard F. "The Salvific Character of Jesus' Death in Lucan Soteriology." *TS* 30 (1969) 420–44.

Zeitlin, Solomon. *Who Crucified Jesus?* 4th ed. New York: Bloch, 1964.

Zias, Joseph, and Eliezer Sekeles. "The Crucified Man from Giv'at ha-Mivtar: A Reappraisal." *IEJ* 35 (1985) 22–27.

INDEX OF MODERN AUTHORS

INDEX OF ANCIENT SOURCES